AFRICAN ETHNOGRAPHIC STUDIES
OF THE 20TH CENTURY

Volume 58

THE JAKHANKE

THE JAKHANKE

The History of an Islamic Clerical People of the Senegambia

LAMIN O. SANNEH

Routledge
Taylor & Francis Group
LONDON AND NEW YORK

First published in 1979 by the International African Institute.

This edition first published in 2018
by Routledge
2 Park Square, Milton Park, Abingdon, Oxon OX14 4RN

and by Routledge
711 Third Avenue, New York, NY 10017

Routledge is an imprint of the Taylor & Francis Group, an informa business

British Library Cataloguing in Publication Data
A catalogue record for this book is available from the British Library

ISBN: 978-0-8153-8713-8 (Set)
ISBN: 978-0-429-48813-9 (Set) (ebk)
ISBN: 978-1-138-59776-1 (Volume 58) (hbk)
ISBN: 978-1-138-59792-1 (Volume 58) (pbk)
ISBN: 978-0-429-48675-3 (Volume 58) (ebk)

Publisher's Note
The publisher has gone to great lengths to ensure the quality of this reprint but points out that some imperfections in the original copies may be apparent.

Disclaimer
The publisher has made every effort to trace copyright holders and would welcome correspondence from those they have been unable to trace.

THE JAKHANKE

The History of an Islamic
Clerical People of the Senegambia

Lamin O. Sanneh

INTERNATIONAL AFRICAN INSTITUTE

INTERNATIONAL AFRICAN INSTITUTE
210 High Holborn, London WC1V 7BW

ISBN 0 85302 059 0

Printed in Great Britain

To Sandra, devoted wife
and mother, with love and admiration

CONTENTS

MAPS

FIGURE

An abridged version of Chapter One appeared as 'The origins of clericalism in West African Islam,' in the *Journal of African History* XVII (1976) 49-72. An expanded version of Chapter Nine appeared as 'Slavery Islam and the Jakhanke people of West Africa,' in *Africa* 46 (1) (1976) 80-97.

Cover photo: Shaykh Farūqi Jakhabi reading from a family history, Sutukung, the Gambia.

ACKNOWLEDGEMENTS

I am grateful to a great number of people for their assistance in the course of preparing this work originally as a thesis for the Ph. D. at the University of London. I can only mention a few. I must thank the Theological Education Fund for a grant to undertake this work and the Central Research Fund of the University of London for helping to finance part of the field-work. I should also like to thank the Methodist Church Overseas Division, London, for valuable assistance on the field. My thanks go to Mr Momodou Jabi, my invaluable Jakhanke field-assistant in Senegambia, for his loyalty and willingness and for giving unstintingly of his time and services, and my friend Fanding who introduced me to him. Mr E.A. N'jie, then Development Engineer at Mansakonko, kindly provided transport for many of the trips into the country. I owe him a profound debt. In this connection the following people helped in facilitating my field-surveys: Mr Salieu Cham, then of the Establishment Office, Banjul; Mr Edward Sowe Jnr, at the Ministry of Local Government, and his colleagues the District Commissioners; the then Medical Officer at Bansang, Dr Lamin Kurang; Mr Larson-Parry of Mansakonko, and Mr Mowdo Joberteh of the Basse Area Council. I would also like to thank Mr Albert Andrews, formerly of the Education Department, Banjul, who lightened my load in numerous ways, and Janko, Seni and Fatu Sise, all of Serrekunda, for love and hospitality, and other friends and relatives who had to suffer neglect during my investigations. My greatest debt of all is due to the many Jakhanke people who placed at my complete disposal their rich knowledge and resources and stimulated me in pursuing what was a new subject for me.

It is traditional for research students to record a word of appreciation to their supervisors and I happily embrace that tradition in sincerely thanking Dr Humphrey Fisher for first bringing the topic to my attention and then for meticulously and painstakingly following every step of the work. I must also, within that tradition, record my gratitude to Dr John B. Taylor of Birmingham whose earlier tutorials introduced me to the study of Arabic and Islamics and thus laid the foundations on which the present enterprise in large measure rests. Dr David Dalby of London read through the revised draft of the work and I am indebted to him for calling my attention to many points of detail.

Many authors speak appreciatively of the contribution of their editors, and none could do so with more reason than myself. I have benefited greatly from the detailed scrutiny under which Nicola Harris has put this book. Her high standards have helped me to avoid many embarrassments over factual details as well as interpretation. It is only with her scrupulous sifting and unyielding precision that this book has reached this stage. I owe her an incalculable debt. But she and all the others are of course absolved from responsibility for any remaining defects, inaccuracies and peculiarities in the work, for which I remain solely responsible.

I owe a special debt of gratitude to my wife, Sandra, for her patience during the strains of composition, and her invaluable expertise which made her bear the brunt of typing the manuscript as a thesis and for stimulating me to revise it. Her unflagging zeal withstood the numerous alterations and changes I made to the text as she was going through it, and her critical eye was responsible for removing many obscurities and inconsistencies. Her sympathy and good humour buoyed me up constantly during a concentrated and strenuous exercise.

A NOTE ON ORTHOGRAPHICAL AND SIMILAR CONVENTIONS

In the transliteration of Arabic I have followed in the main the *Encyclopaedia of Islam*, New Edition, except in the following particulars. I have written *j* for *dj*, *q* for *ḳ*, and the *hamza* at the beginning or end of a word is not shown. Also I have disregarded the ligature for letters like *sh*, *dh* and *gh*. All Qur'ānic quotations, except where otherwise indicated, are from Arberry's translation, *The Koran Interpreted*, but his line arrangements are not followed. The verse-numbering of the Qur'ān is that of the European Flügel version. Also I have differed from the *Encyclopaedia of Islam* in writing the *tā' marbūṭah*. I have shown it by writing *yāh* instead of *yya*, as in Tijāniyāh and Qādiriyāh, rather than Tijāniyya and Qādiriyya. There are a few exceptions, like *ṣalāt*, where usage makes a variant rendition (*ṣalāh*) unwarranted. I have in general kept the spelling of names (like Fadiga, Gassama, Momodou-Lamin) as found in current usage rather than following the Arabic version where that is applicable. I have omitted final é in names (like Fode, Suware, Serakhulle) whether the people concerned are living in francophone or anglophone areas. Towns (like Touba, Diakha) are spelt as they appear on modern maps, in English or French style according to the country, except for certain instances (like Futa Jallon, Bundu, Timbuktu) where English spelling is more familiar to anglophone readers.

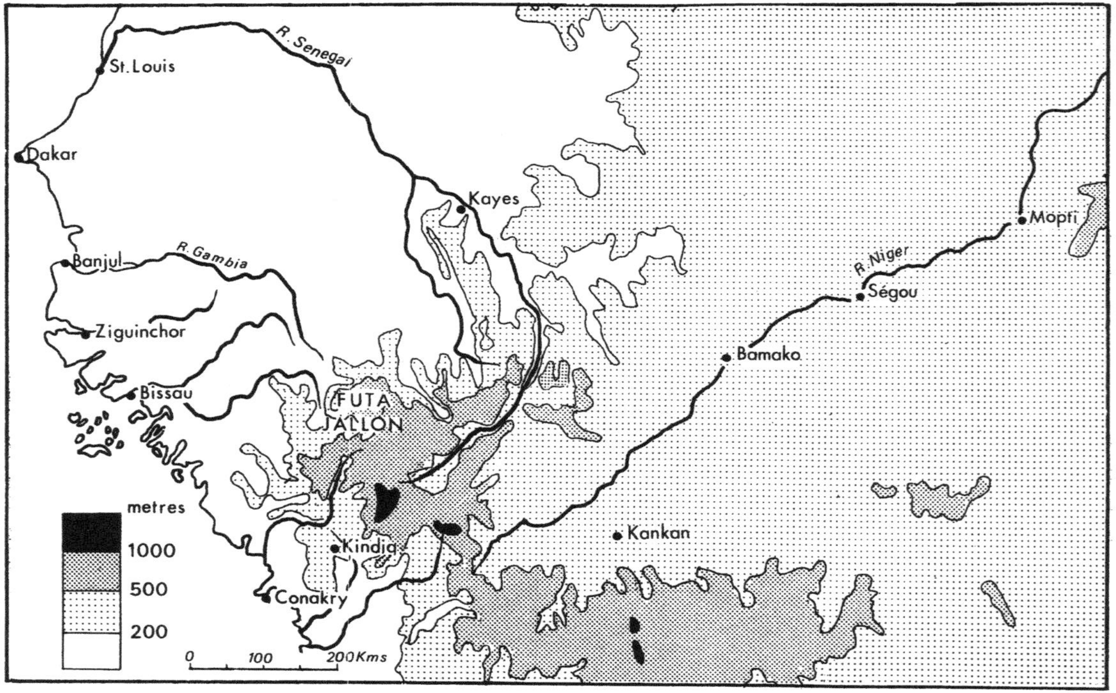

Map 1: The Senegambia Region

INTRODUCTION

HISTORICAL INTERPRETATION AND SOURCES

> The ancient historian, in consequence of the comparative paucity of official reports and the absence of our modern organisation for collecting and circulating news, would have to be his own journalist and do all the labour of obtaining facts orally from the most likely sources; and his sources might largely depend on accidental facilities. His work would rest mainly on information obtained orally by his own inquiries, supplemented by such documents as were available, such as the texts of treaties or official instructions and letters... It is clear that the ancient conditions made the historian's task more difficult, and demanded from him greater energy and initiative. (J.B. Bury: *The Ancient Greek Historians*, Harvard Lane Lectures, 1908, reprinted, New York, 1958: 82-83)

The Jakhanke

The Jakhanke are a specialised caste of Muslim clerics and educators, now mostly Manding speaking, who traditionally look to Dia (or Diakha) in Masina (now in the modern Republic of Mali) as their origin, whence their name Diakhanké or Jakhanke (for further details on nomenclature, see p. 13). Over a period of several centuries[1] they have been identified with a vigorous tradition of Islamic scholarship, education and clerical activity. They are not an ethnic group as such and possess no language of their own. They belong to the Serakhulle (or Soninke) people, in whose language much of their clerical vocational thinking is steeped. A high percentage of Arabic loan words, however, has infiltrated their speech, further setting them apart from their Serakhulle cousins (see pp. 13-17). They are at present found in the geographical area known as Senegambia, that is, the region extending along the Senegal and Gambia rivers from their source in the Futa Jallon highlands (see Map 1). The period of their dispersion into Senegambia covers approximately four centuries, from about 1250 to 1650, with a later stream developing towards Futa Jallon proper in the latter half of the 18th century.

This book investigates their identity rather than looking for a Semitic lineal descent. This approach has allowed me to place the necessary emphasis on intellectual ties with Classical Islam as well as religious/spiritual connections with the Maghrib without necessarily claiming genetic affiliation in either instance. The advantage of this approach can also be seen in the extent to which it has enabled me to spotlight charismatic origins where these are claimed and to take special note of how interest is maintained in such accounts without necessarily attempting to peer behind the accounts, 'for then the characters rapidly assume supernatural qualities and the facts embodied in the traditions begin to lose connection with time and space and the historian's critical apparatus must...be replaced by the tools of other analysts. Otherwise Clio will stumble credulously into the realm of myth' (R. Gray 1973:192-3).

The Jakhanke rose into prominence from the missionary activities of al-Ḥājj Sālim Suware sometime around 1200.[2] At that time they were still part of the Serakhulle people but soon developed into a specialised clerical elite with a reputation for learning and pacifism. From their beginnings in Masina they adhered closely to the teachings of al-Ḥājj Sālim who led them eventually to Diakha-Bambukhu on the River Bafing. From this time on they spread widely in Senegambia and beyond, carrying with them a strong commitment to the peaceful dissemination of Islam. Their significance in the islamisation of much of pre-colonial West Africa is without parallel, and the Islamic educational system as it developed was largely their creation.

The pacific clerical legacy bequeathed by al-Ḥājj Sālim merged in time with Qādirī Ṣūfī teachings, giving a decisive boost to the pacific strain in their tradition as well as reinforcing the educational enterprise. This became the mode of their dispersion, and until recently schools and educational materials were concentrated at dispersion points which sponsored educational and missionary projects among adjacent peoples. Thus without resort to arms the Jakhanke were able to undertake a far-reaching reform programme in local Islam, in contrast to the nineteenth century Muslim divines, the leaders in *jihād*, who saw military measures as indispensable. The Jakhanke position on religious warfare and the conflict to which it led them with respect to their militant co-religionists is frequently discussed below.

In upholding the tradition of learning alongside a pacific and politically neutral Islam, the Jakhanke have based their professional status on the clerical sources inherited from al-Ḥājj Sālim. They are united by a close bond of solidarity based on fidelity to al-Ḥājj Sālim's charismatic legacy and sustained by strong family and professional relationships. The problem, therefore, of their so-called ethnic origin resolves itself around the form their identity took as they emerged into recorded history.

Dispersion

The phrase 'dispersal' or 'dispersion', when used in connection with the Jakhanke, needs to be explained, for it is a key concept among them. There are three main characteristics. As a general phenomenon it means a whole family evacuating one area, with a large following of relatives, and going to another area, to which they might be attracted by the reputation of a holy religious figure, and where, once established, they will regulate their lives according to the strict rules of Islam. Such contact with centres which might reinvigorate a faded Islam was much sought after by the Jakhanke, for they needed that channel of open contacts to keep alive the hope and possibility of religious reform, especially since they seem always to have ruled out as a matter of principle military *jihād* as a legitimate method of religious/political change. In such circumstances, when faced with the danger of religious or moral decay, or, conversely, when attracted by the 'scent of holiness' (Manding: *noro*) of a Jakhanke teacher, a whole section of a *qabīlah* (clan) or several families would emigrate to place themselves under his guidance and direction. Thus dispersion in general terms has come to mean the entire process of communal withdrawal (a *hijrah* following the Prophet's example), with the guiding aim of a search for a revitalised Islamic image through greater adherence to the *Sharīᶜah* (the Law), the eventual adoption of a new religious centre, the careful provision of adequate services and incentives for the enrichment of their devotional and communal life, and the establishment of supporting links with other Jakhanke centres along the path of withdrawal. Along that same path of withdrawal, students and favour-seekers and general support would come pouring into Jakhanke communities now established at the other end. At its fullest extent, the dispersion chain enabled clusters of mutually supporting Jakhanke communities to develop and flourish as tiny enclaves widely scattered among heterogeneous populations, and this further strengthened the reforming zeal which such communities had been desirous of preserving in the first place. Pious families, in danger of compromise, could redeem their falling stature and adopt the path of withdrawal as a purifying undertaking; the gifted or ambitious young, with little prospect of advancement, could follow the dispersion trail in search of fame. Emigration (*hijrah*) and renewal (*tajdīd*) were interconnected in this way within the dispersion process as discussed below in Chapter 7.

This description has been concerned thus far with one type of dispersion, namely, the voluntary type. But there is another type, the involuntary or enforced dispersion in which the Jakhanke were compelled to emigrate and seek fresh pastures elsewhere by forces and pressures over which they appear to have had no direct control. The book dwells in considerable detail on this second aspect, for which the evidence is well established. Even in the case of enforced dispersion, the pattern and the results are comparable with the effects of the first type of dispersion. There is, however, a third and final aspect of dispersion which may be briefly set out here.

The Jakhanke, though confined to definite geographical areas, have no strict territorial boundaries as such and have never been associated with one inspired ethnic ancestor. Thus the traditions which point to Dia or Diakha as their home do not directly claim a particular ethnic origin. Diakhanke or Dia'nke is a generic term and merely means, in Mandinka and Fulbe, 'people of Dia' or 'Diakha'. The Soninke (or Serakhulle) basis of Jakhanke ethnic composition is supplied independently in the sources, nearly all of which hesitate to attribute a fatherland to the Jakhanke but instead fix upon them the characteristics of a landless, immigrant people. The result is that in their multifarious dispersions the Jakhanke have never embarked on what might look like a search for an ancestral home, and the absence of such a motivating ethnic ideology has made it easier to apply Islamic religious criteria to their wanderings. The Jakhanke chose their collective professional solidarity and religious commitment as the purpose around which they organised the dispersion process. The numerous centres which they founded, and many others in which they settled as subsidiary immigrants, served to safeguard their professional interests as clerics and educators. In time those professional interests came to require further dispersions, and the standard around which people rallied was the religious one of renewing Islam and preserving it from corruption, not, for example, the patriotic one of seeking to regain a fatherland.

The Sources

There is no full-scale comprehensive study of the Jakhanke, and the little that has been published appears in the form of articles or chapters devoted to limited aspects of the subject. The bulk of the remaining material is dispersed widely and incidentally in a variety of sources, and the treatment given is often fragmentary. The state of confusion which exists about the Jakhanke is itself a reflection of the fact that they are a far-flung community, scattered across an extensive band in the Western Sudan. Such a scattering of Jakhanke communities is, as we have now seen, a function of the life of dispersion which they have led. Hitherto, no single study has made use of the significant family and *qabīlah* (clan) *tawārīkh* (sing. *ta'rīkh*) (histories) as well as the abundance of oral accounts maintained by the Jakhanke themselves, or indeed the mass of library materials contained in Jakhanke family collections. The Jakhanke are a secretive and withdrawing people, and this has further placed them behind a veil of obscurity. But this veil is not impenetrable, and field experience has proved that what has in the first place led them to cultivate a life of private devotion, with a minimum of interference from political rulers, also encourages them to lift the veil and reveal a remarkable openness and eagerness to talk which has consistently marked their lifestyle within their own communities. Being a scholarly people, they are familiar with the methodology of enquiry, and the value they place on faithfulness to the record makes them willing to produce any documents which may exist, and, where none exist, to reproduce as faithfully as they can what has been handed down from the past. The practice of recording, either on paper or by a memory technique, is highly valued among them, and even an obscure Jakhanke teacher will trace in minute detail every incident of even a casual trip. This provided an ideal situation in which to set up a critical historical apparatus, both for detailing the past and for observing present-day practices.

The early published material on the Jakhanke is concerned to trace their origin on the basis of the Semitic hypothesis. Their ties with the Serakhulle are assumed or ignored, while the Semitic argument is pressed to yield the desired results. The first serious attempt was made by the translators and editors (O. Houdas and M. Delafosse in 1913) of the *Ta'rīkh al-Fattāsh*, by the Timbuktu scholar Maḥmūd al-Kaᶜti, although recent research suggests that his grandson, ibn al-Mukhtār, completed the editing of the work in c. 1664. They argued that Maḥmūd Kaᶜti was a Soninke scholar resident in Timbuktu, but who originally belonged to the circles of Banī Isrā'ila, a name they took at its literal Arabic meaning as the 'Children of Israel', a concept which may have originated with the Silla *qabīlah ta'rīkh* concerning their charismatic origins in Banī Isrā'ila, a village in Bundu (see pp. 49-51). Delafosse especially elaborates on this in a separate work, tracing the Jakhanke to a circle of fugitive elements from Cyrenaica which had originally been the destination of the descendants of Jacob, Joseph and Solomon. The dislocation and dispersal of these Semitic remnants in Cyrenaica followed ravages by the forces of Pharaoh (Delafosse 1912:I 215-6nn). André Rançon (1894a:173), perhaps drawing on a source later utilised by Delafosse, even cites a tradition which purports to go back to proto-Semitic origins. During World War II, the veteran A. Bonnel de Mézières went on a field trip to Bundu principally to test and confirm the Semitic argument, but the fragment of a Hebrew manuscript which he believed to be circulating in the region was nowhere to be found, and he died (in 1942) before he could do substantial work on his limited findings. These were later collected, edited and published, with the help of Raymond Mauny, as 'Les Diakanké de Banisiraïla et du Boundou Méridional (Sénégal)' (Mézières 1949). The original title of the article, subsequently altered by the editors, was 'Les Beni Israël du Soudan, de la Guinée, du Boundou Méridional et de la Gambie, connus sous le nom de Diakanké'. Paul Marty's works did not explicitly propound the Semitic view, discouraged in this probably by the views of his chief informant, himself a Jakhanke, al-Ḥājj Banfa Jabi (see p. 32 n. 6), but the topic crops up in modified form as he looks to Maghribian sources (1921:36-7).

The first attempt to give a composite account of the Jakhanke was made by the anthropologist, Pierre Smith. His work, 'Les Diakhanké: histoire d'une dispersion' (1965a), is, however, limited in scope and subject-matter. His treatment was general, concerned merely with picking out broad themes of Jakhanke history, and in this seldom going beyond published secondary sources, chiefly Marty. Secondly, he was occupied with a Jakhanke region, namely Bundu, which has for a long time been, through the dispersion process, a transitional area. The result is that much of the historical material he obtained in the field, and which, so far as can be seen, he made little use of, was simply copied from original manuscripts circulating in the Gambia.[3] A companion study by Pierre Smith (1965b) is of very limited use for an historian, being an anthropological study of the Jakhanke of Kédougou.

Another work limited in both scope and subject-matter is the study by the French Marxist, Jean Suret-Canale, entitled, 'Touba in Guinea - Holy Place of Islam' (1970). This is an account of one religious figure, al-Ḥājj Sālim Jabi-Gassama of Touba (Karamokho Ba) (see Chapter 5). It is not a study of the Jabi-Gassama *qabīlah*, let alone of the Jakhanke as such. Much of the material is based on a version of a *ta'rīkh* said to have come originally from Karamokho Madi, the first son of Karamokho Qutubo of Touba (d. 1905), although Suret-Canale seems unaware of this. The study is important in one detail, namely, in giving us a local account of the political crisis which in 1911 led to the arrest by the French of local Jakhanke leaders, including the spiritual leader of Touba at the time, Karamokho Sankoung (see Chapter 6). But Suret-Canale was unable to gain access to al-Ḥājj Banfa Jabi, the eldest son of Sankoung, who was instrumental in obtaining his father's release from detention in Mauritania, who had been Paul Marty's informant, and much later was my own.

All these studies are consistent in attempting to present a picture of the Jakhanke based on their own accounts, partial and fragmentary though that picture is. The work of Philip Curtin, however, belongs to a different category altogether. Its paramount concern, using mostly secondary sources, is to examine the Jakhanke primarily as a trading people, expert professionals who knew all the secrets of credit facilities in long-distance trade and maintained dominance over the complexities of trade and currency transactions.[4] It would, however, be misleading to see trade and commerce as the factors which mainly motivated the Jakhanke dispersions, or in fact as activities around which they organised themselves in any significant way. Rather, the picture we get is that of a people largely devoted to Islamic learning and clerical activity, some of whom, much closer to the commercial spirit of their Serakhulle cousins, carried on a tradition of trade, occasionally retiring to clerical Jakhanke enclaves for a period of rest and reflection. Into this group would fall the

Bajo, a part of the Silla and the Jakhite-Kabba, the Fofana-Girasi, Sedi-Mente, Danso and Bayo *qabā'il*.[5] The clear division between the secular and the religious, as Curtin rightly points out, was always a feature of Jakhanke settlements, and there is evidence to show that where the emphasis was laid on the secular side of a settlement, the Jakhanke invariably abandoned the town and transferred their clerical practice somewhere else. For example, Sutukho, in Upper Gambia, belongs to this group. But far more deserving of consideration are the numerous clerical centres in present-day Senegambia which have been deliberately sited in rural locations and removed from any major trade artery, giving the picture of a definitive pattern of Jakhanke settlement more characteristic of them than strategically located commercial entrepôts into which some elements might occasionally drift.

The foregoing analysis is directed at trying to restore the balance against what has been a fashionable line of enquiry in some quarters, namely, the linking in a general way of the progress of islamisation with the growth of trading activities, of which Curtin's work is only one strand. Having said that, it should be pointed out that the Jakhanke have given sanctuary to traders, and took part in their own right as clerical specialists in the wider ramifications of pre-colonial trade, seeing trade in the light of the Prophet's early career, and relating themselves to it again in the light of the Prophet's subsequent active religious life. They kept close to the parallel.

There is a large body of material on clan patronymics under which the Jakhanke have been considered. The anthropological bent of much of this material restricts its use for the historian, but the chronological framework can sometimes be of value and historical interest. Two general works fall into this category. The one by Vuillet (1952) is based on work carried out in Senegambia, and his concern is to link existing Jakhanke communities to a wave of Maghribian immigrants with ultimately Classical Islamic origins. Another account, earlier and taken from a different area, is given by Pierre Humblot (1918) and is based on an Arabic manuscript of a griot (*jeli*) of Téliko. Once again the focus of this account is on the Classical Islamic background of the Mandinka-Mori people of Kankan (Guinea), among whom a number of Jakhanke patronymics are prominent. Related to Humblot's piece, though again somewhat pre-dating it, is the account by André Arcin who devotes a small sub-section to Jakhanke patronymics (1907:308-9). André Rançon may also be mentioned in this connection (1894a). Of a different order is the paper on the Mandinka-Mori community of Baté by Lansine Kaba, himself a Mandinka-Mori from Kankan, though his study is in parts marred by insubstantial speculation (1972).

Field-work: Family Tawārikh, Library Resources and Interviews

Field-work was preceded by an extended period spent collating the existing elusive and scattered published and documentary sources. Archival sources were then examined. Not surprisingly, the archives in Paris did not yield much on the subject, although the military side of more recent events in which the Jakhanke were indirectly involved, concerning the activities of Muḥammad al-Amīn Darame better known as Momodou-Lamin (d. 1887), was well covered (see Chapter 4). As expected, the bulk of the material for this book in fact comes from my own field-notes. I spent some six months of extensive travelling and interviewing which met with a positive response in virtually all Jakhanke communities in the Senegambia area, I spent most of the time in rural areas where the Jakhanke have established centres of Islamic learning, with extensive manpower and library resources to maintain them. The library holdings in some cases turned out to be quite impressive, and it was clear that a vigorous tradition of Islamic learning, sustained over many years, was still being maintained. The love of scholarly pursuits and devotion to saintliness were being cultivated in most of these areas in the belief that that is how history has rewarded the efforts of their forefathers who are believed to have stood within the same tradition. But this self-image, very much the ideologically motivating force of Jakhanke life, will need close examination, particularly in Jakhanke attitudes to the Senegambian *jihād* wars and to slavery (Chapters 8 and 9). At the end of my field-trip I went to Dakar to look at the archives at the Institut Fondamental de l'Afrique Noire (IFAN) and while there I had further meetings with the elderly al-Ḥājj Banfa Jabi and his son al-Ḥājj Soriba Jabi ibn Banfa.

A few themes arising out of the field-work may be touched on here. First, the definition and scope of the research. The topic is too vast to be satisfactorily treated without rigorously limiting the range of the discussion to matters that touch directly on Jakhanke history in the long process of dispersion and eventual settling down.

The practical effect of this is to cut out much of the theological and devotional material. The other way of limiting the scope was to prune the disproportionate amount of material which exists on local heroes. For example, the abundance of material on Momodou-Lamin, the subject of Chapter 4, is sifted in order to underline the essentially religious theme of his career. Secondly, the area under consideration is mainly, though by no means exclusively, Senegambia, and although the Jakhanke have dispersed to other areas it is clear that the main axis of their educational and clerical activity has consistently been shifting towards the Senegambia area, that is, westwards from Bambukhu. The study, in looking to the Senegambia area, will in that sense be following the interest and emphasis of Jakhanke history itself. Thirdly, in order to reflect the extremely rich and diverse sources on Jakhanke life and history, a good deal of attention will be directed to events in the nineteenth century and early decades of this century. The richness and diversity of sources is further illustrated in the thematic material in Chapters 7 to 9. I must, in this connection, point out a limitation of the present study. In a basically historical undertaking such as this, full justice cannot be done to the breadth and depth of many themes in Jakhanke clerical life. Yet, within that restriction, some notion of the content of that clerical life is called for, if only so that we may better appreciate the past. Comparative models based on Ṣūfī Islam are also treated in this thematic section, the aim being to suggest sources of influence and parallels with Jakhanke Islam.

The significant body of family records and *qabīlah tawārikh*, augmented from other sources, will constitute the major source for this book. The four major families who form the clerical core of the Jakhanke have in their possession accounts of their own *qabā'il* (sing. *qabīlah*). A *qabīlah* in this sense means a confederation of families who trace their descent through an identical *nisbah* or genealogical tradition and recognise through that tradition a common ancestral figure from whom they derive the sanctions for the social rules which regulate relationships among the *qabīlah* members. The four major *qabā'il* among the Jakhanke are the chief clerical and educational lines, which have kept a detailed account of themselves. They are the Suware, the Jabi-Gassama, the Jakhite-Kabba[6] and the Silla. Some accounts include Fofana and Darame as well, but I have nowhere come across a separate supporting tradition for either of these. Suware origins are dealt with particularly in Chapter 1; the other three in Chapter 2.

The oral accounts in published sources have been augumented with field-notes. The special memory technique developed by the Jakhanke has also meant a fairly high return on investigation into detail and comparative material as well as fine theoretical distinctions. For example, in discussions with a venerated blind Jakhanke leader I mentioned the accepted sociological maxim that endogamy has been one way in which the Jakhanke are claimed to have preserved their cohesiveness. After some thought he countered by saying that the union of two lax Jakhanke would not lead to a strengthening but a weakening of community life. First, he said, Islam and to be strong before considerations of endogamy could be relevant.[7]

I also participated in a number of Jakhanke activities. I was present at Qur'ān school evening lessons, sessions of public Qur'ānic exegesis, public discussions on consistorial judicial procedures (the Jakhanke avoid initiating law suits, and oath-taking on the Qur'ān is strictly forbidden among them), visits to holy sites such as Sutukho and numerous visits to mosque-tombs of local holy figures where prayers were said at the graveside. Most graves were on the outer perimeter of mosques, on the left side facing the *miḥrab*, and some were adorned with fine cotton material suspended over the entire length of the grave.

Reverting to the question of who the Jakhanke are, field-experience would seem to lead to the following conclusion. Literacy, limited or extensive, and religion emerge as the two general criteria by which they are defined. Their original linguistic affinity with the Serakhulle has little relevance since it was weakened by the wave of islamisation, combined with arabisation, which came over them. The Jakhanke did not completely lose their Serakhulle cultural ties, of which most Jakhanke leaders have retained remnants to the present day. But what happened was that their own language ceased to be important as a way of defining them, and instead Arabic and Islam emerged as the new standards by which they assessed their cultural values. One result of this has been to divert interest from ethnic 'origins' to concern with the point at which a significant Islamic religious experience created a new Muslim consciousness among them, that is, to their formative period at Diakha-Bambukhu. For their subsequent history, literacy and religion (Arabic and Islam) became the source of their self-identity and the basis of their relationship with other people. This is the context in which they surfaced into recorded history, and is examined in some depth in the first chapter.

NOTES

1 Documentary and oral sources look back to the earliest days of Islamic penetration in the Western Sudan for the emergence and identity of the Jakhanke. This long time span has forced many traditional accounts to overstretch into the precarious, but standard, Semitic breeding ground for an origin. Jakhanke lineal ties with their more recent neighbours, the Serakhulle (or Soninke), have been loosened and replaced by supposed links with Classical Islamic heroes. But a series of close investigations has recovered much of this lost Serakhulle ground.

2 For detailed chronological discussion, see pp. 23-6.

3 P. Smith 1965a: 246. The material in question was a copy of a *qabīlah ta'rīkh* on the Jakhite-Kabba lineage, which the *imām* of Kédougou, Dembo Kabba-Jakhite, copied from his teachers in the Gambia. (For the Jakhite-Kabba *qabīlah*'s history, see pp. 38-43.)

4 Curtin 1971b; 1972. Curtin claims that the Jakhanke 'became virtually synonymous with merchants among the Europeans on the Gambia or the upper Senegal' in the last decades of the 17th and early decades of the 18th century (1972: 10).

5 Al-Ḥājj Shaykh Sidiya Jabi, Brikama, 30/10/72. The involvement of the Jakhite-Kabba in commerce happened very late and they have mainly operated in the area which is now Guinea Bissau.

6 In both these cases the patronymics are alternatives: the Jabi are the same as the Gassama; the Jakhite as the Kabba.

7 Karamokho Sankoung Jabi, Nibrās, 4/12/72.

CHAPTER ONE

THE BIRTH OF THE JAKHANKE ISLAMIC CLERICAL TRADITION

c. 1200 - c. 1500

Introduction

A familiar but intractable problem in African history is the question of the identification and origin of nomenclature and ethno-linguistic groups, and the Jakhanke people are no exception. They have been ascribed various names (see p. 27) and even now some confusion remains about how to resolve the problem. Among the Jakhanke themselves the Arabic form *ahl Diakha* (or Dia) is used. The phrase means 'the people of Diakha', and refers to the ancient Sudanic town in Masina visited by Ibn Baṭṭūṭa. The Jakhanke are by origin the same people as the Serakhulle, sometimes also known as Soninke,[1] and are distinguished only by a professional specialisation as Muslim clerics. The appellation 'Jakhanke' merely describes their original geographical home, Diakha-Masina, and does not relate to any theory of ethnic origins. Jakhanke sources indeed use the Arabic word *nawᶜ*, kind, branch, to describe themselves, rather than *jins*, race or species. An historian need not, therefore, be overly exercised about the question of ethnic origins in order to identify and describe the community *ahl Diakha*. That is our approach in this book. It is important to stress this lest an erroneous impression be created that the Jakhanke are a distinct ethno-linguistic grouping with a language of their own. Charlotte Quinn rather hastily describes the Jakhanke as a Mandinka people 'from Futa Tuba [Touba] who spoke a dialect of Mandingo different from their neighbours in the Gambian states' (1972: 172). Jakhanke clerics have until recent times conducted Qur'ānic exegesis (*tafsīr*) in the Serakhulle language, while using relevant languages, such as Susu, Fula, and Wolof in everyday contact with the people living around them. Indeed such ethnic distinctiveness as they may have acquired is usually the result of historical intermixture with adjacent peoples and not of an original linguistic affinity.

The community of ahl Diakha acquired a separate identity by virtue of an occupational clerical tradition on the one hand, and, on the other, of a common acknowledgement of al-Ḥājj Sālim Suware as the originator of their way of life. At a very early date the Jakhanke were characterised by large-scale dispersion (Ar. *tafrīq*) and this accounts in part for the different names by which they are known. Dispersion, as shown in the Introduction, is a grand theme in Jakhanke history, and to this may be added other factors of geographical mobility, such as educational travel, *tournées pastorales* and other special purpose visits such as pilgrimage (Ar. *ḥājj*). What the cleric practises as he moves from place to place, that is, the thematic content of clerical activity, is described in detail in later chapters. For all this the figure of al-Ḥājj Sālim Suware is predominant. As the source and proto-type of Jakhanke clericalism his stature is without parallel and a history of the Jakhanke as *ahl Diakha* must start with him.

Surprisingly little is known of the life and work of al-Ḥājj Sālim, and even hagiographical material is hard to come by. This, no doubt, is connected with the Jakhanke aversion to anything that might appear as blameworthy or heretical (Ar. *bidᶜah*).[2] One or two recent studies have tried to establish the person of al-Ḥājj Sālim but did not get beyond a few intuitive conclusions (P. Smith 1965a; Wilks 1968). That al-Ḥājj Sālim was an historical figure is indubitable, and beyond that his influence is felt in all Jakhanke communities to such an extent that he must have been an exceptional leader in his time. We must now turn our attention to him, drawing principally on local Jakhanke Arabic sources for an outline of his life and career.

Al-Ḥājj Sālim Suware and the Origins of Jakhanke Clericalism

Sometimes called Mbemba Laye Suware,[3] al-Ḥājj Sālim arrived in Diakha-Masina, on the Niger buckle, after his legendary seventh and last pilgrimage to Mecca. It was on his return journey that the nickname (Ar. *laqab*), 'Su-ware', meaning a piebald horse, was applied to him by his admiring entourage.[4] He had not intended to return to Black Africa from Mecca, but a dream he had there urged him to return and undertake missionary work. Thus opened a chapter in his life which was to leave a permanent imprint on West African Islam.

Traditional accounts make al-Ḥājj Sālim a contemporary (but more plausibly a man of equal stature) of Magham Diabe Sise, the founder-king of Wagadu, that is, the ancient Ghana of written sources.[5]

Although some accounts place some emphasis on this contemporaneity, they should not be pressed for their chronological value only. What they might be saying is that if Magham Diabe Sise can be seen as representing a secular/political impulse in Serakhulle history, so can al-Ḥājj Sālim be seen as representing a contrasting and independent religious/clerical line. Magham Diabe and al-Ḥājj Sālim are thus two stylistic representations in oral tradition of a differentiation between political innovation leading in one direction, and in another an autonomous clerical establishment in Serakhulle history. The Jakhanke, arguing their own case rather than the secular triumph of Magham Diabe, ascribe to al-Ḥājj Sālim an importance which, although clearly exaggerated, is not altogether undeserved.

In an Arabic document obtained on the field in Senegambia and to be referred to hereafter as *TSK*,[6] an account is given of how al-Ḥājj Sālim and his large entourage left Diakha-Masina following unspecified political upheavals in that region. Al-Ḥājj Sālim decided to leave because of what the sources describe as a fundamental aversion to assuming secular responsibility or being involved in war, thus introducing the two important themes of Jakhanke history: dispersion, in this instance because of war, and withdrawal from politics and armed conflict.

When al-Ḥājj Sālim left Diakha-Masina to settle first in Jafunu and then in Diakha-Bambukhu, he was accompanied by numerous followers: students, members of his family, *qabīlah* communities (clan segments), and other sympathisers and disciples. Charles Monteil mentions the names of only three of al-Ḥājj Sālim's disciples: Salla Kebe, Baba Kamara, also called Wage and ancestor of the Kamara-Wage of Kagoro, and Fa Abdullahi Marega, whose descendants dispersed to Mulline, near present Kunyakari (Ch. Monteil 1953: 372; on the Marega in Kayes see Brun 1910). *TSK* gives fuller details, and when the list it supplies is conflated with similar information given by al-Ḥājj Soriba Jabi, a Jakhanke scholar of Senegal and the younger brother of al-Ḥājj Banfa Jabi, we have an impressive list of al-Ḥājj Sālim's leading *ṭullāb* (sing. *ṭālib*) (students). *TSK* coincides exactly with al-Ḥājj Soriba with regard to the patronymics represented in al-Ḥājj Sālim's entourage. Both he and *TSK* also stress the Serakhulle composition of al-Ḥājj Sālim's community. Except possibly for the names Kamara and Jawara (Diawara), all can be identified as essentially Serakhulle: Sakho, Karara, Maigha, Fadiga, Kabba, Fofana-Girasi, Darame, Silla,

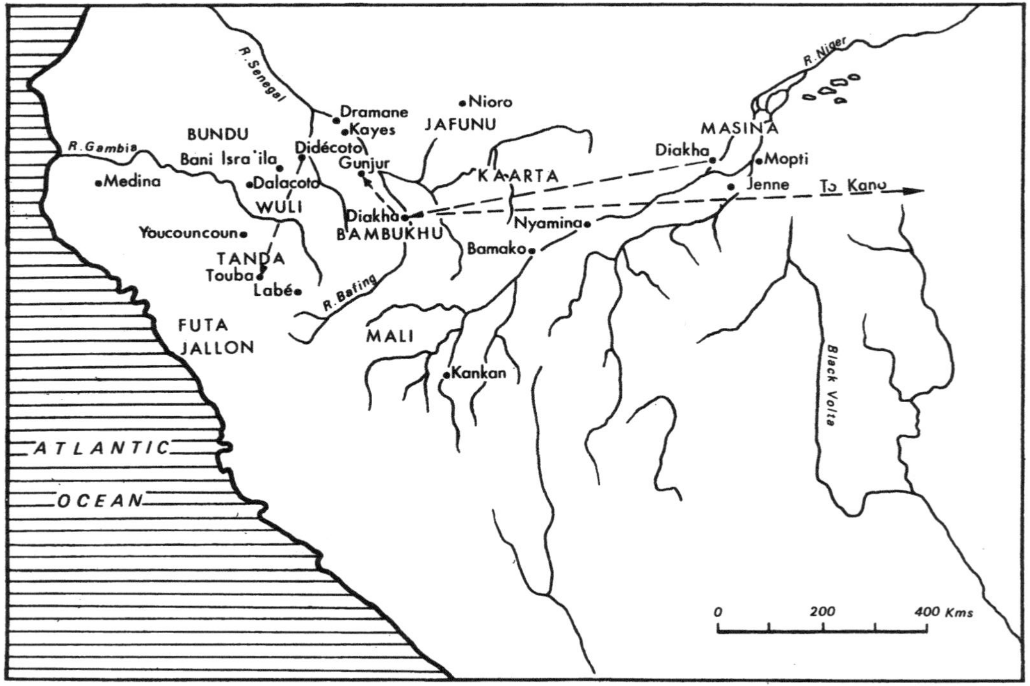

Map 2: Jakhanke Dispersions in West Africa

Gassama and Kayasi (*TSK*: fos. 1 and 2; Sanneh 1974a: 93-4). But al-Ḥājj Soriba's list is slightly longer than *TSK*. The Serakhulle theme is pursued further in the sources. *TSK* says two members of al-Ḥājj Sālim's family, probably his sons, were uterine brothers (Ar. *shaqīqāt*), namely, Darameba and Kharu Muḥammad Fofana-Girasi, and that their names had a Serakhulle origin. Darame, it says, was a *laqab* (honorific) acquired from the practice of cultivating a field located on what is vaguely described as 'the south side of a great river' (*TSK*: fo.2). It was the descendants of this Darameba who founded Gunjūr in Bundu to which we shall return in Chapters 2 and 3 below. As for Kharu Muḥammad, Kharu was a Serakhulle nickname like Tulli Fadiga, which was acquired through the Fadiga being noted for their liking for honey, which they used for making pious offerings to people.[7]

The interest in the Serakhulle background of the early Jakhanke is sustained similarly in respect of al-Ḥājj Sālim's close family. He is credited with four sons, given in order of age: ᶜUthmān Suware, Yūsūf, Fābu, and Fode, and these were all with him (*TSK*: fo. 2) when he went to found Diakha-Bambukhu (also called Diakhaba and Diakha-sur-Bafing). His wives, four in number, are equally all Serakhulle: Saghalle Sudūru (mother of her husband's namesake), Āminata Sudūru (mother of Darameba), Fāṭumata Sudūru (mother of Kharu Muḥammad Fofana-Girasi), and Diba Sudūru (mother of Tulli Fadiga) (*TSK*: fo. 2). The sons of these women are known by different names, the more formal Islamic baptismal names, given above, and the more common house-names, given in some accounts, some of which occur in the list in *TSK*. It is clear from these names that at this early stage al-Ḥājj Sālim and his community were not a separate ethnic group but were part of the Serakhulle people, although a definite clerical orientation was taking shape under al-Ḥājj Sālim's leadership.

It is impossible to be exact about the numerical strength of al-Ḥājj Sālim's following when he withdrew from Diakha-Masina to Bambukhu. Al-Ḥājj Soriba Jabi estimates that well over 100 *qabīlah* sections accompanied al-Ḥājj Sālim on his travels, first to Jafunu, where he lived for thirty years, and then to Diakha-Bambukhu (see Sanneh 1974a: 85). This figure of upwards of 100 *qabā'il* is independently corroborated by a seventeenth century local Arabic chronicle, *Aṣl al-Wanqarayīn*, to which we shall return in another place (pp. 28-31).

Although al-Ḥājj Sālim's name does not occur in that text, nor was he specifically identified by the translator,[8] the description fits him pretty closely:

> Then the *shaykh* [*raḥimahu Allāh*, i.e. 'may God have mercy on him'] emigrated [Ar. *intaqala*] from their country with 160 *qabā'il* to a western land called Mali [read Bambukhu, a province of Mali]. (Ḥājj 1968: Ar. 3)

This points to a substantial number of people, and elsewhere in the same document when the figure of 160 *qabā'il* is mentioned it is claimed to comprise more than 3,600 people. But we cannot be sure even here, for numbers are bound to fluctuate in the course of retelling.

Jakhanke sources pass lightly over the Jafunu episode of al-Ḥājj Sālim's career. When they say he spent thirty years in that place they make almost nothing of it so that we have a curious hiatus in his life. Nevertheless, enough is known about Jafunu's early history, ranging from legends of its founding (Ch. Monteil 1953: 371) to accounts of its great political/commercial supremacy (Lewicki 1971) to suggest that its secular importance may explain its near-eclipse in Jakhanke clerical sources which would be concerned to describe their own religious interest rather than the secular fame which Jafunu achieved. The Jakhanke clerical counterpart to Jafunu is Diakha-Bambukhu, and about this we have relatively more information.

Virtually all Jakhanke and other local sources claim that al-Ḥājj Sālim founded Diakha-Bambukhu. Historians committed to the position that al-Ḥājj Sālim was a late fifteenth century figure, and possibly even later,[9] find it difficult to accept this unanimous tradition. To assign an earlier chronological *floruit* to al-Ḥājj Sālim would upset calculations on which they have based the history of stages of Islamic penetration in Black Africa. The weight of the evidence, however, makes it probable, though by no means proven, that al-Ḥājj Sālim was connected with the origins of Diakha-Bambukhu, whether in the historical sense of creating the town himself, or the clerical sense of baptising an already existing town.[10]

It is only by extreme conjecture that the Jakhanke of Bambukhu, as a composite community, can be identified with the Serakhulle and Manding merchants (classed under the generic term Wangara), who operated the lucrative gold trade of Bambukhu at this period, as some scholars have suggested. In their own accounts, supplemented by outside observers, Bambukhu represented a most formative period of Jakhanke clerical history. They did some trading there, and according to one account al-Ḥājj Sālim assigned the Fofana-Girasi *qabīlah* the commercial franchise of Diakha-Bambukhu, including custody of community property.[11] But it is clear from these accounts that the Jakhanke were not a collective commercial guild and they never undertook trade as professional carriers nor as resident agents with monopoly control, as is sometimes claimed (see e.g. Curtin 1973). According to their own accounts the Jakhanke community was occupied with what has come to be seen as the fundamental triad of clerical life: diligence in learning (Ar. *al-qirā'ah*), farming (*al-ḥarth*), and travel or mobility (*al-safar*), the last of which would undoubtedly include some trading (*TSK*: fo. 3). These activities are regarded by the Jakhanke as constituting legitimate (*ḥalāl*) sources of livelihood. It is obvious that this is a very compressed statement of what actually constitutes the fields of clerical activity. For example, Islamic divination,[12] a vital part of clerical practice, would be included in *al-qirā'ah*; the acquisition and use of slaves in *al-ḥarth*; while the legal and ritual provisions concerning slaves would come under *al-qirā'ah*; and the penetration of distant lands for religious purposes (*ḥājj* and *ziyārah*) and educational reasons (recruitment of students, general educational itinerancy, setting up schools) would fall under the broad category of mobility (*al-safar*) where several other themes overlap.

Diakha-Bambukhu was, especially in its initial stages, a compact clerical corporation, the nucleus of which were the *émigrés*, *al-muhājirūn*,[13] from Diakha-Masina. The community was organised into four clerical wards under the overall leadership and patronage of al-Ḥājj Sālim. The first order (Ar. *al-qasm awwal*) was Suwarekunda, then Daramekunda, Fofana-Girasikunda and, finally, Fadigakunda (*TSK*: fo. 3). The Suwarekunda people were given charge over the entire clerical settlement: they organised its general life and passed rulings on community welfare and political relations with the secular leaders of Bambukhu as a province of Mali. The Darame clerics were treated as the heirs-apparent of al-Ḥājj Sālim. The Fofana, we have seen, were responsible for commercial relations and community property. The Fadiga were responsible for student affairs: welfare, discipline, recruitment and farm labour.[14] It is obvious from this that al-Ḥājj Sālim had set up a personal clerical dynasty with his four eldest sons in titular control. As head of the clerical establishment at Diakha-Bambukhu al-Ḥājj Sālim exercised a profound influence on the members of the *qabīlah* sections who all recognised his authority. He was *imām ratti*, chief presiding *imām*. *TSK*, our only source here, says, because of their devotion and seeking of *barakah*, blessing or virtue, from al-Ḥājj Sālim, the leaders of the four *qabā'il* (they are called *al-rijāl al-ṣāliḥīna*)[15] received his blessing for themselves and posterity. The emergence of the communal clerical core of Jakhanke Islam is traced to this *barakah* of al-Ḥājj Sālim. On this basis the Jakhite-Kabba *qabīlah* became renowned for their efficacious prayers (*mustajību al-daᶜwāt*)[16] and produced notable scholars (*ᶜulamā*) and jurists (*fuqahā*) (*TSK*: fo. 4). Similarly the Darame fathered numerous saints (*awliyā*, sing. *walī*), jurists, ascetics (*zuhhād*, sing. *zāhid*) and scholars, and in time rose to prominence at the holy town of Gunjūr which became the illustrious abode of forty Muslim divines and a famous Darame clerical republic (for a fuller description see pp. 27-8).

Al-Ḥājj Sālim and the Pacifist Tradition

> Travel, both physically and metaphorically, can be an important part of [clerical] activity. The [cleric] travels in his own land (internally) and also through the countryside from land to land (externally). Some spend no more than forty days in one place. 'On dead skins, by tanning, the effects of purity, of softness, and of delicacy of texture appear; even so, by the tanning of travel, and by the departure of natural corruption and innate roughness, appears the purifying softness of devotion and change from obstinacy to faith.' (Idris Shah, *The Sufis*, 1971: 268, quoting from al-Suhrawardī)

Apart from the foundation of Diakha-Bambukhu al-Ḥājj Sālim is best remembered for his extensive peaceful missionary journeys which tradition, relishing the thought, may have embellished with fiction. Seven times to Mecca and back, his appetite seems to have been further stimulated and he toured widely in the western Sudan, primarily to confirm and strengthen existing Muslim populations. Local sources claim he visited Kaabu,[17] Suna-Karantaba and other parts of northern Casamance (the district of Sédhiou),[18] and eastern and western Senegambia. When to this is added the earlier record of the emigration from Masina to Jafunu and Bambukhu, al-Ḥājj Sālim must have been worn to a deep hue from 'the tanning of travel'. Two concrete results of such *tournées pastorales* were, firstly, the establishment of mosques or the upgrading of existing ones (from *masjid* to *jāmiᶜ*, the former being a minor mosque for daily *ṣalāt*, ritual prayer, and the latter a major one, of Cathedral status, in which Friday Congregation prayer is held) and, secondly, the recruitment of large numbers of students and disciples who returned with him to Bambukhu (see Sanneh 1974a: 103-5). Jakhanke clerics from then up to the present day have spent a good deal of their time in similar activities.

This seems the natural point at which to introduce what was a creative and original contribution of al-Ḥājj Sālim to Sudanic Islam, namely, his scrupulous principled disavowal of *jihād* as an instrument of religious and political change. This was a significant development for future Jakhanke communities living in the nineteenth century atmosphere of *jihād* wars of epidemic proportions. During his religious travels al-Ḥājj Sālim is said to have preached to a wide spectrum of believers, including Muslims living in *bilād al-kufr* (pagan territory) (Wilks 1968: 179) and in some places to non-believers as well, and everywhere he eschewed the employment of arms in preference for peaceful witness in the propagation of Islam (see Sanneh 1974a: 106). At the same time he stressed the necessity of Jakhanke clerical solidarity for an effective witness, pointing to the fact that intra-*qabīlah* rivalry, a fragmented Muslim community, was one of the factors successfully exploited in *jihād* situations.[19] Numerous details are given on this theme which may be passed over here. What is clear is that his emphasis on the peaceful propagation of Islam and the establishment of institutions and structures designed to consolidate and bolster the image of Islam in numerous parts of the Western Sudan were among his most original and far-reaching contributions to Sudanic Islam. No one before him had identified or considered this as a viable option in the spread of Islam in this area nor had a community developed and thrived on its basis.[20]

There are many examples of individuals outside the Jakhanke tradition who created a separate clerical identity and also renounced the use of arms in the spread of Islam, particularly among the Kunta Arabs and some Berber peoples.[21] But the Jakhanke are unique in having evolved an independent pacific Sudanic tradition which has adhered stedfastly to the line of separate existence from warrior/secular groups and to the principle of neutrality and refusal to bear arms in conflicts or to sponsor movements for violent change. What is remarkable is that secular champions, such as the warriors and the *mujāhidūn* (leaders in holy war) of the nineteenth century should by and large respect Jakhanke scruples in this regard and should be themselves occasionally amenable to Jakhanke clerical pressure. The fact that their neutrality was not violated then is indicative of the strength and viability of the Jakhanke clerical tradition: it was their prestige and stature as religious savants with a recognised tradition of political neutrality which enabled the Jakhanke to escape conscription into the *jihād* armies and the confiscation of their property.[22]

It may be (although this needs further investigation) because of al-Ḥājj Sālim's profound influence and abiding relevance for Serakhulle/Manding peoples that the *jihād* tradition among them failed to develop into a significant instrument of political change, thus allowing the drive and initiative to pass to the Fulbe *tcherno* (Fula: cleric) elite. The repudiation of the *mujāhidūn* Momodou-Lamin (d. 1887) and Fode Kabba (died c. 1911) by their own Jakhanke communities (the latter even by his own relatives, see pp. 193-5) attests to the insuperable difficulties which similar Jakhanke *mujāhidūn* at earlier times would have faced in struggling to create a committed following from among their people. It also testifies to Jakhanke fidelity to the pacific clerical line insisted on by al-Ḥājj Sālim. In the story of Karamokho Ba of Touba (c. 1730-1824), whose baptismal name was taken from al-Ḥājj Sālim (see Chapter 5), we come across the same meticulous scruple against being embroiled in war or politics; he even (c. 1803) extracted a promise and an undertaking from the Timbo and Labé ruling aristocracies to this effect. Also relevant is the message the Jakhanke cleric, Karamokho Qutubo, sent to Alfa Yahya when the French were beginning to penetrate into Guinea, urging him to surrender and not offer any resistance (see pp. 116-7 below). This evidence might be seen as confirming Thomas Hodgkin's hypothesis (1962: 326) that traditional Islamic institutions and ideas helped to retard the growth of national resistance movements. But it is also direct evidence of the influence and power of clerical opinion and judgement on war, and it is worthy of the tradition usually associated with al-Ḥājj Sālim.

Jakhanke consistency in upholding a tradition of pacifism as a necessary corollary to clerical and missionary activity makes it clear that al-Ḥājj Sālim as the founder and initiator of this tradition holds the key to the absence of significant *jihād* wars among people predominantly influenced by his teachings. Wilks (1968: 179) cautiously suggested this, even though he was working with only limited sources on the life of al-Ḥājj Sālim, and was too hastily set upon by John Hunwick (1972) who, it would seem implausibly, advanced trade as the reason for such clerical pacifism. Jakhanke involvement in trade has, as a rule, been marginal, and anyway commerce itself in terms of competition for markets can equally be the breeding ground of armed conflicts, so that it hardly qualifies as a *sine qua non* of pacifism.[23] The network system of clerical establishments characteristic of the Jakhanke, which Hunwick sees as the weak link as far as military potential is concerned, is in fact an efficient basis for the movement of personnel, resources and materials for the support of clerical communities dotted along the dispersion trail, or, as Hunwick puts it, 'isolated in small pockets'.[24]

Al-Ḥājj Sālim is claimed by the Jakhanke to be the original propounder of their characteristic tradition of communal clerical withdrawal and isolation, on the one hand, and, on the other, of the repudiation of the use of arms and *jihād* in principle. To use the success of this tradition as an argument for introducing other factors like trade and the over-extended diaspora as explanatory reasons seems circuitous. The sanctions for maintaining such a tradition go back to the man who first proclaimed it as a distinctive and inherent principle of the clerical vocation, namely, al-Ḥājj Sālim. Writing specifically of his contribution to and impact on Islamic education, Wilks writes:

> Over a large part of West Africa the institutional framework within which teaching has been organised seems largely his work, and the high esteem in which learning is held...must be attributed in no small part to the existence of regulations which militate against charlatanism and venality. (1968: 179)

The Chronology of al-Ḥājj Sālim

When did al-Ḥājj Sālim Suware live? Wilks' (1968: 178) 'notional date' of 1500 as the probable year of his death is too late to allow us to account for developments initiated by him and carried to other parts of West Africa by the communities which succeeded him. Although it seems that local sources are inclined to exaggerate al-Ḥājj Sālim's antiquity, the date of A.H. 542/A.D. 1147 given as his death in one account should not be hastily dismissed (Wilks 1968: 177). *TSK* says that Diakha-Bambukhu was dissolved after it had been in existence for 500 years, and it was after this that dispersion took place towards the Western Atlantic and other places. The foundation of many clerical centres in Niokholo, Dentilia and other parts of Bundu is claimed in tradition to stem directly from the dissolution of Diakha-Bambukhu (P. Smith 1965b: 279). Other centres like Gunjūr, Qayrawān, and Sutukho are likely to have preceded the decline of Diakha-Bambukhu (see Sanneh 1974a: 150-61). A source emanating from al-Ḥājj Mbalu Fode Jabi, the Jakhanke cleric and Mālikī Muftī of Senegal (*TSB*) says that al-Ḥājj Sālim flourished in the sixth century (500th year) of the Hijrah (that is, the twelfth century A.D.). Another source says that it is '748 years since the Jakhanke dispersed from Diakhaba.'[25] The figure is based on the Islamic lunar calendar, as are most Jakhanke figures of this kind.

Local sources in Bambukhu in the eighteenth century described an invasion of major proportions in about 1100 A.D., but more probably in the course of the twelfth century, which led to the forcible imposition of Islam. The invasion was led by one Abba Manko at the head of some 10,000 troops who occupied the country and put to the sword those who resisted conversion.[26] Whether this episode came before or after Jakhanke settlement in Bambukhu is not stated, but it seems most likely that it preceded the arrival of the Jakhanke, since it is hard to imagine the Jakhanke clerics being attracted to Bambukhu before Islam had been introduced. The Jakhanke probably capitalised on the Muslim presence established by Abba Manko.

Two other events connected with the preceding account may have had a bearing on the Jakhanke in Bambukhu. According to local traditions the Portuguese penetrated the country in the fifteenth century and soon after their arrival they were implicated in sanguinary conflicts with the local inhabitants who finally chased them off. Shortly thereafter local Muslims banded together in an effort to overturn the Manko ruling dynasty, and the Muslims were led or encouraged by a powerful clerical party :

> On sait que ces prêtres mahométans forment une caste particulière, chez toutes les nations noires de l'Afrique, qui suivent la religion de Mahomet...ils formèrent un parti contre l'autorité de chefs du pays... (Golberry 1802: I 423).

Whether this refers to the Jakhanke or to another group is unclear, but it suggests a clerical tradition more or less parallel to their practice, except for the hint of a possible participation in direct military insurgency. The Muslim bid for power in this attempted *coup d'état* failed abysmally and a vengeful dynasty and its supporters put to the sword a large number of suspected dissidents and forced other Muslims to flee the country (Golberry 1802: I 423). Only two kinds of cause are given for the evacuation of Diakha-Bambukhu: one emphasises the external factor of a war breaking out between Bambukhu and the Berbers,[27] and the other points to internal causes of disputes and rivalries between the various *qabīlah* leaders.[28] But it is reasonable to assume that if the Jakhanke were still in Diakha-Bambukhu at the time local Muslims were being rounded up they too would have been affected by these troubles and thus pressed to leave the country. Thus the arrival of the Portuguese and the abortive Muslim uprising may be two events connected with the fate of the Jakhanke in Diakha-Bambukhu.

If the Jakhanke community left Bambukhu for areas in Niokholo, Dentilia, Khasso and Bundu (see Map 3) sometime in the late fifteenth century as our sources claim, then their dispersion to these and other places, including Hausaland, hangs together in a meaningful chronological whole. The first wave of immigrants went to already existing centres like Qayrawān, Banī Isrā'ila, Gunjūr and Sutukho. But a good many, particularly the direct descendants of al-Ḥājj Sālim, stopped just short of Bundu at places in Niokholo and Dentilia. The earliest centres in these places were settlements like Diakha-Madina, Sillacounda and Ballori (where an important Jabi-Gassama lineage, led by a disciple of al-Ḥājj Sālim, according to tradition, went to settle) (P. Smith 1965a: 244, 255; 1965b: 279). The evacuation of Diakha-Bambukhu, if it took place in the late fifteenth century, still leaves open the question of its founding by al-Ḥājj Sālim, but such a terminal date may give a clue to its origin.

Another way to calculate the approximate life-span of Diakha-Bambukhu is to examine the *salāsil* (sing. *silsilah*), chains of transmission, and similar genealogical data. It should be pointed out at once that these materials are far from secure and cannot be relied on entirely. That said, they nevertheless give us an idea, however vague, of the direction in which we should proceed. al-Ḥājj Soriba Jabi gives a list of 21 names of *imām ratti* who reigned after al-Ḥājj Sālim before Diakha-Bambukhu finally broke up.[29] If *TSK* is right in stating that Diakha-Bambukhu existed for 500 years then this gives a generation unit of 23-24 years. But this need not be decisive for our calculations.

An oblique reference to al-Ḥājj Sālim's chronology is contained in the tradition which says that when the Fulbe first appeared in Masina they were received by 'the holy man', al-Ḥājj Sālim Suware. From Masina, according to this tradition, the Fulbe, following the instructions of al-Ḥājj Sālim, travelled southeastwards to arrive eventually in present-day Futa Jallon (Reichardt 1876: 319; see also Jamburiah 1919). If such a conjunction between the Fulbe and al-Ḥājj Sālim is to be of use a rough idea of the epoch in which the Fulbe arrived in Masina has to be provided. According to other Fulbe traditions, they arrived in the Sahil (Masina) in the reign of Banna Bubu (Delafosse 1913), which Trimingham (1962:58) fixes between 1100 and 1120. This also then suggests a twelfth century *floruit* for al-Ḥājj Sālim.

The evidence on the chronology of al-Ḥājj Sālim begins to thin out at this point. However, the early history of Diakha-Bambukhu, assuming that al-Ḥājj Sālim founded the town, is relevant here and is discussed in one or two sources. Charles Monteil writes of the introduction of Islam to the Upper Senegal region in the eleventh century (with reference probably to the conversion of War Diabī, ruler of Takrūr (d. 1041) (Trimingham 1962: 28), and suggests the importance of a clerical tradition on the model of Diakha-Bambukhu:

> Au XIe siècle l'implantation de l'Islam dans le Haut-Sénégal s'accompagna de noyautage sous forme de collectivités disséminées un peu partout, et aussi de la constitution de gros centres quasi exclusivement musulmans comme celui de Diakha-sur-Bafing qui compta dix villages [*qabīlah* sections]...Diakha fut un centre de rayonnement considérable, surtout vers la Gambie et les pays du sud, la Falémé et les pays au nord. (Ch. Monteil 1926: 598)

Elsewhere Monteil hints at a very early date for the foundation of Diakha-Bambukhu, saying that it was founded by immigrants from Diakha-Masina:

> Diakha-sur-Bafing est de notoriété indigène, le point d'où ont essaimé tout les Ouangara de la région aurifère, connue pour cela sous le nom de Diakhanké: la fondation de cette Diakha-sur-Bafing remonte très haut dans le passé et est attribuée à des émigrants de Dia du Macina. (Ch. Monteil 1929: 44-5)

The Legacy of al-Ḥājj Sālim

It would be rash, in the present state of our knowledge, to pronounce a firm verdict on the dates of al-Ḥājj Sālim beyond saying that he and the Diakha-Bambukhu he is claimed to have founded flourished sometime around the twelfth and thirteenth centuries. His achievements and the reasons for the renown of Diakha-Bambukhu are less subject to dispute. An autonomous cohesive clerical solidarity developed at Diakha-Bambukhu where, in addition, a fundamental cultural transformation took place. There the Jakhanke rapidly shed some of their distinguishing Serakhulle traits as they were progressively absorbed into the literary Islamic tradition they so enthusiastically adopted. For example, their racial/ethnic heroes were no longer Ɗinga and his illustrious posterity but Classical Islamic personages: the Four Orthodox Caliphs, Salmān the Persian, Bilāl ibn Rabāḥ and so on (see Sanneh 1974a: 51-2). Another significant cultural wave which helped to submerge some of their Serakhulle identity was the adjacent Manding environment. From their own point of view their alliance with the Manding merely extended the ethnic corridor of their influence, but from the point of view of the historian this is another source of an increasingly complex ethnic riddle. Sources refer to them henceforth under different names: Wangara, Jula (Manding for trader), Mandingoes, Serakhulle, Soninke, as well as professional titles such as Karamokho (teacher), Moriman, Marabout, Muslim priest, bookman, and Jobson's quaint terms, Marybucke and Bissareas (Ar. *bashīr*, pl. *busharā*) ([1623] 1968: 61-2, 78-81, 85).

Diakha-Bambukhu's communal integrity and clerical autonomy were respected by the rulers of Mali of which Bambukhu was a province. The *Ta'rīkh al-Fattāsh*[30] carries a tradition about the town's prestige as a clerical centre, written at a time when it had ceased to exist. It says:

> There was... at the time of the supremacy of Mali, a town called Diakha-Ba (or Diaᶜba), a centre of jurisconsults situated in the interior of the kingdom of Mali. The king of Mali never entered it and no one exercised authority there outside the *qāḍī*. Whoever entered the town had automatic sanctuary from harm or interference from the king. Even if he had killed one of the children of the king, the latter could not exact recompense. They gave it the epithet 'the city of God'. ([my transl.] Kaᶜtī 1913: 314, Ar. 179)[31]

The clerical eminence of Diakha-Bambukhu was not an isolated phenomenon, and in this respect al-Ḥājj Sālim's achievement was both a durable and a cumulative legacy. The rest of this chapter will be devoted to two specific examples showing how this legacy was perpetuated: one concerns a clerical settlement, Gunjūr, and the other a clerical personage, ᶜAbd al-Raḥmān Jakhite.

Diakha-Bambukhu's eminence was shared with another centre,

namely, Gunjūr (Ar. Kunjūru), the holy town of the Darame clerics, situated on the peripheries of Bundu in the area called Kaniaga (sometimes Kanyaga) or Khasso. It is described by the *Ta'rīkh al-Fattāsh* (Ka^c^ti 1913: 314, Ar. 179) which says that according to a local informant, Muḥammad Sire, himself of a clerical Jakhanke lineage, the supreme authority there was the *qāḍī*, assisted by an assembly of *^c^ulamā*. No one represented the secular authority and the power of the king was limited to the observance of certain religious ceremonies. Every year in the fast (*ṣawm*) month of Ramaḍān the king of Kaniaga visited the town as the guest of the *qāḍī*, taking with him appropriate presents and offerings. On the night of the 26/27, regarded in the Muslim religious calendar as a holy night (Qur'ān xcvii; ii: 181), the king ordered cooked meals which he distributed from a dish or calabash perched on his head. He gave the food to Qur'ān school children who afterwards cried down blessings on him. The king was then judged to have satisfied his obligations to the clerical town (Ka^c^ti 1913: 315, Ar. 180). On the face of it the king may have been making an annual religious pilgrimage (did he take an annual tribute as well?) but the clerics definitely held all the diplomatic trumps: they could hold the king to account on the ritual requirements of what had become an obligatory condition of kingship. The later history of Gunjūr is taken up in Chapters 3 and 4 below but it may be remarked here that its clerical autonomy continued to be respected until late in the nineteenth century when the French sacked it as the natal town and military base of the *mujāhid*, Momodou-Lamin, against whom they were fighting.

The dispersions to Khasso, Niokholo, Dentilia and Bundu from Diakha-Bambukhu beginning in the mid-fifteenth century or thereabouts are complemented by a similar clerical settlement in Hausaland, set up at approximately the same time, which suggests a common source of departure. The account of this is contained in *Aṣl al-Wanqarayīn*, a recently discovered seventeenth century chronicle on the origins of the 'Wangara' in Kano. It is one example of how Sudanic Islamic history has created common patterns across vast distances. In the document the name 'Wangara' is used not to describe traders but an ethno-linguistic group of Manding speakers. By that time the Jakhanke, from their contacts in Bambukhu, had assimilated Manding cultural elements. The chronicle says that these 'Wangara' clerics were the descendants of an unidentified '*shaykh*', and the leader of the 'Wangara' party was a certain ^{c}Abd al-Raḥmān Jakhite (Ar. 'Zaite' or 'Zaghite') (Ḥājj 1968: 10, Ar. 3-4). Once ^{c}Abd al-Raḥmān Jakhite is recognised as a Jakhanke cleric, which he has not hitherto been, then it is more than likely that the '*shaykh*' of whose community he was a member was al-Ḥājj Sālim Suware. Such an interpretation of course has far-reaching consequences for an understanding of Jakhanke clerical history in the Western Sudan. This ^{c}Abd al-Raḥmān and his followers left Mali (read Bambukhu as in Ka^{c}ti 1913: 179) in the year A.H. 835 (1431/32 A.D.) with the stated intention of proceeding to Mecca on pilgrimage, accompanied by 3,636 versatile scholars (Ar. *al-^{c}ulamā al-mutafannin bi-kulli fannin*) (Ḥājj 1968: Ar. 5) but other traditions say it was 160 *qabīlah* sections (*ibid*). The confusion (and the touch of hyperbole) may be due to the scribe mixing up the story of al-Ḥājj Sālim with that of ^{c}Abd al-Raḥmān Jakhite. Be that as it may, after ^{c}Abd al-Raḥmān declared his intention to leave on *ḥājj*, the ruler of Mali pressed him in vain to defer his departure. Details of his travel, including a miracle he performed at a river-crossing where it was planned ultimately to thwart him, are then given until his arrival in Kano (Ḥājj 1968: 10, Ar. 6-9). Accompanied by his wives, Sise and Kebe, four sons, three daughters and three brothers, among others, ^{c}Abd al-Raḥmān took up residence in Kano at about the same time as the famous fifteenth century Muslim, ^{c}Abd al-Karīm al-Maghīlī, alias Sīdī Fārī.[32] Recognised by al-Maghīlī as an outstanding scholar (he is reputed to have learnt by heart the Mālikī jurisprudential work of al-Tanūkhī (d. 854 A.D.), *al-Mudawwana al-Kubrā*), ^{c}Abd al-Raḥmān was recommended to the Sarki (ruler) Muḥammad Rimfa (reigned 1463-99).[33] Convinced of the value and prestige of having such a learned man living in his court, Rimfa entreated ^{c}Abd al-Raḥmān to abandon his pilgrimage vows and stay in Kano under his royal patronage, which ^{c}Abd al-Raḥmān agreed to do (Ḥājj 1968: 13, Ar. 16-17).

This raises the question whether ^{c}Abd al-Raḥmān left Bambukhu of his own volition. The details of his travels, his persistence in undertaking the *ḥājj* against royal pressure at Bambukhu, the character and description of his enormous entourage and his subsequent willingness to settle in Kano with his pilgrimage vows still unfulfilled, all suggest that ^{c}Abd al-Raḥmān abandoned Bambukhu for reasons other than the *ḥājj*. Why should he be willing to adopt Rimfa as a royal patron when he had refused similar prospects nearer home, taking considerable risks with his entire community in the process? It is much more likely that ᶜAbd al-Raḥmān Jakhite was a man in the tradition of al-Ḥājj Sālim whose emigration from Diakha-Masina to Bambukhu provides the model for Jakhanke dispersion. We have in ᶜAbd al-Raḥmān an example of a Jakhanke community's withdrawal and transplantation across barriers of culture and language. The pretext of going on *ḥājj* or other business is familiar to us from other Jakhanke clerics, and it may have enabled ᶜAbd al-Raḥmān and his community to withdraw peacefully without the danger of incurring royal reprisal, although an incident at a river-crossing where all the boats were tied at the opposite bank shows that more than a trace of hostility was directed at him.

Once installed in Kano ᶜAbd al-Raḥmān quickly established a definite Islamic image for the city. Kano had probably been introduced to Islam before the arrival of ᶜAbd al-Raḥmān. According to the Kano Chronicle (Palmer 1908: 70) Islam was brought there in the reign of Yājī (1349-85), but this is not consonant with the present analysis in that it says that the man who took Islam there at that time was this same ᶜAbd al-Raḥmān Jakhite. Nevertheless the city was the centre of a strong and vigorous pagan religion. One of ᶜAbd al-Raḥmān's first symbolic public gestures towards the local Islamic circles, apart from his agreement to settle in Kano, was to assist in having a sacred tamarind tree, used for pagan worship, hewn down and the sacred images scattered. The site was used for the erection of a Friday mosque (Ḥājj 1968: 12, Ar. 15-16). Another activity for which ᶜAbd al-Raḥmān was distinguished in Kano was the practice of Qur'ān recital (Ar. *tartīl*) and other devotional exercises at night (*ibid:* 12, Ar. 14). In fact learning and teaching seem to have occupied a large part of his time. We have already seen how he is claimed to have memorised the work of al-Tanūkhī. It was during his stay in Kano that the standard Mālikī legal text, *al-Makhtaṣar* of Khalīl, was introduced there from Cairo by a visitor. ᶜAbd al-Raḥmān had meanwhile lost his sight, and when told of the arrival of a *shaykh* from Egypt he decided to meet him in what turned out to be an intellectual duel. (Was this because ᶜAbd al-Raḥmān felt his tight grip on the city threatened by a learned man like himself?) The Egyptian visitor recited a portion of *al-Mukhtaṣar* from memory, to which ᶜAbd al-Raḥmān listened attentively. At one point in the passage he interrupted the Egyptian with an observation about a slight textual deviation. On reference to the book ᶜAbd al-Raḥmān was found to be right and thus, in the eyes of the audience, vindicated.[34]

ᶜAbd al-Raḥmān Jakhite died in Kano, but even after his death (the year of which is not given) his clerical prestige remained considerable. Muḥammad Rimfa, before his death (1499), asked that he be buried at the side of ᶜAbd al-Raḥmān who had predeceased him, 'so that', in his own words, 'I might obtain his *barakah*' (Ar. *laᶜallī ajidu barakatuhu*) (Ḥājj 1968: 14, Ar. 20). After the death of ᶜAbd al-Raḥmān his sons and others of his community carried his work further into Hausaland. As the author of the chronicle says, ᶜAbd al-Raḥmān had established and consolidated (in typical Jakhanke fashion, we might add) the ties of clerical kinship, and introduced what had been inherited from al-Ḥājj Sālim, namely, the notion of a charismatic community founded and perpetuated in the spirit and style of a peaceful clerical personality. From this point of view al-Ḥājj Sālim's effect on Sudanic Islam has been most profound and widespread.

NOTES

1 I have preferred to keep to the word Serakhulle rather than Soninke because in the Senegambian context the latter is overlaid with ambiguity and is used to refer to pagans. Mungo Park, travelling in 1795-7, whose credibility is discussed below (p. 66n), said that the 'Sonakies' or, in another place, 'Soninkees', were pagans with a strong penchant for alcoholic beverage and were the target of Muslim military action ([1799] 1969: 25, 303). Trimingham said that the terms 'Soninke' was used by the people themselves but that the Wolof referred to them as 'Sera-kule', meaning 'red man' (1959: 13n). But the name 'Serakhulle' occurs in a much wider tradition. A 16th century source says the Serakhulle were engaged in active trade with merchants from Cairo as well as the Maghrib from two principal centres, Jenne and Timbuktu (Lange and Berthoud 1972). Muḥammad Bello (d. 1837) in his *Infāq al-Maisūr* mentions the Serakhulle under the name 'Sarankulli' (1957: Ar. 208-9; Arnett 1922: 137-8). A section of them, according to Trimingham, living in Western Masina in Dia, are called 'Dyakanké'. In French sources these are referred to as Diakhanké and other variants. The Serakhulle of our discussion were estimated by Trimingham to number some 450,000, 'impregnated by Berber and Fulbe. They are agriculturalists attached to the soil, yet also great travellers and out-rival Dyula as traders in the western Sudan. As the basic population of... Ghana they were islamised at an early date and have played a considerable role in the islamisation of the Sudan. Islam has deeply influenced their social life but, like Saharans, the ruling classes and agriculturalists tend to leave practice to clerical clans' (1959: 13-14). A branch of these people are also known as the Marka in the middle Niger area (Levtzion: 1972).

2 In Niokholo and Dentilia, where some of the descendants of al-Ḥājj

Sālim went to settle, there was a quasi-saint cult practised around his name, but this was strictly controlled. Pilgrims and visitors made offerings of kola-nuts - 50 or 100 pieces - to the Suware *qabīlah* and asked for special prayers in return. Such prayers were normally for fertility and rain (P. Smith 1965b: 281). On p. 198ff. below this question of the cult of saints among the Jakhanke is more carefully examined.

3 *Mbemba* means Patriarch, ancestor, and is used of al-Ḥājj Sālim as a pious honorific.

4 *Su-ware*, a compound Manding word, does not mean red horse, as Wilks claims (1968: 178). He may have been misled by Mézières, who says that the name derives from an ancestor of the Jakhanke who was riding a red horse through a Serakhulle village when the title was given him (1949: 23). The context makes it clear that al-Ḥājj Sālim was distinguished among the riders by his piebald mount. *Su* means horse, and *ware* means alternating colourful patterns.

5 Al-Ḥājj Sālim is made one of the three sons of Dinga (or Digna), the ancestor or father of Magham Diabe Sise, and a half-brother of Magham himself. In one account he is referred to simply as 'Diakhaba Foune', literally, a twin of Diakhaba. By Diakhaba of course is meant not Diakha-Masina but Diakha-Bambukhu which al-Ḥājj Sālim is claimed to have founded (Delafosse 1913: 7). Another source says his name is Fode al-Ḥājj Suware (Ch. Monteil 1953). On the identification of Wagadu as the ancient Ghana of written accounts see Levtzion 1973: 20ff.

6 *TSK* emanates from al-Ḥājj Banfa Jabi, eldest son of Karamokho Sankoung of Touba, and was copied by his student and disciple, Fode Khousi Darame, from an original retained by Banfa. This copy is not without flaws but they are easily recognisable. It was submitted to Banfa at his new home in Senegal for his permission to use it. Al-Ḥājj Banfa in his younger days at Touba in Guinea was Paul Marty's informant for the Jakhanke material in *L'Islam en Guinée* where he is referred to as Alfa Oumarou (1921: 112; see also Chapter 6). Banfa died early in the New Year, 1975, at his adopted home in Senegal, Macca-Kolibantang.

7 The text reads: *fa'amma laqabahu bi-tulli fādiqa li-kawnihi yaḥibbu ṣanᶜati al-ḥīja li-ṭalaba bi-ᶜasal li-yataṣadaqa bihi al-nās* (*TSK*: fo. 2). Translation: 'and as for the reason why 'Tulli' was acquired by the Fadiga people, it is because of the fondness of the Fadiga for extracting honey in order to make free-will offerings to the people.' I take *al-ḥīja* to be a mis-spelling for *al-ḥājah*. It is not clear from the context whether the Fadiga were fond of making free-will offerings to the people or of honey extraction as an occupation.

8 Ḥājj 1968: 9 n. 19). The chronicle describes events in the mid-fifteenth century and may have been based on a source, probably written, which was somehow lost. The chronicler does not tell us anything about his own immediate source and is unlikely to have been personally acquainted with the earlier original material.

9 Wilks 1968. Philip Curtin, accepting Wilks' date for al-Ḥājj Sālim, writes: 'Some accounts say that Salimou Soare founded Diakhaba,

which seems unlikely' (1971b: 288; q.v. ff.; see also 1972). Pierre Smith similarly makes light of such claims among the Jakhanke, saying that hagiographical material among the less educated clerics shows that the Jakhanke 'n'ont pas une idée très précise de la profondeur historique et que la conservation de généalogies n'est pas, chez eux, soumise à une exigence de vraisemblance chronologique' (1965a: 236). It is true that the Jakhanke, though literate and on the whole consistent, are by no means critical historians. However, in the fundamental question of clerical pacifism, for example, they are concerned to set forth their views with historical accuracy; see pp. 134-5 for Karamokho Sankoung's statement on this subject.

10 See Delafosse 1913: 7; Ch. Monteil 1953: 372, both of whom say that al-Ḥājj Sālim was the founding father and Patriarch of Diakha-Bambukhu. *TSK* uses the Arabic word from the root *assa*, meaning to found, create: *wa annahum al-mu'assisīna balad zaghāba al-qadīm* ('and they founded the ancient town of Diakhaba') (fo. 2).

11 Oral traditions collected in Jimara-Bakadaji, chiefly from al-Ḥājj Janko Darame, 11/12/72.

12 The standard work on Islamic divination is the massive definitive two-volume opus of ᶜAbd al-Ghanī al-Nābulsī (1641-1731): *Taᶜṭīr al-Anām fī Taᶜbīr al-Manām*, in wide use among the Jakhanke. Muḥammad ibn Sīrīn (d. 728 A.D.) is also a familiar name among the Jakhanke clerics, and a small manual, *Taᶜbīr al-Ru'yā*, is attributed to him. See also Fahd 1966. Humphrey Fisher (1971) discusses prayer in particular. See Chapter 8, for further details on Islamic divination among the Jakhanke.

13 A term originally applied to Muḥammad's companions who accompanied him on the Hijrah (emigration) from Mecca to Medina in A.D. 622, the beginning of the Islamic calendar. See Watt 1962.

14 Al-Ḥājj Janko Darame, Bakadaji, 11/12/72.

15 Literally, the upright or righteous men, but in the clerical context it carries the meaning of 'the four pillars of clerical orthodoxy'. It is obviously patterned on *al-Khulafā'u al-Rāshidūn*, the Rightly Guided Caliphs, used of the first four successors (*khulafā'u*) of the Prophet: Abu Bakr, ᶜUmar, ᶜUthmān and ᶜAlī. *Al-rijāl al-ṣāliḥīna* were the appointments of al-Ḥājj Sālim, and their creation established the principle of collective leadership for Jakhanke communities.

16 The phrase means those whose prayers are always granted, and in Ṣūfī Islam it is one of the qualities of a saint (*walī*), who is a *mujāb al-duᶜā* (Goldziher 1967/71: II 269). For Ṣūfī parallels in Jakhanke Islam see p. 163ff. below. Ṣūfīsm is the system of esoteric religion in which the Seeker (*murīd*) traverses the 'Path' of illuminated knowledge of the Ultimate Reality under the guidance of the Master or Guide (*shaykh*).

17 Kaabu was a state in Upper Guinea founded, according to tradition, by one of Sunjata's generals, Tirimakhan. Whether it was known by that name in al-Ḥājj Sālim's time is hard to say (see Cissoko 1972). Kaabu was destroyed as a state when Kansala, the centre of the main resistance of the Sane-Mane (the two royal families), was taken in 1867 by Fulbe warriors from Labé (see Person 1974: II 287). Kaabu has passed

into tradition as the great epic of Sane-Mane bravery.

18 These oral traditions were collected in the Gambia and southern Senegal (see Map 5 below). The most important Jakhanke clerical establishment in Casamance at present is that under the leadership of al-Ḥājj Mbalu Fode Jabi at Marssassoum. His son, Sidiya Jabi, runs programmes on Radio Senegal at Ziguinchor on Islamic matters. Al-Ḥājj Mbalu Fode is the Mālikī Muftī of Senegal, a position now of theoretical importance only.

19 One account says that before al-Ḥājj Sālim died he was dismayed by signs of *qabīlah* jealousies and uttered a curse which left the Jakhanke fragmented into numerous communities instead of a unified harmonious body (see Sanneh 1974a: 125). But this account must be handled with care. The need for a unified community is keenly felt among many thinking Muslims who are anxious to have the Unity of God (Ar. *tawḥīd*) embodied and reflected as a sociological reality, and it may simply be this desire which is finding expression in this tradition. The environmental factors which determine the proliferation of scattered, if co-ordinated, settlements are discussed on pp. 62-4.

20 Philip Curtin considers the emergence of clerical groups in West African Islam, but in his view this was motivated chiefly by the minority status of Muslims in a predominantly non-Muslim society. In order to safeguard their position, such Muslims, Curtin says, sought autonomy from political rulers and acquired a reputation for neutrality in war time, which enabled them 'to secure safe passage for commerce in long-distance trade' (1971a: 13). But this is somewhat unhelpful speculation, and when applied to the Jakhanke, in the way that Curtin does, it is misleading.

21 Willis has written that the Kunta *shuyūkh* in their *zawāyā* (sing. *zāwiyah*), religious retreats, had 'renounced the use of arms and hence depended upon their *barakah* and diplomatic skills as a means of exercising influence' (1970: 268). Aḥmad al-Bakkā'i also wrote in similar terms to al-Ḥājj ᶜUmar al-Fūtī of his position on repudiation of *jihād* (Willis 1970: 272). On al-Ḥājj ᶜUmar himself some traditions claim that the Saghanogho *ᶜulamā* of Bobo-Dioulasso, Upper Volta, an area traversed by Jakhanke clerics and their disciples, advised al-Ḥājj ᶜUmar against his *jihād* (Wilks 1968: 179n). The work of Thomas Whitcomb, still in progress, among the Berbers of the Western Sahara has also shown the presence of clerical groups among the Tajakant. However, clerical Berber groups belong to a confederacy of warrior and other groups, and many of the clerical groups carry arms (Whitcomb 1972).

22 Jakhanke wealth was most obvious in the large towns and settlements, and the accompanying farmlands and livestock which the more important clerics owned. These would be liable to outright confiscation as a matter of secular policy. Although most clerics did not attain that stature, many owned considerable property, some of it in liquid form. Al-Ḥājj Cherno Silla of Jinani, Casamance, for example, bequeathed £12,000, 5.5 million CFA francs, plus 141 head of cattle, when he died in the 1890s (information from his grandson, al-Ḥājj Khousi Silla, Brikama).

23 Trade as a full-time occupation and long-range exploit can be

disruptive of the cohesion of a clerical centre. The problem of maintaining a viable Qur'ān school tightly controlled by a resident master would be an acute one, if not altogether impossible to handle, if a cleric divided his time between teaching and trading. Farming is better suited to the clerical basis of a sedentary, if at times mobile, community. It is also important to realise that some of the Islamic reformers had an unflattering opinion of traders. ᶜAbdallāh ibn Muḥammad, the brother of ᶜUthmān dan Fūdī, wrote with an ascetic disdain for an irreligious world full of fantasies, saying 'its dogs are the traders' (Hiskett 1973: 148).

24 Hunwick 1972. Network organisation as a general problem is outside the scope of this work, as well as being beyond my competence. It is discussed in Meillassoux 1971, e.g. by Abner Cohen. In the case of the Jakhanke the isolationist feature of their enclaves is more deliberately determined, by reasons other than trade. Some of the better known centres attracted considerable trade, but the siting of a large proportion of clerical settlements in somewhat inaccessible areas (Touba is an excellent example) suggests withdrawal rather than commercial motivation. The religious and educational considerations as well as geographical factors underlying the choice of clerical centres are discussed more fully in Chapters 3 and 7 below.

25 Maḥmūd Jīlānī Jikinne, Sutukung, 16/11/72.

26 Golberry 1802: I 420. Golberry describes at the beginning of this section of his travels how he obtained the oral accounts which, despite his prejudice against them, he decided to include in his writings.

27 *TSK:* fo. 3. Fode Dusu Suware, a descendant of al-Ḥājj Sālim, was the presiding cleric of Diakhaba at this time.

28 Oral materials collected from Muḥammad Khalīfa Silla at Kounti; al-Ḥājj Fode Jabi at Sandu-Jakhaba; and al-Ḥājj Soriba Jabi at Macca-Kolibantang.

29 Al-Ḥājj Soriba Jabi, Macca-Kolibantang, 10/12/72.

30 The *Ta'rīkh al-Fattāsh* was begun by Maḥmūd al-Kaᶜti (b. 1468) in 1519 and completed by his grandson, ibn al-Mukhtār, in about 1664. (On its authorship, see Trimingham 1962: 5; and more fully Levtzion 1971.)

31 The 'Diakha' of Djibril Niane (1971), called 'city of divines', is almost certainly Diakha-Masina, although Wilks erroneously links it with Diakha-Bambukhu (1968: 178). Levtzion confuses the two as well, saying that the 'Diakhaba' described by Kaᶜti is Diakha-Masina (1973: 201).

32 Ḥājj 1968: 12. On al-Maghīlī see Batrān 1973. Al-Maghīlī's death is put by Batrān and Hunwick (1966: 306) at 1503/4 or 1505/6, though Trimingham (1962: 98n) has 1532, probably an error.

33 Ḥājj 1968: 8 suggests this revised date (in the 15th rather than 14th century); but see Kano Chronicle (Palmer 1908: 77).

34 Ḥājj 1968: 13-14, Ar. 18-19. Elaborate preparations were made for

this encounter. Advance notice was given and the visiting *shaykh* was advised to roll up his sleeves and prime himself for the occasion. The visitor, perhaps unnerved, passed a sleepless night in study. Next day ᶜAbd al-Raḥmān arrived in the compound of the visitor mounted. After the recitation and the final outcome of the encounter ᶜAbd al-Raḥmān mounted his horse again, supported by the Egyptian. In the eyes of the townspeople ᶜAbd al-Raḥmān had risen to new heights.

CHAPTER TWO

THE EMERGENCE OF THE CORE CLANS OF JAKHANKE CLERICS

c. 1200 - c. 1700

Although al-Ḥājj Sālim took great care to establish an institutional framework for educational and other types of clerical activity to continue after his death, he remained in his lifetime the primary and overriding influence in Jakhanke clericalism. As long as he was alive he was the source and arbiter of the Bambukhu clerical republic. Moreover, the characteristics Diakha-Bambukhu acquired under his leadership became the model for similar clerical settlements elsewhere. His influence was pervasive and enduring.

The emergence of a durable clerical core in Jakhanke Islam derived from the structural and organisational patterns he had established at Bambukhu. All the major Jakhanke clerical families continued to acknowledge him as their prototype even when they were separated from him by the great gap of several centuries and the dust of dispersion trails had obscured their memory of him as a personal model of inspiration.[1]

Soon after arriving in Bambukhu al-Ḥājj Sālim set about organising the new settlement. He divided Diakha-Bambukhu into four main sections or wards: Suwarekunda, Daramekunda, Fofana-Girasikunda and Fadigakunda (*TSK:* fo. 3). Relations between these *qabīlah* sections were maintained through intermarriage, a common allegiance to al-Ḥājj Sālim's memory after his death and in the celebration of certain communal religious feasts such as at Ramaḍān and Dhū al-Ḥijjah, and especially in the solemnisation of marriage and the observance of ritual obligations related to it (*TSK:* fo. 3). More details are given in *TSK* on some of the specific items exchanged at weddings and how the descendants of these *qabā'il* continued to observe such proprieties. In Chapter 5 we shall see that a much later Jakhanke cleric, in setting up a clerical republic of his own, followed a similar procedure in organising his community. The organisation of the clerical community was centred around the mosque, which became the symbol of community solidarity as well as the opportunity for harnessing and co-ordinating its energies under the four representative leaders, called in the sources *al-rijāl al-ṣāliḥīna*, 'the upright men' (*TSK*: fo. 3).

Although political responsibility for the community was distributed among the four *qabīlah* sections, which in fact were merely the formalisation of al-Ḥājj Sālim's authority through the recognised male agnates, nevertheless this was not a static or fixed arrangement. Within each *qabīlah* section a certain amount of fluidity existed so that newcomers could be incorporated and given precise functions. This internal elasticity was further stretched to apply to the composite character of the town. An important feature of Jakhanke settlements was the principle of an open and undefended centre to which outsiders might, if they wished, come for adoption as clients or members of the community, although full adoption into the clerical vocation was strictly confined to a small section of islamised Serakhulle. This happened in Diakha-Bambukhu. Very soon groups of islamised Serakhulle, among others, gravitated towards the town and were given a place in the community. Of these, the Jakhite-Kabba were one of the most important groups. The others were the Silla and the Jabi-Gassama. Some of these additional members of the Diakha-Bambukhu community were to assume the role of preserving, consolidating and disseminating the legacy of al-Ḥājj Sālim, particularly when a lineage shift in terms of clerical power reduced the parent Suware clan to comparative obscurity. It is necessary, therefore, to provide a detailed sketch of the early history of these three other main clerical families. Attention will also be drawn to the way these three clans relinquished their evident Serakhulle background and adopted Classical Islamic heroes in place of their Sudanic ancestors.

The Jakhite-Kabba

Oral traditions trace the origins of the Jakhite,[2] also known as Kabba, Jakhanke to a certain Hamjatou (Ar. Hamzah), about whose identity there is considerable doubt. Most accounts say this Hamjatou was the Prophet's paternal uncle (Ar. *ᶜamm*) (see, e.g., Rançon 1894a: 173-7; Vuillet 1952; Humblot 1918). But a respected Jakhanke scholar, al-Ḥājj Kemoring Jakhite,[3] has questioned the literal truth of this claim, and to his argument we must turn in a moment. The attempt to link the Jakhite clerical lineage with Classical Islamic sources is not an isolated phenomenon, as a similar claim is made for nearly all the other clerical clans, as well as numerous other groups besides. Historians who have tried to pursue such claims in the hope of obtaining specific chronological data have been let astray (see Introduction). As far as the Jakhanke are concerned we have assumed throughout that their claim to be descended from Classical Islamic or Semitic ancestors is evidence only of their being steeped in a literate Arabic tradition. When other Sudanic groups make similar genealogical claims this may be taken to indicate an identical level of islamisation or a desire to appropriate exotic material to enhance the standing of the clan. Almost all the Jakhanke clans, and a good many of their more important clients, adopt this practice, but in their case it does no more than provide an inspirational source similar to the familiar initiatory filiation of Ṣūfī *ṭarīqāt*.

The present writer obtained an Arabic account of the Kabba clan during a visit to Kuntaur-Fulakunda at the home of the late al-Ḥājj Kemoring. The chronicle hereafter refered to as *TKQ*, gives an account of the history of the various migrations of the Kabba family and their main centres of settlement. The Kabba genealogy claims descent from one Ibrahīm Kabba, though no explanation of the name is given. This Ibrahīm came from the East and travelled via Istanbul and Ḥawḍ to Bakhunu where he died. He had had two sons, Muḥammad Mubarak Kabba and Maḥmūd Kabba, at a place called Dilli in Bakhunu. The two brothers migrated to Jafunu to a place called Kumolo where they separated. Maḥmūd Kabba went to Baté where he founded Kankan with his sons Kabāba Binne, Kumoro, Da'ay, and Umaruba.[4]

TKQ gives a straightforward genealogy of the Kabba clan without making anything of the name of Hamjatou as the ancestor of the Kabba. When Hamjatou's name occurs it is not as an uncle of the Prophet, that is, Hamzah, but as an unidentified Sudanic figure who was a contemporary of al-Ḥājj Sālim Suware. This Hamjatou is said to have left Mecca with al-Ḥājj Sālim Suware to come to Masina. As regards the claim that Hamzah, the Prophet's uncle, and Hamjatou were connected in some way, the accounts are only willing to go as far as saying that a Hamjatou was a namesake of Hamzah and Hamjatou may have been a grandson (or descendant) of Hamzah, though this may just be a fictitious or initiatory relationship (see Sanneh 1974a: 91).

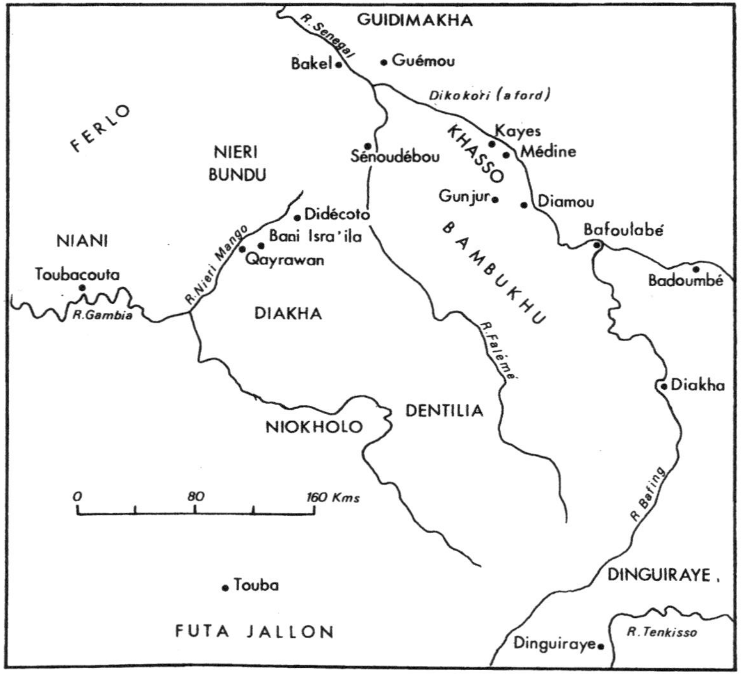

Map 3: Jakhanke Centres in Bundu (Senegal)

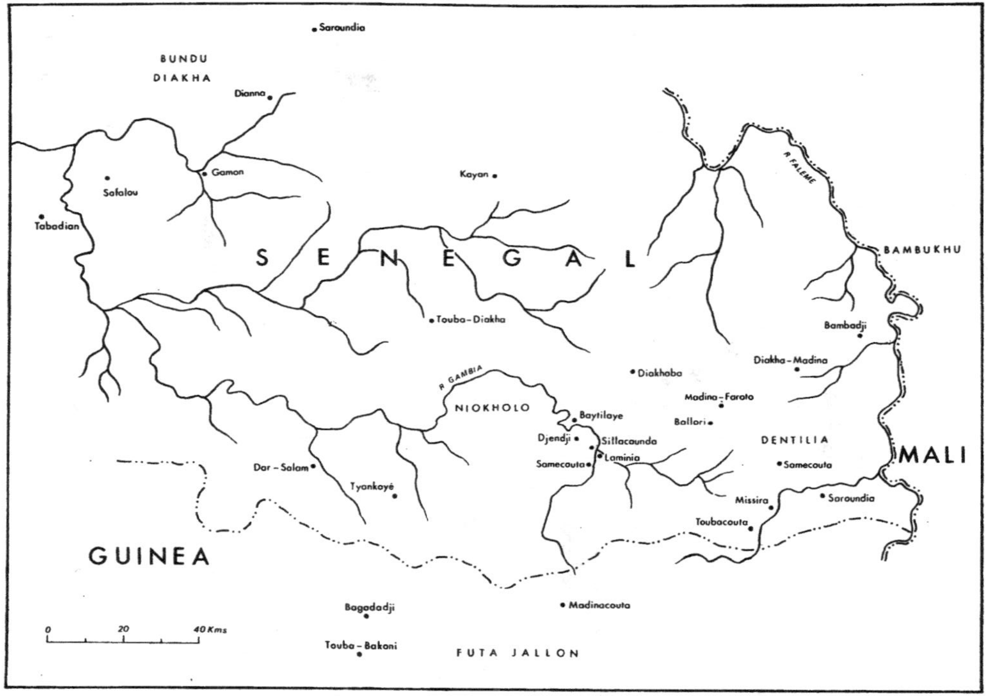

Map 4: Jakhanke Centres in Niokholo and Dentilia (District of Kédougou, Senegal)

Further details are given on the children of Hamjatou. *TKQ* mentions Fode Ibrahīm Kabba who may have been a son of Hamjatou, and this Ibrahīm Kabba is mentioned also by *TSK* as being part of the nucleus of al-Ḥājj Sālim's community at Diakha-Bambukhu. *TSK* suggests that Hamzah and Hamjatou were more likely to have been completely different individuals. This Hamjatou had two sons, ^{c}Amārah and Ya^{c}lā, whom he entrusted to al-Ḥājj Sālim. Before he died Hamjatou left instructions to al-Ḥājj Sālim that a quantity of gold he was leaving behind should be divided between ^{c}Amārah and Ya^{c}lā after they came of age. At the appropriate time al-Ḥājj Sālim turned over the gold to the two sons. The younger of the two, Ya^{c}lā, immediately handed his share back to al-Ḥājj Sālim as a pious gift and asked instead for a prayer that would make him grow in knowledge (*^{c}ilm*) and insight (*ma^{c}rifah*). Ya^{c}lā's posterity, according to *TSK* (fo. 3b) became renowned for erudition and virtue as a consequence. ^{c}Amārah, not to be outdone, imitated his younger brother and was endowed with the gift of efficacious prayer (*ijābah al-du^{c}ā*) (*TSK*: fo. 3b). The tradition of the Jakhite-Kabba leading in the ceremonial pronouncing of *du^{c}ā* is traced to this incident.

The Jakhite-Kabba dispersed widely throughout the Western Sudan. *TKQ* gives many details which we can only present in summary form. Maḥmūd Kabba, we have seen, went with his family to Baté across the Milo river, and his descendants formed the nucleus of the Mandinka-Mori (Maninka-Mori in some sources) Islamic community in Kankan. A history of this section of the Jakhite-Kabba clan of *ahl Diakha* would be a useful complement to what is now known of their Senegambian counterparts. The descendants of Muḥammad Mubarak, on the other hand, followed the westerly direction. His son, Muḥammad Satang, travelled to Guidimakha and Gajaga, both in the Serakhulle heartland (Saint-Père 1925), before continuing on to Didécoto where he died. One settled, probably with Karamokho Ba's original community, at Touba, about which more details are given in Chapter 5. A grandson of Muḥammad Satang, called Ibrahīm, through his son, al-Husayn, founded Dalafing. Many of the Jakhite Jakhanke settled in the general area of Senegambia: at Tyankoye and Samecouta in Niokholo, Madinacouta in eastern Futa Jallon, and Dianna (Janna) and Jīlānī in Bundu. In time Jīlānī became the pre-eminent Jakhite clerical centre.[5] In the Gambian Republic the three chief centres were Kaur-Janekunda, Kuntaur-

Fulakunda and Jarumekoto. Where the Jakhite-Kabba do not form a majority of the population they are recognised in their role as prayer leaders. Smith found in one Dentilia centre, Diakha-Madina, that the head was a member of the Suware clan and the *imām* was a Jakhite-Kabba. There were other Jakhanke groups: Fofana-Girasi, Jabi-Gassama and Jakhabi plus dependant castes (P. Smith 1965a: 255). If the Silla clan are present they normally assume the imāmate, as at Tyankoye in recent times (P. Smith 1965a: 258-9). In such circumstances the Jakhite-Kabba take charge of the many occasions of ceremonial *du*^c*ā*. This division of functions originated at Diakha-Bambukhu.

The Jabi-Gassama

The Founder: Mama Sambou Gassama. The sources maintain that when the Jabi, also known as Gassama, first made their appearance in Diakha-Bambukhu they claimed initiatory filiation from [c]Umar b. Khaṭṭāb and were assigned the task of co-ordinating the functions of the *qabīlah* heads. It was a ceremonial role and carried no executive powers since each *qabīlah* section was autonomous under a sectional head who ruled over its affairs. But the formal responsibility transformed the Jabi-Gassama into a distinctive organised clerical elite with a symbolic ritual identity. Many centuries later, at Touba, this identity was to come to fruition as the Jabi-Gassama took over the intellectual and spiritual leadership of the extensive Jakhanke diaspora (see Chapter 5).

The Jabi-Gassama trace their origin to one Shu[c]aibou, better known as Mama Sambou Gassama. He is said to have been a contemporary of al-Ḥājj Sālim. Mama Sambou is agreed by the sources to have been a warrior. While in Bambukhu he offered his services to the ruler in engagements against the people of Dānya.[6] Although Mama Sambou was in the district he was not himself resident at Diakha-Bambukhu. He knew al-Ḥājj Sālim personally, it is claimed, and emigrated from Jimbala-Diakha, Masina, with twelve *qabā'il* to accompany al-Ḥājj Sālim, more probably in his journey to Jafunu. It is unlikely that the warrior in Mama Sambou allowed him to adopt easily the path of peace and clerical withdrawal with which Diakha-Bambukhu became identified, and the evidence is that he did not.

After operations against the Danya, Mama Sambou moved to Tanda, the region just north of Futa Jallon, where he was involved in military activity against Konya. From there his career took him to Bundu and

Wuli, in upper Gambia.

This proved a turning point for Mama Sambou. The chief of Wuli was one Jalāli.[7] Mama Sambou was welcomed by the Jābai people of Wuli, whom he eventually converted to Islam. He succeeded in putting down a powerful pagan uprising and imposed Islam on the vanquished populations. He founded Sutukho, according to local traditions, built a mosque there and made it a Muslim stronghold. After this he returned to Bambukhu, but not for long. Wuli reneged and a message was sent to Mama Sambou who hastened to restore order and this second visit to Wuli proved decisive. The local populations responded favourably to the personal rule of Mama Sambou, which encouraged him to settle there. Al-Ḥājj Soriba contends that Mama Sambou, confident in the wake of his Wuli victory, went to Fogny (near the Coast between the Gambia and Casamance) and eventually back to Tanda where he remained until his death. This is disputed by informants in Sutukho where Mama Sambou's grave (or the one alleged to be his) now lies outside the new Sutukho village boundaries, and where it is a centre of local pilgrimage (Ar. *ziyārah*). The alleged site of the grave lies close to the ruins of a mosque he is said to have built.

The Sutukho tradition, which directly contradicts al-Ḥājj Soriba, says that the story that Mama Sambou died at Tanda was first circulated by al-Ḥājj Khousi Gassama of Niani-Jarumecuta (d. 1957). Before that, Mama Sambou's death and burial at Sutukho were never challenged, and since then no authority has been cited in support of the theory besides Khousi Gassama. The inference is that such a conspiracy of silence could not have been maintained for so long against the testimony of reliable witnesses. Concern for pilgrimage rights at Sutukho may have motivated such a careful exposition of the nature of historical proof. Although the spirit and manner in which the debate is conducted reflect some familiarity with the canons of meticulous historical enquiry and verification, the context of the dispute makes it hazardous to treat it as a typical example of rigorous sifting of data among the Jakhanke.

What about the view that Mama Sambou was personally acquainted with al-Ḥājj Sālim? The difficulty here is to try to bring together two men who are so diametrically opposed to one another in style and orientation: the one dealing out death with unquenchable energy and the other preaching peace and proclaiming a pacific clerical charter.

However, the sources do not insist that Mama Sambou attached himself to al-Ḥājj Sālim at Diakha-Bambukhu. They suggest rather that al-Ḥājj Sālim remonstrated with Mama Sambou who is unlikely to have heeded his message. They then claim that Mama Sambou's son, Yūsūf, who had met al-Ḥājj Sālim, embraced the latter's clerical vows. An important Jabi-Gassama chronicle, utilised extensively in Chapters 5-6 below, and to be referred to as *TKB*, says that al-Ḥājj Sālim was a personal tutor of Yūsūf,[8] who became the first transmitting link of al-Ḥājj Sālim's heritage among the Jabi-Gassama.

There is a hiatus in nearly all the sources between Mama Sambou and the next leader about whom we are given details, a seventh generation descendant, ᶜAbdallāh. Mama Sambou's descendants are given thus: Yūsūf, father of Abū Bakr, father of Muṣṭafā, father of Muḥammad Sire, father of Sālim, father of Aḥmad, father of ᶜAbdallāh, father of Fode al-Ḥājj, father of Ture Fode (founder of Dougousin-Komé in Bundu), father of Muḥammad Fāṭuma, father of Karamokho Ba (born c. 1730). This list in *TKB* concurs with another provided by al-Ḥājj Soriba, except that in his case the name Aḥmad is missing. Using the generation length of 23-24 years (p. 25), four more generations would still be needed to stretch this genealogical list back to allow Mama Sambou to be a contemporary of al-Ḥājj Sālim Suware.

Nevertheless, it is probably a reflection of al-Ḥājj Sālim's influence that the Jabi-Gassama derive Mama Sambou's religious authenticity through his association, tenuous as that may have been, with al-Ḥājj Sālim, and chiefly through his son, Yūsūf, as a pupil of al-Ḥājj Sālim. Apart from his wide-ranging military exploits and the creation of ancient Sutukho, Mama Sambou is lifted out of obscurity by the prominence which the clerical legacy of al-Ḥājj Sālim acquired among his descendants. The sources are sparing on details about Mama Sambou, but stress the importance of those Jabi-Gassama Jakhanke who lived at and then left Diakha-Bambukhu, presumably at the time of its break up in the fifteenth century.

The Rise of Didécoto in the Seventeenth Century. The man who led a splinter section of the Jabi-Gassama Jakhanke from Diakha-Bambukhu was the seventh generation descendant of Mama Sambou, ᶜAbdallāh. Some accounts say that he came with his son, Fode al-Ḥājj, others that it was with his grandson, Ture Fode. There is some confusion about where ᶜAbdallāh went to settle with his family. Since his migration from place to place is mentioned in the context either of his son, Fode al-Ḥājj, or, more frequently, his grandson, Ture Fode, it is more than likely that ᶜAbdallāh in old age was being looked after by his children. On the other hand, it is conceivable that there was more than one migration, one led by ᶜAbdallāh and a later one led by Ture Fode. ᶜAbdallāh seems to have passed from the scene after the migration to Tanda (*TSK:* fo. 7), or at least makes his reappearance only in the company of Ture Fode. This Ture Fode, according to most accounts, founded both Dougousin-Komé and Safalou in Tanda. All the sources stress that it was a son of Ture Fode, Muḥammad Fāṭuma, who achieved the amalgamation of Jakhanke *qabā'il* at Didécoto.

Before this time *imām* Malik Sy, the Tukulor leader of Futa Toro, had made his appearance in Bundu and this was how Ture Fode made his acquaintance. But the question of which Jakhanke leader met Malik Sy[9] introduces a chronological problem of some complexity which can be resolved by postulating a hiatus between the break-up of Diakha-Bambukhu and the migration to Safalou, perhaps an initial wave of migrants settling at a place like Diakha-Madina. The different versions of the accounts may be set out. According to *TSB*, a source originating from al-Ḥājj Mbalu Fode Jabi, Ture Fode (he is described in the source as Shaykh Muḥammad Fode) acted as court cleric to Malik Sy who utilised his services until he succeeded in subduing Bundu (fo. 3). But al-Ḥājj Soriba Jabi, in a different version, says it was ᶜAbdallāh, Ture Fode's grandfather, who was Malik Sy's chaplain and who prayed for Malik Sy's military success in Bundu.[10] *TSB* says Ture Fode eventually married the daughter of Malik Sy, Fāṭumata Sy. Al-Ḥājj Soriba says that Malik Sy, in gratitude for the clerical services of ᶜAbdallāh, gave him his daughter, whom ᶜAbdallāh promptly turned over to his grandson and heir, Ture Fode. *TSK* (fo. 7) says that both ᶜAbdallāh and his son, Fode al-Ḥājj, died at Safalou, but a son of Fode al-Ḥājj left Safalou, and went to found Didécoto. *TKB* (fo. 2) says Ture Fode founded Safalou, and Dougousin-Komé in southeastern Bundu. All the sources unite on the point that it was from the union of Ture Fode and Fāṭumata Sy that Muḥammad Fāṭuma was born. After the death of his grandfather and father (the order of death is not given) Muḥammad Fāṭuma adopted Didécoto as his home. The details, however, still vary.[11] *TKB* gives one detail omitted by the other sources. It says that Muḥammad Fāṭuma received some of his early education in Baté, across the Milo River, under one ᶜAmara Batan Ture (fo. 2).

Muḥammad Fāṭuma had a large family, to which the sources pay some attention. According to *TSK* (fo. 8) he had four wives: Jaghun Ba, Halīmatu, Sīsāghū and Sise. These wives had ten children, of whom seven were boys: Jagha Salimu, alias Jaghun Jimmo; Jaghun Muḥammad and Jaghun al-Ḥājj were uterine brothers whose mother was Jaghun Ba; ᶜAbdallāh's mother was Sīsāghū; Muḥammad al-Amīn and Yirimaghan were sons of Halīmatu; and, finally, ᶜUthmān was the son of Sise (*TSK:* fo. 8). Muḥammad Fāṭuma's daughters were Jagha Fāṭuma, Fāṭuma Gassama and Fāṭuma Sise (*TKB:* fo. 2). Muḥammad Fāṭuma's son, Jaghun al-Ḥājj, was named after al-Ḥājj Sālim Suware - his baptismal name is al-Ḥājj Sālim Gassama. Jaghun al-Ḥājj, which became his preferred name in the earlier part of his life, simply means 'the al-Ḥājj of Jagha', that is, his earlier namesake. But during the Futa Jallon phase of his career even this popular house-name was overshadowed by the honorific 'Karamokho Ba', meaning 'Great Teacher', a title given him by his Fulbe hosts (*TKB:* fos. 2-3). This title confirmed the place al-Ḥājj Sālim Gassama was to occupy in the history of Jakhanke clericalism, and, thanks to the detailed history of his life and work now available, we have a good picture of the kind of clerical life an earlier figure like al-Ḥājj Sālim Suware may have led (see Chapter 5).

Didécoto, which Muḥammad Fāṭuma is claimed to have founded, was the Diakha-Bambukhu of Bundu. All the major Jakhanke *qabā'il* met there and the present-day Jakhanke communities of Senegambia look to Didécoto, after Diakha-Bambukhu, as their most important home. Al-Ḥājj Soriba Jabi estimates that about 300 compounds of free Jakhanke families made up the Didécoto community in Muḥammad Fāṭuma's time. The endogamous castes, the *jeli* (griots), *numu* (smiths), *garanke* (leatherworkers) and a large number of slaves accounted for a further 60 compounds (see Sanneh 1974a: 140). It is difficult to attach a precise number to a compound. Al-Ḥājj Soriba estimates up to 60 people to a compound, but figures vary widely.[12] One informant spoke of Didécoto's prosperous state and said it had well over 2,000 people, and that Muḥammad Fāṭuma's own *qabīlah*, most probably divided up into many compounds, contained about 1,000 people.[13]

Muḥammad Fāṭuma acquired an enormous reputation for learning and was an active practising teacher. His students came from many areas, but usually, because of Didécoto's geographical position, from the Manding heartland areas, now in the Gambia, Casamance, and Guinea Bissau.[14] Among his helpers was one of his brothers, Mbemba Lasana, who became the founder of a separate branch of the Gassama *qabīlah*.[15] Muḥammad Fāṭuma kept in close touch with other leading scholars, among them his own former student, Shaykh ᶜUthmān Derri, a *tafsīr* specialist in Kounti (see below p. 120 n.4). Fāṭuma left instructions that after his death one of his sons, Jaghun al-Ḥājj (Karamokho Ba) should go there for further studies under Shaykh ᶜUthmān Derri. For his own part, religious and educational itinerancy did not occupy much of Muḥammad Fāṭuma's time; rather he made his mark by presiding closely over the affairs of the Didécoto community.

The sources place some emphasis on the presence of caste groups in the Didécoto community, and this is related to the question of the economic viability of clerical enclaves. Trade was never a major source of livelihood for the families there. On the contrary, it was by tilling the surrounding farmlands and keeping livestock that the clerical settlement was able to support itself. The tools, cloth, wooden slates and building materials, among other things, which the caste specialists produced enabled the settlement to flourish. How such caste families, particularly slaves, were marked off from the rest of the clerical population is treated more fully in Chapter 9. A few examples may suffice here. Richard Jobson, travelling in the Senegambia area in 1620-21, observed that in clerical towns (he was thinking primarily of Sutukho), clerics lived in separate enclosures with their slaves, 'that worke and labour for them, which slaves they suffer to marry and cherish the race that comes of them, which race remains to them, and their heirs or posterity as perpetuall bond-men.' (1968: 78-9). It became important for the continuity and effectiveness of Jakhanke clerical solidarity to rely on slaves and other caste groups to supply the necessary labour for clerical farms. The length and strength of many an *isnād* (educational licence) can be traced to the availability of such additional labour. Cornelius Hodges, who travelled through Senegambia in the 1680s, says that clerics valued slaves and cattle above all else.[16] All the clerical families had a stake in these two commodities, although there was a common interest in farmland, water resources and community real estate, like the main mosque, the town square and grazing land. Additional manpower was obtained by using Qur'ān school pupils who were employed in farm work, domestic chores, and porterage.[17]

The decline of Didécoto as a clerical centre is discussed in Chapter 3. It is only necessary to add that the pre-eminence of the Jabi-Gassama in this town is representative of the supremacy of that *qabīlah* in the Futa Jallon diaspora (for further details see Chapter 5). We must now turn to the Silla clerical clan.

The Silla of Banī Isrā'ila

The source for the early history of the Silla is that used by de Mézières to which reference has already been made in the Introduction. This family chronicle, referred to hereafter as *TBI*, is a short and compressed account which gives the appearance of considerable antiquity, although it is difficult to accept uncritically its chronology.[18]

According to *TBI* the Silla trace their ancestry to Fode al-Ḥasan Silla of Banī Isrā'ila. Fode al-Ḥasan is a revered figure among the Silla, and is looked to as their inspirational ancestor. The stories of his dreams are used to authenticate and hallow his stature as a Patriarch. According to tradition, Fode al-Ḥasan undertook specialised dream-inducing prayers called *al-istikhārah*, literally 'asking favour or seeking choice from God', (see pp. 191-7), and had a dream in which he was surrounded by Old Testament figures like Jacob and his community. In this company was also the Prophet Muḥammad. Fode al-Ḥasan asked what name he should adopt for the town he intended to establish, and at this the Prophet Muḥammad appealed to his dream companions. Jacob stepped out and announced, 'Oh, my children' (Ar. *yā banī*), and withdrew. The Prophet rejoined by telling Fode al-Ḥasan and his companions that they had now heard the name of their centre from what Jacob had said. This was extended by Fode al-Ḥasan to Banī Isrā'ila, 'Children of Israel'. This was how the Banī Isrā'ila of Bundu received its name (*TBI*; Mézières 1949).

Some traditions pass from this to the claim that Fode al-Ḥasan was a descendant of the Quraysh through ᶜAbbās, the Prophet's paternal uncle. De Mézières appears to be following such traditions when he imputes a Hebraic origin to the Silla Jakhanke. But such claims express no more than an active literate interest in early Islamic sources and need not be taken seriously. In a *silsilah*, i.e. a genealogical chain, provided by the Silla themselves, it is clear that Fode al-Ḥasan was not even the first known ancestor of the Silla people, for Silla names are given which pre-date his own name. Here the Silla clerical tradition is traced past Fode al-Ḥasan to one Muḥammad Ba Jafunu, a considerable gap between the two being suggested.[19] But Muḥammad Ba Jafunu has no separate clerical order founded in his name. The inescapable conclusion is that Fode al-Ḥasan is being acknowledged as a religious model and the *qabīlah*'s charismatic founder. His clerical appeal is thus allowed to eclipse earlier precursors.

The identity of this Fode al-Ḥasan himself is far from conclusive in the sources. *TBI* merely says that the earliest ancestor of the Silla left the Quraysh and came to Manding, and from there he went to Diakha (Masina), then to Bambukhu-Diakhaba where, to quote the document, 'our ancestor, al-Ḥājj [Sālim] Suware had gathered together all the *ansāb* (sing. *nasab*) (lineages), including the Silla, the Suware, the Darame, Jakhabi, Gassama, Sise, Kabba, Fadiga, Ture and Fofana and numerous others...' Fode al-Ḥasan emerged as leader after he and his companions had been on a long journey which had taken them through several important Jakhanke towns, including, for example, Bundu-Dianna where, we are told, two eminent Silla clerics were living: Fode Baba Silla and Fode Anas Ibrahīm (*TBI*). From Bundu-Dianna Fode al-Ḥasan went to Qayrawān and then to the spot where he founded Banī Isrā'ila. It was at this point that he emerged as leader. At that time he was accompanied, among others, by his maternal uncle (Ar. *khāl*), Muḥammad Darame, and a student, ᶜAbdallāh Sakho. Other sources add the name of Fode Marena La to Fode al-Ḥasan's companions (Mézières 1949: 21), but this does not appear in *TBI*. In one account the Prophet appeared to Fode al-Ḥasan and his uncle, Muḥammad Darame, in a dream, along with some ancient Hebrew prophets, from which experience Fode al-Ḥasan emerged with the name for his religious centre. The date given in *TBI* is A.H. 635/1237-8 A.D. This seems much too early, although it is relevant for the argument that Fode al-Ḥasan was a contemporary of al-Ḥājj Sālim Suware. But the desire to equate Fode al-Ḥasan with al-Ḥājj Sālim in terms at least of clerical importance might have prompted the evolvement of a corresponding chronology.

Banī Isrā'ila is clearly an ancient centre, even though the long history claimed for it in local sources is unlikely to be entirely accurate. Some of the refugees from Bambukhu fleeing westwards after the dissolution of Diakha-Bambukhu went there. Mungo Park ([1799] 1969: 265-6) visited Banī Isrā'ila, which he described as the principal town of Dentilia, engaged in a prosperous transit trade and having a trickle of slave traffic passing through it. An early eighteenth century traveller, visiting the same region as Park, says that in his time Gunjūr was the chief town of the area, being the capital of a cluster of religious centres ('la république des marabouts') (Labat 1728: III 338). Gunjūr, of course, was an old religious centre (see Chapter 1) but by the time Park visited the area Banī Isrā'ila was the hub of a new political constellation. Its history must therefore go back some considerable time before both Park and Labat. The *Ta'rīkh al-Fattāsh* mentions a Banī Isrā'ila in Masina in connection with the Battle of Tendirma (1496-97) (Ka^cti 1913: 314-5), where it says certain horticultural traces of a flourishing Jewish colony called Banī Isrā'ila were discovered, although that was all that remained of these people (*ibid:* 118-9). The tradition that Fode al-Ḥasan Silla was the founder of Banī Isrā'ila in Bundu may have originated from the area in Masina described by the *Ta'rīkh al-Fattāsh*, or it may have survived among people connected with or familiar with it. As far as its chronology is concerned all we can be certain about at this stage is that the name at least was known at the time of the compiling of the *Ta'rīkh al-Fattāsh*, and that it may go back to the same period as Gunjūr which had a similar history.

NOTES

1 A good example of this is the senior *imām* of Kambia (Sierra Leone), al-Ḥājj Muṣṭafā Suwaray who, in 1969, claimed that his 'great grandfather, Alhaji Salimu Suwaray, went to Mecca seven times to receive instructions in Islam.' This was contained in an oral account given to David Skinner who unfortunately seems to have been no more enlightened than his informant on the identity of al-Ḥājj Sālim (1971).

2 Maḥmūd Jīlānī, with a flair for linguistic etymology, traces the name Jakhite (Zaite or Zaghite in Arabic) to the clan's commercial association with shea-butter. This is traced to the Arabic word *zayt*, olive oil or any kind of oil. A dealer in oil is called *zayyāt*. Taped interview, Sutukung, 16/11/72.

3 The late al-Ḥājj Kemoring Jakhite lived at Kuntaur-Fulakunda. See *Ta'rīkh*, 1968, vol.(2) for a brief account. Widely recognised for his scholarship he was chosen while on *ḥājj* by the Saudi Arabian author-

ities to be *muqaddam* of pilgrims from the Western Sudan. He died in 1972, his work largely uncompleted.

4 *TKQ*: fo. 1. A.le Chatelier records a tradition which says that the first Muslims in Kankan were under the leadership of Shaykh Kadry Sanounou and that the Kabba were led by one al-Ḥājj Fode Kabba and his son, Fode Modou Kabba. It was the younger son of this Fode Modou, Alfa Kalabinne, who established a branch of the Qādiriyāh Ṣūfī *ṭarīqah* there after his initiation into the Bakkayah order (1899: 161). Arcin has a slightly different tradition in which the Sakho clan were the founders of Kankan (1911: 80-81).

5 *TKQ*: fo. 5 ff. Jīlānī was founded by Maḥmūd Kabba, himself nicknamed Jīlānī. More details of its later history are given on pp. 84-5. P. Smith, who did some field-work in the Niokholo area in the district of Kédougou, discovered the Jakhite-Kabba were predominant. The *imām*, Dembo Jakhite-Kabba, possessed a copy of the Kabba *silsilah*, i.e. chain of transmission, which he obtained as a student in the Gambia. Smith also points out that the same Kabba people are classed as Mandinka-Mori or Jula in Kankan (1965a: 246).

6 Al-Ḥājj Soriba Jabi, Macca-Kolibantang, 9/12/72.

7 Interviews at Wuli-Sutukho with the Alkali and others. See Sanneh 1974a: 133.

8 *TKB:* fo. 2. This chronicle says that Mama Sambou had three sons: Yirajang, Yūsūf and a third whose name is not known.

9 Curtin 1971a; Curtin and Skinner 1971 give his dates of rule as 1690-1707. But in Trimingham 1962: 173 his death is given as 1680. Either way, however, a long time seems to have passed since the move from Diakha-Bambukhu.

10 Al-Ḥājj Soriba Jabi, Macca-Kolibantang, 9/12/72. See Sanneh 1974a: 138.

11 *TSK* seems to imply that Muḥammad Fāṭuma founded Didécoto. This version is also carried by al-Ḥājj Soriba Jabi, *TKB*, and the venerable blind Jakhanke scholar Karamokho Sankoung Jabi of Nibrās (see also p. 11). *TSB* is silent on this point.

12 Al-Ḥājj Soriba Jabi, Macca-Kolibantang, 9/12/72. The Jakhanke clerical enclave of Jimara-Bakadaji now has between 2,000 and 3,000 inhabitants. It has, according to the official Area Council Assessment Records, 57 compounds, that is, approximately 35 to 55 people per compound. The more prosperous families would have the larger compounds.

13 Karamokho Sankoung, Nibrās, 4/12/72.

14 Al-Ḥājj Soriba Jabi, Macca-Kolibantang, 9/12/72.

15 Al-Ḥājj Fode Jabi, Sandu-Jakhaba, a descendant of Mbemba Lasana, 9/2/73.

16 Hodges distinguished between professional traders and clerics. He calls the clerics 'Bitcheereen' (Ar. *bashīrūn*) missionaries (1924: 92).

17 The use of pupils for farm work and domestic chores is a standard practice today among the Jakhanke, and Mungo Park observed that it was customary in his time too. He said the boys had their lessons by night, 'for being considered during their scholarship as the domestic slaves of the master, they were employed in planting corn, bringing firewood... through the day' ([1799] 1968: 240). For porterage see Hecquard 1855: 249. See also Chapter 7.

18 Raymond Mauny, who helped in editing de Mézières' manuscript tried to salvage what was left of it apart from the alleged origins. But this salvage operation was carried out mainly in glosses on the work (1949). See earlier discussion on p. 6. *TBI* is widely available. I collected four copies of exactly the same material. The shortness of the text (2 pages) makes it easy to commit to memory.

19 Muḥammad Khalīfa Silla, Kounti, 30/11/72 and 1/12/72.

CHAPTER THREE

JAKHANKE CENTRES IN BUNDU

c. 1700 - c. 1890

The Economic and Historical Setting

Bundu was the bridgehead for Jakhanke penetration into many parts of Senegambia and Futa Jallon. In the late seventeenth century, as we have seen, most Jakhanke families were concentrated at Didécoto under the patronage of Muḥammad Fāṭuma. The town later contracted, from ecological causes rather than from political or commercial ones, and most of its inhabitants dispersed in small communities to settle elsewhere in Bundu. At these centres the Jakhanke continued with their clerical work and spent some of their time in farming and livestock breeding. Some centres were fairly large and became active staging points for the transit trade which passed through Bundu at various points. The role of the Jakhanke clerics in such trade was minimal and certainly not that of professional commercial agents.

Their spread throughout Bundu was facilitated by its cultural and political situation. The Jakhanke had become deeply influenced by Manding culture at Diakha-Bambukhu and felt a natural propensity towards Khasso, Bundu and outlying regions where Manding cultural hegemony was maintained alongside pockets of Serakhulle people. This had been a feature of Jakhanke settlements in the Senegambia area for a very long time: the practice of absorbing Manding cultural traits alongside an increasingly muted espousal of their Serakhulle origin.[1] Politically, the *entente cordiale* that existed in the seventeenth century between the Jakhanke leaders and the masters of Bundu, the Sy family, helped them. The Jakhanke appear to have taken their submission to the Sy family seriously, and much later when Momodou-Lamin, the nineteenth century *mujāhid*, rose against the political leadership of Bundu, he was rejected by his fellow Jakhanke who reiterated their support for Sikunda (the Sy family). Details of this rift are given below in Chapter 4.

There was a third, subsidiary attraction of Bundu, namely, the rich soils of the fertile Senegambia valleys. As two elderly Jakhanke put it, they go to those places: *'seno aning danyining sonoyata dameng'* (where the burdens of farming and livelihood are light).[2]

The understanding with the political leadership meant that the Jakhanke could secure a secular guarantee for their neutrality as a matter of principle and, secondly, that they were free to establish Islamic institutions and offices of the prescriptive variety. Thus the cultural, political and agricultural contexts of Bundu favoured the pursuit of the clerical vocation. When some of the clerical towns developed a lucrative transit trade the Jakhanke clerics acquired an additional source of income.

The Bundu region in general was by the eighteenth century the scene of an active network of trade caravans, though few precise details are available on how this affected the Jakhanke. Bundu was linked to Bambukhu by an artery of gold trade, with a trickle of ivory and slaves flowing in (W. Gray and Dochard 1825: 180). A similar trading link existed with Futa Jallon, as well as with European posts on the Gambia and Senegal rivers from which traders obtained firearms, powder, Indian baft, hardware, amber, coral, glass beads and other luxury items. With the Moors to the north trade was mainly in *gum arabica*.[3] The Almamy of Bundu also imposed a substantial trade levy on all transit goods, according to one source (Walckenaer 1826/31: VII 161 ff.) a second part of such goods, which seems particularly heavy. Also a tenth of the salt brought from the coast was paid in as tax. An annual tribute was paid by vessels of the Senegal Company and by the French government factory at Bakel ('Baquelle') (W. Gray and Dochard 1825:183). Peace contributions were also made by all those who carried on business or wanted to obtain special favours: the gifts included slaves, horses, cattle, poultry, rice, corn, cotton, cloth and gold (*ibid*). The masters of this commercial affluence were the political leadership and the men who specialised in its carriage as traders and creditors. Others benefited at several stages removed from this buoyant circle of entrepreneurs. (For details of the economic history of the area, see Curtin 1975.)

By far the greater attraction of Bundu for the Jakhanke was its climate and agricultural potential. Whereas Bambukhu could be considered 'the Peru of Africa' (Mollien 1820: 79), Bundu can be reckoned its bread-basket: 'Le sol y est, dans les vallées des marigots, éminemment fertile et le Tiali et le Nieri notamment ont toujours été regardés par les Almamys du Bondou comme leur véritable grenier d'abondance' (Rançon 1894a: 6). William Gray and Dochard (1825: 179-80) wrote that the dimensions of Bundu were 90 miles from east to west and 60 miles from north to south; it produced corn in four varieties, plus rice, pumpkins, watermelons, gourds, sorrel,[4] onions, tobacco, red pepper, pistachios, cotton and indigo. The agricultural richness of Bundu also made a great impression on Mungo Park, who describes it in superlatives: 'In native fertility,' he writes, 'the soil is not surpassed, I believe, by any part of Africa' ([1799] 1969: 43).

Of what importance was Islam alongside the two themes of commerce and agriculture considered so far? W. Gray and Dochard who were in the area between 1818 and 1821 say that the government was theocratic, based on the Sharīᶜah which was in turn interpreted by jurisconsults (1825: 181-2). Gray paid particular attention to the way the inhabitants of Bundu scrupulously followed the detailed prescriptions of Islam, and said that every town had a principal Qur'ān school where the children were taught the rudiments of Islamic practice and belief as well as the Arabic Qur'ān. The Muslim religious leaders were distinguished by their cavalry and their dress: prominent white turbans surmounted by red or blue cone-shapes (Walckenaer 1826/31: VII 161 ff.).

Mungo Park, visiting the area thirty years earlier, also makes mention of Islam and the status and influence of Muslim clerics in Bundu. The secular authority of the region was under the influence of the Sharīᶜah, and the leading court counsellors were Muslim clerics, so that 'the authority and laws of the Prophet are everywhere looked upon as sacred and decisive'.[5] Park went on:

> Religious persecution is not known among them, nor is it necessary; for the system of Mahomet is made to extend itself by means abundantly more efficacious. By establishing small schools in the different towns, where many of the Pagans as well as Mahomedan children are taught to read the Koran, and instructed in the tenets of the Prophet, the Mahomedan priests fix a bias on the minds, and form the character of their young disciples, which no accidents of life can ever afterwards remove or alter... With the Mohamedan faith is also introduced the Arabic language. ([1799] 1969: 45)

Three major centres in Bundu at the time: Banī Isrā'ila, Qayrawān and Gunjūr (sometimes placed in Khasso), provide good examples of how the Jakhanke fused these Islamic traditions of clerical activity with farming. Each is discussed in turn.

Banī Isrā'ila

The prestige of Banī (a shortened form of Banī Isrā'ila) was unchallenged among its Bundu neighbours, and for the Silla it was their first clerical republic, created on the model of Diakha-Bambukhu. Its early history has been discussed in Chapter 2. Its material strength rested on the vast agricultural potential of the area, and the transit trade which crossed its borders, due mainly to the sanctuary it could provide for traders concerned over security.[6] The Jakhanke clerics were more directly concerned with cattle and slaves, two commodities essential to their sedentary clerical life.

In Mungo Park's time, slave caravans frequently went through Banī on their way to Bambukhu and Futa Jallon, making a crossing at a point on the Falémé River ([1799] 1969: 265). Park joined one such slave caravan belonging to a Serakhulle merchant. The slave dealers were called Slatees.[7] The acquisition of slaves and cattle for use on clerical farms was a standard practice among the Jakhanke. Banī also featured small-scale ironworking, which again was in keeping with the Jakhanke practice of including leatherworkers and metal specialists as endogamous castes in their clerical settlements. These artisans manufactured the tools needed to work the farm-estates and provided leather for the extensive use of Qur'ānic amulets.[8]

The first references in European sources to Banī speak of the presence there of slaves, and travellers describe how these slaves were put to work as farm labourers. A clerical settlement which was sited, like Banī, in rural agricultural surroundings, required a good and stable labour force to sustain a tradition of Islamic learning in the form practised by the Jakhanke. Slaves were ideal for this, and Qur'ānic students resident in the home of the cleric were another good source. Whatever commercial merits the settlement might have acquired at various times, it relied on slave and student labour to exploit its agricultural resources in order to retain its clerical character.

The political position of the town was similarly typical of Jakhanke clerical centres. It owed fealty to the king of Bundu who resided elsewhere. The king was prayed for and tribute was rendered but the king's edict did not reach Banī in all its force. In return for recognising the king's rule Banī's political neutrality was accepted and it was allowed to exist without secular interference in its internal affairs. Park spoke of the genuine affection with which the inhabitants regarded the ruler.[9] Banī was at the time of Park's visit the principal town of that part of Bundu called Dentilia ([1799] 1969: 305), but this was an indication of the clerical stature of the town. The leading citizen there (a *qāḍī* or *imām*?) was a cleric called Fode Ibrahima. Park spoke warmly of his hospitality and indicated that his host was pleased with a copy of the Arabic New Testament he gave him (Park [1799] 1969: 305).

Large-scale dispersions from Banī late in the nineteenth century completed a process of decline which had already set in. Banī's leading Silla clerics abandoned it, and most of them went farther west into present-day Gambia. Its spirit was broken, and the ancient walls behind which it had been cloistered for so long were reduced to rubble.[10] What remained of the place were a few near deserted corridors along which contact on a much reduced scale of effectiveness was maintained with the surrounding regions.

Qayrawān

Our sources on the early history of Qayrawān are very few. There are a number of scattered references to it but no coherent systematic treatment. Mungo Park, however, gives a relatively full account of it in the late eighteenth century. The prosperity of Qayrawān was based primarily on agriculture. Situated in a valley, the town thrived on the extensive farmlands cultivated in its vicinity. It is worth quoting Park's eye-witness account. He says the extensive farmlands stretched 'for more than a mile round...and [were] well cultivated.' He continues:

> The inhabitants appear to be very active and industrious, and seem to have carried the system of agriculture to some degree of perfection, for they collect the dung of their cattle into large heaps during the dry season, for the purpose of manuring their land with it at the proper time. I saw nothing like this in any other part of Africa. ([1799] 1969: 266)

In order to till their fields the inhabitants used slaves who were treated as beasts of burden. Clerics obtained their slaves mostly, but by no means exclusively, from slave merchants, Slatees. Park met one such merchant in Qayrawān who was so concerned that his slaves from neighbouring Futa Jallon would run away that he felt he could not employ them on his farms. He traded in a Futa Jallon slave for another, presumably from a more distant place, in order to have an additional hand on his farms.[11]

If slaves supplied the necessary labour for clerical farms the endogamous castes provided the skills needed for making farm tools and implements: hoes, sickles, axes, matchets, knives, etc. Qayrawān had a local factory for producing such items. Park describes it thus:

> Near the town are several smelting furnaces, from which the natives obtain very good iron. They afterwards hammer the metal into small bars, about a foot in length and two inches in breadth, one of which bars is sufficient to make two Mandingo corn hoes. ([1799] 1969: 267)

We do not know for certain, apart from a reference to Fode Baba Silla and Fode Ibrahīm Anas in *TBI*, which Jakhanke *qabā'il* first settled in Qayrawān, when it was founded or how it adopted that name. It appears to have been a companion centre to Banī Isrā'ila, and the presence there of the two Silla clerics suggests it had long been settled at the time of Banī's founding by the Silla *qabīlah*, among others. Oral accounts also say al-Ḥājj Sālim visited Qayrawān during the *tournée* which took him through Senegambia. Apart from such dispersed comments there is evidence only that the town existed as an undistinguished clerical settlement. In comparison with Gunjūr, for example, it is shrouded in mystery.

The Holy Town of Gunjūr

A town of great antiquity, Gunjūr was a redoubtable clerical centre founded by immigrant Jakhanke from Diakha-Bambukhu. It was a spiritual and religious heir to Bambukhu, and seems to have succeeded well in conserving the heritage of al-Ḥājj Sālim to whom the leading lights of the town looked for professional inspiration and a personal model. *TSK* affirms this spiritual loyalty of the Darame clerics of Gunjūr to the life and work of al-Ḥājj Sālim by saying that it was after al-Ḥājj Sālim had delivered a powerful prayer for their *qabīlah* that the Darame emerged into prominence. Forty distinguished divines, it is claimed, shone forth at Gunjūr with saintly power on account of the *barakah* with which al-Ḥājj Sālim invested the posterity of Darameba (see p. 20). It is to the later history of the town that we must now turn.

At the turn of the eighteenth century Labat visited Gunjūr and he has left us a description of the town. He estimated the population to be 4-5,000, 'tous Marabouts et marchands, chez lesquels les caravannes de captifs Bambaras ne manquent jamais de passer et de s'y arrêter pour se reposer' (1728: III 357-8). André Brüe, who visited the area in 1698, was assured by the leading cleric of the town that their neutrality was guaranteed in their relations with the 'Tonca Maca' (Tunka Magha), i.e. the ruling Vicegerent, as well as with the king himself (Labat 1728: III 335). A mid-eighteenth century account gives Gunjūr a place in the first rank of clerical centres; its houses were made of stone and covered with tiles, some of which appear to have been imported (Demanet 1767: I 81-2). There is a tantalising reference to the power and authority of the clerics because of the large quantity of amulets they possessed (*ibid*). It is not clear whether this means the amulets were accumulated by clerics out of a collector's curiosity, or, as seems more probable, whether such amulets were in high demand and the clerics made large numbers to attempt to meet this demand, which would as a result make them prosperous as well as powerful (Ch. Monteil 1928).

Gunjūr's reputation for trade derived from its proximity to a trading centre rather than from an original Jakhanke interest in commerce. This trading centre was Kenio, a town of roughly equal size to Gunjūr and situated on the Senegal River east of Kayes. It had a population of around 5,000 and was a transit stage for caravans going to the gold mines of Kessiela (Ch. Monteil 1928: 651). Although there has been some confusion as to the actual site of Gunjūr, Charles Monteil thinks La Courbe (visiting in 1710) was right in locating it on the left bank of the Senegal River south of Kayes and southeast of Kenio.[12]

The rest of our discussion on Gunjūr will be concerned with two specific questions, firstly, the political status of the town and, secondly, the clerical strength of the settlement. On the political side Gunjūr continued to enjoy its autonomous clerical status. Although it entered into a pledge of nominal political subservience to the ruler, it was able in return to extract certain obligations. Demba Sega, who ruled Khasso 1796-1803, was converted to Islam by one Sanjan Babi, and the account says that the latter required him to take the formal position of the *ṣalāt* as a public demonstration of his sincerity, with which he is said to have complied.[13] In his relations with Gunjūr he obtained the annual tribute, a tribute which had a commercial character and was not political (Ch. Monteil 1915: 22). For his part Demba Sega adopted a Jakhanke cleric as a court chaplain and counsellor and recognised Gunjūr as his supreme judicial tribunal where he sent cases 'de gravité exceptionelle' (*ibid*: 27).

As to the clerical strength of Gunjūr, we have seen (Chapter 1) that *TSK* includes the Darame within the legacy of al-Ḥājj Sālim. Gunjūr, as the enclave of the Darame clerics, achieved great fame throughout its history and is thus one example of how al-Ḥājj Sālim's influence persisted down the centuries. Among the local Torodbe people the Darame clerical clan was given the venerable epithet of *Waliabe*, i.e. 'Holy' or priestly people (Rançon 1894a: 39-40). This clerical reputation, protected by secular recognition and guarantees, was supported by the agricultural resources of Gunjūr. Although the early French accounts were oriented towards commercial/political themes, there are references to the farming strength of Gunjūr. Labat, for example, remarked on the fertility of the soil and how slaves were brought there, most probably to till the farms owned by clerics (1728: III 357-8). Labat also explicitly spoke of Gunjūr as the chief town of a cluster of autonomous clerical centres, the capital of 'la république des marabouts' (*ibid*).

French Imperialism and the Decline of Gunjūr

It is ironic that Jakhanke clerics, who had specialised in the science of delineating the shape of things to come through divination, and had successfully adapted to the vacillations of political rulers, should come to rate so low in the reckoning of the French imperial overlords who, during the nineteenth century, were appearing in increasing strength in places where the Jakhanke were settled. The final destruction of Gunjūr in 1886 was the result largely of a breakdown of the institutional arrangement by means of which the Jakhanke had hitherto succeeded in maintaining an *entente cordiale* with their secular partners within a jealously guarded tradition of political neutrality. Environmental factors undoubtedly played an important role in bringing about Gunjūr's eventual demise, but the political causes determined the manner and timing of its collapse.

The political background to the events surrounding Gunjūr's final collapse is discussed more fully in the next chapter. Here we are concerned only with the implications of French confrontation with the Jakhanke. When the French engaged Momodou-Lamin in protracted combat, beginning in about December 1885, and escalating into the military operations of April 1886, they pursued him to Gunjūr, his natal town, which they beseiged. In attacking Gunjūr, which was subsequently burnt down, the French infringed the principle of neutrality which had been the *raison d'être* of the town. Gunjūr disappeared from the map, at least as an autonomous clerical town, which dealt a profound blow to the long tradition of clerical neutrality and the sanctity of the Jakhanke tradition of withdrawal from political involvement. The French, in pursuit of a doctrine of complete political participation in the colonial venture, began to impose conditions on the Jakhanke clerics which threatened the survival of clericalism in the form in which they had understood it. A good example of this, discussed more fully as it affected Touba in Chapter 6 below, was the enforced French ban on slavery among the Jakhanke. But with reference to Gunjūr it was the French lack of regard for Jakhanke scruples over direct political and military involvement that was to have far-reaching consequences for their clerical vocation.

Environmental Factors Affecting the Bundu Centres

The environmental factor is worth considering separately, for it exerted an influence on the siting as well as the size of clerical centres in Bundu and adjacent areas. For example, Gunjūr never acted as a rallying point for the Jakhanke of Senegambia because the town could not support a large population. At the end of the seventeenth century it had about 4,500 inhabitants as we have already seen. When the French entered the town nearly two centuries later the population had altered significantly, reduced far below its former strength. Such a demographic pattern was due in part to the restricted food resources of the area and the unavailability of additional farmland. The Jakhanke site depended on agriculture, whereas Kenio could exist as a neighbouring town because it did not need to draw from the same source for its livelihood but depended on trade. The fate of Didécoto was sealed in large measure by the over-concentration of population and the consequent drain on the agricultural resources of the surrounding countryside. Gunjūr escaped that fate by being able to divert its additional population to other places, but the prospect of critical food shortages through soil exhaustion and periodic climatic variation was real. This restricted the growth of the town and made it potentially vulnerable to adverse environmental factors. In recent times, since the French sacking of Gunjūr, the area has been reduced to a dustbowl by the relentless encroachment of the Ferlo Desert.

The relatively very much greater agricultural prosperity of

Bundu attracted large concentrations of population which, with the methods of cultivation then current, over time proved a strain on the land. These populations therefore existed mainly in dispersed pockets dotted around the country. The advantage of modest clerical enclaves favoured the expansion of Jakhanke clerical power which had always thrived along the dispersion trail. A typical settlement, stunted in this way by internal population pressures, was Diakha-Madina. One tradition says that after the break-up of Diakha-Bambukhu some of the Suware Jakhanke emigrated in the direction of Bundu and established Diakha-Madina in Dentilia (P. Smith 1965a: 244, 253, 255). Rançon, describing Diakha-Madina at the end of the nineteenth century, stressed its smallness, saying it had around 450 inhabitants. Its wealth was derived almost exclusively from the number of its granaries of millet, rice, cous-cous (a form of grain) and groundnuts. There were also about fifty goats and sheep and a herd of cattle (Rançon 1894b: 524-7). In other words it was essentially a purely agricultural settlement. Ballori was a town like Diakha-Madina whose foundation was attributed to the Jabi-Gassama disciples of al-Ḥājj Sālim. The town was later abandoned, probably from environmental causes, and the population moved to another site just to the north of old Ballori. But the Jabi-Gassama maintained the tomb of the founder of Ballori as a venerated site (P. Smith 1965a: 255). The list of such small centres is endless.

Population pressure, as well as stunting the growth of individual settlements, led to migrations both within Bundu and to areas outside it. For example, when the large centre of Didécoto began to disintegrate in the eighteenth century, families and clan sections withdrew in smaller numbers to discrete settlements. One of the effects of such migrations was to produce a proliferation of towns of similar name. After leaving Didécoto, for example, a few Jakhanke families withdrew to the fertile grain-producing area of Nieri to a place they named Didécuta.[14] In more recent times such movements continue. For example, I collected traditions in Sandu-Jakhaba and Danfakunda in the Gambia of a branch of the Jabi *qabīlah* which emigrated from Sandu-Jakhaba to Taybatu, near Basse, under Ba Kambi Gassama and his elder brother, Ba Karamo Gassama. Although, in this case, the emigration was precipitated by a pedagogic dispute, it was clear that Sandu-Jakhaba was reaching the limits of possible population concentration. Another example is Bakadaji (Ar. Baghdād) in Jimara, the Gambia. It is the third centre of the same name of the Darame clerical clan. The first was founded in Bundu by Safiyatu Burema, accompanied by Safiyatu Madi, Safiyatu Sanūsī and Safiyatu Ma Sireng, all of the Darame *qabīlah*. They had settled at Banī Isrā'ila but left it after a dispute with their hosts, the Silla. They went to middle Bundu and founded a second Bakadaji which they likewise abandoned after a split with the *mujāhid*, Momodou-Lamin, and, under Fode Ansumana Darame, they moved to Jimara-Bakadaji. Since then, a stable population has continued to exist at Jimara-Bakadaji and a favourable balance has been maintained between food resources and population.[15]

These migrations and others caused by the upheavals of the nineteenth century created fresh problems of adjustment and of survival. However, in the process of facing these events the Jakhanke in the main succeeded in preserving the basic tenets of their teachings and even in spreading to new areas. The colonial factor, which was to prove such a bane for their clerical practice, was also compounded by forces of Islamic militancy, reducing the clerics to a state of bewilderment. The encounter with Momodou-Lamin in Bundu was the first stage in their eventual humiliation, although the resort to dispersion robbed even that of any finality.

NOTES

1 Pierre Smith discovered in Upper Senegambia that Jakhanke settled close to Serakhulle populations, thus helping to conserve the Serakhulle basis of Jakhanke culture (1965a: 243).

2 Shaykh Farūqi Jakhabi, Sutukung, 16/11/72, and the late al-Ḥajj Ansumana Jakhite-Kabba, Jarumekoto, 30/11/72. See p. 153-4.

3 One of the reasons why the Almamy of Bundu was reluctant to undertake trade with the French, and became suspicious of the French factory at Bakel, was that it might interfere with the gum trade with the Moors. Bundu had relied on Bakel as the main artery for the flow of gum from the north (Communication from the Governor to the French Minister for Colonies, Feb. 1853, ANFOM, Paris, Sénégal 1/37 a.b.).

'These gums', Mungo Park writes, 'being thrown on hot embers, produce a very pleasant odour, and are used by the Mandingoes for perfuming their huts and clothes' ([1799] 1969: 43).

4 The botanical name for this is *Rumex acetosa*, and it is a favourite species of leaf vegetable used in soups and stews with rice meals.

5 Mungo Park [1799] 1969: 45. See note 11 below for a discussion of the reliability of Park's work.

6 This introduces what is itself a topic of considerable scope, namely, clerical or religious sanctuary in West African Islam. Two brief references may suffice here. The renowned Sankore Mosque in Timbuktu was dominated for some time by the Aqit family of whom the leading light was the *qāḍī*. His house became an asylum for deposed rulers and was accorded immunity as an inviolable sanctuary. Governors in revolt and disgraced officials went there to seek asylum and immunity. The other example concerns trade directly. The ruler of Jenne asked the clerics of the city to pray for a prosperous commercial activity in the city so that it might become a refuge for enterprising merchants and traders (Sa^c^dī: 1964 tr. 24; Ar. 12-13).

7 The origin of this word is obscure, and is not explained in the sources. Like the word 'coffle', caravan, with which it is closely associated, it may be of Arabic derivation, from the word *sil^c^atu*, commodity, article or merchandise, or *sala^c^atu*, the process of branding a skin, i.e. inscribing the skins of slaves with the marks of their owners. 'Coffle' comes from the Arabic *qāfilah*, pl. *qawāfil*.

8 See Park ([1799] 1969: 266, where he says he and his party delayed their trip in order to purchase 'native iron' and other articles. For amulets, see below pp. 207-13.

9 He writes of how high the king of Bundu stood in the esteem of the people of Banī: 'few of his subjects wished more earnestly for the continuance of his life and the prosperity of his reign' (Park [1799] 1969: 305).

10 The ancient town walls were destroyed in operations against Momodou-Lamin in Gunjūr, and new ones erected in their place, but even these eventually disappeared (Mézières 1949: 21).

11 Park [1799] 1969: 267. There was some controversy over Park's book after it was published, partly from the fact that the manuscript had undergone considerable editorial revision and its genuineness was therefore questioned, and partly because the book was claimed as supporting material by the powerful Anti-Abolition Planters' lobby in the British Parliament (see *Parliamentary Debates*, Feb. 23rd 1807, 'Slave Trade Abolition Bill', p. 987). When carefully handled Park's account contains rich corroborative material. It is only in select areas that he is used in this work as an independent authority.

12 Ch. Monteil 1928: 651. He was here opposing Robert Arnaud who said that in operations against Momodou-Lamin the French took the town and razed it to the ground (1923: 193ff). Delafosse (1912) carries a similar tradition. But the larger question of identifying actual historical sites is an old and slippery problem in African history.

13 Ch. Monteil 1915: 23-4. From a different area there is a similar account of how the Shehu ^c^Uthmān dan Fūdī had Sarkin Bawa under pledge and proceeded to extract political concessions from him (Hiskett 1973: 45).

14 Interviews with several Jakhanke leaders such as al-Ḥājj Soriba Jabi, al-Ḥājj Mbalu Fode Jabi, both of Senegal, and al-Ḥājj Fode Jabi, Sandu-Jakhaba, and Karamokho Sankoung Jabi, Nibrās, both of the Gambia. See P. Smith 1965a: 244.

15 Al-Ḥājj Janko Darame, Jimara-Bakadaji, 11/12/72. See also p. 85-6 and p. 225-6. Further information on this topic is contained in the field report of the present writer, compiled during December, 1972, p. 5.

CHAPTER FOUR

MOMODOU-LAMIN DARAME AND PATTERNS OF JAKHANKE DISPERSION IN SENEGAMBIA

THE NINETEENTH CENTURY

> A pure and simple mind might perhaps even then have argued that, since all power is derived from God, these princes, if they were loyally and honestly supported by their subjects, must in time improve and lose all traces of their violent origin. But from characters and imaginations inflamed by passion and ambition, reasoning of this kind cannot be expected. Like bad physicians, they thought to cure the disease by removing the symptoms, and fancied that if the tyrant were killed, freedom would naturally follow.
> (J. Burckhardt, *The Civilization of the Renaissance in Italy*, New York, 1961: 74)

The Early Career of Momodou-Lamin

Of all the Senegambian *jihād* wars of the nineteenth century that affected the Jakhanke closely, that of Muḥammad al-Amīn (generally known as Momodou-Lamin) Darame (c. 1835-87) was the one which caused the greatest disturbance. The son of an undistinguished Darame Jakhanke of Safalou and a mother from Jafunu, Momodou-Lamin stands in the tradition of West African Islamic reform which has sought to create a new political *dawlah* for the maintenance of Islamic law and justice. Close ethnic ties as well as the explicit Islamic programme of his movement confronted the Jakhanke on the two bases of ethnic fellow feeling and ideological persuasion. On the first ground he aimed at destroying Tukulor hegemony in Bundu and other parts of Senegambia, and on the second he came into direct conflict with the French.

The main concern of the present study is with the religious theme of Momodou-Lamin's movement: his own personal religious preparation, the degree of support from local Muslim populations, particularly his fellow Jakhanke, and the consequences of his military engagements for religious groups. The military and political dimensions of his career are outside our present purpose.[1] But in order to appreciate his impact on Jakhanke communities in Bundu, a sketch is required of his personal life, his preparations for launching the *jihād*, his relations with political rulers in Bundu, and the growing support he gathered which enabled him to adopt the military option.

Momodou-Lamin was born sometime between 1830 and 1840. There is likewise some uncertainty as to his family background.[2] His real name was Malamine Demba Dibassi.[3] According to Charles Monteil's version, Momodou-Lamin's grandfather, who came from a renowned Jakhanke background, lived in Gunjūr, as did his father. The latter, Mamadou-Khoumba, left Gunjur after the birth of Momodou-Lamin and came to live in Safalou in southern Bundu.[4]

Momodou-Lamin began his Islamic education at Safalou or at Gunjūr[5] 'under the paternal eye', although it is not clear from this phrase whether his father was actually teaching him. After his preliminary studies he transferred to Bakel to continue his education. One version says that he was attached to 'an important branch of the maraboutic family of the Darame to which he was himself related' (Bathily 1970: 22). Two other versions carry more details, saying his teacher at Bakel was the famous Fode Muḥammad Saloum (Ch. Monteil 1915: 373; Rançon 1894a: 109), presumably of the Darame lineage.

Some accounts stress his particular educational endowments: 'Mamadou-Lamine aurait été un élève particulièrement doué dans ses études' (Bathily 1970: 22). His intellectual qualities were remarked upon by those who came into contact with him. Frey wrote: 'La persuasion de sa parole, son ardente foi, et la dignité de son attitude avaient déjà attiré sur lui l'attention et le respect de tous...' (1888: 252). When he went to Mecca to accomplish the *ḥajj*, '...il s'y fit remarquer par sa piété et son intelligence' (Nyambarza 1969: 126).

There is some controversy as to whether he enrolled in the forces of al-Ḥājj ᶜUmar Ṭāll, the Tukulor *mujāhid* of Segu. Rançon says that in about 1854, while Momodou-Lamin was studying at Bakel, al-Ḥājj ᶜUmar, already committed to his *jihād* programme, passed through Bakel on a drive to rally support in Futa Toro.[6] During that visit Momodou-Lamin, then aged 14 according to Rançon, went to see al-Ḥājj ᶜUmar and obtained his blessing.

The precise nature of Momodou-Lamin's association with al-Ḥājj ᶜUmar has been a subject of controversy. At about the time when Rançon says that Momodou-Lamin went to pay a visit of respect to al-Ḥājj ᶜUmar, other accounts say that he had enrolled as an active soldier in al-Ḥājj ᶜUmar's forces and had taken part in the attack on Medina, southeast of Bakel on the Senegal River.[7] Some local sources go even further and say that Momodou-Lamin and al-Ḥājj ᶜUmar first met on the *ḥājj* in Mecca (see Fisher 1970: 56). This is certainly apocryphal, for al-Ḥājj ᶜUmar is known to have left for the *ḥājj* in about 1826, long before Momodou-Lamin's earliest possible date of birth, and to have returned to Masina in December, 1838 or early 1839 (Oloruntimehin 1972: 40-1). All these accounts have one thing in common, namely, the suggestion that Momodou-Lamin and al-Ḥājj ᶜUmar enjoyed a religious *entente cordiale*, and that their aims, were the same, that is, the overthrow of pagan powers and their compromised Muslim supporters, on the one hand, and, on the other, the institution of a reformed Islamic political order. Whether or not Momodou-Lamin completely identified himself with the political project of al-Ḥājj ᶜUmar at the beginning, as opposed to using the religious association to enhance his own prestige, his later attitude to al-Ḥājj ᶜUmar's achievements indicates that he saw himself rather as the leader of a Serakhulle/Jakhanke alliance against Tukulor/Fulbe domination.[8] It was in this struggle to overthrow the yoke of Tukolor/Fulbe authority, to be complicated by French intervention on the side of the latter, that he lost his life.

An event of paramount importance in the subsequent career of Momodou-Lamin concerned his relations with Gamon, a state to the south of Bundu. It is probable that this event took place before his pilgrimage,but some sources place it afterwards. One detailed account of what happened is supplied by Rançon (1894b: 383). According to him, Momodou-Lamin and his mother were on a journey to a village in the vicinity to obtain some dye-stuffs when they were overtaken by some strapping fellows from Gamon who captured them and demanded a ransom. A passing caravan decided to pay the ransom for them, but before they could collect enough money, the frail mother died in detention. This was an incident which continued to rankle in the mind of her son. To the extent that,some time later,he planned military operations against Gamon in retaliation. Another account says that when Momodou-Lamin was about twenty he took part in operations against Gamon organised by the people of Kamera and Guoy. During those operations he was seized, put in fetters and beaten. After a long captivity he was finally released (Frey 1888: 250-1). But this story has been discounted on account of the formidable logistics required for such a long-range military operation (Fisher 1970: 55). Rançon, however, describes the traditional hostility between Gamon and Bundu, saying that in one operation the forces of Boubakar Sa^c^ada, ruler of Bundu 1857-85, lost heavily to Gamon, some 300 men being killed in action and 200 taken captive and sold into slavery in Niani (1894b: 383 ff.). Momodou-Lamin's alliance with Boubakar Sa^c^ada was strengthened by this incident, for it united both men in a common desire to humble Gamon. By the time Momodou-Lamin was himself able to mount operations against Gamon he had accomplished the *ḥājj* (c. 1885) and returned to Bundu and Boubakar Sa^c^ada had died (18th December, 1885) (Rançon 1894a: 116, quoting Frey).

The Ḥājj of Momodou-Lamin

Most authorities treat the pilgrimage as of decisive importance in Momodou-Lamin's religious preparation, and see the events connected with that journey as a significant contribution to the style he ultimately adopted in his movement. There is, however, a great deal of variance on the actual date given for his departure for the *ḥājj*, and the estimates range between 1850 (Marty 1915/6: 280) and 1874 (Trimingham 1962: 174n). Part of the difficulty, as Fisher (1970) has already pointed out, is how much of his travels should be included as part of the pilgrimage trip. Momodou-Lamin himself, in a letter to the Governor of Senegal, says that he was absent from Gunjūr, his natal town, for 36 years during which time he had been to Mecca on the *ḥājj*.[9] But this figure is likely to have been arrived at by including all his travelling from the time he left Gunjūr via Segu to his final return from Mecca.

When Momodou-Lamin left for the pilgrimage he went by way of Segu, Northern Nigeria and Waday. According to Le Chatelier, he purposely toured every possible religious centre on his pilgrimage route: Gando [?Gwandu], Wurnu [northeast of Sokoto] and Bornu. He stayed for a long time in Waday where a disciple of the Sanūsiyāh order, Fakir Ali ibn Fakir Baraouala, educated at Noumero, gave him his daughter, Miriam, in marriage.[10] Momodou-Lamin then proceeded on his way to Mecca, spending some time in Cairo and Medina (Chatelier 1899: 216). According to one report he boasted on his return of having spent some years in Constantinople (Nyambarza 1969: 125). Frey (1888: 251-2) says that he spent seven years in Mecca itself, devoting himself to prayer exercises and study. According to Le Chatelier, while Momodou-Lamin was in Mecca, he cultivated the Tijāniyāh association which he first entered into after leaving Senegal. He was associated with the *zāwiyah* of the Tijānī Sidi Soliman al-Kabīr in Mecca, a familiar Negro Tijānī hospice (Chatelier 1899: 216). Fisher carries a story that Momodou-Lamin received his Tijāniyāh initiation from the Prophet, in a dream in Medina,[11] but is inclined to impute the dream initiation to al-Ḥājj ᶜUmar about whom a similar story is told (see also Abun-Nasr 1965: 111).

The pilgrimage of Momodou Lamin conferred on him a high status, and everywhere he went he was held in great esteem by the general public. One story says that some eleven kings beseeched him in vain to accept their hospitality and remain among them (Frey 1888: 252). His reason for refusing was that God had other business for him to accomplish, though he did not make it clear what his plans were. Brosselard, a French officer in the War Ministry, was sent on a mission to the Senegal in April, 1886. He travelled to Bakel where he found a strong following for Momodou-Lamin whom he described as 'no ordinary man'.[12] Some comment unfavourably on his religious endowments. Brosselard, for example, describes him as an impostor who claimed an equal status with the Prophet. This stems from the fact that Momodou-Lamin is reputed to have said that while in Mecca he slept close to the body of the Prophet which was hardly taller than he was,[13] implying that he was of almost equal stature with the Prophet. Nyambarza, following these reports, says that Momodou-Lamin returned from the pilgrimage with the idea that he was a great prophet and that he enjoyed an equal status with the founder of Islam (1969: 126).

That the *ḥājj* had profound effects on Momodou-Lamin is without doubt, but what is not so certain is whether it was responsible for resolving him to wage a *jihād* on his return. French official sources are in no doubt that his resolve to foment a revolution against the French colonial administration was formed because of his *ḥājj*. Local Jakhanke sources are not so definite, and emphasise the religious programme of the conversion of pagans rather than military and political aims. A surprising feature of local Jakhanke accounts is the absence of any reference to Momodou-Lamin's anti-Tukulor platform, and in fact many sources stress co-operation between him and al-Ḥājj ᶜUmar.[14] This is in consonance with the Jakhanke tradition of underplaying the ethnic factor. One effect has been to dissociate the Jakhanke clerical families from any sectarian crusades relying on appeals to ethnic and similar loyalties. Their attitude to Momodou-Lamin was no exception.

He received numerous presents on his return journey. He had 300 copies of the Qur'ān, all of them richly bound in fine leather.[15] These books, or most of them, were destroyed by the French at the Battle of Kydira on 24th April, 1886. Frey says that these copies of the Qur'ān were Momodou-Lamin's pride and joy, for they were given to him by rulers of the countries through which he passed (1888: 388). Marty describes how the books were carried by ten slaves elaborately dressed and marching pompously (1915/6: 280; see also Fisher 1970: 59n).

Momodou-Lamin's sojourn in Masina represents a watershed in his career. Frey's account says that not far from Timbuktu Momodou-Lamin was forewarned that the king had dispatched a force to arrest him. Momodou-Lamin broke the news to his enraged disciples whom he then led in prayers, facing the tomb of the Prophet, asking for courage and victory. After the prayers he told his followers that they had nothing to fear, implying by this that his prayers for safety had been answered, to which his enthusiastic disciples responded with shouts of joy. When the enemy forces appeared Momodou-Lamin marched straight through the numerous troops unharmed for he had become invisible. His enemies meanwhile continued their search for him.[16] The story does not say what happened to his numerous disciples in that incident, although it seems unlikely that they all shared Momodou-Lamin's miraculous transformation.

In Masina, by contrast to this hostile reception, he was well received by the current ruler, al-Tijānī, the nephew of al-Ḥājj ᶜUmar. Al-Tijānī was also the cousin of Ahmadou, the ruler of Segu. Al-Tijānī gave Momodou-Lamin a slave girl whom he married (Frey 1888: 253-4). There is some disagreement as to where he actually met al-Tijānī; one source says Bandiagara (Bathily 1970: 22), but other authorities would have it at Hamdallahi, the political centre of Masina (Frey 1888: 253-4). After a short stay at Hamdallahi, during which, according to one oral tradition, al-Tijānī asked to be instructed in some Tijāniyāh recitations,[17] Momodou-Lamin went on to Segu. There a new chapter in his career opened.

The Sojourn at Segu, 1880–85

Momodou-Lamin probably arrived in Segu sometime in 1880, although some accounts suggest 1878.[18] The oral traditions collected by Fisher contain some important details on the manner of Momodou-Lamin's reception by the *sulṭān* Ahmadou Shaykhu. According to these, Momodou-Lamin arrived in Segu bringing Ahmadou greetings from al-Tijānī. This, however, occasioned some heated exchanges in which Momodou-Lamin was reproached for belonging to the Serakhulle nation, a people, Ahmadou said, notorious for spreading evil reports. Nevertheless, Momodou-Lamin was royally entertained: Ahmadou gave him a compound with six women slaves. The *sulṭān* also killed a bull and provided ten gallons of oil as his welcome present (Fisher 1970: 62). Other accounts agree with the first part of this story which indicates that Momodou-Lamin's initial welcome in Segu was a rough affair. After he arrived in Segu Ahmadou immediately set about trying to capture the slave girl al-Tijānī had given to Momodou-Lamin and even to seize and kill Momodou-Lamin himself, but found the latter's students too influenced by a veneration for Momodou-Lamin to co-operate. Ahmadou was forced to abandon his plan. He certainly received the traveller with a measure of reserve and had him confined outside the city to a derelict village, Salām.[19] It was here that the programme of religious militancy began to acquire definite shape.

Momodou-Lamin's fame began to spread, taken to numerous corners of the Western Sudan by Serakhulle long-distance traders who circulated reports of his supernatural powers, accrediting to him numerous miracles. Trade caravans coming from Sangaran and Kankan and bound for points on the Senegal carried stories about him after paying him a visit to the village of his exile. At this time a comet appeared in the skies with its tail turned towards the North Pole and was visible for three months. This was seized on by the Serakhulle sympathisers of Momodou-Lamin as a sign that God was about to launch a prophet into the world, who in their eyes was to be none other than Momodou-Lamin (Rançon 1894a:111). French accounts of his political ambitions, and imputations that he claimed Messianic or apocalyptic titles need to be carefully handled, for the danger is apparent that in attempting to explain his hold on the imagination and sympathy of his devoted following they were also projecting their own fears and frustrations on to the situation. It is in this light that French reports about the Serakhulle looking to Momodou-Lamin as the promised Mahdi who would restore the Serakhulle people to their former glory must be seen.[20] Reports about his religious and supernatural powers continued to spread in all the surrounding area, and everywhere people waited with expectancy for the apocalypse. Meanwhile in Segu itself he was kept under constant surveillance, for Ahmadou remained deeply suspicious of his political motives, and was angry when his own personal life was denounced by the holy man (Chatelier 1899: 217).

Accounts of Momodou-Lamin's eventual departure from Segu vary. According to one version, Ahmadou was apprehensive about conducting military operations against Kaarta and leaving behind him a man whose ambitions he feared and whose following was great, deep in the heart of his empire. Thus, according to Le Chatelier, Momodou-Lamin was released as a consequence of this fear that he had become a political liability (1899: 217).

According to Frey, however, stronger measures were taken and several miraculous incidents preceded Momodou-Lamin's final departure from Segu. Afraid to leave a man of Momodou-Lamin's stature behind him, the *sulṭān* persuaded some of his followers to go and keep him prisoner in his house. When the arrest party arrived, on horseback, eight monstrous fishes appeared before them at the entrance to the village. Distraught, the horsemen fled. A second attempt was made the following day, led by the *sulṭān* himself, but the arrest could still not be made. Ahmadou alighted from his horse and walked towards Momodou-Lamin's dwelling. Before he could appear within the walls of the house eight monstrous fishes appeared and barred his way. At that point Momodou-Lamin came forward, chided the *sulṭān* and charged him with having betrayed his faith. He ordered him to return to Segu, and the *sulṭān*, deserted by his men, was obliged to withdraw (Frey 1888: 256-7). Having failed through confrontation, Ahmadou tried indirect means: he tried to kill Momodou-Lamin with a poisoned kola-nut, but that scheme proved abortive too (*ibid*).

Oral traditions collected by Fisher (1970: 63) similarly stress miraculous interventions on Momodou-Lamin's behalf although the details are considerably different. According to one, the first attempt to dispose of Momodou-Lamin came when the two first met: the *sulṭān* had dug a well and placed a covering over it, and he then invited Momodou-Lamin to sit on it, which the pilgrim did without falling in. This kind of test is a recurrent feature of miracle stories about West African religious figures: the *askiya* Muḥammad passed a similar trial ordeal when Sonni Ali tried to trap him in the same way (Rouch 1953: 187); the Fula *mujāhid*, ᶜUthmān dan Fūdī, escaped a similar fate at the hands of the *sulṭān* of Gobir, Yunfa (Muḥammad 1963: 132-3).

The second attempt took place when fifty young men waylaid the pilgrim on his way to the *sulṭān* at night, ready to pounce upon him, but he passed unnoticed in their midst both ways (Fisher 1970: 63). As already indicated by Fisher, this story of becoming invisible could have been confused with the incident already described as happening near Timbuktu, although other explanations are possible.[21]

A third attempt on Momodou-Lamin's life, still following Fisher, was made when the *sulṭān* invited him to undertake a religious exercise for him involving retreat. The *sulṭān* first made sure that the house was impenetrable from all sides so that Momodou-Lamin, once he stepped inside, would in effect be setting the seal on his own death, for no one would be allowed to take him food or drink. It is said that Momodou-Lamin walked straight into this trap and remained in solitary confinement for one month and twelve days, during which time his family wept for him as one dead. At the end of that period the house was entered and the retreatant found alive and well, with all manner of food next to him. The oral account goes on to say that when Momodou-Lamin was released from the house he upbraided the *sulṭān* for putting him to a test which he himself would not have been able to pass. The *sulṭān* acknowledged his deficiency, taking comfort in the thought that his own father, al-Ḥājj ᶜUmar, was greater than Momodou-Lamin. Nevertheless, the account goes on, Ahmadou gave his own mother, Aissa, to Momodou-Lamin in marriage, and the holy man then left Segu (Fisher 1970: 64).

However, according to Frey's account (1888: 261-3), Momodou-Lamin was still in Segu when Ahmadou left for the Kaarta campaigns. The *sulṭān* had heaped presents on Momodou-Lamin and promised him a large part of any booty, all this, says our source, in order to attach Momodou-Lamin to his cause and to control his ambition. However, Ahmadou still nursed suspicions against his redoubtable guest and ended by reiterating his former threats and vaunting his power. Ahmadou left his son, al-Madani, behind and charged him with the responsibility of running the state. This source says that al-Madani harboured a secret respect for Momodou-Lamin, and took the first opportunity after Ahmadou's departure to accord him his liberty (Frey 1888: 261-3). As we have seen, according to Le Chatelier, it was Ahmadou himself rather who set Momodou-Lamin free and chased him out of Segu, and he left sorely grieved at his treatment (1899: 217).

Why should Momodou-Lamin, a highly respected religious figure returning from a sacred mission, who, into the bargain, was widely acclaimed for his zeal in propagating the Tijāniyāh *tarīqah* (Brigaud 1962: 55; Fisher 1970: 65), be ill-treated by the son and heir of al-Ḥājj ᶜUmar, the arch-Tijānī of Black Africa? What was at the source of this grave misunderstanding? It can hardly be explained by Momodou-Lamin's visit to al-Tijānī in Masina, a subordinate, at least in theory, of Ahmadou, or the rapport he enjoyed with him. Normally renowned religious figures were sought and courted by princes whatever their previous record of friendship with other rulers. It is surprising that Ahmadou did not see in Momodou-Lamin a possible ally but rather appears to have mistrusted his Tijāniyāh connections. One tradition, originating in Bamako, says that the only occasion on which Ahmadou called attention to Momodou-Lamin's links with the Tijāniyāh brotherhood was to call even that into question (al-Naqar 1972: 19-21). It seems in fact that the relationship between the two men was doomed to failure before they even met. As the quarrel between them developed and intensified, with miraculous powers coming to the aid of Momodou-Lamin, grounds for a possible rapprochement receded, and Ahmadou's departing words underlined further the lack of rapport. The official French explanation focused on Momodou-Lamin's supposed political intentions, that is, the creation of a Serakhulle empire which would displace the Tukulor in Masina. Their reports of secret agents actively recruiting on Momodou-Lamin's behalf and plots due to be hatched as soon as he was reunited with his Serakhulle sympathisers are unsubstantiated and unlikely. The differences with Ahmadou seem to have been more a question of a basic personality clash whose origin remains unclear.

The Triumphant Return to Bundu, 1885

According to Frey, Momodou-Lamin left Segu in 1885, travelling across the Niger to Nyamina, 150 kilometres northeast of Bamako. En route he met a deputation from Tabacoura asking him to lead a military operation against Ahmadou. He is said to have declined and to have said that his time had not yet come (Frey 1888: 261-3). Momodou-Lamin arrived in his natal town, Gunjūr, sometime in early July 1885. His return caused great excitement among the population, and the leading citizens received him triumphantly. The king of Khasso,

Dioukha Samballa, went forward to meet him, and a massive cortège of people from the region gathered together to express their support and sympathy for the returning son of their town (Bathily 1970: 22; Ch. Monteil 1915: 374). Large and numerous gifts were brought to him. His rising fame from the time of his detention at Salām had spread to all the neighbouring towns, and there was a general expectancy in religious circles that great events would trail his arrival home. The French, on the defensive, feared precisely the same.

The spontaneous upsurge of feeling which Momodou-Lamin excited among his compatriots, and the apparent ease with which coteries of sympathisers formed among religious elements, especially in the initial stages of his movements, can be explained partly by the enormous popular appeal his personality exercised upon these individuals. His physical stature was impressive, and those who knew him describe him as of extraordinary demeanour. Frey, for example, hostile in his attitude, was nevertheless impressed:

> Dévoré d'une ambition insatiable, très intelligent et très ambitieux, d'un langage meilleur et d'une grande audace dans l'action, il ne dédaigne pas de faire usage pour frapper des esprits naïfs et crédules des tours de prestidigitation qu'il a appris dans ses voyages. (*Rapport Frey*, 1886, cited in Nyambarza 1969: 129)

Commandant Brosselard described his physical appearance thus:

> Il était bien doué pour le rôle qu'il s'était choisi; il était de haute taille, il avait la physionomie d'un homme qui était fait pour commander. Il parlait bien, il était instruit..., et il s'était montré aussi rusé dans sa propagande qu'audacieux dans l'action. (*ibid*)

Such descriptions would suggest that Momodou-Lamin was a natural leader, although the French insisted on their view of him as unscrupulously prepared to capitalise on the credulity and naïveté of his following. This assessment is, however, unjust, for he was able to attract men of sound moral judgement and among his supporters were citizens of high respect, and not only from among his own Serakhulle people.

Military Activities and Relations with the French

All the sources are unanimous in maintaining that upon his return to Gunjūr, Momodou-Lamin was bent on avenging the ill-treatment he and his mother had received in Gamon before his departure for the pilgrimage, and that this fever for revenge was aggravated by his bad relationship with Ahmadou of Segu. He had, the reports say, irreconcilably adopted the war path. For a time he was able to rely on his old friend, Boubakar Sa^{c}ada, by then an ally of the French, who also had some old scores to settle with Gamon. But Boubakar Sa^{c}ada died in mid-December, 1885, a few months after Momoodu-Lamin's arrival in Bundu.

Relations between the Serakhulle and the French in Bundu had for a long time been uneasy. Forced labour and an active French presence at Bakel from July, 1874, had antagonised the local Serakhulle populations. The French, led by Captain Zimmermann, had attacked villages, massacred the inhabitants and burnt houses in July, 1875.[22] Henceforth the French presence in the Serakhulle towns was considered tantamount to imposed servitude (see Nyambarza 1969: 135). The French response to what they considered Serakhulle stubbornness was to maintain vigilantly their preparedness to crack down decisively on dissident populations. The whole area was thus seething with revolt, or at least ready for one, when Momodu-Lamin arrived on the scene, a godsend in the eyes of the disaffected elements and a natural hero of the anti-French forces simmering beneath the surface.

Nevertheless Momodou-Lamin himself explicitly foreswore any plan or ambition to unsheath the sword against the French. Between July and December, 1885, he maintained adamantly that his intentions towards the French were peaceful and he constantly reassured them of his friendship and support. 'I am the friend of the French,' he wrote in August, 1885, 'and will never cease to follow their orders wherever I may be.' As far as his rumoured plots in Gunjūr were concerned he would brushed these aside. 'I have come,' he said, and his words have the ring of sincerity, 'to inhabit the soil of my ancestors and my natal town, in order to follow the way of righteousness and of wisdom, and to counsel my people to follow in my footsteps without committing any acts of brigandage or theft, as is the custom of our neighbours and most other groups.'[23] Even when Momodou-Lamin was actively amassing gunpowder, guns, and men for war, he was profuse in his protestations of friendship towards the French. In a letter dated 24th September, 1886, that is, well into his active recruiting campaigns, he appealed to the Governor proffering sincerity and arguing that even if he had not needed the French on the grounds of friendship alone, he would have needed them on the grounds of trade and political expediency: the French were his only source of arms and his most powerful commercial allies (Nyambarza 1969: 130). In some of this correspondence his overriding religious concern about the alleged growing power of pagans (*kuffār*, sing. *kāfir*) is evident.

It is outside our purpose to analyse the political components of Momodou Lamin's revolutionary programme or within that to assess the military developments which grew out of his overall strategy. Was he in the event more anti-French than anti-Tukulor? Did the course of subsequent military engagements provide any pattern of an unfolding political ambition?[24] We do, however, need to discuss the kind of support he obtained and, in so far as this can be determined, how much weight religious criteria had in attracting followers. This will have a direct bearing on the question of Momodou-Lamin's sincerity and whether charges of his being an impostor and a freak religious adventurer can be properly sustained.

Le Chatelier's account of the social composition of Momodou-Lamin's followers is unflattering. He said they were a disparate assortment, mostly floating members of society and rejects of the colonial bureaucracy: '...population flottante des escales, laptots, tirailleurs et mariniers, congédiés du service de l'Etat ou des particuliers...une foule de Soninké du Guoy, du Guidimakha...' (1899: 218, 219). Many other sources also focus on the Serakhulle (Soninke) ethnic factor as the basis of support for Momodou-Lamin (P. Smith 1965a: 248; Frey 1888: 210; Sabatié 1925: 214, 215). The ethnic or tribal factor touched on here is a Pandora's box in African history. That the Serakhulle supported Momodou-Lamin is certain, but to interpret his movement purely in terms of a recrudescence of Serakhulle political ambition is to edge towards the conspiracy theory of his French opponents, and that explanation excludes too many other important factors to be satisfactory.

Marty, who wrote some time afterwards, collected information on who Momodou-Lamin's supporters were and gave a detailed account of them. Even at that date the possibility that such information was highly incriminating cannot be entirely ruled out. In Nioro, Serakhulle territory, he found evidence of wide and influential support for Momodou-Lamin. One Adietou Sinde (b. 1850), the old chief of Boully, and his brother, Shaykhu Mamadou Jawara (b. 1872) of Moulizimo, also in Nioro, played supporting roles in the movement (Marty 1915/6: 310). At Arténou, in Nioro, the Muslim, i.e. pro-Momodou-Lamin, faction was led by the Sokhona family: Mamadou Sokhona (b. c. 1853), in collaboration with the chief of Selibaby, Amady Sise, the latter's brother, Seydi Bambi of Gambi Sara, Doike Sokhona and Demba Awa (b. 1865). At Ralli, still in Nioro, the leading Serakhulle *imām* was Mamadi Wagui Korena (b. 1844). He was originally of Moorish descent and was a disciple of Fode Diamou of Bakel. He was known for his pro-Momodou-Lamin sympathies. A leading Jakhanke cleric, Abdoulaye Kabba-Jakhite, originally from Jafunu, was a close supporter (Marty 1915/6: 311). The great and distinguished Soumare Serakhulle family also rallied to Momodou-Lamin's support. Ali Koumba Soumare (b. 1849), a Tijānī disciple of Samba Dia of Mounderi (Bakel), and his brothers, Ousman and Boulaye, supported him, as well as Fode Tālibe Sise (b. 1845) (*ibid*: 312).

Some Wolof elements were also on Momodou-Lamin's side. For example, the disciples of Fode Bakary Ndiaye were among his most prominent followers: Bakary Ndiaye's son, Adietou, his nephews and cousins Daouda, Bakary, Bakari Silli, Souleyman, Nafi (*imām* of Gandji mosque) and Sire Ndiaye. These men, according to Marty, carried arms for Momodou-Lamin in operations against the French in 1886 (1915/6: 313).

Jakhanke Attitudes and Responses, 1886–87

The specific Jakhanke response to Momodou-Lamin may be divided into two phases. In the initial stages of the campaign Jakhanke populations by and large gave him moral and in some cases token military support. In the latter phase of his career the Jakhanke withdrew support and eventually adopted a positively hostile attitude towards him. This breach with Momodou-Lamin was to have far-reaching effects on the Jakhanke in Bundu and other parts of Senegambia.

But why did the Jakhanke, a traditionally pacific people, espouse this *jihād* in the first place, albeit for a limited time? And what precise form did this espousal take? Although these questions are not adequately answered by our sources, they are fundamental enough to require close consideration. The fact that Momodou-Lamin himself came from a Jakhanke background had a considerable effect on his ability to arouse the spontaneous sympathy of the Jakhanke. This ethnic factor played a similar role in the career of Fode Kabba (see pp. 193-5). In Momodou-Lamin's case it was strengthened by another important factor. The enormous religious and spiritual stature Momodou-Lamin acquired as a celebrated returned pilgrim strengthened his hand and made his general endorsement by the consensus of clerical opinion among his Jakhanke kin a fairly natural course of events. The detailed miracle stories about him circulating among the Jakhanke suggest that his religious stature was considerable in their eyes.[25] This much is conceded by some oral traditions which accept that Momodou-Lamin's pilgrimage had made him a formidable religious figure although the same traditions would question his *jihād* credentials. The support Momodou-Lamin received from the Jakhanke took the form of prayers, and, more tangibly, recruits for his first campaigns, and possibly food for his troops. It is not clear, however, whether the recruits sent were Jakhanke themselves, and from comparative knowledge one would be inclined to say not. The French, who meticulously followed Momodou-Lamin's every move, do not mention Jakhanke recruits specifically. It is more likely, therefore, that the men drafted from the Jakhanke side were clients, students, and possibly slaves.

Marty adduces as a reason for Jakhanke support for Momodou-Lamin a long-standing opposition to the Tukulor (1915/6: 317ff), an opinion which is hardly supported by the evidence. It does not explain, for example, their later abandonment of their principal ethnic advocate at a time when the Tukulor menace was still far from being dismissed.

Why then did the Jakhanke abandon Momodou-Lamin? Oral accounts stress the intervention of religious and moral scruples as leading to the split. The French officer, Lt Bonaccorsi, in a despatch to Lt Col Galliéni, wrote that the Jakhanke population of Bundu followed Momodou-Lamin to Diakha, in southwest Bundu. Soon afterwards, however, they broke off all relations with him. According to the despatch, Momodou-Lamin sent a request for fresh recruits from the Jakhanke, but:

> '...on lui a répondu qu'on lui fournirait quand les 300 hommes qu'il avait laisser en route seraient de retour...'[26]

According to this source Momodou-Lamin reacted sharply to the Jakhanke refusal of his request. He sent back a stern message advising them to 'quitter les petites villages et de se masser dans deux ou trois qu'ils fortifiraient bien pour résister en cas d'attaque.'[26] This was interpreted to mean that Momodou-Lamin would withold protection from the Jakhanke in the event of an attack, possibly by his own forces. In a despatch of 14th November, 1886, Lt Guiguandon said that Dianna, an early base of Momodou-Lamin's movement, was the principal town among a group of settlements in the Diakha region. The population of the entire region was estimated at 5,500 scattered in some 32 villages.

Dianna, the chief village, had between 450 and 500 inhabitants. It was reckoned that of these 5,500 inhabitants, only a tiny proportion, with a possible total armament of no more than 600 guns, might at any given moment support Momodou-Lamin. The overwhelming majority would be neutral because 'les Diakhanké ne sont pas guerriers.'[26]

The widescale Jakhanke desertion from the cause of Momodou-Lamin needs explaining in the light of their earlier espousal of it. What precisely had changed about Momodou-Lamin's movement which prompted the withdrawal of the Jakhanke from his side? The answer to this question turns almost exclusively on the fundamental soundness or unsoundness of the earlier position of support for him. It was time, and the rapid turn of events which finally exposed the unsoundness of the original support for a *jihād* effort. The operation against Gamon, seen by the Jakhanke as a limited and justifiable campaign against a pagan people, and undertaken at a time when the returned pilgrim was riding the crest of popular acclaim, turned out to be part of a much wider ambition of political domination. The early reverses in his campaigns as well as this deeper involvement in a military and political plan than they had anticipated offered the Jakhanke an opportunity to extricate themselves. The changing character of Momodou-Lamin's movement completed Jakhanke estrangement from him. The turning point came in April, 1886, with his declaration of war against the Sy family (Sikunda), the Bundu political leadership and confirmed Muslims. When it became clear that Momodou-Lamin was not content with limiting his operations to punitive action against Gamon but that indeed he was taking on the French as well as their Muslim Bundu allies, the Jakhanke repudiated his *jihād* by formally withdrawing from areas under his control or sympathetic to him.

Up until April, 1886, Momodou-Lamin was bent on teaching Gamon a lesson in what was little more than a personal dispute. He had been preparing for this operation in the months of January and February, 1886. But within a very short time he had both Omar Penda, the ruler of Bundu, and the French hard on his heels. It became clear that the Gamon enterprise could not be separated from the wider and more suffocating mesh of local political forces delicately poised for a new role under the imperial mandate. The Jakhanke populations of Bundu, relatively insulated and unaware of the logic of colonial military conquest, found themselves caught in the wider ramifications of an action to which only a tenuous moral strand bound them. Neither they nor Momodou-Lamin could have clearly understood the meaning of what they envisaged as a legitimate cause against perfidy.

The sources certainly suggest that the issues were not clear, at least to Momodou-Lamin's supporters. In the early stages of his campaigns he insisted on his status as a religious savant, 'a man of God', as he described himself to the French.[27] The people that Frey interrogated at Bakel at the beginning of Momodou-Lamin's campaigns were convinced that he was waging a limited religious war, a *jihād* (Nyambarza 1969: 136). In numerous protestations to the French and his own disciples, he said his quarrel was only with the pagans of Gamon and elsewhere. The large following of students he attracted soon after arriving in Gunjūr were similarly persuaded that the enterprise for which he was preparing them involved the extension of the rule of *dār al-Islām*, the abode of peace, to the *dār al-ḥarb*, the sphere of warfare. They did not imagine their aim was to overthrow French power, which the French thought Momodou-Lamin had long decided to challenge even before he arrived in Bundu. Despite some of the claims to the contrary, Momodou-Lamin did not, from the evidence of his early campaigns, envisage opening a war front against the French in addition to his avowed aim of taking action against the pagans.

However, as remarked earlier, even if he had spelt out in strict terms what his quarrel with Gamon was, that would not necessarily entitle him to the loyalty and support of the Jakhanke as a whole as we have come to understand that tradition of loyalty and support. Many would not support war on any terms. It should be stressed, indeed, that only certain sections of the Jakhanke community did lend him support, mainly those from the Diakha region of Bundu, and that the vast majority, for example all the Silla, Kabba-Jakhite and the Jabi-Gassama were not only uncommitted to him throughout but in the end diametrically opposed to him.

The circumstances in which such a majority Jakhanke view was asserted must be looked closely, but one point concerning French confusion over the issues involved needs to be cleared up. The French, who credited themselves with the ability to discern Momodou-Lamin's plans, accepted his offers of friendship and fidelity to the extent of supplying him with the necessary arms and equipment. If the faith which they reposed in him turned out to be misplaced and they were led astray as a consequence, the Jakhanke can hardly be seen as more gullible for the limited support they lent him under similar circumstances.

The circumstances under which Jakhanke families renounced or repudiated the cause of Momodou-Lamin are worth investigating more closely. Jakhanke accounts emphasise the point that once Momodou-Lamin took steps which brought him nearer to secular leadership their estrangement from him was inevitable. One explanation was that 'a Muslim is someone who prays, fasts, pays out the *zakāt* and goes to Mecca. But if that same Muslim fights, than that is just to take a district from someone else, which is not right.'[28] In what appears to have been a doctrinal dispute with Momodou-Lamin, some of the leading Jakhanke clerics of Bundu challenged his right to wage war for political office. In one incident, Fode Mamadou Jīlānī, a respected Jakhanke leader of Bundu, led the challenge. He said Momodou-Lamin had been given a Qur'ān to read in Mecca,[29] not a gun to come and fight. 'God had not given Bondu to Muḥammad al-Amīn; he was not a chief: he had been to Mecca, and was famous, but he was not a chief.'[30] As we shall see throughout this study, the distinction between a political career, even with an explicit Islamic appeal, on the one hand, and a religious/clerical vocation, on the other, is a sharp and consistent one among the Jakhanke. That distinction has a much wider application than specific Jakhanke quarrels with Muslim (or non-Muslim) aspirants to political power.[31]

The Fode Mamadou Jīlānī of the account cited above who resisted Momodou-Lamin's war aims may be the same individual as the Fode Maḥmūd Jīlānī of another account. This Fode Maḥmūd was a member of the Kabba-Jakhite *qabīlah* who had at one time over 600 students studying under him.[32] In a dream during his travels he is reported to have encountered ᶜAbd al-Qādir Jīlānī, who asked him to return to where he came from and found a clerical centre there. Fode Maḥmūd then went back to Bundu and founded the village of Jīlānī. He was recognised as the Qādirī *muqaddam* in the Western Sudan by the Kabba-Jakhite *qabīlah*. After the split with Momodou-Lamin, who attacked his centre in the initial stages of his campaigns and forced the evacuation of all Jakhanke families in Bundu, he came to a place called Pakeba in Senegal Orientale where he died.[33] A tradition maintained among the Kabba-Jakhite *qabīlah* is the annual visit to the grave of Fode Maḥmūd

Jīlānī at Pakeba. The children of Fode Maḥmūd dispersed from Bundu and came to settle in the Gambia river basin. His eldest son, ᶜAbd al-Qādir Kabba, went to live in Kaur-Jannehkunda. His grandson, ᶜUthmān Kabba, was still the leading cleric at Jannehkunda in early 1973. Another grandson of Fode Maḥmūd Jīlānī was the late al-Ḥājj Kemoring Jakhite of Kuntaur-Fulakunda, a highly respected scholar in the region.[34] Karamokho Bātuo Kabba, a son of Fode Maḥmūd Jīlānī, founded the Jakhanke clerical centre at Jarumekoto.[35] His Qur'ān school won wide acclaim and students flocked there from numerous parts of Senegambia including Bundu.[36]

Another Jakhanke *qabīlah* adversely affected by Momodou-Lamin's *jihād* in Bundu was the Silla section led by Muḥammad Sanūsī. Confronted by Momodou-Lamin at Neteboulou (Bundu), he took formal leave of him and came to Jarra-Bureng,[37] and from there he eventually went to Kounti as the clerical leader. This took place between 1885 and 1886 (see p. 195).

Momodou-Lamin's most serious setback was the collective repudiation of his *jihād* efforts by members of his own clerical *qabīlah*, the Darame. According to Jakhanke accounts, after Momodou-Lamin warned the Jakhanke in Bundu not to expect to be spared from his military operations, numerous families came to Neteboulou.[38] The Bundu Darame were led by Safiatu Burema, Safiatu Madi, Safiatu Sanūsī and Safiatu Ma Sireng. One account says that when Safiatu Burema arrived in Banī Isrā'ila in Bundu he and his following were hosted by the Silla. However, a dispute broke out and Safiatu Burema and his disciples went to found the village of Bakadaji in Bundu.[39] Fode Ansumana Darame succeeded Safiatu Burema when he died, and the Darame moved to middle Bundu where a second Bakadaji was founded. It was at this point, around 1885, that the dispute with Momodou-Lamin erupted and precipitated a fresh dispersion to the existing Jimara-Bakadaji in the Gambia Republic.[39]

The details of this dispute, involving a dispute over prayers, are discussed on pp. 195-6. Fode Ansumana had spurned Momodou-Lamin's appeal for help which provoked threats and counter-threats between the two, resulting in Fode Ansumana leaving Bundu. It is said that when Fode Ansumana left Bundu and came to Fuladu he found Musa Mola and Bakary Demba in power. Musa Molo is said to have tried to entice him to adopt Fuladu as his home but he declined the offer. Instead, he adopted a site near some riverain swamps so that his people could cultivate crops (mainly swamp rice, grains and groundnuts) and lead a quiet life of study and religious work.[39] This is how he came to live in Jimara-Bakadaji. Musa Molo is said to have acceded to his wish, and paid him visits at his new home in Bakadaji, bringing him presents of slaves, among other things. A story is told about one Danso who was the other member of the triumvirate with Musa Molo and Bakary Demba. Danso came to visit Fode Ansumana once and was lodged at the home of Safiatu Sanūsī. The house in which he was lodged was near a goat-pen, which Danso took as a personal slight, so that he left in a temper, vowing to sack Bakadaji on his return. Before he could mobilise against Bakadaji he quarrelled with Musa Molo who attacked and killed him.[39] Bakary Demba, the other member of the triumvirate, also split with Musa Molo and came to a place later called Bakary-Dembakunda, close to Jimara-Bakadaji, daring Musa Molo to pursue him there. It is said that Fode Ansumana, concerned about what appears to have been an attempt to embroil his clerical centre in a political/ secular issue, pronounced a curse that Bakary-Dembakunda would never have a future and that its size and importance would be insignificant.[39] It is said that the effect of that curse has never been broken, and Bakary-Dembakunda has remained an insignificant village. Bakadaji made a brisk and promising start under Fode Ansumana, but just before his death a disastrous fire engulfed the town, destroying the house of Fode Ansumana himself. Whether he was hurt in that fire is not clear, but the sources say that he died soon afterwards - ten years from the time he first arrived there.[40]

Such wide-ranging dispersal trails triggered by Momodou-Lamin's military operations in Bundu suggest that overall he found little sympathy among the Jakhanke. In view of this, it is difficult to explain why the French authorities did not encourage the Jakhanke to remain in Bundu taking advantage of the fact that their attitude to Momodou-Lamin was unsympathetic. By capitalising on his breach with the Jakhanke the French might have been able to widen the rift and alienate further local sympathy from him. On the Jakhanke side, it was feared that a general mobilisation of local populations by the French would result from their policy of direct involvement in local affairs, and that in those circumstances the Jakhanke would not be spared. The Jakhanke were also quick to sense that their ethnic connection with Momodou-Lamin might place them in a highly ambiguous position vis-à-vis the French. In reprisal operations during 1886-7 against Momodou-Lamin, particularly against Dianna and Toubacouta, the Jakhanke were at the mercy of French military power. They fled in different directions, most of them heading for the Gambia river basin (P. Smith 1965a: 248).

At about the same time the Jakhanke came under fresh suspicion of links with Samori Toure from whom they obtained a large number of slaves (see p. 196f.). After killing Momodou-Lamin and destroying his movement, the French turned their attention to the question of slavery. In 1893, the French officer Hostains, accompanied by the Almamy of Bundu, Mālik Toure, laid seige to the three most important Jakhanke centres in Bundu: Sillacounda, Laminia and Samecouta. At first the Jakhanke thought of defending themselves but quickly dismissed the idea as futile, if we may believe the story handed down by tradition. They voluntarily surrendered, but, according to one source, they were still severely punished 'pour des raisons qu'ils ignorent aujourd'hui et que personne n'a pu donner' (P. Smith 1965a: 256). The result of these political measures was again to encourage dispersion to the Gambia 'où l'administration indirecte des Anglais convient mieux désormais à leur esprit d'indépendance et à leur goût pour le commerce et le prosélytisme. Plus tard, un certain nombre de familles reviendront dans leurs villages du Boundou mais c'est dorénavant en Gambie que les meilleurs iront chercher l'enseignement de grands marabouts' (P. Smith 1965a: 248-9).

The Jakhanke themselves were fully aware of the difference between French and British policy, and conscious that the position of the latter was more conducive to their clerical practice. Two specific examples may suffice. After the split with Boubakar Sa^{c}ada, the Jakhanke cleric Bakary Jabi came to Sandu where he created Jakhaba.[41] A sizeable number of refugees fleeing from the wars of Momodou-Lamin soon after Jakhaba was founded came to settle there. At first, the Jakhanke there continued to pay taxes to the French post at Bakel ('Bakili'), largely because lines of British and French jurisdiction were not firmly drawn at that time, but also because the Jakhanke had still not decided which way they were going to turn. Two years later they started paying taxes to the British. They had decided on Jakhaba and British protection rather than submission to French direct rule in Bundu.[42] The second example is contained in an account by al-Ḥājj Ansumana Jakhite. According to him, when the Jakhanke decided to leave Bundu they specifically wanted to place themselves under British protection.[43] This is supplemented by another informant who says that the British tolerated Jakhanke clerical independence and did not require them to attend courts where they would be forced to take the judicial oath.[44] This reference to oath-taking and law courts relates to the Jakhanke tradition of refusal to take oaths upon the Qur'ān and the British policy of non-interference in the internal institutions and structures of their protectorates. While it is a matter of record that the Jakhanke came to settle in the British controlled area because of the greater potential for escaping from political interference, I have not been able to substantiate the claim of Pierre Smith that they were also attracted there by trading opportunities.

Conclusion

Three general observations may be made in a final summary of the Jakhanke response to Momodou-Lamin. The first is that the dispersion trail again proved a safety valve for the survival of Jakhanke clerical tradition. According to one oral account such a dispersion from Bundu had two broad implications for Jakhanke clerical activity, one being a loss and the other a gain. The loss was that it dispersed and so reduced the strength of Jakhanke witness and effectiveness and exposed each dispersed segment to one of several different influences; and the gain was that it scattered and spread their clerical influence and educational practice, helping to make a wider diffusion of Jakhanke Islam possible.[45]

The second general observation has to do with Islam as a political creed. The Jakhanke dissociated themselves from the programme of Momodou-Lamin when he, in their eyes, set Islam on the path of political power. In spite of their ethnic affinity with him, they found his vision and programme and his methods for a triumphant Islamic political *dawlah* ideologically unacceptable. It seems to have been on a similar issue that the Jakhanke some thousand years before splintered away from their original Serakhulle cousins who may have been the founders of ancient Ghana, Old Wagadu. For many Jakhanke families the attack in April 1886 upon Sikunda, the Bundu political leadership, recognised as fellow Muslims, was the deciding factor, and from then on the

Jakhanke were permanently alienated from Momodou-Lamin.[46]

The French attack on Gunjūr in March, 1886, opened the round of military confrontation which was to end in Momodou-Lamin's defeat. The forces ranged against him were formidable. Lt Galliéni was in charge of French operations and was able to mobilise two columns against Momodou-Lamin. The rulers of Wuli and Bundu, under French instructions, also mobilised against him. The people of Gamon, already antagonistic, joined forces with the French, and Musa Molo, capitalising on Fulbe/Tukulor antipathy to him, similarly backed the French against Momodou-Lamin. The British denied him haven as the French closed the net around him. He was finally cornered in the district of Niani in early December, 1887, and killed. He was decapitated by local troops and his head taken to the French as a trophy. Despite the lack of Jakhanke involvement by this stage, his defeat also accomplished the demise of Jakhanke clericalism in Bundu, although the clerical practice there did not disappear completely.[47]

As a third and final point it may be fruitful to draw a parallel with the later history of Touba in Guinea, the prosperous clerical centre founded by Karamokho Ba. There too the Jakhanke faced equally imponderable questions as the active presence of the French began transforming political events in hinterland territories. As with Momodou-Lamin and the events surrounding him in Bundu, here too they resorted to dispersion. But that method of escaping political involvement was hardly adequate in an era of universal colonial subjugation. In reassessing their future the clerics found that the crisis was due to a lack of understanding of the new forces, not to any inherent weakness in their traditional attitudes of neutrality and pacifism. Nevertheless, while they lost the immediate struggle to gain French recognition for their religious autonomy, they succeeded even in defeat in preserving their reputation as men of religion and peace.

NOTES

1 The Czech scholar, Yvan Hrbek, has been working on Momodou-Lamin for some years now, and his study will provide a comprehensive account of the movement. Three articles already published dwell on his relations with the French and the Tukulor: Oloruntimehin 1968, 1971, and Bathily 1970.

2 According to one account, Demba Sega, the founder and first king

of Khasso, concluded an alliance with the ruling Moorish clan of Axiri by giving his daughter, Khoumba, in marriage. From that marriage was born a son, Mahmadou, who also had two sons, Bou Seydi, from whom the Fall descended (to become chiefs of the Moors of Sero), and the founder of Déya, Mamadou Khoumba, who became the father of Momodou-Lamin (Ch. Monteil 1915: 28, 373).

3 Frey 1888: 250; Rançon 1894a: 107; Marty 1915/6: 280; V. Monteil 1964: 99; Nyambarza 1969: 124.

4 Ch. Monteil 1915: 373. Mamadou or Mahmadou is also given as his father's name by Chatelier (1899: 216) and Nyambarza (1969: 124). Rançon, however, says that his father's real name was Alfa Ahmadou (1894a: 107-8).

5 Ch. Monteil (1915: 373) says Safalou; other accounts Gunjūr (Frey 1888: 250; Nyambarza 1969: 125; Fisher 1970: 53). Bathily does not say explicitly that Momodou-Lamin began his studies at Gunjūr, but that is the impression he leaves (1970: 22).

6 Rançon 1894a: 109. There is a conflict about dates here if another account of ᶜUmar's movements is to be accepted. This latter account says that while ᶜUmar was fully aware that the French had engineered a powerful anti-ᶜUmar bastion at Bakel, with Boubakar Saᶜada, ruler of Bundu, as the cornerstone, military engagements against the Bambara in Kaarta kept him pinned down in that theatre of the war from about the middle of 1855 to August, 1858. His first opportunity to visit Bundu and Futa Toro came in August, 1858. See Oloruntimehin 1972: 85-92, 106 (which gives the account of his campaign in Bundu and Futa Toro). However, ᶜUmar's military operations in Bundu may be a separate incident from a goodwill visit in or around 1854 for a preliminary on-the-spot assessment of feeling there. Rançon implies that such a visit, if indeed it ever took place, preceded the actual opening of hostilities against the Bambara (*loc. cit.*). Much earlier, ᶜUmar visited Bundu prior to his *ḥājj* to seek blessing from a Jakhanke cleric, ᶜUmar Kabba, 'a much venerated *shayk* of that region' (Willis 1970: 51).

7 Chatelier 1899: 216; see also Tyam 1935: 34, the first source to mention the connection between an unidentified Momodou-Lamin and al-Ḥājj ᶜUmar in this fashion.

8 Fisher wrote: 'The yoke from which he sought to liberate his own Soninké was not French, but Tokolor...' (1970: 51); see also Rançon 1894a: 115. Tukulor and Fulbe are the same people with a slight regional difference. The Jakhanke are the Serakhulle clerical specialists.

9 Nyambarza 1969: 130, where the letter, dated August, 1885, is reproduced.

10 Chatelier 1899: 216. Faidherbe (1889: 477n) suggests a connection between the Sanūsī and Momodou-Lamin, and Frey (1888: 243-4 and n) sees links between Jakhanke clerical ritual and the Sanūsiyāh. Fisher (1970: 58), however, does not think the evidence is sufficiently strong to support theories of Sanūsī allegiance among the Jakhanke, even for Momodou-Lamin.

11 Fisher 1970: 59. The story originated from the Serakhulle town of Alunhare, Upper Gambia.

12 Nyambarza 1969: 126, quoting from ANSOM, Paris: Sénégal III, 11f, *Rapport Brosselard sur la situation dans la vallée du Sénégal en 1886*, p. 94.

13 *ibid*; also Faidherbe 1889: 420; Marty 1915/6: 280.

14 Karamokho Sankoung Jabi, Nibrās, 4/12/72. The alliance with the Tukulor leader could, however, also be a protection for the Serakhulle/Jakhanke.

15 Nyambarza 1969: 128, quoting from ANSOM, Paris: Sénégal IV, 85a, *Rapport Frey* (22 juin, 1886).

16 Frey 1888: 253-4; Rançon 1894a: 110ff. Rançon follows Frey's account faithfully, and so reference to him is omitted in what follows.

17 This oral account is contained in Fisher 1970: 61, and according to this source Momodou-Lamin stayed three years in Masina.

18 The date 1880 is given in Chatelier 1899: 216; Marty 1915/6: 280. Fisher (1970: 62) also thinks it the most likely. 1878 is given by Oloruntimehin (1968: 380), citing a French report of 1880.

19 Frey 1888: 255. He translates 'Salām' as 'prayer', followed in this by Nyambarza (1969: 128), but the word in fact means 'peace'. Fisher carries an oral account which says that Momodou-Lamin lived at a village called Tugu, just outside Segu, and that the place where he went to pray every Friday was called by him 'Salām' or 'Ya'Salām' (1970: 62n). This tradition was collected in Bamako.

20 Frey 1888: 255. Marty says, without foundation, that Momodou-Lamin was a Tijānī Mahdi (1915/6: 280). Galliéni (1891) and Chatelier (1899) do not make this assertion.

21 Fisher gives the example of an amulet known to have this power, as reported in Tremearne 1913: 171. He also cites al-Naqar who says that an amulet of this description was highly esteemed by pilgrims (Fisher 1970: 63; see al-Naqar 1972).

22 The incidents are reported in detail in ANSOM, Paris: Sénégal, IV, 44d, *Affaire Zimmermann et les Sarakolé, Rapport fait à l'enquête ordonnée le 22 juillet, 1875.*

23 Letter to Governor of Sénégal, August, 1885, quoted in Nyambarza 1969: 130.

24 For attempts to answer such questions see Oloruntimehin 1971. Trimingham (1962: 174n) suggests Momodou-Lamin's ambition was to create a Jakhanke state.

25 This is conceded, while his *jihād* is deplored, by traditions collected by Fisher (1970) to be referred to presently. Although these traditions are looking back, with the inherent danger of inventing arguments not formulated at the time, nevertheless they make a

distinction between a secular programme and a religious one and to that extent faithfully preserve a long standing Jakhanke tradition.

26 ANSOM, Paris: *Mission 18, d'après Mission Galliéni - Campagne 1886-87* - 'Mission de Capitaine Martin en Bambouk'.

27 In a letter of August, 1885, to the Governor of Senegal, quoted in Nyambarza 1969: 136.

28 Fisher 1970: 59, reporting a tradition from Kabba Kunda, a Jakhanke clerical centre near Basse (Kabba Kamma?).

29 Perhaps a reference to the numerous copies of the Qur'ān acquired as gifts on his pilgrimage trip.

30 Oral tradition from Danfakunda, Upper Gambia, collected by Fisher 1970: 60.

31 Muḥammad al-Ghālī, al-Ḥājj ᶜUmar's *shaykh* in Mecca, warned his *murīd* after initiating him into the Tijāniyāh *wird* and conferring on him the status of most favoured *murīd*, that al-Ḥājj ᶜUmar should 'cease associating with kings or *sulṭāns*' and that he should never himself seek temporal power on pain that the *shaykh* would cease 'sustaining him in his prayers and intercessions' (Willis 1970: 62). It is said that Muḥammad al-Ghālī pressed the importance of abstaining from temporal power upon his disciple. He reminded him of the words of the Prophet: 'the best *amīrs* are those who comply with the wishes of the *ᶜulamā*, and the worst *ᶜulamā* are those who comply with the wishes of the *amīrs*', and again: 'the *ᶜulamā* have the security of the Messengers of God as long as they spurn association with *sulṭāns*. But if they associate themselves with *sulṭāns*, they are unfaithful to the Messengers' (*ibid*: 62-3).

32 Muḥammad Lamin Jakhite-Kabba, Kuntaur-Fulakinda, 6/12/72. A different source says he had 400 students under him when he established a mosque in Jīlānī (al-Ḥājj Ansumana Jakhite-Kabba, Jarumekoto, 30/11/72).

33 *TKQ* and interviews referred to in n.32.

34 There is a brief notice on al-Ḥājj Kemoring in an article on the Stone Circles of Senegambia in *Ta'rīkh*, vol. 2, no. 2, London, 1968, where al-Ḥājj Kemoring discusses not only the possible origins of these ancient megaliths but also indicates some of the sources of Jakhanke scholarship.

35 Al-Ḥājj Ansumana (ᶜUthmān) Kabba-Jakhite, son of Karamokho Bātuo, Jarumekoto, 30/11/72.

36 Al-Ḥājj Khousi Silla, Brikama, 11/11/72. Although he is not a member of the Kabba-Jakhite *qabīlah*, al-Ḥājj Khousi, echoing many other witnesses, testified to the success of Karamokho Bātuo's educational establishment.

37 Al-Ḥājj Ansumana Jakhite Kabba, Jarumekoto, 30/11/72.

38 Al-Ḥājj Khousi Darame, Danfakunda, 12/12/72.

39 Al-Ḥājj Janko Darame, Jimara-Bakadaji, 11/12/72. See also pp. 63-4 and pp. 225-6.

40 The informant, Al-Ḥājj Janko Darame, is the grandson of Fode Ansumana through his son, Safiong Darame, a former Alkali of Bakadaji.

41 Bakary Jabi himself and his brother, Yusufa, first went to live at a place called Misira, but some time later, with the influx of refugees from the disturbances in Bundu, the new settlement was created at Jakhaba.

42 Al-Ḥājj Fode Jabi, Sandu-Jakhaba, 9/2/73.

43 Al-Ḥājj Ansumana Jakhite-Kabba, Jarumekoto, 30/11/72.

44 Muḥammad Khalīfa Silla, Kounti, 30/11/72.

45 Al-Ḥājj Fode Jabi, Sandu-Jakhaba, 9/2/73.

46 *ibid;* also Karamokho Sankoung Jabi, Nibrās, 4/12/72, and al-Ḥājj Ansumana Jakhite-Kabba, Jarumekoto, 30/11/72.

47 On the fall of Momodou-Lamin there are numerous sources (see e.g. Galliéni 1891: 107ff; Faidherbe 1889: 449; also Quinn 1971: 437). Galliéni said that even after the rout of Momodou-Lamin's forces at Dianna, the people of Diakha laboured under a stigma. 'Je bornai là les mesures de répression prises contre les gens du Diakha' because of 'leur obstination à suivre le marabout' (Galliéni 1891: 109). The remains of Momodou-Lamin are contained in an unmarked grave in Yona, a small village in Niani. According to local sources Momodou-Lamin was killed in Niani-Kayaye and his body taken to Yona where it was placed in the village stockade to avoid detection by colonial forces. Al-Ḥājj Banfa Jabi told the present writer that he had plans to erect a tomb for Momodou-Lamin at Yona as a fitting tribute to his career. Quinn (1971) says that Momodou-Lamin was killed at Lamin-Koto, but most local sources disagree with this version.

CHAPTER FIVE

THE JAKHANKE IN FUTA JALLON
THE NINETEENTH CENTURY

The Islamic and Colonial Background

The Jakhanke move to Futa Jallon at the beginning of the nineteenth century, under the charismatic leadership of al-Ḥājj Sālim Gassama, better known as Karamokho Ba, is an example of a further elaboration of the theme of dispersion in the interests, not of recovering a fatherland, but of preserving the values of a professional clerical tradition. Settling in Futa Jallon, deep in the heart of Fula country, is a striking example of Jakhanke clerical withdrawal and rootlessness.

Futa Jallon was itself heir to a reform Islamic tradition sponsored largely by Karamokho Alfa (d.1751) and his party. Also known as Alfa Ibrahima, Karamokho Alfa went to Kankan to study under Qādir Sanūsī (Marty 1921: 3), a highly respected scholar from a Jakhanke background. The Islamic revolution which Karamokho Alfa led completed Fulbe domination over the original Jallonke inhabitants of Futa Jallon, the Jallonke being one of the two important autochthonous groups of the area. When he died Karamokho Alfa left a strong Islamic tradition bound up with his own charismatic appeal. Marty refers to him as the epitome of the entire century, 'comme le résumé d'une époque et d'une grande oeuvre' (1921: 4). The Old Testament, Marty continues, and the records of the early days of Islam offer many examples of the characteristic figure or type of an epoch. 'Karamokho Alfa est le prophète d'Israël venu secouer la torpeur de ses frères, réveiller leur foi somnolente et les lancer dans la voie des grands destins'(1921: 4-5).

This Islamic legacy soon came under heavy strain. Karamokho Alfa was succeeded by his cousin, Ibrahima Sori (d.1784) a warrior with strong political and commercial ambitions. He sequestered the political heritage of Konde Buraima, a pagan conqueror from Wassoulou whose centre of power was in Kankan,[1] and in its place created a powerful political state (Marty 1921: 5). The different emphasis placed on the *jihād* by Ibrahima Sori produced a divergence from Karamokho Alfa's line. Henceforth Futa Jallon Islam was split between the faction of Karamokho Alfa and that of Ibrahima Sori into the Alfaya, of a zealous Islamic orthodoxy, and the Soriya, with a programme for Fulbe political and commercial domination of the entire Futa Jallon area. Ibrahima Sori, who restored the *jihād* effort to an effective fighting capability, after Karamokho Alfa's death had left it in some disarray, changed his title from the religious one of *imām al-ṣalāt* (lit. prayer leader) to the political/secular one of *imām al-ṭā*ᶜ*a* (which can be translated as 'commander of obedience'). This change came after he had achieved the triumph of his cause in 1776 in alliance with the hitherto anti-Fulbe Solima people (Trimingham 1962: 166-7). When the Jakhanke arrived in Futa Jallon in the late eighteenth and early nineteenth centuries, this division in Futa Islam persisted, but, as our study shows, the Jakhanke were able to bridge the divide.

A second important political element in the Futa Jallon was the French commercial and, in the nineteenth century, colonial presence. Jakhanke records do not tell us much about this, and when they mention it, it is late in terms of French penetration of what in French official circles were called *les rivières du sud*. It is necessary, therefore, to fill in from other sources the background of French penetration into Guinea and Futa Jallon in view of the fact that it was to have a profound impact on the Jakhanke there.

French interest in the *rivières du sud* region (today the coast of Guinea) began with Faidherbe's explicit policy of extending French power in Black Africa. In 1860 he created a political agent in the Rio Pongas. In the same year he sent Lt Lambert to the interior of Futa Jallon. Pinet-Laprade, Faidherbe's successor, signed a number of treaties with riverain princes between November, 1865 and February, 1866. He established a military post at Boké in the Nuñez (Hargreaves 1963:129). Direct French intervention, precipitated by local political troubles and the clamour of both French and (the majority) British and Freetown merchants for protection in the Mellacourie region (now just north of Sierra Leone's borders), led to the establishment of a French military post of 25 men on the south bank of the Mellacourie at Binty in February, 1867 (Hargreaves 1963: 134). The French continued active presence in the area, largely in order to forestall suspected British influence spreading from Sierra Leone and creating a political corridor from there to the Gambia, and also in order to protect French trade in the area. On 15th February, 1876, Colonel Canard, a commandant of the second *arrondissement* in Senegal, signed, so the French claimed, a treaty of protection over the ruler of Rio Pongas, John Catty, giving the French commercial rights and land to establish a post, in return for which John Catty received an annual pension of 5,000 francs, a sum that was twice that offered to him by the British (Terrier et Mourey 1910: 124-5). In June of the same year the British redoubled their efforts to establish a presence in the Mellacourie area (Hargreaves 1963: 217). One of the most important protégés of the French was Youra, sovereign of the Nalou, whose friendship they had cultivated since 1865. On 30th January, 1884, the French, through Dr. Bayol, signed a treaty with Youra. But after his death in 1887 he was succeeded by Dinah Salifou, with French connivance, although they abandoned him in due course and sent him to Senegal in forced exile in 1890 (Terrier et Mourey 1910: 126). Meanwhile the French, under Colonel Brière de l'Isle, the new governor of Senegal, pursued a vigorous policy of expansion in the Mellacourie area. In about April, 1877 he dispatched the political director in Senegal, Boilève, to conclude treaties in the region. The French exploited the fears of local chiefs about the future of their domestic slaves threatened by avowed British policy on the issue (Hargreaves 1963: 223). Brière de l'Isle, restless about suspected British aims in the *rivières du sud*, anticipated Governor Rowe of Sierra Leone and signed a treaty with the superior chief of Konakry, Balla Demba, ruler of the Kaloum Baga, in June, 1880 (*ibid*: 247). Four years later Balla Demba disclaimed all knowledge of a previous treaty (*ibid*: 290). The French continued their penetration into Futa Jallon from the south, impelled by fears of a British manoeuvre, and, later, by signs of German interest on the coast and in the riverain territories. In 1880, Aimé Olivier, 'a pretentious Marseillais adventurer in a tartan *boubou*', visited Timbo, the chief town of Futa Jallon (*ibid*: 267). A series of treaties and conventions drawn up between July, 1881 and December, 1885 sealed the fate of Futa Jallon under French political control.[2] French determination to contain British designs, or what they imagined to be British designs, launched them on a career of treaty-making even after the formal conventions were drawn up with other European interests in the area. The French were still preoccupied with the idea that the British had secret plans to connect their possessions in Sierra Leone with the Gambia and saw the Futa Jallon and the Mellacourie region as ideal buffer zones to prevent such a grand plan from coming into effect. On 30th May, 1888, the French signed yet another treaty with the Almamy of Futa Jallon establishing a French Protectorate over the area, and coupled this with a treaty with Britain signed on 10th Auguust, 1889 (ratified on 12th October), formally recognising French rights over Futa Jallon.[3]

This French policy of direct involvement in the politics of the *rivières du sud* and an aggressive pursuit of an imperial mandate further inland contrasts sharply with the British approach based on the classical policies of the 'informal empire'. As far as the Jakhanke were concerned the current of direct rule which buoyed the French ran counter to their tradition of withdrawal from external politics and internal self-rule. The conflict that this clash of attitudes was to generate was a fundamental one, although Jakhanke failure to arrive at a *modus vivendi* with the French need not be seen as a lack of perception or awareness of the issues involved. Indeed, the eventual breakdown in relations with the French could be seen as an index of Jakhanke consistency to their philosophy of political neutralism, for it was that primary ideology of neutralism which made their encounter with the French a painful one. However warily they walked with their French colonial masters, if they stuck to this ideology sooner or later the tide was going to turn against them,unless there was a basic shift in French policy.

The Early Life of Karamokho Ba c.1730-1824

> Thucydides does not seem to have grasped fully that in estimating the action of an individual in history his whole character must be taken into account; he is a psychical unity, and it is not possible to detach and isolate certain qualities. Psychological reconstruction is one of the most important as well as delicate problems which encounter the historian, and Thucydides failed to realise all that it means. In his impatience of biographical trivialities, he went to the extreme of neglecting biography altogether...(J.B. Bury, *The Ancient Greek Historians*, Harvard Lane Lectures, 1908, reprinted, New York, 1958: 146-7)

Jakhanke clerical and missionary zeal was given a fresh impetus by the personal life and career of al-Ḥājj Sālim Gassama, otherwise known as Jaghun al-Ḥājj, the son of Muḥammad Fāṭuma by his wife Jaghun Ba (see p. 47). As the name indicates, he was called after al-Ḥājj Sālim Suware, but the honorific 'Karamokho Ba', 'the Great Teacher', given him by his impressed Fulbe hosts and admirers during his long peripatetic career, came to stick and to replace the other names. Consciously modelling himself on his nominal prototype, he symbolised the independent clerical and missionary spirit of the Jakhanke at its most developed and effective stage. Two broad themes stand out clearly in his career: the long educational journeys he undertook, during which time he also increased his personal following, leaving behind an impressive reputation of learning and holiness, and, secondly, the creation of a settled clerical community to which people came for instruction and guidance.

The accumulation of scholarly merit and religious virtue from a long travelling career and the subsequent founding of a burgeoning settlement, with the potential for further emigration, have consistently marked out the Jakhanke cleric. Karamokho Ba's biography thus gives us an insight into the lives of others before and after. His biographical details, framed and gilded in laudatory terms, portray a fairly typical career pattern. He undertook no major departures from traditional Jakhanke norms, and no innovations of clerical enterprise can be accredited to him. Yet, in undertaking to bring the weight of Jakhanke clerical values to bear on contemporary political and social problems, he gave those values a fresh articulation and a new meaning and appeal for his generation. Whatever durability was infused into Jakhanke Islam, a large part of it was his doing.

Born about 1730 at Didécoto, Karamokho Ba undertook his early studies under his father. When his father died in about 1750, he transferred his studies on his father's instructions to Kounti under the leading *tafsīr* specialist in the area, a former pupil of his own father, Shaykh ᶜUthmān Derri.[4] His educational career, as outlined in considerable detail in local sources, provides invaluable evidence on the state of learning in islamised Africa at that time. The wide ethnic background of the scholars he encountered indicates the range of intercourse between people of different backgrounds under the common influence of Islam. The course of his studies is therefore followed in this account.

After the completion of his studies under Shaykh ʿUthmān Derri, his teacher conferred on him a mantle (Ar. *khirqah* of scholarly merit.[5] Following this, 'he was stirred by a high ambition to go to those places where real men of God resided, and for this reason he undertook a travel career which led him first to Gunjūr' (Soriba n.d. 192). The text reads:

ثمّ نهضت به الهمة العلية
إلى مقامات رجال الله تعالى
فعمل الرّحلة وتوجه إلى
ناحية مشرق التّكرور فوصل إلى
كُنجور... الاقصى أيضا وتعلم
فيها...

According to *TKB*, Karamokho Ba first went to Didécoto before continuing on to Gunjūr, but he may just have been on his way to the latter, for there is no mention of any educational motive for the visit. At Gunjūr his teacher was Ibrahīm Jane, sometimes known by his *laqab* (honorific), Gunjūru-Ba. Under Ibrahīm Jane he studies the *Mukhtaṣar* of Khalīl, a book on Mālikī jurisprudence (*fiqh*). Then in the same place he studies the *Maqāmāt*[6] ('Assemblies') of al-Ḥarīrī under Fode Hasan Gakou. He followed this up with a *fanna* (branch) of *tafsīr* with Fode Muḥammad Jawara. After his sojourn in Bundu he travelled to Diombokho in Khasso where he studied *naḥw* (grammar) under Fode ʿAmar Ture. In addition he studied *taṣrīf*[7] under the same teacher. From there he went to Bakhunu and under Fode al-Hasan Fulānī he studied a two-volume commentary, *al-Makīkī*, on *tawḥīd* (theology). At Bakhunu his teachers included Fode Bakari Jebaghate, with whom he studied the works of al-Sanūsī, in five volumes, and who greatly impressed him. Karamokho Ba travelled farther afield to Jenne with the specific intention of studying Islamic jurisprudence (*li-qasdi taʿallam al-shifā*). While in Jenne, he made the acquaintance of numerous scholars, among them one Alfa Nūḥi, the Fulani. Alfa Nūḥi left an indelible impression on Karamokho Ba, and he is represented in the account as a man with a prodigious memory, a master of forty branches (*funūn*) of learning.[8] Other teachers included Alfa Ḥāṭib, under whom he continued his study of Muslim jurisprudence from the *Shifā*, a work by Abī al-Faḍl ᶜIyāḍ bin Mūsā (twelfth century) as well as the *Ṣaḥīḥ* (Traditions) of al-Bukhārī. He proceeded to higher studies (*fanna al-awfāq*) under Alfa Rāha, and then began serious study of a formidable work on *naḥw* (grammar), called *al-Fiyah* by ibn Mālik, in which he was guided by ᶜUmar, nicknamed Naḥawī. Muḥammad Naḥawī taught him more *taṣrīf*, and according to *TKB*, also *lūghah* (linguistics). His other teachers included Muḥammad Tumāju, Muḥammad Kharāshī, Muḥammad Ghullī and Muḥammad Kamisātu.

Among all his teachers, Alfa Nūḥi, who came originally from Masina, appears to have had the most profound spiritual impact on him. The accounts say that it was Alfa Nūḥi who led him to an intellectual and spiritual weaning stage.[9] This is most likely a reference to the fact that Karamokho Ba was said to have been initiated into the *Qādiriyāh wird* by Alfa Nūḥi, who received it himself from Shaykh Mukhtār al-Kuntī.[10] The practical effect of this spiritual influence was to enable Karamokho Ba to start an independent clerical order and establish a school of his own. His long association with Alfa Nūḥi, which some authorities say lasted seventeen years,[11] brought to an end his formal educational career, and from then on whenever he went to meet leading divines it was to confirm his scholarly status and to seek *barakah*.

Karamokho Ba then left Jenne and went to Masina where he made the acquaintance of a charismatic scholar, Muḥammad Taslīmī Saghanukhu, who left a lasting impression on him. The chronology of events at this point is unclear, for between the time Karamokho Ba was in Masina and the time he went to Futa Jallon a number of significant developments took place about which the sources vary. What follows is a reconstruction of the order in which events most probably took place, although care is taken not to tamper with the substance of the accounts themselves.

After Karamokho Ba left Jenne and travelled to Masina, he was looking, not for any more teachers, but for a place to settle. His encounter with Muḥammad Taslīmī, who impressed him greatly, gave him the idea of founding a settlement under the latter's spiritual shadow. He built a new centre in Masina and named it Taslīmī (*TSK*: fo. 7; Soriba n.d.: 193). He lived there for three years. At this point a divergence occurs in the sources. *TKB* (fo. 4), followed by both Marty

(1921: 107-8) and Suret-Canale (1970: 57), says that Karamokho Ba left Masina and went to Kankan where he lived for three years. Oral accounts and *TSK*, however, contain a journey to what is now Sierra Leone which is supposed to have taken place between the time he left Masina and the time he arrived in Kankan.

TSK says that after Karamokho Ba left Masina he travelled to Konya, and after a brief stay he continued to a place called Faye, or Failung. His visit to Faye (Mfailo, Sierra Leone) was distinguished by an outstanding miracle he performed. Oral accounts say that during his travels he met a man who told him that in a forthcoming visit he would ask to marry a princess who would bear him his spiritual heir and successor.[12] Reluctantly Karamokho Ba went to Faye where he was hosted by King Isḥāq Kamara. Karamokho Ba, as predicted, became acquainted with the daughter of King Isḥāq, Aisatou Kamara, and asked for her hand in marriage, offering a large marriage payment in gold. King Isḥāq pleaded the girl's youth as an excuse for turning down the request, but on perceiving Karamokho Ba's earnestness in the matter, he yielded on one condition. A large piece of rock had become implanted in the middle of the river (the St. Paul?), obstructing shipping. Isḥāq asked Karamokho Ba to pray so that this impediment to shipping would be removed. He refused the large quantity of gold he was offered but agreed to the king's request for help. The sources say Karamokho Ba performed a specialised devotion, *ᶜilm al-asrār*, which was accompanied by a request-granting dream, *ru'yā al-ṣāliḥah*, and God answered his prayers (*TSK*: fo. 7). He then married Aisatou.

Both al-Ḥājj Soriba Jabi and al-Ḥājj Mbalu Fode Jabi say that Karamokho Ba possessed a large quantity of gold. According to Mbalu Fode, King Isḥāq returned the gold Karamokho gave him as dowry, dividing it into three portions. The first portion was to be distributed to feed the poor and destitute, the second to be set up as capital outlay towards a *bayt al-māl* charitable endowment, which would be used for the purposes of maintenance and upkeep of mosques, aid to pilgrims, etc. The third and final portion was to be retained by Karamokho Ba himself to help him set up house with his new bride. It was from this union with Aisatou Kamara that Muḥammad Taslīmī (Karang Taslimanka), his spiritual successor, was born. From Faye he went to Kankan by retracing his steps to Konya.

A large student body accompanied him to most of these places.

Al-Ḥājj Soriba Jabi said he was accompanied by some 160 *ṭullāb* (sing. *ṭālib*), students.[13] *TSK* supplies a list of the names and home towns of the leading ones which is given in full here in a note.[14] These students went with him to Kankan where he was most warmly received (*TSK*: fo. 10).

Although he intended to proceed beyond Kankan, the leading citizens persuaded him to settle there for a while. Some Muslim notables had arrived from Jenne, and it was they who made him a gift of a cow, so that, it is said, Karamokho Ba, moved by the gesture, relented. He accepted the offer and asked one of his senior students, Karam Dawda Suware, to kill the animal (*yadhbaḥuhā*).[15] The cow was the gift made by the people of Jenne, but the people of Kankan itself would not be left out. They gave Karamokho Ba four men as his personal assistants: Karamokho Khadījata Mādī [the grandfather of Muḥammad Sharīf, better known as Sharīf Fanta-Mādī (d. 1955) and of wide fame],a son of Alfa Maḥmūd Kabba, Karam Ṭālib Silla and Karam ᶜUthmān Kamara (*TSK*: fo. 10). He made a deep impression on the people of Kankan during the three years he taught there. The inflated claim in one account which says that Karamokho Ba was 'the founder of Qur'ānic teaching [in Kankan]' (Suret-Canale 1970: 57) has its basis in the wide currency which his teaching and ideas had there.[16] But Kankan also contributed enormously to Karamokho Ba's personal stature and it was there also that his sixth son by Aisatou Kamara, and heir to his title, was born. He duly named this son after his charismatic clerical patron, Muḥammad Taslīmī, whom he had met at Jenne. It is evident that Kankan provided Karamokho Ba with a good and keen audience, for it was thither that a branch of the Jakhite-Kabba Jakhanke lineage had emigrated, under Maḥmūd Kabba (see *TKQ* and above p. 39). The descendants of these early immigrants appear to have given him every facility he needed in his work.

He then went to Lako in the canton of Oualada, a strong Manding centre. He was well received by an enthusiastic and admiring following and lived there for a year, making wide-ranging contacts with the Fulbe inhabitants of Timbo. Also he met Imām Bademba, the Fula leader of the Alfaya Muslim faction.[17] It is said that Imām Bademba lavished honours on Karamokho Ba and conferred a special status on him in recognition of his scholarly achievements by awarding him a special burnous which had cost him one hundred dinars. He also met Imām ᶜAbd al-Qādir of the Soriya party who paid him similar high honours and made him a personal gift of seven slaves and a thoroughbred horse.[18]

While still at Lako he came across a man of considerable local renown and a versatile scholar (*al-mutafannin*), Alfa Muḥammad Woinke. He recalled (*tadhākara*) with Alfa Woinke some of his earlier studies in *tawḥīd* and other disciplines. By this time his personal following had swelled with more people coming from Timbo (*TKB*: fo. 4). Pressure was brought to bear on him to accept political office in Futa Jallon but he remained adamant about his clerical priorities. *TKB* gives further details on this question, and Karamokho Ba's attitude, which is examined here, is crucial to an understanding of Jakhanke notions about secular power. It is said that the people of Timbo offered him a lucrative position as Paramount Chief, at a place of his own choosing, but he turned it down. His reasons were crisp: he never saw himself as destined for a political career nor did he ever entertain any ambitions for a chieftaincy.[19] All that he desired was the right of unrestricted movement, full control over his personal destiny, peace and tranquillity for himself and his clerical community and the absence of any subservience to secular authority. He called all the people together in the open and made a public declaration in which he enumerated some of his conditions for being willing to settle in Futa Jallon. *TKB* says that he appeared before the assembly as a spiritual guide and appealed to a Ḥadīth from the Prophet, to the effect that every Muslim is a shepherd of the flock entrusted to him, and made the people promise that they would renounce *jihād* and all strife and divisiveness in the area. He made it plain that he would accept their invitation on his own conditions. It is a measure of his spiritual and moral stature that the political leadership of Futa Jallon kept faith with him and never embroiled him in any compromising scheme. The public declaration was followed up by extracting a pledge of good faith from his hosts. The principle of clerical independence and neutrality was accepted and ratified.

It was on this basis that Karamokho Ba left for Futa Jallon, and a new and brilliant chapter in his career opened. When he arrived in southern Futa Jallon, of which Timbo was the chief town, the ruler there was a vassal chief (*al-amīr al-mutawallī*), Modi ᶜAbdallāh Wura. The latter, like so many before him, was impressed with Karamokho Ba and entrusted to his keeping his son, Alfa Ṣāliḥu. He met some scholars there as well: Bakari Bote and Sa^{c}d bin Ibrahīm al-Dalmī from whom he sought *barakah* (*TKB*: fo. 4). Shortly after arriving in Labé, Karamokho Ba convened a general meeting to which the local people came. At that gathering he gave a public disquisition on the relevant portions of the Ḥadīth, and in what appeared as a spontaneous gesture, the rulers and their representatives undertook not to wage *jihād* any more nor to persist in pressing him to assume political office, but that instead they would leave him to live his religion in peace and security. This understanding well suited Karamokho Ba's plans. His earlier message at Lako had seeped through to his audience. He then left for Wura, accompanied by Alfa Ṣāliḥu and other members of his community. His intention was to found a permanent settlement and to devote himself exclusively to scholarship and clerical practice. The symbolic 'gift' (Ar. *tawallā*) of Alfa Ṣāliḥu made by Modi ^{c}Abdallāh Wura was the sign that secular authority had accepted his terms and an assurance of their support and co-operation. With his token hostage, and weighed down by age, for he was by now well over 70, he adopted a sedentary life. Although he was to do some more travelling later, he did so from a fixed base.

When he left Wura, Karamokho Ba went to Bakoni to found Touba-coto (c. 1804) in which he was aided by Alfa Ṣāliḥu and others of his following. He is said to have owned some 400 compounds there, and remained there with his community for eleven years. He attracted a large number of other Jakhanke clerics to his centre as well as other groups who came there to be instructed and he built a large mosque. But trouble broke out with the people of Tanda, the Bassari, who mounted raids on the centre. In one fatal sortie, the people of Tanda sacked Touba-coto, spread wide slaughter among its inhabitants, and took numerous captives, including a son of Karamokho Ba, Muḥammad al-Kabīr, whom they took away as hostage. Muḥammad al-Kabīr was later able to escape to safety. The attack precipitated a fresh dispersion, and at this point Karamokho Ba went to Binani where he was hosted by the incumbent ruler, Modi al-Ḥussayn. This welcome made him determined to make another attempt to settle in Futa Jallon, and he founded another Touba in Binani, Touba-cuta ('New Touba'). According to the sources, he created this Touba following a dream (*ru'yā al-ṣāliḥah*) by his senior wife, Nana Ba (*TKB*: fo. 5). The new town was destined to play a significant role in the islamisation of Futa Jallon and beyond.

The Touba Clerical Community

In normal circumstances, the arrival of a Jakhanke clerical community in a new place is signalled by the building of a major mosque which becomes the solidifying symbol and focus of community loyalty. At Touba circumstances were different and the building of a mosque took some time to achieve. Memories of the misadventure at Old Touba were still fresh, and so Karamokho Ba delayed for seven years before finally approving a mosque scheme. When the mosque was completed he was automatically adopted as the *imām ratti* (Chief Imām) a function he performed for another seven years before he died. Although the impression is given that the foundation of both Old and New Touba were relatively simple affairs, the facts appear to belie this. Support by secular authorities, if not expressly solicited, was nevertheless willingly accepted, and one source says that Alfa ᶜAbdallāh, who had earlier given him his son, Alfā Ṣāliḥu, provided him with large manpower support and with this Karamokho Ba was able to erect a large number of houses and thus set Old Touba off to a brisk start. He had been given an introduction to Alfa ᶜAbdallāh by Imām ᶜAbd al-Qādir. In the transfer to New Touba, similar support was given and Karamokho Ba was able to guarantee his large community a new start at fairly short notice.[20]

The sources speak of a large concentration of population at Old Touba and most of these people, including most of the 400 compounds owned by Karamokho Ba himself, transferred to Touba-Binani. The earlier experience at Old Touba in matters of organisation and administrative details proved invaluable. The fruits of this experience were effectively applied in the new establishment. The population was divided into four principal wards or sections, each one being assigned specific tasks concerned with the maintenance and upkeep of the mosque. The mosque,after its erection, became the focus around which the clerical community lived. The first order (*al-qasm al-awwal*) was the Karambaya, or more properly, Karamokho-Baya, and consisted of the following patronymics: Kabba, Silla, Darame, Ture, Suware, Sawane, Fadiga, Dabo and Jallo. This section of the community was apportioned certain members of the endogamous professional castes: leather-specialists (*garanke*) and smiths (*numu*). The second ward consisted of

Gassama Temoto (Middle Gassama), Gassama Santo (Upper Gassama) and a number of dependent caste families. The third consisted of the Fofana-Girasi, Sise, Dumbuya, Jawara and Kamara. These also had some members of the lower castes assigned to them. The final ward comprised the Fofana-Jula, Bajo, Dansokho, Tamanate, Jakhabi Temoto, Jakhabi Santo, Danfakha and Minte. These families were likewise served by dependent castes. (*TKB*: fo. 6 and *TSK*: fo. 14 supply identical lists.) Presiding over all these families was Karamokho Ba, technically head of the Karambaya ward, who occupied the position of supreme pontiff. His jurisdiction extended over all the free clerical families, although the dependent castes were directly subservient to their respective clerical patrons. Included among these endogamous castes was a large and growing slave population.

Community relations at Touba followed the normal Jakhanke pattern. The political aspirations of the Jabi-Gassama lineage were automatically fulfilled through the leadership role assumed by Karamokho Ba. The Sharī^{c}ah rules were uniformly applied by sittings of *qabīlah* representatives, on such questions as, for example, *zakāt* (alms), imāmate and divorce and inheritance. These *qabīlah* representatives were also responsible for insuring that their respective wards discharged their communal obligations, such as services in mosque maintenance, and providing a fair quota of the common granary. The agricultural setting of Touba is obvious, and the large manpower resources available to it meant that this potential could be exploited fully, as indeed it seems to have been. A small trading interest was represented by the fourth ward consisting of the Fofana-Jula, Bajo, Dansokho, Danfakha and Minte, among others, and some of the descendants of these families continued to be traders long after they left Touba.[21] But the indications are that even this modest representation of traders voluntarily abandoned long-range exploits in favour of a settled life in a clerical community.

A network of voluntary obligations and ties bound the various *qabīlah* leaders to Karamokho Ba. Schemes which concerned the community were submitted to him for consultation, plans to be absent from Touba were reported to him, and newcomers presented to him. Visitors were introduced to him and their mission explained. Permission to undertake schemes outside the normal community routine was sought from him. He could in certain situations, like approving an endowment, act alone, but in most cases he relied on the co-operation of the other three *qabīlah* leaders. The sources do not tell us how frequently this council of *qabīlah* leaders met, but what is known about other Jakhanke communities indicates that their sessions were closely tied to the Muslim religious calendar, and at the New Year or the fast (*ṣiyām*) of Ramaḍān, new measures would be announced relating to the welfare of the community. Consistorial deliberations disposed of community disputes, settled individual grievances and awarded penalties and compensation where necessary. The care of the individual educational institutions, called by the Jakhanke *majālis* (sing. *majlis*), was left to the respective heads of the *qabā'il*, but the general standards of educational performance, curriculum and discipline were matters very much within the province of the council of elders. Uniformity of practice throughout Jakhanke Islam has remained highly valued, and at Touba this was a matter under constant scrutiny.[22] The unity of the *ummah*, community, symbolised for the Touba Jakhanke by the chief mosque, was maintained and reflected in the unanimous decisions and rulings of the council. The choice of four *qabīlah* elders to preside over the Touba clerical settlement was deliberate and recalls the familiar model of the *Khulafā'u al-Rāshidūn*, and more recently the experiments at Diakha-Bambukhu and Didécoto (see pp. 37-8, 47). What was original about Touba was the scale on which it transplanted and conserved the heritage of Diakha-Bambukhu. Numerous people, and not only the Jakhanke, flocked to it and participated in the clerical vocation. The sanctions and the norms were based on claims to old models, but the application of these norms and the specific situation of Touba to which they were directed constitutes an original or new interpretation.

Touba's reputation for sanctity and learning increased, and numerous students flocked there from Mandinkaland and from such groups as the Sangare (Bambara), Kuranko, Jallonke, and from Baté, Konya, Kaabu, Pakao, Wuli, Niani, Niamina, Bundu, Jarra, Kiang, Guidimakha, Gajaga, Kakandi and other areas (*TSK*: fo. 15). Most of these areas are within the Manding heartlands, but other people than Manding were also involved, particularly people from Futa Jallon.

Karamokho Ba had a large family of twelve sons[23] and eight daughters. Of his sons nine survived and had families of their own. These families eventually subdivided into five sections or sub-

qabīlah branches, and only one son, Muḥammad Khasso, established a separate section at Kanjalong (in Casamance).[24]

The Miracles of Karamokho Ba

Some outside researchers have encountered difficulties in obtaining material on this subject,[25] but this is highly untypical. In general, the Jakhanke are not only willing but eager to discuss the miracles of Karamokho Ba and members of his entourage.

The famous miracle attributed to Karamokho Ba concerning his removal of a large piece of rock from the middle of a river has already been discussed. This is described by nearly all the sources. Another incident tells how Karamokho Ba suddenly became visibly distressed one day at Touba because he had been miraculously made aware that a student of his was in distress:

ومنها بعض مُريديه غرق في بحر
كمب انقلب به المركب فأستغاث
بالشيخ فاذا الشيخ قد خرج مِن البحر
وَاخرج المُريد منه سالما صحيحا وَلم
يغب عَن القوم في طوبى الا قدر نصف
ساعة أو ادنى مِن ذالك فاذا هُو حاضر
فسئل عنه فقال...

> A miracle of his was when a student of his was drowning in the sea at Kombo [20 miles away] after he fell from a capsized boat. He cried for help from the Shaykh. The Shaykh then rescued him from the sea and he was safe and sound. The Shaykh was not absent from Touba for more than half an hour or thereabouts. When he re-appeared someone asked him and he explained...(Soriba n.d.: 195)

Oral accounts embellish this story. It is said that Karamokho sat among his astonished students, dripping with water. He explained that he had just saved a drowning student of his at Kombo. In this version it was his physical appearance which prompted the question.[26]

Again, it is recounted that one day Karamokho Ba went out to lead the *ᶜaṣr* prayers at the main mosque. He opened the prayers with the usual *takbīr*, finished one standing position and then, contrary to normal practice, broke off with a *taslīm*. He was promptly asked why, and he explained that Shaykh Mukhtār al-Kuntī had died in the early part of the afternoon of that day (*ḍaḥwah al-yawm*) and that the prayer they had just performed as well as the unseen prayers of the saints were to mourn that death. This happened on Wednesday, the 15th day of Jumādā al-Ākhiratu in the year A.H. 1226 (A.D. 1811).[27] Nobody, it is claimed, had brought him the news before, nor had he heard about it from any source till that point in the prayer when he was miraculously given the knowledge. This happened while Karamokho Ba was still at Old Touba.

Another miracle concerns the integrity of clerical power vis-à-vis secular authority. It is related that a Jallonke ruler, Bakari Tamba, took a dislike to a son of Karamokho Ba, Muḥammad (?al-Kabīr). Bakari Tamba did not recognise him as Karamokho Ba's son, and had him arrested one evening with the intention of killing him. Muḥammad was locked up in a room. Karamokho Ba was supernaturally informed of the incident during the night of the arrest and he prayed to God and besieged Him (*fa'ibtahala ilā allāh*) on behalf of his son. Immediately Bakari Tamba appeared in Karamokho Ba's house. Karamokho Ba asked him a number of questions: Did he know where he was? Did he know before whom he was now standing? To both of these Bakari Tamba answered 'No'. Karamokho Ba told him he was in Touba, and that he was the father of the man Bakari Tamba had arrested and was intending to execute. And then, taking full advantage of the situation, Karamokho Ba demanded the immediate and unconditional release of his son, threatening to incite the wrath of God against Bakari Tamba if he failed to do as he was told. After that Karamokho Ba llowed Bakari Tamba to return home, and when he arrived he carried out Karamokho Ba's wishes and released Muḥammad. But, shaken by his recent experience, he went further than that. After releasing Muḥammad he made him a gift of his daughter, Sukhurung Sakho, and set apart handsome gifts and presents which he took to Karamokho Ba every year.[28]

Another supernatural story is recounted of Karamokho Ba which took place when he was in Kankan, shortly after he was given the cow by the people of Jenne. It is said that a body of *jinn*, spiritual beings, appeared to him and posed many teasing questions. This spiritual company was joined by another of orthodox Muslim saints (*awliyā'a al-ummah al-muḥammadiyāh*) such as Shaykh ᶜAbd al-Qādir al-Jīlī (d. A.D. 1410),[29] al-Suhrawardī (d. 1168), al-Shādhilī (d. 1258), Aḥmad al-Badawī (d. 1276), al-Shaᶜrānī (d. 1565),[30] Muḥammad Riqqād, Mukhtār al-Kuntī (d. 1811), and his son, Muḥammad Khalīfa (d. 1825).

Al-Sha^c^rānī then, according to the source, took up the gauntlet and made brilliant passes with the *jinn*, providing authoritative answers based on the approved opinions of the orthodox saints. Then Muḥammad Khalīfa, taken by the scene, broke into speech and declared that the *jinn* had gathered together and formed such an impressive spectacle as men had never seen before, and plied all manner of strange and taxing questions which were capably dealt with by al-Sha^c^rānī. The *jinn* appeared as different religious groups: Jews, Christians, Magians (Zorastrans), idol-worshippers (*^c^ibādah al-aṣnām*) and heterodox people (Soriba n.d.: 196). It appears that the outcome of this confrontation with the *jinn* was decided in favour of the orthodox Muslim party, and the source quotes a verse of the Qur'ān:

> And some of us have surrendered, and some of us have deviated. (lxxii: 14)

This story has many complex features, and is suffused with an element of marvel. It would appear that Karamokho Ba's religious and spiritual stature was increased by his being a part of such company, and the account speaks of his nearness to God under those circumstances (Soriba n.d.: 196). The list given of the pious authorities of Islam suggests sources of influence on Jakhanke Islam and indicates the close ties shared with a number of Ṣūfī orders, most of them associated with the Qādiriyāh *ṭarīqah*, of which the Jakhanke have long been members. This material was incorporated into the teaching programme of Touba, from where it was carried to other places by returning students. It invested Karamokho Ba with a venerable status in the eyes of his community. The story adds that Karamokho Ba's spirit, consecrated by communion with the saints, was elevated by being summoned before God and admitted to Paradise.

Karamokho Ba's Personal Legacy to Touba

Karamokho Ba was 99 when he died according to the Muslim lunar calendar (*TKB*: fo. 8), or 96 according to the Christian one. His personal initiative in founding Touba made his contribution to the wider sphere of Jakhanke Islam a more permanent one. Touba's clerical prosperity in terms of an influx of students there derived originally from Karamokho Ba himself and the career of extensive travel he undertook. These students and other sympathisers came initially from the Manding heartlands, but it was not long before the Fulbe, the Jallonke, the Susu, and Bambara and other ethnic groups were represented. It is clear from the list of Karamokho Ba's teachers that the majority were Manding scholars, including a sizeable proportion of Jakhanke figures. But the number of such scholars did not necessarily outweigh, or at any rate exclude, a significant contribution from non-Manding scholars. The sources are unanimous in attributing to two such non-Manding scholars a high degree of spiritual influence. One was Alfa Nūḥi, a Fula scholar from Masina. His spiritual impact on Karamokho Ba was profound. The other was Muḥammad Taslīmī, whom he promptly honoured by founding a clerical centre and naming it after him. Karamokho Ba also named the son who was to be his spiritual heir after Taslīmī. Both men 'wafted on him the breath of felicity'. Recognising that his own intellectual pedigree was mixed, Karamokho Ba encouraged students from various ethnic backgrounds to come to Touba and strengthened his appeal to adjacent communities by sending religious deputations to them. One such deputation was led by his brother, Muḥammad Khaira. His relationship with different ethnic groups was more than a policy of accomodation to his neighbours. It was founded on the principle that a clerical vocation committed the Jakhanke to a life style which opened them to contact with people, Muslim and non-Muslim alike, who desired to use their services, provided such demands left them free of any compromising obligations.

Clerical enterprise aiming to strengthen Jakhanke Islam and ensuring that Jakhanke communities are not burdened with unbearable and irreconcilable political demands is a recurrent and familiar feature of Jakhanke settlements. A corollary to that is the wide-ranging contact with both centres of political power and areas of non-Muslim population concentration. Touba embodied this attitude.

The sources speak of the reason why Karamokho Ba led a somewhat rootless life at the beginning of his religious career. The discussion on this does not allow for the fact that Shaykh-seeking has a long tradition and a respectable history in West African Islam. Nevertheless the view superimposed on the picture needs to be taken into account. One account says that the reason why Karamokho Ba fled from 'town to town and from one country to another was because of fear of violent strife (*fitnah*) and of political oppression as well as a search for a hospitable place to live.[31] *TKB* then quotes a Ḥadīth in support of this practice to the effect that, 'a man of religion is he who flees from trouble spot to trouble spot until he reaches the pinnacle of a mountain [of security]', because his only reason, with that of his followers, is nothing except to teach and search after knowledge, and alongside this to work with his hands and to farm and labour. His aim is never to seek for a political kingdom nor to seek for worldly leadership.[32] It is clear, as will be shown in a subsequent section, that Karamokho Ba's long career of Shaykh-seeking was not imitated by his successors, but the tradition was exploited at Touba to encourage students to come there. In this sense Karamokho Ba's example was an asset to the Touba community.

Karamokho Ba's greatest legacy to Touba was the large number of children who succeeded him and consolidated his reputation. Each of his sons brought his own individual contribution to Jakhanke Islam, and many of them ranged far outside the immediate surroundings of Touba. All of them bore the name of Muḥammad, which broadcast their Islamic identity for all to know.

After his death Karamokho Ba was buried within the mosque precincts,a tradition to show reverence for founders of clerical centres which was prevalent among the Jakhanke. Traditions say that he died peacefully in bed on the 2nd/3rd of Ṣafar al-Khayri, the second month of the Muslim calendar (*TKB*: fo. 8). He was succeeded by his sixth son, Muḥammad Taslīmī (Karang Taslimanka), thus fulfilling a prophecy made to him before he married this son's mother, Aisatou Kamara, the princess from Faye (see p. 101).

The Consolidation of the Touba Clerical Establishment

Enough religious and educational merit had accumulated under Karamokho Ba's leadership and guidance for his successors to concentrate their attention on the internal life of Touba without having to make extensive religious *tournées* in the manner of Karamokho Ba. Muḥammad Taslīmī, more commonly known as Karang (or Karamokho) Taslimanka, and occasionally as Karamokho Sankoung (Marty 1921: 109), had already proved his ability before his father died. Widely recognised as a man of religious virtue and scholarly endowments, his succession was universally welcomed. Like his grandfather, Muḥammad Fāṭuma at Didécoto, Karang Taslimanka distinguished himself as a resident scholar. He remained at Touba for some twenty years without ever leaving it, except on one occasion when he travelled to the Sahil to be inducted into the Qādiriyāh *wird*, first by Shaykh ᶜAbd al-Laṭīf of the Kounta, and then by Muḥammad Khalīfa, son of Shaykh Sidiya al-Kabīr, of the Walad Biri of Trarza (Marty 1921: 109).

Numerous details are provided by local sources on the introduction of the Qādiriyāh *ṭarīqah* into the Touba community. The story is told that Karang Taslimanka was prompted to go and meet ᶜAbd al-Laṭīf after one of his students passed through Touba. But before he did so he sent one of his own students, al-Ḥājj Kamara, more commonly known as N'Dar Bambo, to try to obtain a book by Shaykh Mukhtār al-Kountī on Qadīrī litanies.[33] Al-Ḥājj Kamara was accompanied by another student, Sahil Binne, originally from Badibu Salikeni.[34] Al-Ḥājj Kamara returned with the book, *Kawkab Waqqād*, which became the chief instrument for introducing members of the Touba clerical community to Qādirī devotions and practices.[35] Karang Taslimanka did some writing, but his output was very small. Three works are known, two of which are eulogies (*madīḥ*) on the Prophet, *Safīnat al-Khalaṣ* and *Dhakīrat al-Muḥibb fī Takhmīs Ṣalāt Rabbī*, while a third concerns *adab* (literature), *Tanbīḥ al-ᶜAṣīf ᶜalā Mawārid al-Ta'līf* (Marty 1921: annexe xx).

The sources speak of numerous miracles wrought by Karang Taslimanka, but only as a formal and complimentary way of closing the discussion on him, no more detail is given. Such polite references are but a standardised pious formula to set the seal of religious authenticity on established clerical figures. But the practice is based on a notion that religion should have a practical utility. Among the Jakhanke this is known as *fidā'atu*, and the idea of instrumental religion which it signifies will be discussed in Chapter 8. Suffice it to say here that Karang Taslimanka has little explicit claim to any outstanding miracles, and that his reputation, and main contribution, was in providing stable leadership and an increased religious and spiritual potential by encouraging affiliation to the Qādiriyāh *ṭarīqah*. He was 55 when he died (c.1829) (*TKB*: fo. 8).

Karang Taslimanka was succeeded by his eldest son, Karamokho Ba Madi, who ruled the Touba community for eight years. He died on a journey through Dabola in central Guinea. His brother, Muḥammad Khasso, followed him and ruled for 40 years. His period of leadership is particularly remembered for the distinguished manner in which he discharged his office as *imām ratti*. He is referred to in *TKB* (fo. 8) as a servant and shepherd of the flock, godly and upright (*ᶜābidan waraᶜan*). He died in about 1877 and was followed by his brother, Muḥammad bin ᶜAlī, and then by Muḥammad Muṣṭafā ibn Muḥammad Taslīmī,

Fig. 1 The descendants of Karamokho Ba who succeeded to spiritual leadership of the Jakhanke community at Touba

b. = born s. = succeeded d. = died

All dates are approximate

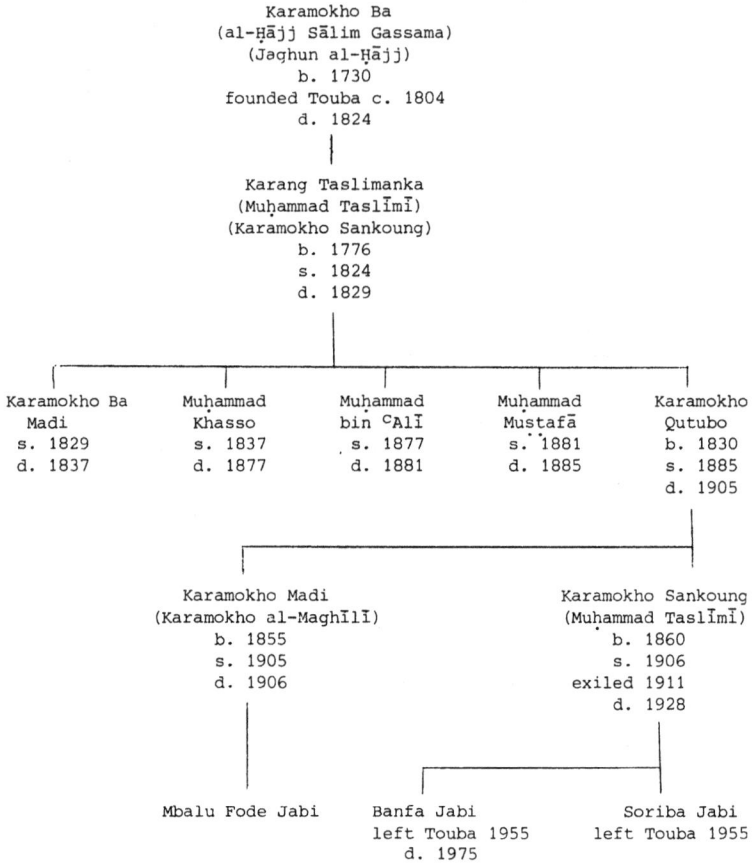

Karamokho Ba
(al-Ḥājj Sālim Gassama)
(Jaghun al-Ḥājj)
b. 1730
founded Touba c. 1804
d. 1824

Karang Taslimanka
(Muḥammad Taslīmī)
(Karamokho Sankoung)
b. 1776
s. 1824
d. 1829

Karamokho Ba Madi	Muḥammad Khasso	Muḥammad bin ʿAlī	Muḥammad Muṣṭafā	Karamokho Qutubo
s. 1829	s. 1837	s. 1877	s. 1881	b. 1830
d. 1837	d. 1877	d. 1881	d. 1885	s. 1885
				d. 1905

Children of Karamokho Qutubo:

Karamokho Madi (Karamokho al-Maghīlī)	Karamokho Sankoung (Muḥammad Taslīmī)
b. 1855	b. 1860
s. 1905	s. 1906
d. 1906	exiled 1911
	d. 1928

Mbalu Fode Jabi (son of Karamokho Madi)

Banfa Jabi, left Touba 1955, d. 1975 (son of Karamokho Sankoung)

Soriba Jabi, left Touba 1955 (son of Karamokho Sankoung)

but each died after four years. During the latter's term of office the French made their first appearance in the area (*TKB*: fo. 8). Muṣṭafā is also singled out for the life of prayer he led, and is said to have performed numerous efficacious prayers. But the sources give no further details.

Muṣṭafā was succeeded (in about 1885) by his brother, Karamokho Qutubo (Ar. *Quṭb*, pole, axis) (c.1830-1905). His name at birth was ᶜAbd al-Qadīr. He was born too late to see his grandfather, Karamokho Ba, unlike his other brothers, but like all of them he was educated at Touba. Karamokho Qutubo appears to have achieved considerable renown. He is referred to as *shaykh al-kabīr wa al-ustādh al-shahīr.. wa kāna mujaddid al-dīn wa mujtahid fīhi* ('the great Shaykh and the renowned teacher...He was a renewer of religion and diligent and conscientious concerning it') (*TKB*: fo. 9). He owned a vast library containing 700 books and small manuals. He wrote fifteen works himself on grammar, law, theology, literature and eulogies on the Prophet (Marty 1921: 110). In about 1860, Karamokho Qutubo went on a long and circuitous journey which took him finally to Mauritania where he met Shaykh Sidiya al-Kabīr. On this particular trip he also visited Pakao, Jarra, Badibu, Niani, Wuli, Sandu, Bundu, Futa Toro and outlying regions.[36] When he finally returned to Touba he had a personal following of a huge number of students, 780 according to one source.[37]

The written account lays great stress on the teaching activities of Karamokho Qutubo. It is said that a great number of students who passed through his hands emerged as fully-fledged scholars, and that people travelled great distances to come and seek instruction from him (*TKB*: fo. 9). Marty, whose chief informant was a descendant of Karamokho Qutubo, Banfa Jabi (although referred to by him as Alfa Oumarou) (Marty 1921: 112), records a tradition which essentially concerns the educational and religious stature of Karamokho Qutubo. He writes:

> ...le jeune marabout s'imposa tout de suite par ses connaissances, ses vertues, et ses qualités de commandement. Sous son pontificat d'un demi-siècle (1860-1905), Touba prit un essor incomparable. Les étudiants y affluèrent de toutes parts; les dioula-missionaires portèrent la bonne parole dans les trois Guinées; les études islamiques s'y développèrent considérablement. Touba fut plus que jamais la ville sainte de toute la région. (Marty 1921: 109-10)

Nearly all the sources pay some attention to the political influence Karamokho Qutubo was able to exercise on local political leaders. He appears to have intervened willingly in what were essentially political matters and to have directly altered the course of events. Such a role was possible largely because he was highly regarded by the Fulbe political leaders who relied on his friendship and respected his scruples about secular leadership.

He was a great personal friend of Alfa Yahya, in practice the Almamy of Labé at that time, although he did not carry the title, for fear perhaps of grasping the Futa Jallon religious nettle. The two men first met in the 1890s and it appears that Alfa Yahya approached Karamokho Qutubo and made a voluntary avowal of amity. He travelled to meet Karamokho Qutubo, and took his son, Modi Aguibou, with him. Sometime later, Aguibou, to improve his chances of succeeding his father, assassinated his brother (c.1897). Embittered by this episode, his father led a troop movement against him to avenge the murder. Alfa Yahha commenced operations from Kadé, at the head of a column of troops. Aguibou mobilised from Toubandé and brought the military confrontation nearer. By this time Alfa Yahya had arrived in Touba. Karamokho Qutubo, appalled by the imminent conflict, stepped in. He defused the situation, persuaded Alfa Yahya to desist and obtained Aguibou's submission to his father (Marty 1921: 110).

It was during the time of Karamokho Qutubo that the French began to strengthen their position in Futa Jallon by adopting a more active role in the political developments of the area. The penetration of French power eventually forced the Jakhanke to spell out yet again their position on politics, an exercise, as will be shown in Chapter 6, in which they did not altogether succeed. The French had acquired too many definite ideas on the inherent hostility of marabout power to French colonial expansion to make an exception.

There were two versions of the way the Jakhanke, led by Karamokho Qutubo, reacted to the French presence in the area. Marty, representing the colonial view, says that the Jakhanke were dismayed by the coming of the French, and adopted a chilly reserved attitude. Gradually, however, relations warmed between the two, and in 1903 Karamokho Qutubo pledged the co-operation of the Jakhanke community (Marty 1921: 110). The Jakhanke view is contained in *TKB*, and differs in a rather fundamental way. According to *TKB*, when French power came to Labé, Alfa Yahya sent a message to Karamokho Qutubo informing him of the fact and requesting advice as to how best to relate to this.

During this time, the Jakhanke themselves had been personally confronted by the French who established an administrative post in Touba and put one Commandant Faye in charge (*TKB*: fo. 9). Karamokho Qutubo had written to Alfa Yahya urging surrender to French power (*fa-amarahu bi-taslīm*). He had also sent secret word to all the leading citizens urging on them a similar act of submission, and the account says that all these heeded Karamokho Qutubo's message.[38]

Marty's version is surprising in view of the fact that he had already noted Karamokho Qutubo's peace-making role in the breach between Alfa Yahya and his son, Aguibou, a role Qutubo could fulfil because of his fundamental political neutrality. To imply that this neutrality was half-hearted and circumscribed by events derives from a fundamental misconception of the nature of Jakhanke withdrawal from politics. The version carried by *TKB* may not have been accessible to the French at the time, but it is a logical extension of arguments made at other times.

This divergence of views was to have far-reaching consequences for the future of Jakhanke relations with the French (see Chapter 6). But, to return to Qutubo, he had established a standard of co-operation with the French to which the Jakhanke remained faithful. This policy was not Qutubo's personal idiosyncratic attitude but is integral to notions of an autonomous and cohesive clerical tradition. What was at stake was not the survival of Qutubo's personal leadership but the whole basis of Jakhanke community solidarity and the validity which the rulings and judgements of past patriarchs had for the Jakhanke. The way in which new communities modelled themselves closely on past practice is enough to dispel doubts about Jakhanke flirtations with political power. Marty (1921: 110) himself says that by the time Qutubo died (1905), he had established very good relations with the French, a development which did not appear to have been achieved either through coercion or through formal negotiation. It is hard to advance any reason why the Jakhanke should have moved so quickly to the side of the French except by assuming an original intention to co-operate.

Suret-Canale collected some details which confirm the picture of Jakhanke co-operation with the French *ab initio*. Qutubo is reported to have sent a message to Alfa Yahya as follows:

> The fact that the French are in our country is the will of God. You must avoid war. You have already spilt a great

> deal of blood and if you persevere in this fashion, you will not enter Paradise...If you do not comply with the orders you have received, you are sure not to enter Paradise. (Suret-Canale 1970: 63)

It is doubtful whether the text of this passage represents faithfully the message as it was originally sent. It does not do justice to the friendship which existed between the two men for it is a message of confrontation, not of conciliation. Its tone is too inflexible and rigid for it to have come from a man of Qutubo's temperament, and the spirit of self-justification suggests it was produced for apologetic purposes and is not an original transcript of Qutubo's message. But Jakhanke attitudes to French colonial power were broadly what the message purports to convey.

All the accounts say that Alfa Yahya complied with Karamokho Qutubo's message of surrender to the French. In 1897, he, with several others, including Oumarou Bademba of the Alfaya, Alfa Ibrahima Sori Elely of the Soriya and Alfa Ibrahima, who was grand marabout of Fugumba, signed a treaty of capitulation and recognised French power in Futa Jallon. The terms of the treaty were dictated by the French and secured for them, among other things, the right to nominate successors to political office as well as a guarantee of French monopoly of commerce in the area. (For the text of the treaty, including an Arabic version, see Marty 1921: 535-8.)

A remarkable theory has been propounded that 'the marabouts of Touba...[with] certain malice on their part', were not 'altogether displeased to see the redoubtable King of Labé (Alfa Yahya) humbled' (Suret-Canale 1970: 63). This implies that either the Jakhanke had lent support to a conspiracy to subdue Alfa Yahya and the Fulbe aristocracy, in which case there was no ground for later French suspicions of a grand marabout alliance with Alfa Yahya (see Chapter 6 below), or that they kept out of any such schemes but retained a secret wish to see Alfa Yahya defeated, a wish which they succeeded in concealing both from the French and Alfa Yahya. There is no foundation in fact for this theory. Suret-Canale himself quotes a report to the effect that Karamokho Qutubo, after securing Alfa Yahya's compliance to his message, assured him in return of a continuance of his personal rule in Labé (1970: 63). It is hard to imagine why Karamokho Qutubo, under no particular military threat from Alfa Yahya, should give this undertaking if his friendship with Alfa Yahya were not a genuine one.

It is a misunderstanding of the Jakhanke to impute to them political double-dealing on this scale, or, as Suret-Canale does on a different scale, to speculate on their antipathy towards the Fulbe because of a difference of ethnic origin.[39]

Karamokho Qutubo died on 6th/7th July, 1905. He was 78 by the Islamic calendar, or 75 by the Christian one. Touba acquired a pre-eminent status in the Western Sudan as a result of his life and teaching. He gave the clerical community a spiritual and intellectual respectability in the eyes of surrounding populations, Muslim and non-Muslim alike. The traditional withdrawal of the Jakhanke from scenes of political strife was maintained and strengthened. The principle of disavowal of *jihād* was unwaveringly adhered to. This had two broad consequences for their relationship with outsiders. Secular political leaders respected their consistency on this point and approached them for counsel and religious help. Secondly, other non-Muslim ethnic groups, who had been traditionally alienated from Islam by being made the targets of Muslim military action, were reconciled by other forms of Islamic activity represented by the Jakhanke. The Jakhanke consolidated their gains among non-Muslim peoples by establishing Qur'ān schools and appointing agents and organising periodic religious visits.

Touba succeeded in achieving a workable *modus vivendi* with the local secular power. It was relatively easy to obtain secular co-operation. Touba did not need any elaborate expensive defences. The existence of such a clerical settlement like that was hardly a security risk for the secular authorities. Their open-door policy made the Jakhanke of Touba a welcome presence. There was nothing to lose and everything to gain by having them.

In fact the Jakhanke seem to have had little difficulty in finding people who were willing and sometimes eager to host them. Their problem was often in deciding which offers to accept and which to turn down. The evident viability of Touba in what by other criteria was a hostile environment suggests the warm welcome usually extended to Jakhanke communities. Karamokho Ba had created a centre which embodied the power and prestige of religion. His tomb became a centre for religious pilgrimage (*ziyārah*) to which people came from great distances to satisfy their multifarious needs.[40] In a very vivid sense, Karamokho Ba's voice, and that of his successors, continued to be listened to in Touba, a mark of his deep and abiding influence on a wide variety of peoples. Karamokho Qutubo nurtured this legacy and added his own measure to it.[41]

NOTES

1 Konde Buraima had been finally encountered and killed at *tiangol* Sirakouré, near Timbo, by Karamokho Alfa's forces (Noirot 1889: 195; Chatelier 1899: 162; Marty 1921: 5). On the reliability of the Kankan material in le Chatelier see Y. Person's review article in *Journal of African History* XV (4), 1974.

2 Hargreaves 1963: 268-9, 323; Terrier et Mourey 1910: 125, 130-31; ANSOM, Paris, Colonial Ministry Correspondence *MC/I série: Sénégal et Dépendances 1850-1886*, folios 37-73, *MC/IV série: Sénégal: Expansion territoriale et politique indigène 1820-1895*, folios 24, 50, 60, 104-5, 127.

3 ANSOM, *loc. cit.*

4 ᶜUthmān Derri lived all of his later life at Kounti and his descendants still live there. He appears to have succeeded in making Kounti a renowned educational centre, and although he did not belong to any Jakhanke lineage, his scholarship was respected by them. It is said that his work was facilitated by a good supply of writing paper from the then Portuguese post at Georgetown (Al-Ḥājj Soriba Jabi, Jnr, son of al-Ḥājj Banfa, 28/2/73).

5 Soriba n.d.: 192 (also one of the author's most useful oral informants). There are numerous sources on Karamokho Ba, but when all these are collated it is clear that they stem from one main version. Those furnished by Marty (1921) and by Suret-Canale (1970) are the best known, but they are by no means the most reliable. *TSB* carries another version which is distinguished for its emphasis on the religious/dogmatic interpretation, while *TKB* and *TSK*, both identical in many details, give a coherent narrative account followed by al-Ḥājj Soriba, whose version is valuable for providing numerous details omitted by the other sources. I have preferred to follow his version in the main, but have drawn on the others when this is necessary. *TKB* is the oldest surviving account I have come across, written on the instructions of Karamokho Madi (born c.1855) (see p. below) from a source the latter had in his possession, and further expanded in the time of Karamokho Sankoung (born c.1860), al-Ḥājj Soriba's father. Its factual accuracy is nowhere seriously challenged.

6 This is a highly popular and excellently written twelfth century religious and philological work in 50 parts.

7 *Taṣrīf* literally means 'disposal' and is used in grammar to mean declension and conjugation. Among the Jakhanke it became a formal discipline, teaching the cleric how to alter the course of fate through amulets and special prayers. Mastery of this art conferred a privileged status. See pp. 158-9 below.

8 The sources say he was *ḥafiẓ arbaᶜīna fanna min funūn* (a knower by heart of forty branches of learning) (Soriba n.d.: 193) but it is difficult to take this at face-value. *TSK* (fo. 6) makes an identical claim, saying that Alfa Nūḥi taught Karamokho Ba forty different branches of Islamic science and that Alfa Nūḥi himself was a competent master in those branches.

9 The text reads: *wa kāna fiṭāmahu ᶜalā yaddi shaykhihi wa ustādhihi al-shaykh Alfa Nūḥi* ('and he was weaned at the hands of his tutor and guide Alfa Nūḥi') (Soriba n.d.: 193).

10 Al-Ḥājj Soriba Jabi, Macca-Kolibantang, 9/12/72.

11 Soriba n.d., but most other sources pass over this initiation episode in silence.

12 al-Ḥājj Mbalu Fode Jabi, Marssassoum, 18/1/73, and al-Ḥājj Soriba Jabi, Macca-Kolibantang, 9/12/22.

13 Al-Ḥājj Soriba Jabi, Macca-Kolibantang, 9/12/72.

14 The students, according to *TSK* (fos. 8-10), were: Mori Wulli Karfala, also called Konya Kabba, Kendo, Karamokho Dawda Suware (from Konya), Karamokho Suware (Konya), Morike Konte, Karam Bakari Sise and his son Mori Wulli Sise, Fode Bakari Darame, Karam ᶜUthmān Sanqaranko (all of Konya). (It was this ᶜUthmān Sanqaranko who helped Karamokho Ba build Mau Touba in Masina, Mali.) Also the following: Karam Baba Berete, Man Fara Kulukalan Sangare, Karam Ṭālib Silla, who founded a clerical centre at Banaba Touba, Saghanokho Ba, Karam Yaᶜqūb Konte Dandankara, Fode Ibrahīm Sinbā, Fode Muḥammad Sire, Fode Ismaᶜīl, Karam Fode Bintu, Kabba Darame (from Dar Salam), Kabbaba (from Laya in Guinea), Karam Laye Sumaya, Karam Fode Tarawalli, Fofana, nicknamed Kiskisi Bulli, Fode Sama Silla (from Pakao in Casamance), Karam Fode ᶜUthmān Kabba, Karam Kabba Saghanokho, better known as Kabba Binne, Karam Banora, Karam al-Ḥājj Kanyi, Karam Bada (from Jarra-Sutukung), Karam Ibrahīm Silla and Karam Fode Ibrahīm Jakhite (both from Pakao-Janna), Karam Fode Ibrahīm (from Pakao-Sonkodu), Fode Lalimata and Fode Muḥammad Sire (both from Pakao-Mankanonba), Fode Manjang (from Pakao-Njama), Karam Fode, Yirimakhan Suware (from Baddibu-Suwarekunda [Ripp]), Fode ᶜUthmān (from Badibu), Mbemba Suware, Fode Bakari Jakhite, better known as Ja'itejang (from Badibu-Njakunda), Fode Janko Sise (from Pakao-Dar Salam), Fode Gassama (from Niani-Laminkoto), Karam Yaqin Fofana (from Jenne), Karam Mankaman Dabo (from Niani-Dobo), Fode Kanyi and Karam Yaqin Fofana [the latter already mentioned], both of whom died at Binani-Laya, and Idrisa Sakho among others.

15 *TSK*: fo. 10. The appeal to a leading cleric to settle in a place is a standard practice in many communities, and the Jakhanke have traditionally waited for such requests to be made before deciding to settle among other people. Compare also the manner of ᶜAbd al-Raḥmān's settling in Kano, p. 29 , above.

16 Soriba (n.d.: 193) represents it thus: *wa baqī fīhā āthāra ᶜilmihi ilā zamāninā hadhā...* ('he bequeathed to it a scholarly influence which has remained up to our own times...')

17 The Alfaya party were closely identified with the Jakhanke

clerical tradition of Kankan where Karamokho Alfa, their founder, did his Islamic studies and 'grew up within the precincts of the mosque' (Tauxier 1937: 287; see also Arcin 1911: 71-82; Trimingham and Fyfe 1960; W. Rodney, *J. Hist. Soc. Nig.* IV (2), 1968).

18 That Karamokho Ba in fact straddled the divide between the Alfaya and the Soriya is a typical example of Jakhanke clerical neutrality and independence which endowed them with powers of conciliation and safeguarded their corporateness. *TKB* (fo. 4) reads: *fa'akramahu wa a^{c}ṭāhu sab^{c}ah ^{c}abīd wa farsan ^{c}atīqan.*

19 A similar view is propounded by Aḥmad al-Bakka'ī who wrote to al-Ḥājj ^{c}Umar explaining his position on *jihād*. He wrote 'My conditions are the conditions of my forefathers. We teach the ignorant, put right those who have deviated, and meet the needs of those who seek our help. We do not master anyone, nor will we be mastered by anyone... I replied to these people [the followers of Muḥammad Bello who wrote to him], 'I am fully aware of the merits of *jihād*, but *jihād* leads to *mulk* [political office and kingship] - and *mulk* leads to tyranny [*ẓalm*]. Our present condition as it is is more suitable to us for not having indulged in *jihād*, and more assuring to us for not having indulged in unlawful things which *jihād* would entail...' (Willis 1970: 272).

20 Soriba n.d.: 194. *TSK* (fo. 12) says that Alfa ^{c}Abdallāh Wura, accompanied by a large number of people, went with Karamokho Ba in search of a place to the latter's liking. When Karamokho Ba decided on a site, this was adopted and a large number of dwellings were soon raised.

21 Al-Ḥājj Shaykh Sidiya Jabi, Brikama, Oct. 1972.

22 In a concentrated discussion on the process of *tajdīd*, communal self-renewal, al-Ḥājj Ba Jakhite described uniformity of practice as one of the four cardinal principles, Sutukho, 10/12/72.

23 The twelve sons of Karamokho Ba were: Muḥammad al-Kabīr, M. Diakhaba, M. Sanūsī, M. Khasso, M. Bukhārī, M. Taslīmī (or Taslimanka), M. Sire, M. Kamisātū, M. Khirāsī, M. Ghullī, M. Tumāju and M. bin ^{c}Alī (The information comes from Al-Ḥājj Soriba, Macca-Kolibantang, 9/12/72; also Marty 1921: 108.) Most of these names were given in honour of some of the teachers of Karamokho Ba. His first son, Muḥammad al-Kabīr, was so named following a Jakhanke practice of calling their first sons after the Prophet, a name commonly altered to Momodou-Lamin (Ar. Muḥammad al-Amīn). Occasionally they are also known as Muḥammad Awwalī. This is still current practice, not only among the Jakhanke but also among adjacent islamised Manding people.

24 Al-Ḥājj Mbalu Fode Jabi, Marssassoum, 18/1/73.

25 Suret-Canale 1970: 61. The circumstances under which Suret-Canale was working had a lot to do with the unwillingness of his informants in this matter. Touba had ceased to be a major Jakhanke centre following the emigration of al-Ḥājj Banfa Jabi and al-Ḥājj Soriba Jabi to the Senegal (c. 1955). With their dispersion went a considerable section of Jakhanke clerical initiative and Touba succumbed to the nationalist political pressures of the Partie Démocratique de Guinée (PDG). This has inhibited and restrained clerical remnants there.

[26] Al-Ḥājj Soriba Jabi, Macca-Kolibantang, 9/12/72.

[27] Soriba n.d.: 195. Shaykh Mukhtār al-Kuntī's dates are 1729-1811; he remains to this day an important influence in the Jakhanke Qādiriyāh tradition. See also Trimingham 1959: 94ff. A similar story is told of Mukhtār al-Kuntī himself who interrupted leading public prayers once because, as he later explained, he had learnt of the birth of an exceptional child, ^{c}Umar b. Fūtī (Willis 1970: 45).

[28] Soriba n.d.: 195. Is this miracle based on the incident where Muḥammad al-Kabīr was taken hostage by the Bassari shortly before Old Touba was abandoned? The details on Bakari Tamba would tend to suggest not, but this could be the result of deliberate editing.

[29] The context would suggest ^{c}Abd al-Qādir al-Jīlānī, who is also known in other sources as al-Jīlī.

[30] The mention of these four Ṣūfī saints indicates clearly the importance of Ṣūfī Islam to the Jakhanke clerics. For more on the famous al-Suhrawardī, see Trimingham 1971: 34-5. The second saint mentioned, Abū al-Hasan ^{c}Alī al-Shādhilī, was born in the village of Ghumāra in Morocco (1196), and received his first *khirqah*, the Ṣūfī symbol of office, from Abū ^{c}Abdallāh Muḥammad bin Ḥarāzim (d. 1236). ^{c}Abd al-Salām ibn Mashish of Fez initiated him into a Ṣūfī office, *wilāyah*, and eventually he left Morocco and went into retreat in a cave near Shādhila, a village in Ifrīqiyāh (Tunisia), hence his *nisbah*. (See Trimingham 1971: 48-9.) For more on the third saint, the Egyptian, al-Badawī, see Trimingham 1971: 45. Finally, ^{c}Abd al-Wahhāb ibn Aḥmad al-Sha^{c}rānī was born in Egypt in 1492 and made his most important contribution from there. A *zāwiyah* was built for al-Sha^{c}rānī right in the centre of Cairo which attracted some 200 students, including 29 blind. Al-Sha^{c}rānī was conscious of the social role which Ṣūfī *ṭarīqāt* could play in Egyptian society and turned the material prosperity of his *zāwiyah* to the welfare needs of ordinary people. (See Trimingham 1971: 221-5.)

[31] *TKB*: fo. 6.

[32] *TKB*: fos. 6-7. The original has the following:

في الحديث عنه صلّى الله عليه وسلّم
لا يسلمُ لذي دين دينه، إلّا مَن فرّ
من شاهق إلى شاهق وَالشاهق رأس
الجبل إذ ليس إشتغاله مع جماعته
إلا في التعلّم وتعليم وَ إلّا إكتساب
من حراثة وزراعة لا ملك وَلا رياسة
دُنيوية

33 Alieu Sajjalī Jabi, *imām* of Nibrās, 8/2/73.

34 Al-Ḥājj Banfa Jabi, Macca-Kolibantang, 10/2/73.

35 Al-Ḥājj Kamara's parents originally came from Kankan, but he himself was born at Touba. He was named after Karamokho Ba, and when his parents returned to Kankan they left him at Touba. He eventually migrated to N'Dar in Senegal, from whence his *nasab* (patronymic) and acted as Aḥmad Bamba's spiritual guide (*muqaddam*), eventually initiating him into the Qādiriyāh Way. He died in 1889. Aḥmad Bamba was later to launch the separatist Murīd Brotherhood. He died in 1927. (Alieu Sajjalī Jabi, Nibrās, 8/2/73). Cf. Dumont 1975: 41 .

36 Al-Ḥājj Mbalu Fode Jabi, Marssassoum, 18/1/73.

37 *ibid*. This looks like an inflated number, but I have no means of evaluating it. It is, however, difficult to see how such a large number of people could all travel together in convoy without putting unbearable strain on the hospitality of towns through which they passed.

38 The crucial words are:

'And he sent (a message) to all the elders of the country concerning it [i.e. his earlier message to Alfa Yahya], and they received his word...' (*TKB*; fo. 9).

39 Suret-Canale (1970: 63) says: 'One notes that the Jakhanke of Touba received pupils from all over West Africa with the exception of precisely the Peul [Fulbe] country surrounding them... The religious and commercial vocations of the Jakhanke and their publicly expressed aversion to war hardly led them to find themselves in sympathy with the warlike and plundering ways that characterised the aristocracy of the Fouta, and that of Labé in particular.' This view can only be advanced by maintaining an ignorance or disregard of the facts, many of which are within easy access.

40 Soriba n.d.: 196. This says that the tradition of pilgrimage which grew up around Karamokho Ba's tomb was the greatest miracle with which God blessed him.

41 Qutubo carried out restoration works on the mosque at Touba built by Karamokho Ba. This was the first major work on the religious building since it was first constructed (Marty: 1921: 127).

وَ أُرسل إلى كبراء البلاد بذالك
فقبلو كلامه

CHAPTER SIX

TOUBA AND THE COLONIAL MISFORTUNE

THE EXPROPRIATION OF TOUBA'S CLERICAL PRIVILEGE

1905-1911

> Our judgement must proceed from the countless spiritual possibilities included in the word 'stimulus', which, though they cannot be computed, can, on closer study, be practically demonstrated in particular cases... The sack of Rome in the year 1527 scattered the scholars no less than the artists in every direction, and spread the fame of the great departed Maecenas to the farthest boundaries of Italy. (J. Burckhardt, *The Civilization of the Renaissance in Italy*, New York, 1961: 174-5)

The cumulative impact of the life and work of Karamokho Ba, Karang Taslimanka and Karamokho Qutubo, among others, reinforced the Touba clerical tradition and extended its missionary range. Qutubo's successors stepped into this tradition at a time when the essential pioneering work had been done. What Touba needed was a period of comparative quiet to strengthen the work of consolidation begun under Karamokho Qutubo's tenure of pontifical office. Karamokho Sankoung, the most brilliant of Qutubo's successors to office, was clearly moving in this direction when disaster struck. What happened has been confused in the accounts, but the events themselves produced unmitigated hardship for the Jakhanke. First let us examine the background and stages leading up to the catastrophe.

Early Career and Leadership of Karamokho Sankoung c.1860-1928
Many of the children of Karamokho Qutubo left Touba and went to settle in other places. But his two eldest sons, Karamokho al-Maghīlī,[1] better known as Karamokho Madi, and Karamokho Sankoung, remained at Touba and presided over the clerical community. By this time the clerical leadership (the *majlis tio*) was distinguished from the secular (the *alkali*). Karamokho Madi was a respected Qādirī *muqaddam*, whose chief interest seems to have been in deepening spiritual insights and acquiring religious sanctity.[2] When he died (c.1906) he was succeeded by Karamokho Sankoung, a man of great popularity and fame.

Named after his grandfather, Karang Taslimanka, Sankoung was called Muḥammad Taslīmī, but the name Sankoung, also a *nasab* (patronymic) of Karang Taslimanka, acquired a distinctive characteristic and became his preferred form of address.[3] He was born about 1860. His mother was Fāṭumata, more popularly known as Fanta. He was his mother's only son, but had two sisters, Khadijatou and Aisatou, also called Mbinki, both married at Touba (Marty 1921: 111).

Sankoung himself had four wives, the legally prescribed limit in Qur'ānic Law. His first wife was Kadi, the daughter of a Wolof of Kakandi (Casamance), who bore him two daughters: Mariama, named after the mother of Shaykh Sidiya Baba (of Boutilimit), and Maḥjūba, named in honour of the grandmother of Shaykh Sidiya. The second wife was Jan-Kemba, daughter of the *alkali* of Touba, Karamokho Dawda. The third was Fanta Kabba, daughter of a Touba Jakhanke, and finally came Umuna, another local girl, of whom we shall hear more below. Two of his wives, Kadi and Fanta Kabba, were later to leave him during his long internment by the French. Karamokho Sankoung had five sons: Banfa Jabi, Soriba Jabi, Ba Fode (deceased), Karam Ba Qutubo and Sidiya. The last two have continued to live in Touba, but Banfa and Soriba left for Senegal in c. 1955. Banfa and Soriba are Sankoung's heirs.[4]

Karamokho Sankoung began his educational career under the paternal eye, and then transferred to study under Karamokho Sakho, a man versed in Muslim healing and divination. Karamokho Sakho died in 1895 while Sankoung was in the middle of his studies. With advanced training from some of the leading scholars at Touba, including his father, Sankoung was able to establish a separate Qur'ān school of his own, a stage widely recognised among the Jakhanke as of crucial importance in proving one's leadership and scholarly qualities. Sankoung's Qur'ān school was a huge success, attracting to it large numbers of students. It is said that his scholarly reputation spread throughout all Futa Jallon, and it was widely assumed that he would succeed his father. From about 1890 until 1905, when his father died, his school attracted students from Casamance and Kaabu, as well as from different areas of Futa Jallon (Marty 1921: 112). On many of these students he conferred the Qādiriyāh *wird*, which he himself received from his father, and in this way his spiritual influence radiated to distant places in the Western Sudan (Marty 1921: 113).

The career of travel on which he embarked was a characteristic one. His numerous *tournées pastorales* made him a familiar personality to neighbouring peoples and spread his personal influence. He also obtained new sources of material wealth for the Touba Jakhanke community from the generous disbursements and pious gifts his hosts made to him. In some of these areas he was visiting local Jakhanke communities, for example, at Biké, Kakandé, Boffa, Kindia and Conakry (Marty 1921: 113), where his presence was designed to strengthen Jakhanke clerical and missionary work. In some cases, however, Sankoung was visiting not only non-Jakhanke areas but also non-Muslim people. Marty, who found his following still impressive in the Guinea area, says of him: 'Il est très connu et très populaire dans toute cette région, même chez les fidèles des bannières rivales, même chez les peuples fétichistes' (1921: 113).

But Sankoung did not always travel with the sole aim of pastoral work. On one occasion at least he travelled with the explicit purpose of personal improvement. This was in 1909 when he went to meet Shaykh Sidiya Baba at Boutilimit. He wanted to be confirmed in the Qādiriyāh *wird* by Shaykh Sidiya, just as the latter's father had initiated his own father earlier (1860) (Marty 1921: 113). He travelled to Dakar from Conakry by sea, accompanied by his brother, Khairaba, and then up the Senegal river through Podor. His month's sojourn at Boutilimit was highly successful. He struck up a friendship with Shaykh Sidiya who welcomed him with high honours and received him afresh into the Qādiriyāh brotherhood.[5] On his departure Shaykh Sidiya presented him with a number of religious books. They parted on excellent terms, and some years later Shaykh Sidiya was to intercede on his behalf with the French, prompted by the importunate pleas of Sankoung's eldest son, Banfa Jabi.[6]

Internal Disputes at Touba, 1908

Shortly after Karamokho Qutubo's death and the succession of Sankoung, a dispute erupted in the Touba community which brought about the intervention of the French. That incident was the prelude to an unfolding drama that was to lead to the political defeat of Touba's main clerical personalities. The published sources which discuss this aspect of Touba's crisis, Marty (1921) and Suret-Canale (1970), principally, are rather cautious about suggesting a connection between this early dispute and later events which paralysed the centre.[7] The sequence of events as given by Sankoung's sons, al-Ḥājj Banfa Jabi and his brother Soriba, differs in some details from the only extended published account we have so far, that of Suret-Canale (1970).

The principal characters of the drama were Ba Gassama and Sankoung. These men were closely related as their fathers had been brothers. Ba Gassama was a man of considerable political influence, and his alliance with Alfa Yahya, the Almamy of Labé (see p. 116 ff. above) was well-known. Banfa and Soriba say that Ba Gassama had a lurking ambition to assume the leadership of the Touba clerical settlement and had relied on the tacit support of Alfa Yahya for this. But Alfa Yahya, already committed to Karamokho Qutubo and his son, Karamokho Sankoung, was not in a position to promote Ba Gassama's cause.[8] In addition, Alfa Yahya's relations with the French had by now deteriorated and he was arrested and exiled to Dahomey in November, 1905. Ba then, according to Soriba, turned to the French, but it is clear from both Marty (1921) and Suret-Canale (1970) that in his later relations with the French Ba did not get much help from that quarter.

Meanwhile events took a turn for the worse and Ba and the Touba leadership seemed set on a collision course. The French were moving towards a decisive banning of slavery. On 12th December, 1905, a decree was promulgated forbidding trade in slaves throughout the interior of French West Africa (up until then only trading by sea had been banned) (Suret-Canale 1970: 64; Klein 1968: 169-70). This measure set the whole Touba community on edge. To begin to understand the complexity of the crisis at Touba it is necessary to understand how profoundly the French position on the slave-trade affected the Jakhanke. This has so far been analysed in purely economic terms, but far more pertinent is the way it split Jakhanke community solidarity, provoking a deep and fundamental crisis of clerical unity and ethnic solidarity. Ba Gassama's conflict with Karamokho Sankoung has to be seen in this context.

Ba Gassama had accumulated capital from the trade in slaves. It seems that, unlike the other Jakhanke at Touba, he had engaged in this trade on a wide scale and he tried to use the wealth he amassed from this for political ends. But just at that time, to his disappointment, the French banned the inland trade in slaves (Suret-Canale 1970: 68). Local sources imply that Ba Gassama could never reconcile himself to this, and continued to trade in clandestine fashion. But the Touba leadership, nervous about Ba's political motives, kept a close eye on him and Karamokho Bambo Gassama, the *alkali* of Touba and an ally and protégé of Sankoung, reported violations to the French administrative authorities. The possibility that the Jakhanke, now labouring under the disadvantage of a divided loyalty, would end up before a secular colonial arbiter to resolve differences previously dealt with by their own religious judicial procedures was very real. In fact, Ba Gassama lost no opportunity in taking his dispute with the Karambaya ward to the Poste.[9]

From that moment the quarrel escalated. The outcome of that particular litigation proceeding is not known, but Ba, presumably dissatisfied, took matters into his own hands and proceeded to withdraw his daughters and other members of his family married into Sankoung's *qabīlah*. Al-Ḥājj Soriba says that Ba's sisters were married to Sankoung and to Mukhtār, a brother of Sankoung; another was married to Karamokho Khairaba, a third brother.[10] The leading woman involved was Umuna. It is said that one day Ba went to ask back Umuna, who was married to Sankoung himself. This was coupled with a simultaneous demand to both Mukhtār and Khairaba to relinquish their claims to their wives. There is some variance about the names of these women. Al-Ḥājj Soriba says that Nsamma Gassama was married to Mukhtār, but does not give the name of the third one. Suret-Canale (1970: 68) says that Gouno Jabi was the name of the woman married to Mukhtār, and Na Binta of the one married to Khairaba.

Ba's determination to pursue his dispute with the Touba leadership knew no bounds, and by dragging in family matters he gave events a bitter and inexorable twist. For with the introduction of marriage disputes he was technically able to widen the area of disagreement to include property rights as well, which he proceeded to do. He and his sister, Umuna, shared a piece of rice field, and it is said that Ba promptly seized it from Karambaya where his sister had been resident.[11] He also tried to alienate his sister's sons in Karambaya from any allegiance to Sankoung.[12] Meanwhile Ba had tried to establish an independent centre at Nāta, a few miles south of Touba, to which he had been forced by administrative decree to transfer, and from that base he pressed his demands aimed at destroying Sankoung's credibility. He is said to have been opposed to Sankoung's leadership of Touba, claiming it for himself.[13] It happened that at Nāta Karambaya also had certain property rights tied up in farm land. These rights were eventually consigned to Ba, under French aegis, in return for abandoning his claims to the disputed rights at Touba.[14] Apparently, Ba's transfer to Nāta had been forced by an expulsion order which Karamokho Bambo Gassama had taken out against him and his family, which banned them from Touba, including the nearby fields (Suret-Canale 1970: 68). But this does not appear to have soothed matters, and Ba went to Nāta only to nurse his grievances. His mother, Hawa, approached Monsieur Legeay, the administrative head of the Poste, for permission to harvest the rice sown by Ba's party at Fofanakunda before the transfer to Nāta. The *chef de poste* granted the request but failed to notify the *chef de village*, Karamokho Bambo, who had acted as the intermediary between Touba and the French on previous occasions.

On 28th October, 1908, Soriba, Kajali and Mbemba, three of Ba's brothers, turned up on the rice fields at Touba, but the *chef de village*, having earlier obtained an order from the *chef de poste* denying rights of access to Ba, refused them entry (Suret-Canale 1970: 68-9). Too much should not be made of this oversight on the part of the *chef de poste*. In truth Ba's relationship with Touba had deteriorated beyond repair. The French, equipped only to deal with overt breaches of the peace, could not be expected either to understand clearly the underlying causes of the trouble or to provide the kind of answer that would have reconciled the protagonists and allayed deeply ingrained fears and mutual suspicions. The omission by the *chef de poste* merely helped to speed up the inevitable confrontation.

When Ba's party were turned away, they reported back to the *chef de poste*, who confirmed his earlier order allowing them to harvest the rice at Touba. At the second attempt fighting broke out, apparently more than once. The first incident took place on the rice fields where some injuries were sustained.[15] Another account says that after Ba's party had been refused entry they were seen in the vicinity of Touba by some local people who reminded them of the ban.[16] Some angry words were exchanged during which the visiting party were asked to leave. Meanwhile an excited crowd had gathered and a mêlée broke out. Ba's brother, Soriba, had his arm broken, and from the other side Mukhtār sustained a sabre wound on his right hand and Ba Boukaria was wounded on the temple.[17] Following that particular incident the *commandant* sent a platoon of riflemen to effect the arrest of those responsible for the troubles. He then summoned the *chef de village* and reprimanded him (Suret-Canale 1970: 70). It is said that the *chef de village* held the *chef de poste* responsible for the incident which had taken place, reminding him that it was he himself who had ordered the original ban on Ba Gassama.[18]

A second incident took place in which some members of the Karambaya ward organised an ambush with which to surprise Ba Gassama (who had been summoned from Nāta) and his party on their way home. The ambush was organised by Soriba, Sidina, Sidia, Bahio, Demba and Sankoung, a tradesman (Suret-Canale 1970: 70). They were seen, and M. Legeay informed of their presence. To try to avoid trouble, the *chef de poste* put a guard, Mamadou Kourouma, in charge of Ba Gassama and his party. On the way back, at Béréla, fighting broke out in spite of the efforts of Sankoung, the tradesman, to prevent violence. Ba was set upon, badly mauled, and seemed to be dead. He was being carried off when his attackers were stopped and Ba was taken to the Poste where he regained consciousness (Suret-Canale 1970: 70).

Another version of the troubles, possibly describing a third incident, says that a party of Ba's supporters appeared one morning at the market place at Touba. They were questioned by local people in view of the ban on their entry to Touba. They drew arms, probably sensing danger, and a fracas seemed imminent. Word of this came to the *chef de village*, who had the visiting party apprehended. He then sent for Ba Gassama who came, accompanied by 300 slaves, a most ominous and provocative gesture. However, although some firearms were displayed, only one shot was fired, allegedly from Ba's side. It wounded a member of the Karambaya *qabīlah* on the leg, at which point a Karambaya student, originally from Niani-Dobo, stepped in and overpowered Ba.[19]

In these second and third incidents, there is no mention either in oral accounts or documentary sources, of the precise nature of French response to these local troubles. For example, Soriba is simply content to say that the French intervened and resolved the matter. Although the Jakhanke believed that these incidents made them culpable in the eyes of the French, whom they wrongly suspected of having prepared elaborate plans for taking punitive measures, there is no evidence that the French saw the troubles as more than a local family feud (Suret-Canale 1970: 70). Pobéguin, administrator of the Cercle of Kadé, of which Touba was a part, reported that the troubles had 'neither a religious nor a political character.'[20]

Jakhanke suspicious that in taking especially harsh measures against them in 1911 the French were bringing them to account for their earlier behaviour, though deficient in material fact, had a firm psychological basis. The Jakhanke leaders had succeeded in bringing the French right inside the intimate life of the Touba community, an eventuality that could only mean increased French interference with their way of life. Whereas previously the Jakhanke had obtained secular co-operation and guarantees for their neutrality on the basis that they were by themselves capable of running successfully their clerical republics, now such an assurance could no longer be given. On the contrary, Touba had proved a security risk for the French, slithering clumsily from one intractable incident to another, with no end in sight. The leadership at Touba saw quite clearly that they had proved their collective incompetence and forfeited their right to an independent existence by letting events slip out of control. They were playing straight into the hands of the French. The belief, though naīve at first sight, was widely shared that retribution by the French was only a matter of time, and the nervousness that the leadership at Touba showed reflects a defeatist self-abasement, before the French actually imposed the reality of humiliation on them. They did not have to wait long.

Confrontation with the French, 1911

The incidents of 1908, although indicative of a fundamental breakdown of internal relations at Touba, were side issues compared to the events of March, 1911. On 30th March, Liurette, the *commandant* of the district of Kadé, sent a detachment of 40 sharpshooters, commanded by Lieutenant Amberger, to occupy Touba. Karamokho Sankoung, Ba Gassama and one Jamīlatou Sekou, a prominent name on the French blacklist, were arrested. Ba Gassama was picked up at the Poste where he had been held two days earlier because of fears that he might escape from Touba to Portuguese territory. Karamokho Sankoung, having had a presentiment of impending trouble, decided on the day after Ba Gassama's arrest to visit the grave of his father, Qutubo, accompanied by a small devotional party. On the same night a similar demonstration of religious feeling was expressed at Touba and the kettle-drum at the mosque sounded the call to prayer (Marty 1921: 116). Jamīlatou Sekou, a resident of Touba and a renowned friend and ally of Alfa Yahya, announced the imminent return of the latter from detention in Dahomey and promised that Alfa Yahya would recover the Jakhanke slaves emancipated by the French decree, and would henceforth ensure that the Jakhanke were protected from further French interference (Marty 1921: 116). This inflamed French anxieties about the extent of support for Alfa Yahya,who had in fact been rearrested on his release,and Aguibou, who had been arrested and interned at Conakry on 9th February, and the incarceration of Sankoung, Jamīlatou and Ba Gassama was ordered forthwith. The French also ordered a widescale search for arms in the whole district, apparently in an effort to forestall a suspected insurrection.

At about the same time a search party led by Capt Talay and Lt Bornand headed for Goumba to arrest the *walī* (the district chief), Tcherno Alieu. Forewarned, Tcherno Alieu fled to Sierra Leone, and the French detachment was massacred by the local inhabitants (see Guy 1911a). Tcherno Alieu was known by the French to have maintained cordial relations with Sankoung, whose arrest was part of a concerted drive to contain an imagined marabout uprising which the French suspected was being fomented (Marty 1921: 118). Tcherno Alieu was later rounded up by the British following an appeal for extradition, but he died in detention before he reached Guinea (Suret-Canale 1964: 160-4; 1970: 70).

The search for arms was meticulously carried out, but the results did not bear out French anxieties. They discovered only 30 guns in Touba and 773 more in the whole district.[21] Such a quantity was not surprising, given the fact that the population of Guinea had never been disarmed and that all religious ceremony was accompanied by an enormous consumption of gun-powder. As for European arms, they did not find anything except two Portuguese carbines and four double-barrelled hunting rifles and even these were owned by Modi Oumar Binani, who engaged fitfully in commerce (Marty 1921: 116). At Sankoung's house they found a huge quantity of religious objects: charms and amulets, but nothing else (*ibid*: 118).

The arrests and the search for arms were carried out in an atmosphere of calm and orderliness. The Touba Jakhanke, even when faced with the supreme humiliation of the incarceration of their spiritual leader, Sankoung, took it without protest or signs of non-co-operation. It is reported that only one supporter of Ba Gassama raised his voice as a timid, ineffectual reaction (Marty 1921: 118).

Taken to Conakry, the prisoners were eventually sentenced by the Governor-General, on 21st June, 1911, to ten years' internment with hard labour and exile in Port-Etienne, Mauritania, where they were immediately transported (Marty 1921: 118). Touba reacted with a stunned silence.[22] The prisoners themselves conformed strictly to French orders, and it appears that Sankoung accepted his personal misfortune with a philosophical resignation. Marty gives an account of his detention at Port-Etienne:

> On a peut-être eu tort de ne pas signaler au commandant de la baie du Lévrier la situation de Karamokho, son passé, les possibilités de son avenir. Soumis à l'obligation du pénible travail de casser des pierres ou de faire des terrassements, il a été tout de suite incapable de suivre ce régime, et ses camarades d'infortune, émus et respectueux, lui ont immédiatement et d'un commun accord, abandonné la tâche considérée comme la plus douce du poste: la vidange des tinettes. La chose est à la fois touchante et pénible (1921: 117).

Some of the immediate circumstances of Sankoung's arrest followed what appears to be an orchestrated pattern, and will be discussed presently. Following the rearrest of Alfa Yahya in February, 1911, Abdoul Bakar, the Landouman chief of Boké, frightened for his own safety, had denounced a so-called conspiracy of which Sankoung was said to be the chief instigator and Ba Gassama the organising genius. Ba, he alleged, had called a meeting of Landouman chiefs and notables at which they discussed schemes of revolt (Marty 1921: 114). Another accomplice in the trumped-up charge was said to be Kalli Salifou, son of the chief of Nalou and at that time an interpreter to the government of Guinea. Even the local French administration found this a wild and absurb story. Ba's relations with the Landouman chiefs concerned resistance to the suppression of slavery, not plans to lead a political uprising (Marty 1921: 114). The theory that Ba and Sankoung were allies against the French was similarly dismissed, and administrative reports speak of the traditional enmity between the family of Ba and that of Sankoung. Nevertheless, in arresting both Ba and Sankoung the French appear to have ignored these conclusions.[23] And when a letter written by Sankoung came into the hands of de Coutouly, the assistant administrator in Conakry who was investigating the supposed plot, professing his innocence, it was disregarded on the grounds that it was insincere and full of clever tricks (Suret-Canale 1970: 74). In the letter Sankoung spelled out the traditional Jakhanke position on warfare and political leadership, and showed how throughout the history of the Western Sudan the Jakhanke had maintained a rigid adherence to principles of neutrality and abstention from political office:

> Au cours des échanges de sympathie, Sankoun lui remettait un petit *mémoire* historique relatant avec une précision remarquable l'ascension et la chute des grands marabouts et conquérants du Sénégal, du Soudan et de la Guinée. Il formulait de conclusions, empreintes de loyalisme, et remarquait au surplus que sa fidélité, ne fût-elle pas née de ses sympathies naturelles, serait pour lui une nécessité de la logique et de l'histoire. (Marty 1921: 115)[24]

But all this was to no avail, he was at a massive disadvantage.

Yet it is possible to approach the matter from a different angle and to try to fit the complex pieces together in order to arrive at a better understanding of why the French and the Jakhanke finally, almost inevitably, were drawn into confrontation. Starting from a negative position, the French assumed that marabout power was inherently a force of insurrection.[25] Marty says that this fear of what he calls the 'Islamic peril' resolved the local administration to stage what was dramatically referred to as 'the St. Bartholemew's massacre of the marabouts.'[26] A notice had been circulated before the arrests which alleged that there was a plot afoot in which all the principal religious personalities of the area were involved, and that their aim was to organise a general anti-French uprising. The people involved were named as Tcherno Alieu of Goumba, Karamokho Sankoung and Ba Gassama, both of Touba, Tcherno Alieu Bouba Jong of Labé, and Karamokho Dalen of Timbo. There is no evidence to contradict Marty when he says of the allegation that it was 'pure imagination' (1921: 117).

The situation had been aggravated by the release of Alfa Yahya from his five-year sentence in Dahomey. He had returned from Dahomey at the end of November, 1910, but was confined in Conakry from then until 11th February, 1911. Even then on his release, he was rearrested and sent to Mauritania. Governor Camille Guy of Senegal, who was also responsible for Guinea and was orchestrator of the French response, sent a memorandum to the *commandant* of the district of Labé saying that definite information had reached him that Alfa Yahya was in touch with an underground religious movement which was acting as a cover for the advancement of his political ideas. According to

Guy, the principal architects of this movement were Alfa Yahya, Sankoung and the *walī* of Goumba, Tcherno Alieu. The letter was dated 25th February, 1911 (Suret-Canale 1970: 72). Once again, such suspicions were never substantiated, and the conclusion must be that the French were moved 'par un sentiment irraisonné de crainte' (Marty 1921: 117). Suret-Canale makes the point much more explicitly: 'Karamokho Sankoung and the *walī* of Goumba were selected for the role of expiatory victims of French repression on the basis of their reputation alone' (1970: 73).

Whatever fragile and slender chance the clerical leaders enjoyed was irreparably jeopardised by the incident at Goumba when the French party dispatched to arrest the *walī* was routed by the local people (Suret-Canale 1970: 71). The French reaction to this incident was swift and decisive. A reprisal column was sent which burnt villages, confiscated cattle and freed captives (*ibid*). The fact that the attempt to arrest the *walī* of Goumba was timed to coincide with a similar move against Karamokho Sankoung (both incidents took place on the same day, 30th March, 1911) means that the one was not induced or caused by the other. Yet Marty believes that the arrest of Sankoung was a direct consequence of the affair at Goumba. His reasoning is that Sankoung's cordial relationship with the leading cleric of Goumba rendered Sankoung culpable in the eyes of the French (1921: 118). The coincidence of timing, however, suggests that the affair at Goumba and the arrest of Sankoung both sprang from a similar justification, and this is what requires explanation and clarification.

The Issue of Slavery

The sources are at pains to settle on the ban on slavery as the principal source of grievance which supposedly embittered the Jakhanke and turned them into collaborators with political malcontents like Alfa Yahya, and, by implication, into an anti-French faction. Slavery was certainly a live issue, for it deeply affected the continued viability of Touba as a clerical republic. Indeed, without realising it, the French threatened to remove the lynch-pin of Touba's social and clerical stability by outlawing the trade in slaves and forcing the Jakhanke to emancipate their slaves. Although the Touba leadership was at variance with Ba Gassama on other issues, from these policies they both suffered. All the sources say that Touba's population fell dramatically with the freeing of captives. Suret-Canale estimates that it fell from 7,000 in 1908 to 3,000 in 1911 (1970: 65). Other sources suggest a still more drastic change of fortune, for in one day alone 4,800 slaves were freed on the orders of the French.[27]

There is in fact no evidence that the Jakhanke saw emancipation as much more than a hard and painful blow dealt them by fate, and faced with the reality they accepted the need for a scaling down of clerical activity at Touba. The measures adopted included the dispersion of large families to the Senegambia area as well as wider use of Qur'ān school students who were now relied upon to provide services previously rendered by slaves. Another way which seems to have been prevalent was for slave families to continue to be attached to their clerical patrons who put them to domestic work.

The question of slavery, although predominantly of importance to the economic basis of life at Touba, touched on other problems as well. Following Muslim Law, many Jakhanke patrons had adopted slave women as concubines, while others had been theoretically emancipated in order to become wives.[28] Emancipation and the mass evacuation of ex-slave families, therefore, seriously disrupted family life. Slave children of Jakhanke fathers were torn from their roots as they left with their mothers for their places of origin. The Jakhanke reacted by trying to prevent their departure through persuasion, and, when this failed, by an appeal to their contacts in Landouman where the slaves were heading. Then, in desperation, they approached the Governor in Conakry for a scheme whereby the slaves would be partially free, working two or three days a week for their masters during a few transition years. They took handsome presents to the Governor to appeal for favour. Nothing, however, could deflect the French from the course on which they had been set, and the administration pressed ahead in spite of these peaceful Jakhanke initiatives (Marty 1921: 119).

Overt Jakhanke activity on the slavery question vis-à-vis the local colonial administration seems to have been limited to such peaceful if ineffectual appeals. The import appears to be that the Jakhanke were anxious to come to a workable arrangement with the French, and it is unlikely that they would have gone to such lengths if they believed there were other resources on which they could fall back, such as, for example, a maraboutic coalition with Alfa Yahya, to help them recover their slaves. Some political dissidents made much of known Jakhanke anxieties about the great loss which emancipation had brought them, but the clamour of a few frustrated and isolated malcontents about regaining all they had lost, though seized on by the French, can hardly be construed as secret political ambitions harboured by the Jakhanke as a whole.[29] The issue of slavery is further discussed in Chapter 9. In the meantime, the scenario of a hatred for emancipation leading to a deliberate Jakhanke plot to rid themselves of the French menace seems unlikely and certainly unproven. It remains now to assess events in the context of Jakhanke theories of why they happened and to try to relate them to other factors in the widescale reaction of the French to marabout power in Western Africa.

The Issue of Islam

The Jakhanke belief is that the French acted against Karamokho Sankoung as part of an overall policy of containing an imagined anti-colonial marabout league being fomented in various parts of West Africa.[30] The rounding up of notable personalities is quoted in support. At the same time as Sankoung was arrested the French also held Tcherno Ibrahima Dama, Seringe Aḥmad Bamba and Almamy Sori.[31] French fears of a Muslim uprising were real enough. In the Senegambia they had come up against the revolutionary campaigns of Maba operating in Sine and Saloum (see Klein 1968; Quinn 1972), the destructive wars of Fode Kabba in Casamance (Marty 1915/6), the religious agitation of Momodou-Lamin in Bundu,[32] and in Futa Jallon and beyond they were involved in action against al-Ḥājj ᶜUmar Ṭāll, and against his successor Shaykhu Ahmadou (Mage 1868; Oloruntimehin 1972). At the same time they were engaged in protracted war against Samori Toure (Person 1968/70). Probably as a direct result of their experience in these wars, the French adopted an offensive against Islam and what Governor-General Ponty in 1913 called the 'native feudality'.

> Islam acquired something of the status of an 'anti-colonial religion' during French expansion, as the warrior marabouts led much of the most tenacious and effective local resistance. The leading warrior marabouts were killed in battle, and their empires did not survive them, but later and less militant marabouts were able to inherit some of the prestige of the dead leaders, and also to inherit a following whose devotion could be turned to economic rather than warlike purposes. (Cruise O'Brien 1971: 32)

Touba and the great chieftaincies, thus stigmatised as part of the 'native feudality', could no longer enjoy the protection given by earlier colonial administrators working under less militant orders. At the end of the Ballay-Cousturier administration, the first two

Governors of French Guinea, a change occurred and the local administration took on a radical image with the tenure of Governor Frezouls, beginning in 1904.

> He was a declared enemy of the economic feudality (the powerful Compagnie Française de l'Afrique Occidentale - the CFAO - with which, according to him, his predecessors had been too directly connected), and of the native feudality, the great chieftaincies, to which he opposed the ideal of direct administration as more in conformity with the principles of Republican France. (Suret-Canale 1970: 64)

Although French anti-Islamic phobia[33] was later to undergo radical change, and indeed eventually the French came to be seen more as the sponsors of Islamic expansion than as obstacles to it, events in Touba in the first decade of the century led the Jakhanke to believe that, on the one hand, the French were acting from an inherent hostility towards Islam, and, on the other and more specifically, from suspicions that the Touba Karamokho family were trying to use traditional political discontent as an expedient for redress on the slavery question. The only way the Jakhanke leadership connected the events of 1908 with those of 1911 was to say that the bitter fratricidal feud of 1908 gave the French an image of Touba Jakhanke as a culpable people, and destroyed their credibility and reputation for impartiality.

According to one version, the direct cause of this disastrous loss of credibility was an incident even earlier than 1908 in which a local aspirant to power, Kudai Ba, probably Ba Gassama's father (Marty 1921: 124), and the incumbent Karamokho Bambo, were in dispute over the right to political leadership in Touba (c. 1905). It is said that the dispute flared up into actual confrontation, and that Karamokho Sankoung intervened, most probably on the side of his protégé, Karamokho Bambo. This dispute may have completed Ba Gassama's alienation from Touba. It was during these troubles that information reached the French that the Touba marabouts were intent on mounting an anti-French uprising, and that a general call to arms had gone out to all the ex-students and sympathisers of Sankoung throughout the Western Sudan. This version is careful to stress that Liurette, *commandant* of the district of Kadé, rejected this conspiracy story.[34] However, this is curiously at odds with the fact that it was Liurette who in 1911 ordered the arrest column which rounded up Sankoung and the others. It would be surprising if Touba had enjoyed the total confidence of the local French administration, and Liurette may have been disguising true French feelings about the incidents at Touba.

Certainly by 1911 there had been a breakdown of mutual confidence which is demonstrated by the unrestrained French response in sending an armed column to make the arrests. Clearly there was a discrepancy between the actual intentions of the Jakhanke leadership and French beliefs about a massive plot of insurrection. The relationship between the events of 1908 and of 1911 and between the return of Alfa Yahya and the arrest of Sankoung remain obscure in the sources. The very fact of the complete dislocation of Touba society in the face of the offensive by the much stronger colonial power makes the causation of the events which led up to it more difficult to analyse. What is clear is that French attitudes hardened in the period 1905-11, finally resolving them to break the spirit of the clerical community of Touba. In this they seem to have succeeded.

The Exile and Return of Karamokho Sankoung, 1911-17

Karamokho Sankoung did not in fact serve the full ten-year sentence in detention. He was to be released and placed under official surveillance at Dakar in April, 1916. Before his final release came, however, intense activity was needed to obtain a remission of sentence. On the official level, attempts were made to prove his political innocence. The Governor-General wrote to the Lieutenant-Governor of Guinea requesting a reconsideration of remission of sentence. He stated that during the eighteen months that Sankoung had lived in Dakar after his transfer from Mauritania there had been no cause for holding him to account, and that 'his culpability in the affair of the *walī* was very limited'[35] The Head of the Political Affairs Department minuted in a Report to the Permanent Commission of the Council of Government that Shaykh Sidiya, a favourite ally of the French, had given a personal guarantee on the political intentions of Sankoung and of his loyalty. Shaykh Sidiya was commended in this report as a man 'whose devotion to the French cause and high moral worth are indisputable.'[36] It appears that these official pronouncements achieved their objective and on 10th September, 1917, Sankoung was granted remission of sentence and allowed to return to Touba (Suret-Canale 1970: 77). He died there, according to different traditions, some eleven or twelve years later (1928/9).

The oral accounts give much more detail about Sankoung's

imprisonment and release, most of which represents the eye-witness account of Karamokho Sankoung's eldest son, al-Ḥājj Banfa Jabi, supplemented by his younger brother, al-Ḥājj Soriba.[37] According to this combined account, which follows in detail, Karamokho Sankoung was arrested at Touba and taken to Conakry. Then he was transported by sea to Gorée before being transferred to Port-Etienne in Mauritania. His prisoner-companions were Alfa Yahya, his son, Aguibou, and Ba Gassama. Alfa Yahya was to die at Port-Etienne. In about 1914, al-Ḥājj Banfa left Touba on a mission to try to obtain his father's release. He travelled to Boké before continuing to Dakar. From there he went to Boutilimit to see Shaykh Sidiya Baba and appealed to him to intercede with the French authorities on his father's behalf. He then went to Port-Etienne to visit his father. The French authorities had informed Port-Etienne of his arrival in general terms (Suret-Canale 1970: 76). According to Banfa and Soriba, al-Ḥājj Banfa spent two years with his father at Port-Etienne, during which time he was able to put fresh heart into the surviving prisoners. After this, he returned to Boutilimit to see Shaykh Sidiya once more. This time he left Boutilimit in Shaykh Sidiya's company, and headed for Dakar. In Dakar they approached a certain Capt Martin to help them obtain Sankoung's release. At about the same time Banfa saw the Senegalese politician, Blaise Diagne, later a deputy in the French Assembly (cf. Johnson 1973). Blaise is reported to have promised help, but at a price: Banfa was to write to both Shaykh Sidiya and Sankoung to ask for their spiritual help for Blaise as he faced impending elections which were crucial to his political career. Banfa wrote letters to Shaykh Sidiya and Sankoung putting the request of Blaise before them. After the elections, in which Blaise wes successful, new efforts were made to secure Sankoung's pardon. Sankoung was eventually transferred from Mauritania to Dakar, where he spent two years under observation. At this point the oral version merges into the written sources.

There is, however, some confusion as to the fate of Ba Gassama, and whether he also benefited from the amnesty granted to Sankoung. One account says that he was never released from detention and died at Port-Etienne before the expiry of his ten-year term of imprisonment. It does not give the date (Suret-Canale 1970: 77). This conflicts with the eye-witness account of Banfa, who says that Ba Gassama was granted release along with Sankoung, but on the way from

Port-Etienne Ba fell ill and died on the voyage. He was buried at sea. Alfa Yahya also died before he was granted pardon, and Banfa himself performed the funeral rites in Port-Etienne.

All sources agree that neither man made the return voyage to Conakry. Ba's death did nothing to assuage the bitter memories at Touba of the results of his quarrel with Sankoung. His detention left his family in complete disarray; his wives deserted his home and remarried; his goods were confiscated by neighbours and enemies (Marty 1921: 124). Marty found great bitterness against Ba Gassama at Touba and little following for his cause. 'Les Diakanké sont encore très montés contre lui, et son retour de Port-Etienne n'est l'objet d'aucun désir... Ba Gassama est un homme instruit et intelligent, mais remuant et brouillon ' (Marty 1921: 124-5).

The Jakhanke continued to flock into Touba during the eleven or so years that Karamokho Sankoung was there after his return. But Touba never regained the eminence achieved during the time of Qutubo which Sankoung had once promised to reinforce. Its clerical status had been impaired and although the Jakhanke rallied round Sankoung on his return, a spirit of defeat and compromise had settled on the community. Ba Gassama, though repudiated, remained a haunting symbol of failure and divisiveness. The plot of land which was Ba's concession remained deliberately unoccupied and became a memorial to the bitter and schismatic events of which he was the central figure. Having confiscated Touba's clerical rights, the French allowed its continued existence in obscurity. The Poste there was abandoned and local administration diverted to other parts. All the major communications networks bypassed it. Touba lingered on as a clerical centre, but its dynamism was greatly weakened by memories of the recent unhappy times. Suret-Canale aptly sums up its fate in these terms:

> It remained scarred by the drama of 1911. The injustice then suffered broke the spirit of confident loyalty which had characterised it before this date. Touba remained faithful to its rule of political loyalty on principle, but now it stemmed from suspicion and distrust. (1970: 78)

The number of students enrolled in Qur'ān schools slumped drastically during Sankoung's absence (1911-17), and the educational reputation of the place fell to a very low point.

> L'université de Touba a suivi la décadence de la ville. Ils sont loin les temps où les Toubakayes s'enorgueillissaient de compter dans leurs murs 25 professeurs éminents et plus de 300 élèves venus de tous les points de la Guinée

> et de la Casamance. Aujourd'hui, si l'instruction coranique, qui s'adresse aux enfants de la ville, y est toujours en honneur, l'enseignement supérieur y est fortement tombé. (Marty 1921: 128)

Karamokho Sankoung died in 1928, when he was, according to oral sources, 68. The decline of Touba did not necessarily mean a weakening of the Jakhanke missionary impulse. Touba was only a localised problem, and, itself a dispersion point for the Jakhanke, its demise led to a diversion of clerical effort elsewhere. The Karambaya, the depository of Karamokho Ba's heritage, eventually emigrated to Upper Niani (in the Oriental province of Senegal) under the leadership of Sankoung's two eldest sons, in 1955. The two brothers complemented each other: Banfa, the itinerant cleric and energetic sponsor of mosque building in various parts of Senegambia, and Soriba, the resident scholar-mystic and prolific author of religious works. The lateral descendants of Karamokho Ba similarly left Touba and founded clerical centres in Senegambia. The cumulative impact of such a proliferation of Jakhanke clerical centres meant that the eclipse of Touba was of very little long-term consequence for the future of Jakhanke Islam in Western Africa. Its short-term significance lies in the way the Jakhanke were forced to adapt to circumstances entirely beyond their control, and in so doing to stimulate a recrudescence of their clerical esprit de corps, and a reassertion of their traditional loyalty to the principle of political neutralism. Karamokho Sankoung's letter to de Coutouly, already referred to (see p. 134-5), suggests that some stock-taking had taken place, but the initiative had passed from the cleric to the administrator. Yet it appears that the Jakhanke survived the pressures brought to bear on them, first by the aggressive policy of direct rule, and secondly, much later, by the militancy of African nationalist parties, in this case the Partie Démocratique de Guinée (PDG), and the diversity of political regimes provided them with real choice as they again took to the dispersion trail.

NOTES

1 The name al-Maghīlī is borrowed from the famous ᶜAbd al-Karīm al-Maghīlī (d. 1505/6) who is highly esteemed among the Jakhanke. See p. 29 above.

2 Al-Ḥājj Mbalu Fode Jabi, son of Karamokho Madi, Marssassoum, 18/1/73. *TKB* is said to have originated from Karamokho Madi.

3 The word 'Sankoung' means 'rain-cloud' in Manding, and by implication, 'source of blessing'. It was ascribed to Karamokho Sankoung in recognition of his wide appeal and stature among the surrounding people.

4 The source followed for most of the account given in this chapter is Marty 1921. Marty, as we have seen before, obtained much of his information from 'Alfa Oumarou' who was in fact al-Ḥājj Banfa Jabi, son of Karamokho Sankoung. Al-Ḥājj Banfa and al-Ḥājj Soriba, now living in Macca-Kolibantang, were two of the present author's main informants in 1972-3 and are much quoted below in this chapter, particularly where they add information vital to our understanding of Karamokho Sankoung's exile and release. Where al-Ḥājj Banfa's information given orally is the same as that found in Marty, as is the case for most of the early part of the chapter, I cite only Marty's published account. (See also p.32 n.6, and n. 37 below).

5 This is part of the religious process of *tajdīd*, and the Jakhanke observe it by having their students make periodic return visits to their teachers.

6 Al-Ḥājj Banfa Jabi, Macca-Kolibantang, 10/2/73.

7 Suret-Canale in fact denies any connection at all. He says categorically: 'there was no connection between the events of 1911 and the earlier quarrel except that the weight of French authority was to fall particularly on those who had earlier drawn its attention to themselves' (1970: 68).

8 Al-Ḥājj Soriba Jabi, Macca-Kolibantang, 9/12/72.

9 Al-Ḥājj Soriba Jabi, Macca-Kolibantang, 9/12/72. For the ward system in Touba, see. p. 105 ff.

10 *ibid.* Suret-Canale (1970: 68) says that these women were Ba's daughters, but it is hard to imagine how al-Ḥājj Soriba, personally acquainted with the detail of the incident he is describing, can have been mistaken on a point like this.

11 Al-Ḥājj Soriba Jabi, Macca-Koligantang, 9/12/72.

12 *ibid.*

13 Marty says that Ba Gassama was the leader of a faction which had been opposed to Sankoung since Qutubo's death (1921: 124). This was supported by al-Ḥājj Soriba who said that Ba Gassama was contender

14 Al-Ḥājj Soriba Jabi, Macca-Kolibantang, 9/12/72.

15 *ibid.*

16 Suret-Canale 1970: 69. According to this it was the sons of the *chef de village*, Bambo Jabi, Mukhtār and Ba Boukaria, who apprehended the visiting party.

17 *ibid.*: 70. Al-Ḥājj Soriba merely says each side sustained injuries.

18 It is highly unlikely that the *chef de village* had confronted the *chef de poste* in this way, particularly if the meeting took place in the intimidating presence of armed soldiers. This may be another example of apologetic material being produced for propaganda purposes. Suret-Canale (1970: 70) quotes the actual words reported to have been used by the *chef de village*, which portray him as seizing the initiative and sounding very belligerent, a most improbable posture for a subordinate political title-holder to assume before a superior officer.

19 Al-Ḥājj Soriba Jabi, Macca-Kolibantang, 9/12/72.

20 Letter of 22nd March, 1909, *Archives Nationales de Guinée* (ANG) 1.E. 17, quoted in Suret-Canale 1970: 70.

21 Guy 1911a. Marty actually gives the figures as 50 guns in the houses of the suspects, and 775 percussion guns in the whole district (1921: 116).

22 Suret-Canale expresses it thus: 'At most there was a muffled tension expressing itself notably in prophecies of the imminent collapse of French domination. But it gave rise to alarm and fear in some colonial circles, where it expressed itself in demands for repressive and punitive action' (1970: 72).

23 The investigation by de Coutouly 9-19 February, 1911, established quite firmly that Ba and Sankoung had had a long history of bitter and factious relationships,yet such evidence as was available became distorted by an imagined subjective fear that hatred of the French, more feared and suspected than known among the local people, was enough to unite two implacable enemies like Ba and Sankoung, and on the basis of this shaky hypothesis, Ba and Sankoung acquired the common status of culprit (ANG, 1.E. 17, quoted in Suret-Canale 1970: 64n, 74).

24 The full Arabic may be found in ANG, 1.E. 17, cited by Suret-Canale 1970: 74).

25 The suggestion of French antipathy towards Islam is not entirely fanciful. Sometime around 1892 Lt Col Deporter, an officer in the Algerian colonial service, visited West Africa in order to take account, in the official language, 'des progrès que l'Islamisme a accomplis depuis ces dernières années dans l'intérieur de l'Afrique et de la possibilité que nous pouvons avoir de lui opposer enfin une barrière maintenant que nous sommes maîtres des pays qui ne l'ont accepté que pour une faible partie de leurs habitants.' Deporter died during his wide travels in West Africa on 15th July, 1893

(Terrier et Mourey 1910: 234). Both al-Ḥājj Banfa Jabi and al-Ḥājj Soriba Jabi emphasise this overall French policy of an anti-Islamic strategy.

26 Marty 1921: 117. He is referring, of course, to the famous massacre of the Huguenots in Paris on 24 August 1572.

27 Al-Ḥājj Soriba Jabi, Macca-Kolibantang, 9/12/72. The same figure was given by al-Ḥājj Mbalu Fode Jabi, Marssassoum, 18/1/73. See also p. 235.

28 Marty 1921: 119. The Qur'ān allows the marrying of slave women. Elsewhere the verse says that slave women can be freed by contract (xxiv: 32-3). See Chapter 9 for further details.

29 Marty tries to build a case on the vain boasts of, for example, Jamīlatou Sekou, leader of the Fofanakunda *qabīlah* and a professed supporter of Sankoung, but apart from a few impolitic remarks no evidence could be adduced even against Jamīlatou (1921: 115).

30 Camille Guy refers to the intelligence reports of officials in the French colonial service which 'montraient l'attitude de plus en plus équivoque de la caste maraboutique et ses efforts pour enrayer notre influence civilisatrice dans les milieux dont elle avait jusque là gouverné la conscience' (1911b: 2).

31 Al-Ḥājj Soriba Jabi, Macca-Kolibantang, 9/12/72.

32 Galliéni 1891: 183-5; Frey 1888: 210; Rançon 1894b: 383ff; and the discussion in Chapter 4 above.

33 Other examples of the French offensive against Muslims c. 1905-10 are the arrest of Aḥmad Bamba of Jolof (Cruise O'Brien 1971: 42-6); and Muḥammad ᶜUthmān in Bonduku (Marty 1922: 69-70).

34 Al-Ḥājj Soriba Jabi, Macca-Kolibantang, 9/12/72.

35 AFD, 17.G.48, quoted in Suret-Canale 1970: 77.

36 AFD, 17.G.47, *Indigénat-Internements et Amendes* (Guinée), quoted in Suret-Canale 1970: 77.

37 Suret-Canale does point out (1970: 76) that Banfa Jabi was personally active in obtaining his father's release, but no details are given of what form Banfa's endeavours took. I have preferred to combine the evidence of Banfa and Soriba because I interviewed both men at their new home in Macca-Kolibantang Senegal at the same time. (See n. 4 above.) I had further meetings with each of them in which the material obtained was compared and found to be identical, except in cases where Banfa was travelling and thus describing episodes and incidents connected with those travels. But most of this independent material has long been committed to Soriba and to other members of the *qabīlah* for whom it has become common property. Banfa was at the time himself producing a version of his remembered account of his father's last days in order to share it among a much wider Jakhanke community. He died in 1975.

CHAPTER SEVEN

JAKHANKE EDUCATIONAL ENTERPRISE

> To form an accurate picture of the method of instruction pursued at that time, we must turn our eyes as far as possible from our present academic system. Personal intercourse between teacher and pupils, public disputations, the constant use of...[language], the frequent changes of lecturers and the scarcity of books, gave the studies of that time a colour that we cannot visualise without effect... [Some teachers are said to have educated] the gifted poor 'per l'amore di Dio'...(J. Burckhardt *The Civilization of the Renaissance in Italy*, New York, 1961: 168)

At the heart of the Jakhanke clerical or missionary enterprise lies education. This, far more than trade, has been the instrument of their expansion and spread. It is the form in which their clerical activity has survived most vigorously and distinctively. The abundance of references in the sources to this aspect of their work indicates not only that this was of paramount importance to them but also that the Jakhanke may have realised that it was the vital focus for their competition with traditional pagan powers for the soul of Black Africa. It is clear that they concentrated enormous manpower resources in this sector, and the indications are that the yield in material power and prestige was high. Prospects of a wider spread of influence were enhanced by the success of each educational centre, and the cumulative effect was to strengthen their own cohesion as well as their impact on local populations.

The Tools of the Trade

The wooden slate on which verses of the Qur'ān are inscribed and then learnt by heart has formed the basic springboard of all Jakhanke educational establishments. It is called *walā*, and is said to prefigure the perfect heavenly Masterpiece, *lawḥ maḥfūẓ*, termed by the Jakhanke *walābā*.[1] The teachers instruct their pupils that when a portion of the

Qur'ān, which is a copy of 'the Mother of the Book',[2] appears on a wooden slate, such a slate acquires a religious significance derived from the wisdom originally condensed in the heavenly Masterpiece. Such a theoretical exposition of the value and status of the wooden slate is possible because of its prevalent use in education and other types of clerical work. But concealed behind such lofty notions about the value of using the wooden slate was the highly practical side of the matter: the wooden slate was considerably cheaper to obtain and preserve than other forms of writing material.

In the early days, writing paper (*lēro*) was a very scarce and expensive luxury for the Jakhanke. Some of their supplies came from the Middle East and the Maghrib, but not in sufficient quantities to justify indiscriminate use. Later, from their contacts with European traders, further supplies were obtained, although restrictions on its use continued to apply in general teaching activities. Jobson (1623: 85-6) says that in his time paper was scarce and expensive, and that the students used as 'copy books' small smooth boards which they carried in their hands. Durand, writing in 1785/6, reports a similar observation, saying that Qur'ān school pupils had their lessons written out on small wooden boards although the teachers preferred writing paper which they obtained from French trading posts (1802: 69). Well into this century the Jakhanke continued to look upon plain writing paper as a precious commodity, and even when supplies were relatively easy to come by, paper retained its high value.[3]

The tree from which the wooden slate is obtained is chosen for its fine grain and resistant surface, for example, the blackwood or mahogany tree. This ensures it years of use and means that the writing can be washed off fairly easily. There is no ritual stipulation about the wood; the choice is based on utility. Similarly, the ink has to be made from substances which are soluble in water. Traditionally, the ink is extracted from accumulated soot on cooking-pots. Charcoal does not easily make a smooth paste to allow its wide use in this way. The ink is collected in earthen or glass jugs. The slates themselves are smoothed out on both sides, measuring approximately ten to twelve inches in width and three times that in length. Sometimes they are pierced at the rounded or pyramid-shaped top and a piece of string is threaded through the hole to hang them up. At other times the slates are either stood up against the walls of the Qur'ān school or stacked away on suspended platforms under a roof. The slates do not carry the names of the pupils, who identify individual pieces by the shape of the slate, the style of writing, or the stage of recitation. Students have a slate each, but the more advanced, normally those who are part of an ᶜIlm school, do not use slates but instead go directly to the written text. They may still attend Qur'ān school to help supervise junior pupils.[4]

The transition from wooden slate to writing paper is an important one. It is widely assumed that material written on paper has enhanced status as against that on a wooden slate, and a variety of circumstances call for its use. In educational practice it is more used by copyists. A rare religious book is often copied by hand for wide distribution. This was one way in which copies of standard texts like al-Harīrī's *Maqāmāt* or parts of the *tafsīr* of Jalālayn were available along an extensive teaching corridor. The ink used for writing paper is quite different from that used on wooden slates and is obtained through a more complex chemical process. Some chippings from the *dūta* tree trunk are placed in a large earthen cauldron to boil over an open fire. The operation takes place in two stages. Initially the pot is left to boil for about 90 minutes. After that, a random selection of rusty old metal and pieces of iron is collected and added to the mixture. It is then left on the fire for between 24 and 36 hours. To test whether the solution is properly cooked a small drop is placed on the thumbnail, and if it leaves a trace the mixture is taken off the fire and allowed to cool down. If the ring mark is faint or easily rubbed off then further boiling is necessary. This is the chemical ink used for writing documents and amulets, and the numerous *qabīlah tawārikh* on which most of the present book rests were written with this type of ink.[5] Some of these family records have had water spilled on them and others are torn at the edges from normal wear and tear but the ink shows no signs of fading. This is a factor worthy of consideration when assessing the soundness of an educational chain of transmission over a given historical time-span. It also makes the work of the copyist of cardinal importance in the sharing of educational resources. The Jakhanke call this chemical ink *tabiduwa*, a descriptive term meaning 'manufactured ink'. It comes in various shades - I have seen black, blue-black, orange, rust and turquoise - and the colours are fast. Unlike the wooden slate, which is normally produced by a caste of woodcutters (*laibe*), the ink is manufactured by the Jakhanke themselves, or anyone who wishes.

It appears that the red ink could even be used on the wooden slate. At least one source mentions this, but adds that the writing was then washed off.[6] Also, a metal stylus was sometimes used for writing on a slate, after the surface of the slate had first been covered with a thin coat of bees' wax. The writing was removed by friction with any smooth and hard substance (Moister 1866: 156). Charcoal was also used, but only in solid pieces, not mixed into ink.[7]

Qur'ān slates are also used in 'extra-curricular' activities of clerics. External sources for this aspect of Jakhanke activity are poor, but that merely reflects the relative secrecy by which such matters are guarded among the Jakhanke. The extra-curricular activity is concerned with the manufacture of Holy Water. The uses to which this substance is put are discussed below (pp.158-9). Here it is its relation to educational work which needs to be pointed out. Sometimes, particularly when the demand is high, a teacher will have some slates specially set aside for this purpose.[8] The Jakhanke teachers charge a fee for this which is one form of supplementary income for them.

The Student

The most important asset of a school is the student body and the strength of a school varies in direct proportion to its intake/output record. It is clear that the Jakhanke regard the years at Qur'ān school as crucial, not only in the development of the individual child but also in the effectiveness of Jakhanke work and presence in a given area, where they are more likely than not to be, in lineage terms, outsiders and foreigners. The degree to which they succeed in attracting the children of surrounding populations is seen as the measure of their welcome as well as the test of their future relations with their neighbours.

The Qur'ān school pupil is admitted at nursery school age, between three and four; the standard enrolment day is Wednesday. A formal ceremony takes place when the pupil has his head shaved to remove the plait or band of hair which characterises his earlier uninitiated status. Some clerics, however, delay removing all the hair until the passing out ceremony. The pupil is also asked to stretch out both hands and part of the *Basmala* (the phrase which begins every chapter of the Qur'ān except one) is written on his two palms. While the writing is still fresh he is asked to lick it. Then he stretches out his hands again and a small ball of pounded grain is placed in each palm. The pupil takes these balls of pounded grain to his parents, first to his father and then to his mother.[9]

The organisation of the daily curriculum seems to be uniform, with only slight local variations. The school is open every day of the week except Thursday and Friday; the day starts at about 7:30 a.m. and goes into recess at about 12:30 midday. Younger *talāmīdh* (sing. *tilmīdh*, pupil) attend this early morning session. It reassembles again two hours later, at which time all the students come together and the schoolmaster himself takes classes. This afternoon session is mandatory.[10] The number of years pupils spend at Qur'ān school varies enormously: from seven to twenty.[11] The circumstances under which a student may terminate his studies also vary, but normally the parents make a formal request for his release.[12]

The student is the focus of much of the social and economic functioning of a Jakhanke centre. There are two general categories of student: the permanent residents, living on the premises of the schoolteacher and his brothers, and the day-scholars resident in the town in other compounds. Presiding over the two types of student is a head-student, normally a permanent resident himself. He is responsible for the practical organisation of student labour. His chief symbol of office is the horn, usually a cow's horn, which he sounds to summon the students into work camps.[13] Early in the morning the senior student sounds the horn and all the older resident students assemble. In the rainy season the horn is the signal for them to depart for the farms of the schoolteacher.[14] Later in the morning, the women prepare breakfast which they carry on their heads to the students on the farms.[15] No meals are served at the school at this time of day so that students have an extra incentive for going to work on the farms. Delinquents are blacklisted by the senior student who accordingly informs the schoolteacher. Younger pupils are normally exempt from farm labour and meal restrictions.

On Thursday mornings when the horn is sounded it is a signal for day-scholars to gather for their one-day contribution to the farms of the schoolteacher.[16] On Fridays, the day of the canonical Congregation Prayers (at 1 p.m.), the students are allowed to spend time on farm plots which they are allowed to enclose for their own use.[17]

Qur'ān school is suspended on Thursdays, and the full-time students go to the farms of the assistant teacher or the eldest son of the schoolteacher. In some places students spend a part of the late afternoons on their own farms, and the more mature students who have families to support are allowed more time to cultivate their fields. Such senior students are expected, however, to make generous contributions from their produce.[18]

Work on the farms, like the school timetable itself, is regulated by the prescribed prayers. This means that the students stay on the farms between Dawn Prayers and the first Afternoon Prayers (*ṣalāt al-fajr* or *al-ṣubḥ* and *ṣalāt al-ẓuhr* respectively), approximately between 7 a.m. and 1 p.m. An early lunch is served on the farms.[19] The entire school reassembles afterwards at the premises of the schoolteacher for instruction.

This farm labour takes place only during the rainy season, for some three or four months of the year. During the rest of the year the students are employed in various domestic chores. The same division holds between day-scholars and permanent residents: on Thursdays day-scholars attend the schoolteacher who assigns them to various jobs around the compound. These students also help to fetch the domestic supply of fuel on Thursdays. The other students are employed throughout the week in such chores and carrying out repairs to the premises. In the days before roofs were made of imported corrugated iron and the walls of cement-bricks, major repairs and renovation were an annual affair. Such large-scale work was undertaken in the dry season, at a time when all farm work had ceased or been reduced to the minimum. It was the responsibility of the students to carry out such necessary work. The students were thus fully stretched throughout the whole calendar year. The school makes no provision for a long holiday break except at Ramaḍān and the two *ᶜīd* festivals.

By employing students on the farms, the schoolteacher is making sure that there are enough food reserves to maintain his community. He is responsible, in theory at least, for feeding and looking after his students, and, in exchange for this responsibility, he has extensive rights over them. This in itself considerably enhances the power and stature of the schoolteacher, for it means he has an enormous material strength at his disposal, both in terms of farm produce and manpower resources.

The teacher's farms worked by the students produce mainly grains and groundnuts. Some of the produce is laid aside as a cash earner, particularly groundnuts.[20] The money is sometimes used to stock up the school library, but the bulk of it goes into providing a minimum of clothing for the children, and towards improving the wardrobes of the women. The excess grain is used for feeding strangers and guests at the school. Sometimes slave and caste families are also maintained from this source.[21] Clerical journeys are also financed out of extra capital accumulated at the school, although the fact that the cleric can count on the hospitality of the towns through which he passes reduces his dependence on this source.[22]

Mungo Park records that during his travels he came across Qur'ān schools where the students, 'being considered, during their scholarship, as the domestic slaves of the master, ...were employed in planting corn, bringing firewood, and in other servile offices through the day ([1799] 1969: 240). Another observer writes that during the day boys go with the schoolteacher to his field, 'and there he teaches them by word and example the native mode of cultivation' (Mitchinson 1881: 128).

One general conclusion may be drawn from the use of student labour on farms. The rural setting of most Jakhanke clerical establishments means that a good deal of their educational activity has had to be integrated with agriculture. The surprising fact is that the Jakhanke appear to have taken an interest in agriculture only for the purposes of maintaining a viable autonomous life. They never became masters of the art of cultivation, land-use or soil conservation. Primarily interested in clerical and educational activity they leaned on agriculture for necessary support, but no more.[23] The Jakhanke themselves emphasise that farming (called by them *seno*) is a legitimate occupation which every clerical community ought to encourage, if only to inculcate values of diligence, honesty and moral uprightness in their students.[24] When asked specifically why the Jakhanke continued to live in remote rural settings like Nibrās and Sutukung, it was emphasised that living conditions were good at those places while their relative seclusion ensured the flourishing of a quiet and vigorous pursuit of learning. The deliberate pastoral setting of many Jakhanke centres shows a predisposition against commercial market towns and towards more religiously oriented rustic settlements. But apart from a general theory that farming, which may sometimes include livestock breeding, is a necessary and required employment for a clerical community, there is no attempt to concentrate resources in this area. The Jakhanke in Touba, for example, while producing renowned savants had no corresponding reputation for agricultural skills.[25]

Stages in the Curriculum and the Passing Out Ceremony

There are two categories of scholar: the elementary Qur'ān school pupils and the more advanced ᶜIlm school students. The first category of student is called by the Jakhanke *tilmīdh* (pl. *talāmīdh*, an Arabic word) and the more advanced *ṭālib*, (pl. *ṭullāb*, or other Arabic variants). During their time at Qur'ān school students go through five stages and at each stage there is a small formal ceremony to mark the promotion. The educational course begins with learning the letters of the Arabic alphabet. Then follows vowelling, and at this point the pupil is made to practise cursive writing in which the consonants run together with the appropriate vowelling. Once this step is reached and the student can decipher individual words, he starts to commit to memory parts of the Arabic Qur'ān, beginning with the shortest *ṣūrāt*. Thus commence the first steps towards memorising the entire Qur'ān, with pauses along the way.[26] According to one experienced teacher, a student can under normal conditions finish memorising the Qur'ān completely in five years.[27]

The first stage in Qur'ān recitation is completed when the student has reached *ṣūrah al-mulk* (The Kingdom), i.e. the 67th chapter of the Qur'ān. This is a *ṣūrah* with many memorable passages, such as the following:

> Thou seest not in the creation of the All-merciful any imperfection. Return thy gaze; seest thou any fissure? Then return thy gaze again, and again, and thy gaze comes back to thee dazzled, a-weary. (lxvii: 3)
>
> Have they not regarded the birds above them spreading their wings, and closing them? Naught holds them but the All-merciful. (lxvii: 19)

A small token freewill offering, *ṣadaqah*, is made, consisting of kolanuts, pounded grain, and sometimes a sacrificial animal, preferably a white sheep, is killed. After the 2:30 p.m. prayer the Muslim community gathers at the school to offer prayers for the matriculating students.[28] The same ceremony is repeated at the second, third and fourth stages. The second stage is reached at *Yā Sīn*, chapter 36, an esoteric *ṣūrah* much used in Black Africa. There are 83 verses, mostly of a short staccato nature. The third stage is at *ṣūrah al-maryam* (Mary), a chapter devoted mainly to the Holy Family of the Lord, with somewhat fitful and scattered comment on Old Testament figures. The chapter ends by pronouncing an anathema on the doctrine of 'Association' (Ar. *shirk*), in this instance attributed to Christians, and a standard note of warning and eschatological threat. The fourth stage is completed with *ṣūrah al-aᶜrāf* (The Battlements), chapter 7, a *ṣūrah* with more narrative material than most, concerned mainly with Moses and the destiny of the Jews in their captivity and eventual exodus from Egypt. A different and more elaborate ceremony is organised at the end of Qur'ān school, reached when the pupil has mastered *ṣurāh al-baqarah* (The Cow), chapter 2.[29]

Most students leave Qur'ān school when they reach this stage of their education, although a good number will go on to the first stages of *tafsīr*, the exegesis of the Qur'ān. Most parents come to ask for their children back when they have been informed of their progress up to this point. If this happens, a ceremony is organised on the pattern of earlier ones, except that in this instance it is a passing out ceremony with a farewell. It is expected that the parents will pay some money to redeem their children. Destitute parents can have their son back provided they undertake to pay up if they come into better fortune. Although there is no fixed sum, Jakhanke teachers make sure that they have enough grip on their students to make their parents pay a fairly substantial fee at the end. Most students in fact maintain a polite and respectful link with their teachers which sometimes takes the form of monetary payments and gifts in kind for the past labours of the teachers.

One eye-witness account of a passing out ceremony gives the following details.[30] A group of senior students were about to end their school career. A notice of intention to leave was communicated to the teacher through another senior student who was not himself leaving. They bought some kola-nuts and gave them to the teacher through the intermediary, in order to formalise the notice of intention already given. Then the teacher set a date and announced it to the immediate families of those concerned as well as to his followers and supporters in the school compound. Afterwards word was sent to the townspeople. When the day of departure arrived a large crowd gathered in the compound. Two prayer ceremonies were organised. At the first one about 80 people came together. This one was private and restricted. At the second one the school kept open house to all the local people. Sometimes over 300 people would gather on such occasions. The central focus of such ceremonies was the practice of supererogatory public prayers, *ad^ciyah* (sing. *du^cā*), on behalf of the departing students. 'But the student himself does not pray as he is the recipient of blessing, not the giver.'

The passing out of fully fledged Qur'ān students is timed to coincide with the enrolment of new recruits in the lower echelons of the school. This maintains a constant supply of students, and in some cases schools have to be enlarged to cope with increased intake. The system is adaptable and the gap between intake and output can be regulated by adjusting the size of ^{c}Ilm school enrolment. More students graduating from Qur'ān school can be persuaded to stay on into the later phases if recruitment prospects appear dull; advanced students (*ṭullāb*) are drafted into actual teaching duties if the inflow of new recruits outgrows the teaching capacity of the school.

One of the most elaborately staged educational ceremonies is *naw mini*, the canonical investiture of a *tafsīr* scholar. The ceremony is also a solemn religious occasion for endowing the scholar with the power and virtues of *fidā'atu*, insights into the efficacy and benefits of applied religion. A person thus invested becomes known as *fode*, and as his insignia of office receives the long turban. Among the Fulbe he is called Alfa.

The Jakhanke teachers have a rich reservoir of accounts of this which purport to go back to al-Ḥājj Sālim Suware and ultimately to the Prophet himself. Many of these stories are legendary and apocryphal in character, but they serve a most useful purpose in the Jakhanke educational enterprise. It is said that the Prophet turbaned one of his generals to protect him from evil and hell fire. This general was called Tījān al-Malā'ikatu.[31] In the same vein it is said that at the Battle of Badr (March, 624 A.D.) 5,000 angels were all turbaned as Muḥammad's allies. Gabriel, one of the four archangels, was himself turbaned and preceded the Prophet into Medina riding a horse called Haijūm.[31] It is probable that the headgear worn by Muslim armies, particularly in the early days at Medina, became a symbol of distinction and acquired both a social and religious significance. It is certainly true that willingness to fight in the Muslim armies was the crucial test the Prophet applied to determine the faithfulness of his following.[32] The Jakhanke are very lenient and not too scrupulous about conferring the office of *fode* on their protégés, although the overriding aim of a strategic deployment of Muslim agents is kept constantly in view.

The ceremony itself can be a colourful and ornate occasion. The turban is seven arms in length and one arm in width. It can be black, white or mixed colours, but must not include any red.[33] As the ceremony of investiture proceeds, the cleric allows the turban to be wound around his head and below his chin. The ordinand stands facing west. The officiating cleric advances towards him from the front, both standing for the ceremony. The congregation then sits while the cleric recites the *Basmala* and spatters certain phrases on the turban before winding it round the head of the candidate. After the *Basmala* and the consecrating laying on of hands, the cleric recites a formal prayer in which he asks for the gifts of faith (*īmān*) and miracles (*karāmāt*) for the candidate. He also asks for 'powers of the tongue', that is, the gift of preaching and authority in Scriptural interpretation.[34] The turban is called *nawo* by the Jakhanke. It is indicative that the Jakhanke, desirous of impregnating traditional religious thinking with Islamic values, teach that a person not canonised as a *fode* can also use the turban both as a protection from personal calamities like drowning and as immunity from theft and similar misadventures.[35] Similarly, the prayer which the cleric recites at the turbaning ceremony is written on wooden slates and then washed off and the water dispensed for sacred healing. Further removed from the ceremony but deriving from it is the practice of adopting the name Fode for children as a mark of dignity, which also indicates the direction in which parents intend their children to grow. A renowned example of this name-borrowing is Fode Silla, the nineteenth century Senegambian *mujāhid*, whose real name was Ture. Following a visit to Gunjūr in Kombo by a Jakhanke cleric, Fode Jikiba Silla, who went there to inaugurate a new mosque, Ture was named in full after him, although it was the shorter form, Fode Silla, which survived.[36]

The *naw mini* ceremony can also be the passing out ritual for students of ᶜIlm schools. In that case the title of *fode* is invested at the end of a student's career. Another practice, though rather uncommon, is to delay the ceremony until a scholar has become well established in life. Two examples of this were the late *imām* of Georgetown, Muḥammad Fatti, and Fa Bakari Marong, also of Georgetown. The latter was created *fode* only in his last years.[37]

If a student decides to defer becoming a *fode* in favour of pursuing higher studies, his schedule will include more concentration on *tafsīr*, going beyond the elementary stages of Jalālayn. Then follows *tawḥīd* (theology), Ḥadīth, i.e. the six authoritative anthologies on the subject - Bukhārī (870), Muslim (815), Abū Dā^c^ūd (888), al-Nasā'ī (916), ibn Māja (886) and al-Tirmidhī (892) - *lūghah* (linguistics), i.e. mainly the *Maqāmāt* of al-Ḥarīrī and the *Qāmūs* of Majd al-Dīn, eulogies on the Prophet (*madā'iḥ*), Sharī^c^ah (the law) and *fiqh* (jurisprudence) - particularly the *Muwaṭṭa* of Mālik ibn Anas, and the *Risālah* of ibn Abī Zayd al-Qayrawānī - and *naḥw* (philology/grammar), usually the work of ibn Mālik called *al-Fiyah*. This is a stiff programme which can take several years.[38]

The Jakhanke also allow some time for a discipline called *taṣrīf*. This might be called vocational clerical training. It is indispensable in clerical practice. It concerns the ability to conduct occult work, amulet-making, undertake religious healing (to be distinguished from faith healing, see pp.207-13 below), and in general to participate fully in the assault on the spiritual enemies of man. *Taṣrīf* gives the formal training for a Jakhanke Muslim to do this kind of work within a clearly delineated Islamic framework. It is fundamentally based on Islamic legal casuistry (*ḥiyāl*) whereby an apparently contradictory or even heretical custom (*^c^ādah*) can be skilfully adjusted so as to conform to established Muslim practice (*taqlīd*) and accepted precedents (*taḥlīl*). Acts and practices which cannot be integrated with legal conventions in this way and are seen to violate normative Islamic standards are repudiated under the category of *bida^c^*, innovations or heresies.[39] For the Jakhanke cleric this is a significant aspect of the work of educating a class of men who have to be able to function with apparent competence in societies where spirit-divination, religious healing, fortune-telling, necromancy and various forms of religious practice maintain a dominant role. The attempt to construct a set of cogent and expressly Islamic principles whereby the cleric has 'freedom of action', that is, he knows the rules of *taṣrīf*, gives Islam a wide range of applicability and a greater spectrum of effectiveness. It comes very late in the Jakhanke curriculum, perhaps so that by the time students arrive at that stage they have had a firm and thorough grounding in the other branches (*funūn*) of Islamic learning. Karamokho Ba, for example, (see pp. 99-100) returned to the study of *taṣrīf* a second time, studying it once under Fode ᶜAmar Ture at Diombokho in Khasso, and then under Muḥammad Naḥawī in the ancient Sudanic town of Jenne, a repetition which meant either that his first grasp of the subject was unsure or that the field was too vast to be taken in one stride. Through the accepted technique of legal casuistry, the Jakhanke scholars have drawn on *qiyās*, analogical reasoning, one of the four 'sources' (*uṣūl*, sing. *aṣl*) of Sharīᶜah, and tried, on the whole successfully, to accommodate the entire area of spirit power within an Islamic social setting by the method of 'evident interpretation' (*mafhūm*). This guards their orthodoxy and at the same time confirms their African status. It certainly makes their teaching of enormous practical value and appeal.

The Qur'ān School in the Past

Some outside observers and travellers have left descriptions of life in Qur'ān or ᶜIlm schools. One early nineteenth century account gives numerous details of what appears to be an ᶜIlm school. The teacher was reciting aloud, apparently from memory, while his students followed him in their books. One blind student, called ᶜAbdallāh, who seems to have been the senior student, explained the difficult passages to the class. The discussion afterwards turned upon the more doubtful sense of some parts of the book, which was a history of the life of Muḥammad. One of the other students took the book and read aloud. The others, under the direction of the schoolmaster, corrected the faults which had crept into their copies of the same book, which they held in their hands. The effect was not lost on the outside observer. 'The most profound silence prevailed among these young men, who appeared to be really studious.'[40]

Mungo Park describes an occasion when he was present at a Qur'ān school passing out ceremony, and his account carries the description of an ᶜIlm school several stages further. At the end of his term of Qur'ān studies, a feast was prepared for the student. A meeting of examiners was convened, composed of 'Bushreens' (Ar. *bashīrūn*), professional clerics. When the examiners were satisfied of the ability and competence of the student, a page of the Qur'ān was put into his hand and he proceeded to read it aloud. At the end of this recital he pressed the sheet against his forehead and pronounced the word 'Amen'. Following this all the examiners rose from their seats, shook the student cordially by the hand and conferred on him the title of graduate.[41] But it would appear that this was only one part of the proceedings, and that the other, earlier part, followed a different order. Park says that he attended 'at three different inaugurations of this sort, and heard with pleasure the distinct and intelligent answers which the scholars frequently gave to the Bushreens who assembled on those occasions, and acted as examiners'.[42] It was not until the student had got over that preliminary hurdle that he was allowed to proceed to what was essentially a ceremonial taking of his 'degree'.

At the end of his school term a student was redeemed by his parents. At the time of Park the parents gave the teacher a slave, or the price of one, in order to get back their son. In the case of parents unable to pay for their sons this way, the students remained the property of the teacher (Park calls them his 'domestic slaves') until they could work hard enough, usually on the farms of their teacher and a small plot of their own, and from their labours earn their freedom.[43] Under such circumstances only the teacher could determine when a student had worked hard enough for his freedom.

Travel and Education

Many clerics spend a good deal of their lives travelling from place to place. It is a way of canvassing for student-recruits. It makes it possible for them to visit old students and avail themselves of the largesse of local Muslim generosity. Such visits also serve to strengthen the bond of professional solidarity and a common Islamic awareness across spatially dispersed Muslim centres. The Jakhanke undertake it at periodic intervals because wherever they happen to be they are an immigrant people, the local version of the much wider Jakhanke diaspora, and geographical mobility both extends their range and consolidates their common identity.

During such periodic visitations the Qur'ān school travels with the cleric. The students' studies are disrupted, but the travel experience provides a new dimension to them. They come to terms with a makeshift arrangement in order to break away from home and be established in a much wider context. By abandoning home in the arduous pursuit of learning, the cleric hopes that the student may learn to shed his dependence on the home environment and be integrated into a

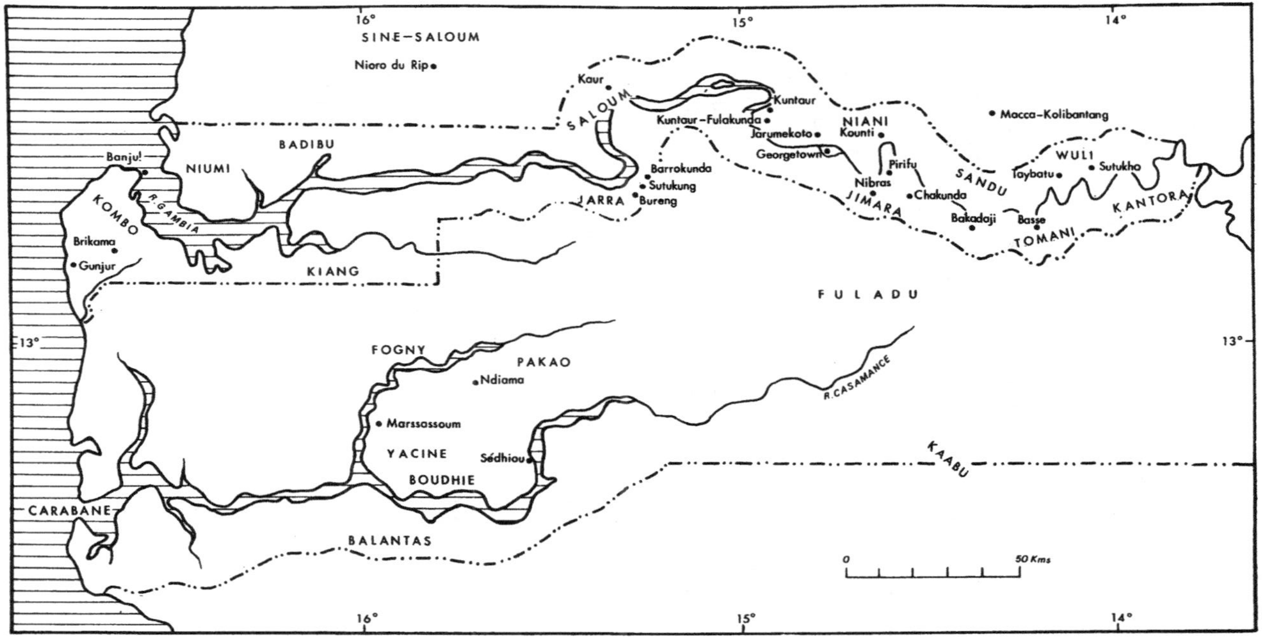

Map 5: Jakhanke Centres in the Gambia and Casamance (Senegal)

more flexible pattern of itinerancy. During the travels the student experiences the fraternal bond which links all Muslims, and, equally important, the high esteem in which Muslim communities are generally held by their neighbours.

Active teaching takes place while the cleric is on his travels, though the schedule is not strictly adhered to. Al-Ḥājj Sālim Suware is said to have instructed Yūsūf, son of Mama Sambou, at Wuli-Sutukho, presumably when al-Ḥājj Sālim was on his travels in Senegambia (*TKB*: fo. 2). When he originally left Diakha-Masina, al-Ḥājj Sālim travelled with a large student contingent, and was accompanied by his students as he moved first to Jafunu and then to Diakha-Bambukhu (see p. 17 above). According to the Arabic chronicle, *Aṣl al-Wanqarayīn*, 'the Origin of the Wangara People', the Jakhanke cleric, ᶜAbd al-Raḥmān Jakhite ('Zaghite') left Mali and travelled to Hausaland with a following of students, among others (Al-Ḥājj 1968; for the story of his travels see pp. 29-31). One of the most important assets possessed by itinerant teaching clerics is a prodigious memory, and in this ᶜAbd al-Raḥmān was typical, having committed to memory the jurisprudential work of Sayd Saḥnūn al-Tanūkhī (d.854).[44] It is possible with such scholastic endowments to undertake serious teaching without being unduly restricted by the paucity of books. Alfa Nuhī, the spiritual mentor of Karamokho Ba, also stands in this tradition.

It appears that the large numbers of students with whom clerics travelled did not inhibit or deter local populations from offering hospitality. The example of Karamokho Ba in this seems typical (see pp. 99-103). When Karamokho Qutubo, the grandson of Karamokho Ba, went to meet Shaykh Sidiya al-Kabīr in Mauritania in 1860, he combined this with an extended visit to numerous places in Senegambia. As a result of the visit his student following is said to have swelled to 780.[45] It is not clear how much teaching Qutubo did on this trip, but it is unlikely that he interrupted his teaching career for any significant length of time, and the phenomenal number of students he is claimed to have acquired probably attests to demonstration of his skills before admiring and appreciative audiences.

In another example, a Jakhanke cleric, Fode Shaykhu Silla, whose relatives de Mézières found living in Banī Isrā'ila (1949: 21), was travelling with some 100 students in the Gambia when war broke out in Bundu (c. 1885, this was the *jihād* of Momodou-Lamin Darame). Fode Baba

Silla, his brother, was anxious about the safety of his family in Bundu and had sent him to bring word on their well-being.[46] It appears that at the time Fode Shaykhu Silla was a visiting chaplain to Musa Molo, the nineteenth century warrior of Fuladu.[47] Eventually Fode Shaykhu returned safely from Bundu when he was warmly welcomed by the Jakhanke and local people of Jarra-Bureng. Six months before Fode Baba died he designated Fode Shaykhu Silla his heir and successor. He was to sever ties with Molo.

Fode Baba Silla himself is reputed to have had a following of 500 students with whom he travelled from place to place.[48] When he left Bundu he went to Dār Salām where he stayed for six years and a well was sunk which continued to bear his name. Then he went to Badibu-Gunjūr and lived there for another six years. When he reached Farafenyi (in Ripp), he met with his younger brother, Fode Shaykhu Silla. The two moved, accompanied by 500 followers, together to Jarra-Bureng, where Fode Baba later died.[48] Fode Shaykhu's break with Musa Molo came after he learnt of the latter's impending attack on Bureng where a cleric, Muḥammad Sanūsī Silla, was teaching at the time. Both of them evacuated Bureng with a large student population, and Fode Shaykhu was to end up at Kounti as the resident cleric.[49]

From European travellers' accounts we have a similar picture of educational activity among clerics. Jobson described how the cleric travelled with his books, manuscripts, his family and his school; at points along the way he would stop to give instruction to his school (1623: 97). Another account says that a teacher was on what appears to have been a *tournée pastorale*, accompanied by eight students. En route the teacher would give the boys their lessons, which consisted of teaching them to read and write Arabic. The students carried the luggage of their teacher. During the day they would go out begging for food and other things which they brought back to the teacher and at night they received their instruction (Hecquard 1851: 249). About such students William Gray and Dochard said: 'they go about, when not at their lessons, begging, and sewing the country cloths together, for any who may want to employ them; the produce of those callings are brought to the master...and appropriated to his use' (1825: 184).

Teacher and Student: Some Ṣūfī Comparisons

The complete and absolute control of the Jakhanke teacher over his student follows a uniform pattern in all Jakhanke educational organisation and leadership. Into this pattern have been infused elements of Ṣūfī teaching and practice so that the novice or seeker (*murīd*) holds the spiritual and educational guide (*murshid*) in the utmost, unquestioning respect. Versed in the writings of the great Ṣūfī masters, the Jakhanke cleric observes towards his pupil a similar attitude of spiritual superiority.[50] His model might well be the Guide-Seeker nexus of Ṣūfī tradition.[51] In this tradition, representative of mainstream Ṣūfīsm, the *murīd* 'ever beareth his *shaykh* in mind; in him effaceth himself through meditation; maketh him his shield against evil thoughts; and regardeth his spirit as his guardian spirit. This is "effacement in the *shaykh*"' (Suhrawardī, trans. 1891: 3). The necessity of the Guide or Director to the one who seeks guidance is paramount in Ṣūfīsm, and this central position of the teacher is reflected in Jakhanke educational activity. A remark made about the Ṣūfī could equally well apply to the Jakhanke set-up: 'The teacher's acceptance is the nearest thing to divine acceptance, and represents it as far as it can...The disciple must honour the *shaykh* deeply. Therein lies his hope.'[52]

The initiation into Qur'ān school takes the form of a conditional sale, with the difference that at the end of his term of schooling the student is purchased back by his parents. Such initiation is similar to the more technical Ṣūfī initiation rite (*talqīn*), called the Pledge (*bay^{c}ah*) (see Suhrawardī, trans. 1891: 160-4), which stresses this dual aspect of the transaction, particularly in the Ṣūfī Dervish Orders.[53] This initiation practice has been the hallmark of the Mouride Brotherhood where the role of the *shaykh* in leading the disciple (*murīd*) to eternal salvation is vital. At the initiation ceremony, the would-be disciple declares (in Wolof):

> Jebbel nā la sama jemmu ak sama bakan. Lo ma diggel ma def ko: lo ma terre ma bai ko.
>
> 'I submit my body and soul to you.[54] Whatever you command me I shall do, and whatever you forbid me I shall refrain from.' (Cruise O'Brien 1971: 85)

After this ceremonial submission the newcomer may make a small symbolic offering to the *shaykh* signifying his new subservient status. 'Mouride ritual and ideology require that the *ṭālibé* should be entirely submitted to the will of his *shaikh*.'[55]

The esteem in which the Jakhanke *ṭālib*, a term which can also describe the position of the Seeker, regarded his teacher is brought out in the following story. In 1904, Karamokho Qutubo issued a general call for his students to clear away a heap of unsanitary waste which had for some time sullied the centre of Touba. The message went unattended for various reasons. Fearful of an epidemic breaking out, and having given vent to his fears in vain, Qutubo, in desperation, decided one morning to go and clean up the mess himself, aided by two of his *ṭullāb*. The entire town immediately flocked to his side. People were running to beg his pardon. They carried him away in triumph while some 200 *ṭullāb* took to cleaning out the town. In three days it became a model as one of the best kept in the area. The epidemic was averted and 'le mérite en fut attribué à la *baraka* du saint Qutubo, qui récompensait ainsi le zèle et l'obéissance de ses talibés' (Marty 1921: 131-2). The fact that his word went unheeded in the first place does not seem to have affected the final issue.

The interaction between the teacher and the student is a recurrent theme in European travellers' accounts. Park describes a school which had seventeen students, including two girls.[56] He was impressed with the schoolteacher whom he described in these terms:

> The schoolmaster, to whose care I was entrusted...was a man of mild disposition and gentle manner...and although he himself adhered strictly to the religion of Mahomet, he was by no means intolerant in his principles towards others who differed from him. He spent much of his time in reading; and teaching appeared to be his pleasure, as well as employment. ([1799] 1969: 240)

In this particular case the Qur'ān school was a hospice for travellers as well, thus fulfilling one important aspect of a *zāwiyah*, a Ṣūfī retreat for strangers. In another example, the teacher and the student come together in what is a normal regular routine. Once again the outside observer seems impressed with the spectacle:

> It is a pleasant and instructive scene to watch a grey, reverend-looking marabout surrounded by boys, listening attentively to his teaching, or all joining in and chanting a repetition of the lessons he gives them from the Koran, or busily engaged under his supervision in practising their writing lessons on boards. The discipline maintained by the marabouts in their schools presents an example of order and attention not to be excelled... (Mitchinson 1881: 127-8)

The Establishment of New Schools and Centres

A Jakhanke cleric must satisfy three basic qualifications before he can operate a Qur'ān school. He must have gone through the stages of a Qur'ān school himself. He must also be a graduate of an ᶜIlm school, and finally, he must be in possession of an *ᶜijāzah* or *isnād* (sometimes also called *silsilah*), educational licence, normally linked to one or other of the better-known Qādirī schools.[57] This enables him to create Muslim clerics (*fode*) on the basis of *fidā'ah* (or *fidā'atu*). Many are in their late thirties or early forties before they qualify for a *majlis* in this way. The word literally means 'council', 'collegium', or 'assembly'. Among the Jakhanke it means an educational parish, in the sense of the recognition of a cleric's right to operate an educational practice in a given area without any conditions and with full accreditation from similar establishments elsewhere. The missionary implications of this concept of the educational *majlis* become apparent when a Jakhanke cleric, in order to maintain an independent *majlis*, withdraws from a town where one already exists and goes to another where none exists. Quite often he will create a completely new centre where he can exercise the functions of a *majlistio* (a local modification of the word), i.e. a director/proprietor of a *majlis*. Some examples of the founding of Qur'ān schools by the Jakhanke may help to elucidate both the concept and the process.

One of the first Qur'ān schools in Jarra-Sutukung was opened by an immigrant Jakhanke cleric, Karang Ya. Behind the story of his eventual migration to Sutukung lies a myriad record of travel, unsettlement, migration and transitoriness. His father was Fode Amara Silla who travelled to Pakao (in Casamance) where he married the daughter of ᶜUthmān Kabba. He had with him at the time some 70 *ṭullāb*. Fode Amara later went to live in Badibu-Kachang where the Danso people were his hosts and students. He built a mosque there although local opposition to his assuming the office of *imām* led to a withdrawal to Pakao, then to Bāsāfu and finally to Sonkodu (both in Casamance) where he died.[58] Karang Ya, his eldest son, succeeded him.

Karang Ya was forced to leave Casamance because of French pressure directed at conscripting his students into the colonial army (c.1915). He left and came to settle in Sutukung. His original intention was to go to Misira (a village near Bansang, the Gambia, in Fula country) where a student of his, Afang Madi Fati, had invited him to take over leadership of the *majlis* in the area. But his cousin, then resident at Sutukung, appealed to him to come there, which he eventually did. After he had been in Sutukung a short time Karang Ya asked permission from the chief man of the village, Alkali

Kalilou Biyai, a Balanta, to open a Qur'ān school. This request was made in addition to another, already granted, to set up house.[59] Karang Ya sent his brothers with kola-nuts as a present to the *alkali*. He also discussed the project with his brothers who were to help him establish the Qur'ān school and be part of the teaching staff as well. Some of his distant relatives came from Bundu to study under him. As part of the process of creating the school, blacksmiths manufactured tools and implements such as machetes, hoes, spears, which became the property of the school. These blacksmiths were a caste group and they lived in special quarters in the village.[60] There were also leather-smiths, woodcutters and cloth manufacturers. A slave quarter was maintained to provide additional labour on the farms which the students cultivated. Apart from the staple grain-produce, the school also worked on cotton-fields. The local cotton reduced dependence on outside supplies. Local production of cotton cloth helped to clothe members of the clerical community as well as the students themselves who were normally very sparsely clad, sometimes only in a loin cloth. Younger girls wore two strips of cloth for the front and back.

One of the biggest Qur'ān schools Sutukung ever saw was the one established by Karang Sambu Lamin, originally from Touba. He left Touba during the time of Karamokho Qutubo, about 1894, and came to Niani-Dobo where some ex-students lived. He stayed there for one year and then went to Niani-Toubanding where he spent four years. Students were attracted there, on account of the successful Qur'ān school he opened, from Pakao, Kaabu and Pirassu (now in Guinea-Bissau).[61] From Niani, Karang Sambu went to Pachang, in Fuladu, where he stayed for three years. He had three sons there. Afterwards he went to Niamina-Jāfai and lived there for seven years. He had two sons there and acquired a good number of students. From there he travelled to Jarra-Sutukung, whose *alkali* had issued a strong request for him to come. He had spent more than fifteen years travelling from place to place since he first left Touba.[61] One of the students who had followed Karang Sambu Lamin in some of his travels was Ba Fode Jakhabi, a previous *imām* of Georgetown. He travelled with Karang Sambu Lamin from Jāfai to Sutukung where he completed his studies.[62] At Jāfai, the senior student of Karang Sambu's Qur'ān school was Woinke Seidi, who was not himself a Jakhanke. The school had about 100 students in residence, most of them members of the complementary ᶜIlm school. Half of the advanced students were married with families of their own.[63] One student at least took leave of absence from the school and went on *ḥājj* to Mecca. He returned afterwards to the school, then at Sutukung.[64]

When Karang Sambu opened his school at Sutukung he had a nucleus of students, including his own growing family, with whom he started. In addition the *alkali* had provided some more students as an incentive for him to stay. The Qur'ān school was set up out of doors in the middle of the compound. Before long Karang Sambu was getting an influx of students from the surrounding villages. The physical surroundings of the first open-air school, with a small raised daïs called *samako*, from which the teacher supervised the students, proved inadequate. Karang Sambu then transferred to more spacious accommodation called *tungi* (a word which may originally have been a Fula term). About fifty students made this transfer.[65] In the meantime the school had been increasing its accumulation of assets like farming implements, leather supplies, quality wood and cotton goods. A special storehouse for some of the tools was built, called *bilo*.[65]

Like most Jakhanke *majālis*, Karang Sambu's school at Sutukung relied for admission of new recruits on the extensive and active network of ex-students who acted as agents in their different localities. Some of these ex-students came to Sutukung once a year to render homage to Karang Sambu, bringing with them numerous gifts. The reputation of a school depended very much on the local renown of its alumni, and verbal communication spread its fame with great rapidity. Karang Sambu had a close network of former students who kept him constantly informed as well as maintaining a continuous supply of fresh recruits. Some of these students lived not too far away, for example, al-Ḥājj Jali Samate at nearby Jappeni. Others were more widely scattered, in Casamance mainly, but also in Kiang, like Tankular Sise. At Kanikunda his leading student was Afang Sire Seide, and at Dankunku, al-Ḥājj Khousi Fati and Afang Bakari Silla.[65]

In addition to the large number of students under him, estimated at some 250, Karang Sambu also owned a number of slave families. Their exclusion from office in the clerical order was complete, and long after Karang Sambu's death they remained outside the free family structure of Sutukung. Most of them eventually dispersed from Sutukung to pledge themselves to new masters. The slaves shared with the griots, and the other professional castes, the status of *nyamakala*.[66]

The accounts say that Karang Sambu allowed a host of such dependents to exist in his clerical community because by providing them with protection (from hunger and nakedness and loneliness) he was providing a useful social service.[67] But this is misleadingly evasive. The *nyamakala* provided invaluable practical and economic service in freeing Jakhanke students from many hours of physical labour, time which they could and did spend on their lessons. In their turn the members of the *nyamakala* were accorded protection inside their accepted social limits. Considered as 'straw' by the free families they lived in a state of ritual uncleanness with a corresponding exemption from the *tana*, ritual prohibitions.

When Karang Sambu was teaching at Jāfai he was once visited by Major Brooke, then a District Commissioner in Georgetown. The Qur'ān school had sixty students at the time.[68] Although favourably impressed with the general standard of the school, he afterwards tried to persuade Karang Sambu to send the children to a Western school, which Karang Sambu refused to do. Major Brooke also discussed with him the peculiar hair-styles the students were wearing.[69] Karang Sambu is reported to have replied that if his students attended Western style school he would eventually lose them to Christianity. Major Brooke appears to have been impressed with Karang Sambu Lamin, nonetheless, and suggested some form of official government recognition of his abilities, if not a regular stipend of some sort. Karang Sambu shied away from the idea of involvement with official circles although he and Major Brooke maintained the most cordial of relations.[70] This may have decided one of Karang Sambu's students, Ba Fode Jakhabi, to settle in Georgetown at the end of his studies: he would be living within the jurisdiction of a colonial official not unsympathetic to Jakhanke educational work.[71]

Karang Sambu's school was typical of other Jakhanke schools. An account by his eldest son of the passing out ceremony has already been given (p. 155-6). Many students asked Karang Sambu Lamin as their teacher to designate areas in which they could establish their own *majālis*. After two years such former students came back to Karang Sambu to pay their respects, bringing with them numerous presents. Like most other students they sent their own sons to study under their former teacher and some of the students sought and obtained the Qādirī *wird* from Karang Sambu.[72]

Another Jakhanke cleric who left Touba during the lifetime of Karamokho Qutubo and came to live in Senegambia was Aḥmad Bakkai, so called in honour of the son of Shaykh Sidiya al-Kabīr of the Kounta. He became better known as Karamokho Bekkai, or Karam Bekkai. In fact, Karam Bekkai was the fourth son of Karamokho Qutubo, a half brother of Karamokho Sankoung. He left Touba early and Marty does not seem to have found out much about him at Touba (1921: 111). Karam Bekkai first went to Kerewan-Dumbokono, Fuladu, where he and his family and students were cordially received by the *alkali*. They stayed there for a few years and then Karam Bekkai asked the *alkali* for permission to go and settle in his own centre. It is said that the *alkali* refused this request at first, but reluctantly yielded when he discovered Karam Bekkai was insistent on leaving. Karam Bekkai for his part agreed to make an important concession to the *alkali* by founding his centre in the same region, which is how he came to establish Nibrās, not very far from Kerewan-Dumbokono.[73]

The name Nibrās was chosen because of its Arabic associations. It means 'lantern' or 'light', because, it is said, Karam Bekkai envisaged the centre as a lighthouse diffusing the light of religion to all the surrounding area. Islam had made very little impact in the area, where most of the Fulbe population were resistant to conversion because of their unfavourable contact with the *mujāhidūn*, particularly Fode Kabba. Karam Bekkai wanted Islamic values and ideas to be diffused throughout the whole cultural complex of Fulbe society, and his emphasis on a quiet and peaceful revolutionary influence turned Nibrās into a model teaching centre to which the pagan Fulbe sent their children and from which they carried impressions back into the heart of their own societies. No record has survived of the names of these Fulbe students or of their performance in later years. The Jakhanke themselves acquired a fluent knowledge of the Fula language and won the confidence of the Fulbe aristocracy. Nibrās flourished and its clientele expanded. A mosque (*masjid*) was erected as soon as Karam Bekkai arrived in Nibrās, though it was many years later before it was up-graded to a major mosque (*jāmiᶜ*). In addition to the Fulbe pupils, Nibrās also received a large contingent of Jola from Buluf, Casamance (their chief town being Bignona). Some of the pagan Wolof, of whom there was a sizeable population, also sent their children there. Students came from Sierra Leone,

Dakar, Kombo and Bathurst (now Banjul).[74]

Nibrās also contained members of the *nyamakala* in Karam Bekkai's time. Particularly prominent were the *garanke* (leather-workers, and *numu* (smiths), as well as a slave community. The leader of the slave community, himself a slave, was Tentu Mansa. He had six children.[74] After emancipation the slaves dispersed from Nibrās, although the *nyamakala* quarter was maintained for a long time. Slaves were in general resident in the same ward as members of the *nyamakala*. More specifically, they belonged to *jongkunda*, the slave caste.

The farming potential of Nibrās is most evident, and its seclusion guarantees isolation from the main commercial routes of the region. The swamp behind which it lies tucked away constitutes its greatest source of food, mainly rice. Adjoining the swamp fields is excellent groundnut farmland. Pasture for livestock also abounds. Students labour, and slave labour when this was available, made these great agricultural assets yield a comfortable living for the clerical community. Clients approached the leading clerics there in the knowledge that they would be immune from unfavourable publicity or the need to divulge a secret mission. More important for the Jakhanke teachers, it meant that their students would be safely insulated from outside distractions and able to devote undivided attention to their lessons. Similar factors weighed, for instance, in the choice of Sutukung by Karang Sambu Lamin.[75]

Education and the Spread of Islam to Non-Muslims

Jakhanke involvement in the education of non-Muslim children was deliberate: an attempt to spread Islamic influence, and in consequence to increase and widen support for their own activities. But the most concentrated effort of Jakhanke educational practice was directed at their own children whom they wanted to educate for leadership roles in the Jakhanke tradition. This explains why a Jakhanke cleric would start with the nucleus of his own children and other children of relatives as the stepping stone for his educational work, and when these were joined by other students from surrounding villages the work-load on the farms was spread around the latter category while the first group of students took on more teaching and supervisory functions. This has laid the Jakhanke open to the charge of exploitation from some of their neighbours who could not understand why a Jakhanke student of ten years' standing should be given more educational responsibility than his non-Jakhanke counterpart of fifteen or more years' seniority. The Jakhanke clerics, however, were not heedless to such grievances, and there are examples of non-Jakhanke students assuming the leadership of Qur'ān and ᶜIlm schools. Karang Sambu Lamin had Woinke Seidi, a non-Jakhanke as his head student. Two non-Jakhanke students who studied at Touba and rose to leadership, one in Niani and the other in Casamance, were Sulayman Janko and Fode Kadiali. Some idea of the influence and work of such men may emerge from the story of these two.

Fode Kadiali was born about 1850 at N'Diama (Ar. *jāmiᶜ*) in the district of Yacine (Casamance). His paternal grandfather, Ousman Jah, was a Tukulor of Futa Toro. He left Futa in about 1790 in search of adventure.[76] He came to Yacine where he founded N'Diama. His son, Fode Kadiali's father, Mamudu Ousman, was born there and took an active part in Muslim military action against the pagans of the area between 1860 and 1880. The Bagnouk suffered particularly from such action (Marty 1915/6: 456).

Kadiali, named after the ethical theologian, Abū Ḥāmid al-Ghazālī (d. 1111), did his preliminary studies at Bidjini (Guinea-Bissau) under Fode Amara. His most important teacher was Qutubo at Touba, under whom he undertook the study of *fiqh*, *naḥw*, and *adab*. Qutubo conferred on him the Qādirī *wird*. Kadiali followed this up with a personal visit to Shaykh Sidiya Baba at Boutilimit who confirmed him in the Order.

Kadiali opened a Qur'ān school in N'Diama which quickly acquired a high reputation. During that time he undertook the customary *tournée pastorale* with a number of his students, which took him to the Sudan and lasted several years. When he returned he founded a village at Diakha in Casamance and settled there (Marty 1915/6: 457). But soon endemic local upheavals made life untenable for him at Diakha and he and his community removed to a new place he named Bakadaji (Ar. Baghdad) (in 1890), after the birthplace of the founder of the Qādiriyāh. A similar fate befell him there when the *mujāhid*, Fode Kabba, spurned by all the leading Muslim centres in Casamance, directed attacks against him (Leary 1971: 239-41; Marty 1915/6: 457). Fode Kadiali then returned to his paternal village N'Diama but was later reinstated at Bakadaji under French aegis. A few years later he performed the pilgrimage to Mecca (1908), an occasion he used to pass through Metropolitan France and Egypt (Marty 1915/6: 457).

Fode Kadiali's four wives and three concubines all belonged to the Mandinka nation. He had a large number of sons and daughters and nine of his sons rose to some importance. He also owned a large herd of cattle and a number of fields cultivated by his students. He maintained close links with some of his students, many of whom he appointed as his chief contacts in different parts: Yakouba (Ya^{c}qūb) Mente was installed in Badibu (Ripp); Abou Dakar was closer at hand at Pakao; Dimbo Damfa ('Danfa') was the chief agent in Upper Gambia; Arfang Lamin in Badibu; Arfang Kaba and Lamin Secka were both based in Kiang (*ibid*: 458). Fode Kadiali was still in active practice when Marty wrote about him.

Sulayman Janko, about whom little is known, was established at Niani-Kayaye (near the port of Kuntaur), a one time redoubtable anti-Islamic centre. It was at Kayaye that the militant Muslim leader, Shaykh Momodou-Lamin, was eventually captured by a pursuing French military detachment, supported by Musa Molo, probably betrayed by the local population, and was killed in 1887. Kayaye became a byword in clerical circles for its avowedly secular stance, and local traditions abound with details on how remnants of the Kaabu aristocracy, fiercely anti-Muslim, took sanctuary there but were promptly followed by enemy forces, which led to their dispersion to Niani-Sukuta, appropriately called by the Kaabu immigrants, Nījī, meaning 'repose'. Sulayman Janko set up his Qur'ān school in that environment. He acquired a tremendous reputation, perhaps a reflection of the exposed position of the Muslims there who needed such a charismatic umbrella to serve as protection from potential local hostility, particularly in view of the fact that Sulayman Janko had lost his sight. One of his best known students was Muḥammad Fati who came from Faraba, some miles to the south of Kayaye. He eventually became the *imām* of Georgetown where he left a venerable reputation for deep spiritual insight and quietistic piety.[77] He lived to a ripe old age and died in 1954.

Numerous examples can be given of vigorous Jakhanke educational networks which stretched from one end of the diaspora to the other. In some cases the Jakhanke failed to penetrate the non-Muslim cultures into which they were sent, but the system of mutual support which traditionally sustained and nurtured dispersion centres, fashioning a strong link of professional solidarity across a long corridor, has considerably minimised failure. The twin purpose of conversion and confirmation of membership to which their educational activities were directed did not mean that the Jakhanke achieved an even record. The edge turned more in favour of confirming existing Muslim populations than of any large-scale conversions. But by strengthening the base rather than widening it the Jakhanke gave local Muslim expression a far greater self-confidence and a wider vision of the potential of an informed Muslim awareness. When conversions occurred as a result of this self-confidence, the converts were absorbed within a sustaining Muslim community alive to its responsibilities.

The educational establishment at Touba appears to have had its share of impact in the strengthening of Islam among Muslim and non-Muslim populations. The pattern seems to be to establish a relatively strong clerical centre in a predominantly pagan environment and then to branch out from there and establish a modest presence in adjacent areas, within easy access. For example, about two hours' travelling distance from Touba, Toubanding, i.e. 'Little Touba', was created. It was divided into several wards, including quarters for slaves and *nyamakala*. A number of Jakhanke clerics practised there (Marty 1921: 133-4). In the district of Kadé several students of Karamokho Dembo of Touba went to settle: Karamokho Sitafa (born c. 1875), Mamadou (born c. 1880), Siré-Modi (born c. 1870), and Shaykhu (born c. 1862). In Labé, in the heart of Futa Jallon, three centres were founded at Touba-koto, Fetoyembi and Summa. At Summa the Jakhanke were greeted with delight by the local Fulbe population who gave up leadership of the community and instead installed a Jakhanke, Karamokho Alfa, in the position of supreme power. In line with Jakhanke practice, Karamokho Alfa appears to have declined the actual office although he continued to hold tremendous sway over the political leadership which consulted him on all judicial matters. Alfa Alimou, the old chief of the district, held him in great esteem, and proudly placed on his chest the amulet Karamokho Alfa had made for him (Marty 1921: 133-4). At Fetoyembi a student of Karamokho Alfa, Karamokho Sori, was the resident cleric and had a handsome library (*ibid*).

In the district of Dinguiraye a centre was created at Bissikrima from the descendants of Jubba Almamy who was originally a Serakhulle from Jafunu. He emigrated to Bissikrima at the beginning of the nineteenth century and died about 1840. His children intermarried with the local Manding population, and, like the Jakhanke at Diakha-Bambukhu, they lost their Serakhulle background as they became assimilated into the Manding culture. Jubba's eldest son, Kankan Fode, founded a new centre called Kankan-Fodeya which was eventually abandoned as the population moved to Bissikrima. Kankan Fode's two brothers were Mori Sallou and Bouba. Mori Sallou was the father of Fode Yaya, and Bouba of Fode Baba. Fode Yaya and Fode Baba were spiritual disciples of Touba. A student of Qutubo, Alfa Ibrahima Gassama, passed through Bissikrima in 1907. He was prevailed upon to spend some time in Bissikrima, and after a few months of persistent entreaty by Fode Yaya and Fode Baba he agreed to confer the Qādirī *wird* on these two, each of whom he also created *muqaddam* for the entire area. 'Ils ont eux-mêmes distribué l'ouird à leurs talibés de la région' (Marty 1921: 136).

Fode Yaya (born c. 1855) was named chief of one part of Bissikrima in 1910. He presided over a prosperous settlement which attracted trade into the area. The opening of the Conakry-Niger railway, however, brought to Bissikrima a new set of problems. The influx of large number of strangers created tension and placed an unbearable strain on the Bissikrima community. A conflict broke out in which the powerful stranger-community succeeded in displacing the settler population. Fode Yaya and his people returned to Bissikrima-Koura (New Bissikrima). But Fode Yaya, in allying himself with the *nouveaux riches* at Old Bissikrima, had sown the dragon's teeth. He was denounced for his misrule as chief of the village and president of the provincial Tribunal at Dinguiraye. He was divested of all authority, tried and condemned to two years' imprisonment in September, 1914. On 8th January, 1915, his students, ostensibly on a recruitment drive, went on the rampage at Bissikrima, raising a spectre of revolt against the new chief, Mukhtār Fall. Twenty-two of the demonstrating crowd were arrested, including the sons, brothers and principal disciples of Fode Yaya. They were all sentenced to various terms of imprisonment and confined at Fotoba with Fode Yaya himself (Marty

1921: 136-7). The Qur'ān school was proscribed.

In one example the Jakhanke of Touba equipped a religious deputation with the explicit purpose of doing missionary work among non-Muslim Susu in Kindia (Guinea). Around 1890, Karamokho Qutubo sent as his personal envoy, Fode Sekou, to spread Islam among the Susu. When Fode Sekou arrived in Kindia he found one Fode Ansoumana in charge of a small Qur'ān school. Fode Ansoumana was also the *imām* of the local mosque. Fode Sekou conferred on him the Qādirī *wird* and established him as the personal representative of Karamokho Qutubo. One practical consequence of this religious drive was to open the way for Fode Ansoumana's sons, Fode Bokari (born c. 1885) and Fode Musa (born c. 1890), to rise to positions of clerical leadership. Most clerical functions were carried out through the medium of Manding: the weekly *khuṭbah* at the Friday Congregation Prayer, Qur'ānic exegesis (*tafsīr*) and verbal commentaries. The Susu language was still considered profane, on account probably of the predominantly pagan population (Marty 1921: 140-42). The Jakhanke, however, spoke Susu fluently as a necessary means of reaching and serving their Susu clients.

An example of specific links with the Susu is given by Blyden who came across one Fode Tarawali who, he claims, was a Susu, and was educated at Touba. He left Touba and went to settle in the Kambia district of Sierra Leone at a place called Gbileh. There he founded a successful educational centre which Blyden visited in January 1872 and called 'the Oxford of this region - where are collected over 500 young men studying Arabic and Koranic literature'.[78] Blyden, who knew of Touba only from hearsay, described it as 'of great literary repute'.

An intricate matrix of semi-autonomous clerical centres developed in which Touba remained the prominent strand. The sons of some of the leading clerics, such as Karamokho Qutubo, Karamokho Khasso, Muḥammad Taslīmī, went outside Touba to set up Qur'ān schools (Marty 1921: 144). Non-Jakhanke students returned home and opened Qur'ān schools. The Jakhanke themselves actively sponsored Qur'ān schools outside Touba. Karamokho Qutubo sent religious deputations on periodic visits to the Baga and Susu quarters of Conakry where schools were run for pagan children (*ibid*: 145). In the Rio Nuñez region Touba directed a sustained and vigorous campaign of proselytisation. Some converts were made among the Nalou, but the pagans of Tanda,

Mikiforé and Landouman remained inveterate non-believers (*ibid*: 145-6). In a less obvious way, Jakhanke slaves, after their liberation, returned among pagan populations with a residue of Muslim habits and ideas which they transmitted to their non-Muslim neighbours. The Jakhanke reinforced this flickering impulse by keeping contact with their ex-slaves and fostering their taste for Islam by opening Qur'ān schools among them (*ibid*: 146).

NOTES

1 Some *salāsil* (sing. *silsilah*), chains of transmission, are traced through this wooden slate to the Pen before terminating in God. Al-Ḥājj Madi Hawa of Barrokunda possesses a *tafsīr silsilah* which is joined this way. The principal *silsilah* at Touba likewise contains such a reference to the original wooden slate (Marty 1921: Annexe XIX). There is only one crisp reference in the Qur'ān to what seems to have taken on such enormous significance for the Jakhanke, and that reference is found in lxxxv: 25, where it is used in the context of the Qur'ān being preserved 'in a guarded tablet' (Arberry's translation). The word translated as 'guarded' is in the passive in Arabic, *maḥfūẓ*, and also means 'preserved in a pure form'.

2 The phrase *umm al-kitāb* occurs in xliii: 3. The word *umm* is translated as 'essence' by Arberry. It also has the meaning of 'source' or 'mother'. As a technical term it is applied to the Virgin Mary in the form *umm al-nūr* (source of light), and to Mecca, *umm al-qurā* (mother of cities). Related to this idea of the Mother of the Book as the heavenly Masterpiece which is the source of the Qur'ān is the ᶜAsharite view, originally intended as a compromise with the Muᶜtazilites, that the Qur'ān is unique in its 'inimitable eloquence' (Ar. *iᶜjāz*), xvii: 90.

3 Jakhanke clerics would prescribe - along with kola-nuts, milk, meal-offerings, strips of cloth, silverware, rams, fowl, etc. - unstated quantities of writing paper as pious votive offerings for their clients, who often made the offerings to the clerics themselves. To dispel fear or ensure a safe journey, a cleric would advise his client to give away any amount of writing paper. Living clerics like al-Ḥājj Shaykh Sidiya Jabi and al-Ḥājj Madi Hawa have continued to work in this tradition.

4 These details summarise observations and discussions in many Jakhanke centres in Senegambia. The sources are too numerous to list individually, but the schools of Karang Sambu Lamin at Sutukung, and al-Ḥājj Madi Hawa, at Jarra-Barrokunda, both in the Gambia, may be mentioned. The first one was nearly extinct while the second was going through a boom period in 1972/3. See also Map 5 below.

5 The description of the manufacture of writing ink comes from interviews conducted at Kounti.

6 Moister 1866: 156. This may in fact be a reference to the metallic colour sometimes present in that layer of the soot nearest to the surface of the pot.

7 Reade (1864:396) describes a Qur'ān school in which each pupil had a wooden slate on which he wrote Arabic characters by means of a charcoal pencil. Provided the charcoal used is smooth and well-burnt it can easily be washed off.

8 Virtually all the major Jakhanke teachers engage in making Holy Water. Its use by traders and military troops to ensure success are two of the best known instances of clerical service to agents of change and mobility. Cf Trimingham 1959: 115.

9 Muḥammad Kebba Silla, Sutukung, 17/11/72. This was corroborated by al-Ḥājj Madi Hawa, Barrokunda.

10 Al-Ḥājj Shaykh Sidiya Jabi, Brikama, 28/10/72.

11 Khalīfa Silla, himself a student aged 32, Sutukung, 17/11/72.

12 Kalāmullāh Sise, Jimara-Bakadaji, 11/12/72.

13 Al-Ḥājj Shaykh Sidiya Jabi, Brikama, 28/10/72.

14 Muḥammad Kebba Silla, Sutukung, 16/11/72.

15 Al-Ḥājj Mukhtār Jabi, Sutukung, 16/11/72.

16 Al-Ḥājj Shaykh Sidiya Jabi, Brikama, 28/10/72 and Al-Ḥājj Mukhtār Jabi, Sutukung, 16/11/72.

17 Muḥammad Kebba Silla, Sutukung, 16/11/72 and Al-Ḥājj Mukhtār Silla, Brikama, 11/11/72.

18 Kalāmullāh Sise, Bakadaji, 11/12/72.

19 Khalīfa Silla, Sutukung, 17/11/72.

20 Kalāmullāh Sise, Bakadaji, 11/12/72.

21 Al-Ḥajj Mukhtār Jabi, Sutukung, 16/11/72.

22 In fact, successful clerics are known to have gained considerable wealth from religious treks, and this is certainly one of the motives for going on long journeys. The way Karamokho Ba was entreated to stay in town after town during his religious treks indicates his success in this line (see Chapter 5).

23 De Mézières writes that the Jakhanke in Bundu are 'agriculturists' only in the sense that they inhabit rich fertile farming regions and produce subsistence crops like millet, groundnuts, rice, *fonio* (a species of cereal grain), and honey (1949: 21 see pp. 54-6 above for earlier comments.)

24 This is the stress laid on farming by the late al-Ḥājj Ansumana Jakhite-Kabba, Jarumekoto. Shaykh Farūqi Jakhabi, Sutukung, and

Karamokho Sankoung Jabi, Nibrās, make an equally strong case for farming.

25 Karamokho Ba's vision of agriculture as merely a useful background is given in *TKB* (fos 6-7).

26 Khalīfa Silla, Sutukung, 17/11/72.

27 Al-Ḥājj Madi Hawa, Barrokunda, 17/11/72.

28 Al-Ḥājj Shaykh Sidiya Jabi, Brikama, 28/10/72.

29 Chapter 1 of the Qur'ān is *ṣūrah al-fātiḥah*, The Opening, an all-purpose *ṣūrah*, which is memorised before any of the rest of the Qur'ān. It is a ritual *ṣūrah*, necessary for the set prescribed prayer of the *ṣalāt*, as well as a ceremonial formula for every occasion on which Muslims may meet. The *ḥizb* division of the Qur'ān into 16 parts is not related to these stages of the curriculum.

30 Al-Ḥājj Shaykh Sidiya Jabi, Brikama, 28/10/72, described the ceremony at the Qur'ān school of his father, Karang Sambu Lamin, at Sutukung.

31 Al-Ḥājj Madi Hawa, Barrokunda, 17/11/72.

32 *Ṣūrah al-tawbah* (ix: 20, 38-40, etc). The reference to the angels sent down to help the hard-pressed Muslim armies at Badr and their consequent miraculous victory may be related to the verse in the Qur'ān on this topic (ix: 26).

33 Al-Ḥājj Madi Hawa, Barrokunda, 17/11/72. The reference to colour opens a wide subject, discussed at greater length by Shah (1971: 187-9: 368-9). According to al-Ḥājj Madi Hawa the Prophet turbaned one of his leading generals in black. The use of black has a venerable tradition in Islamic Ṣūfī practice, and beyond. There are two Arabic words for black, *aswad* and *faḥum*. The latter is similar in sound to another Arabic word, *fahim*, meaning to understand, to know. It is the play on these two words which has produced phrases like Black Art, the Black Virgins of mediaeval times, and the Freemasons (called in Arabic *faḥḥāmah*, sing. *faḥḥām*, from the word for black). In mainstream Islamic tradition the central religious shrine at Mecca is called the Black Stone (*ḥajar al-aswad*). By substituting the other word, we get *ḥajar al-faḥum*, and by a further slight shift of sound we get, not the Black Stone, but the Stone of Wisdom, of Understanding. Muslim tradition holds that the colour of the Prophet's flag was black, denoting lordship and wisdom. The connection between 'black' and 'wise' is a familiar one in Ṣūfī teaching. Shabistarī, a Ṣūfī dervish, wrote that 'The dervish path is dark in both worlds; yet it is but the gloom that on the horizon of the desert gladdens the wayfarer and tells the tents are near at hand...Within a day of darkness shineth light' (*Secret Garden*, composed in 1319, quoted in Shah 1971: 189).

34 Al-Ḥājj Madi Hawa, Barrokunda, 17/11/72.

35 *ibid.* ᶜUthmān dan Fūdī said he received the turban appointing him a leader of his time (Hiskett 1973: 66). In a more secular tradi-

tion, the turban is used by Bori priestesses as a symbol of authority (Mary Smith 1954: 64).

36 Al-Ḥājj Khousi Silla, Brikama, 11/11/72. The same material was given me by Muḥammad Khalīfa Silla, Kounti. There seems to be wide acceptance of this story. However, my sources deny Quinn's contention that Fode Silla was himself a Jakhanke. For the history of his *jihād*, see Quinn 1972: 170ff.

37 The present *imām*, a Jakhanke cleric, Ba Fode Jakhabi, said that these were the only two occasions he remembered since he came to live in Georgetown in 1928. He had spent his early years at Touba where he was a student before leaving for the Gambia.

38 Al-Ḥājj Ba Jakhite, Wuli-Sutukho, 10/12/72.

39 Al-Ḥājj Soriba Jabi ibn Banfa, Dakar, Feb. 1973. In the West African Islamic reform tradition this was an important area of disagreement between the militant Islamic reform leaders and their pagan or nominally Muslim counterparts whom they accused of perpetrating innovations, stigmatised by them as Satanic practices. It was the conventional *casus belli* for many a *jihād*. The leaders of compromising Muslims of this sort were called *ᶜulamā al-sū'i* 'venal malams' (see Hiskett 1962). The Jakhanke traditional position is that lax Muslims or mixers qualify for consideration just like other Muslims in a *jihād* situation: no one can judge them except God.

40 Mollien 1825: 251. It is evident that the schoolteachers were aware of the shortcomings of the method of multiplying copies of a rare book, and devised ways of controlling the quality of reproduction.

41 Park [1799] 1969: 243. Park says the last page of the Qur'ān was placed in the hands of the student, but this seems highly unlikely. Most probably it was a portion of *ṣūrah al-baqarah* (The Cow), the last stage in Qur'ān studies. Park's account would make it the *Fātiḥah*, a *ṣūrah* so widely known and used that it would be superfluous to test even an elementary student on reciting it from memory, let alone reading it from a script. The fact that a sheet of the Qur'ān was lifted from the volume refers to the practice of carrying the Qur'ān in loose separate sheets rather than in bound volumes.

42 Moister makes mention of this fact (1866: 156). It is not clear if this was the same ceremony as becoming a *fode*.

43 *ibid*. The attitude of Jakhanke clerics towards their students until very recent times was to regard them fundamentally as indentured servants, a class of domestic slaves tied in bondage to their masters with the understanding that after certain unwritten but nonetheless binding contractual obligations were met they could regain possession of their personal and economic rights. It was this persistent and pervasive system of educational servitude which cushioned the Jakhanke clerics against the hard blow which sudden statutory emancipation dealt them (see p. 137 and p. 234 ff.).

44 This is probably the same individual as the one who delivered an authoritative ruling from Mālik b. Anas that the people of the Fezzān should be treated as *jizyah* (poll-tax) paying *dhimmī* rather than as

kuffār pure and simple (*Mudawwana al-Kubrā*, vol. i, p.406, cited in Trimingham 1962: 16n). At the root of this distinction is probably the question of the legality of enslavement.

45 Al-Ḥājj Mbalu Fode Jabi, Marssassoum, 18/1/73; see pp. 115-19 above.

46 Al-Ḥājj Khousi Silla, Brikama, 11/11/72.

47 Muḥammad Khalīfa Silla, Kounti, 30/11-1/12/72. See also p. 195.

48 Al-Ḥājj Khousi Silla, Brikama, 11/11/72.

49 Muḥammad Khalīfa Silla, Kounti, 30/11-1/12/72.

50 For example, a student cannot offer prayers for his master and the master does not seek prayer favours from his student. It is considered that a student achieves the stature of a praying man only after he has been infused with his teacher's *barakah*. But schoolchildren can, in groups, offer 'innocent prayers' for people as such prayers do not require of them any diagnostic competence.

51 Al-Suhrawardī (d. 1234), the spiritual founder of the Suhrawardī *ṭarīqah*, for example, in his influential work, *ᶜAwārif al-Maᶜārif* ('Bounties of Divine Knowledge'), spells out in detail the proper conduct of the *murīd* towards the *murshid* (and elsewhere vice versa), and lists fifteen rules of conduct. Ten of these are relevant to our discussion: 1) reposing complete faith in the Guide in instructing, directing and purifying the Seeker; 2) attending the teacher carefully and closely; 3) complete obedience to the *shaykh* 'in respect to his soul and his wealth'; 4) abandoning all opposition, outward and inward; 5) according his will with that of the teacher: 'without the *shaykh*'s permission, he should not eat, drink, sleep, take, give, look'; 6) observing the *shaykh*'s thoughts; 7) referring his dreams to the Guide for interpretation and diagnosis; 8) lowering his voice when he is before the Guide; 9) addressing his *shaykh* as *sayīd* (prince) or *mawlā* (lord or master); 10) revealing to the *shaykh* his own experiences (1939: VI. 4; trans. 1891: 18-23). This, or identical material, was available to al-Ḥājj Soriba Jabi and some of his students freely admitted to me that it was to obtain some of his *barakah* that many students travelled great distances to come under his direction.

52 Shah 1971: 266. Marty (1921: 131-2) reported a similar attitude on the part of Qutubo's students, see p. 115 ff.

53 The current *shaykh al-mushaykh* (a title implying supreme *shaykh*-like qualities) of the Azmiyāh Order, founded by Muḥammad Maḍī al-ᶜAza'im (1870-1936), gives a precise description of the procedure and symbolic significance of the rite:

> The word *bayᶜah* means taking the pledge, pact engagement or undertaking, and it signifies the occasion when the Seeker places his hands between those of the Spiritual Guide for the dual pledge. One, on his part, binds him to seek the Way indicated by the Guide. The other, on his own part, undertakes to guide the Seeker on the Path (*ṭarīqah*). This is a special, solemn, meaningful moment. There is a dual, mutual interaction in the pledge; a contractual relationship is formalised by it. It is at this juncture that the Seeker may be allowed to call himself *murīd* (disciple), Directed One (Shah 1971: 301-2).

54 The Wolof word *bakan* means both 'soul' and 'nose'. This derives from the Wolof belief that man's soul entered his body through his nose.

55 Cruise O'Brien 1971: 83, where he suggests that the model of a Guide-Seeker, so prominent in Mouride thinking and practice, has its roots in Wolof society rather than in the Ṣūfī Qādiriyāh *tarīqah* from which the Mourides broke away. In fact, this model has a much wider provenance than that, being the core of Ṣūfī orders in Islam. Trimingham writes that, 'the foundation of the orders is the system and relationship of master and disciple...*murshid*...and *murīd*' (1971: 3). It was for this reason that many traditional Ṣūfī orders dismissed the ethical theologian, Abū Ḥāmid al-Ghazālī, on account of the latter's 'inability to submit himself unreservedly to guidance,' saying that his 'books are the mysticism of the legalists' (*inna kutub al-Ghazālī taṣawwuf al-fuqahā*) (al-Sanūsī, *Salsabīl*, p. 9 quoted in Trimingham 1971: 3, 243).

56 Girls in Qur'ān schools seem to have been a rare phenomenon and nowhere in the sources are they given attention. In one other example, mention is made of a girl who was specially educated with a *sharif* in mind as suitor, although the match did not in the end come off (Momodou Jabi, eldest son of Mba Fanta, Mansakonko, 13/12/72. Today, however, there are many instances of girls being put through Qur'ān school, at least up to the elementary stages of recitation (for ritual reasons). In Hausaland it was one of the complaints of ᶜUthmān dan Fūdī and his lieutenants that the old Muslim establishment had neglected the education of women.

57 *Ijāzāt* are not, however, all connected with the Qādiriyāh, and they are also used by a number of other Muslim orders and fraternities.

58 Muḥammad Kebba Silla, Sutukung, 17/11/72.

59 *ibid.* and al-Ḥājj Mukhtār Jabi, Sutukung, 16-17/11/72.

60 Muḥammad Kebba Silla, Sutukung, 16/11/72.

61 Al-Ḥājj Shaykh Sidiya Jabi ibn Karang Sambu Lamin, Brikama, 28/20/72.

62 Ba Fode Jakhabi, Georgetown, 2/12/72.

63 Al-Ḥājj Shaykh Sidiya Jabi, Brikama, 28/10/72.

64 This was al-Ḥājj Ibrahima Sise, better known by his *nasab*, Tankular Sise, now with a *majlis* of his own at Jiroffe, Kiang, Lower Gambia, a predominantly Fula town.

65 Al-Ḥājj Mukhtār Jabi son of Karang Sambu Lamin, on site, Sutukung, 16/11/72.

66 This term has acquired a technical meaning, but its etymology throws significant light on the social nuances which have made it relatively resistant to change. Literally it means 'grass stalk', and has the meaning of grass weeds that need separating from the true and genuine seeds. A derivative meaning is that just as grass weeds

are unregenerative of any kind of crops, so the *nyamakala* cannot produce, or qualify for, inheritable status. Free families safeguard their purity and cohesiveness by maintaining a distance from, and prohibiting union with *nyamakala*.

67 Al-Ḥājj Mukhtār Jabi, Sutukung, 16/11/72.

68 Al-Ḥājj Shaykh Sidiya Jabi, Brikama, 28/10/72.

69 The student in the initial stages of Qur'ān school is considered an uninitiate, usually signified by a partially shaven head with a band of hair extending from front to back, with a circular patch of hair on either side of the band. Sometimes there is only one small patch above the forehead. At the completion of school the student is shaved completely at the passing out ceremony when the patches are removed as a mark of full initiation (al-Ḥājj Shaykh Sidiya Jabi, Brikama, 28/10/72).

70 Al-Ḥājj Shaykh Sidiya Jabi, Brikama, 28/10/72.

71 Ba Fode Jakhabi was to fall foul of the colonial administration in Georgetown many years later (1951) when he was apprehended, charged, tried and convicted of handling stolen cartridges from the colonial stock, and sentenced to imprisonment with hard labour. This was during the time of the Welsh District Commissioner, Glyn Davis. Ba Fode engaged sporadically in hunting and apparently bought some cartridges which, unbeknown to him, had been illicitly obtained from the district office. He cut a particularly sorry figure as he sloped daily to the prison labour camp to work on the rice fields run for convicts, and sat behind bars for the rest of the day.

72 Al-Ḥājj Shaykh Sidiya Jabi, Brikama, 28/10/72. The Qādirī *wird* consisted of the following formula:

1 حَسْبُنا الله وَنِعْمَة الوَكِيل

2 أَسْتَغْفِر الله

3 لا إله إلّا الله الملك الحقّ المُبين

4 أللّهمّ سلّ على محمّد وعلى آل محمّد وتسلّم

The first two sentences are said 200 times; the last two 100 times.

We reckon God our sufficiency and trust in His grace.
(I) beg forgiveness of God.
(We testify that) there is no divinity except God, the true and perspicacious King.
O my God! Peace be upon Muḥammad and upon his family, and blessing.

Cf Gibb 1953: 106. The notion of trust (*al-wakīl*) is a familiar one in Ṣūfī thought in the form *tawwakul* (cf Massignon 1954). A prayer in popular use is called *ᶜalayka tawakkaltu* ('in Thee I have put my trust') (Cragg 1956: 137). Cf. Trimingham 1971: 206n.

73 Karamokho Sankoung Jabi, eldest son of Karam Bekkai, Nibrās 4/12/72. Both Nibrās and Kerewan are situated in a geographical area characterised by an extended depression in the soil where water collects in the rains, and for most of the year it is impossible to reach places behind this loop except by going a long way round it. Hence the name Dumbokono (loop).

74 Karamokho Sankoung Jabi, Nibrās, 4/12/72.

75 Al-Ḥājj Shaykh Sidiya Jabi, Brikama, 28/10/72. Muḥammad Khalīfa Silla enunciated similar motives for establishing the *majlis* at Kounti. He pointed out that the Jakhanke have particularly avoided busy towns, trading posts and colonial administrative centres in order to preserve their students from secular pressures.

76 Marty 1915/6: 456. Marty, improbably, has 1890 as the date of leaving Futa Toro, possibly a misprint.

77 Ba Fode Jakhabi, Georgetown, 2/12/72, his close assistant (*nā'ib*) and later successor. Ba Fode said Muḥammad Fati's pacific turn of mind had the danger of isolating him from the real problems people had, but added that this was the charge to which a saintly life was open.

78 Church Missionary Society Archives: CA 1/047, E.W. Blyden to Venn, 19/1/1872, quoted in D.E. Skinner 1972.

CHAPTER EIGHT

PRAYER, DREAMS AND RELIGIOUS HEALING

> The more innocent form of the superstition, in which the mendicant friar could venture to appear as the competitor of the witch, is shown, for example, in the case of the witch of Gaeta...His traveller Suppatius reaches her dwelling while she is giving audience to a girl and a servant maid, who came to her with a black hen, nine eggs laid on a Friday, a duck, and some white thread...They are sent away, and told to return at twilight...The mistress of the servant maid is pregnant by a monk; the girl's lover has proved untrue and has entered a monastery. The witch complains: 'Since my husband's death I support myself in this way, and I would make a good thing of it, since the Gaetan women have plenty of faith, were it not that the monks balk me of my gains by explaining dreams, appeasing the anger of the saints for money, promising husbands to the girls, men children to the pregnant women, offspring to the barren...' (J. Burckhardt, *The Civilization of the Renaissance in Italy*, New York, 1961: 367)

The Different Kinds of Prayer

The Jakhanke are much concerned with prayer, and prayer itself, in different forms, covers the entire spectrum of clerical work. But first it is necessary to distinguish between the various types of prayer and the categories into which they fall.

Ṣalāt, or ritual obligatory prayer, occupies a prominent place in Jakhanke, as in all Muslim, life. The obligatory ritual prayers are five in number. The first is the Dawn Prayer (*ṣalāt al-ṣubḥ* or *al-fajr*), a prayer consisting of two prayer positions (*rakaᶜāt, rukūᶜ*, sing. *rakᶜah, rakaᶜa*) and comes, as the name indicates just before daybreak. Then there is the *ṣalāt al-ẓuhr* (four *rukūᶜ*) which is performed after midday, *ṣalāt al-ᶜaṣr* (four *rukūᶜ*) performed before sunset, *ṣalāt al-maghrib* (three *rukūᶜ*) at sunset, and *ṣalāt al-ᶜishā* (four *rukūᶜ*) between early evening and bedtime. Muslim tradition has accepted this number of five prayers as binding, although in the Qur'ān itself only fours prayers are mentioned, and even there in a most imprecise way.[1] The *ṣalāt* prayers of this category are a necessity (*farḍ*, *farīḍah*) in Muslim Law for all Muslims.

There are other forms of *ṣalāt* which do not fall into this category but are embraced in a less formal and more voluntary category of supererogatory prayer, called *duᶜā*. In addition to that there are times when a prayer ritual is performed, for example, upon first entering a mosque for prayer (e.g. Friday Congregation Prayer) or before the commencement of Qur'ān recital, or before going to bed. This kind of prayer is called *nāfilah*, additional. In Muslim Law it comes into the category of recommended or meritorious acts (*mandūb*).

Duᶜā,[2] because of its informality and flexibility, is used in varying circumstances, and in clerical activity is usually associated with the possession of *barakah* by whoever performs it. Among the Jakhanke it is used widely to include informal and spontaneous calling down of blessings on clients as well as a more rigorous and disciplined practice of religious retreat, *khalwah*. The length of such retreats also varies, from three days to the traditional Qādirī pattern of forty days as practised by initiates of the Suhrawardī branch of the Qādiriyāh *ṭarīqah*.[3]

Khalwah belongs to a category of prayer activity in which Jakhanke clerical practice has been most prominent. The other forms of prayer may also be listed: the *ṣalāt al-istisqā*, which is a prayer for rain; the *ṣalāt al-khawf*, a prayer in time of fear or anxiety, and *ṣalāt al-istighfār*, a prayer of penitence or asking forgiveness of God. A prayer similar to *khalwah* but much more specific and goal-oriented is the *ṣalāt al-riyāḍat*. Another is *ṣalāt al-ittiqāf*, a prayer of stillness and silence, undertaken for ten days and devoted to recital of the Qur'ān and the performance of *ṣalāt* (of the *nāfilah* category). Another prayer devotion, *ṣalāt al-iᶜtikāf*, requires fasting and may be spent in seclusion in a mosque. Much shorter and less demanding is the *ṣalāt ᶜalā al-nabī*, a prayer of memorial to the Prophet used in intercessory prayer as well as at *mawlīd*, the birthday of the Prophet. This prayer is related to the prayer of greeting to the Prophet (*taḥiyāh*) based on the Qur'ān (xxxiii: 56). A spiritual exercise, called *ᶜilm al-asrār* ('secret, esoteric knowledge') is usually accompanied by prayer devotions; its aim is to bring miracles to pass.[4] There is a large category of prayers known as *ṣalāt al-istikhārah*, prayer of seeking guidance on a choice of action in given circumstances. Its wide use in Muslim clerical activity is well-documented, particularly in the dramatic setting of the clash of armies and similar confrontations. We shall return to this form of prayer presently.

Jakhanke involvement in the practice of prayer commences at the naming ceremony (Ar. *ᶜaqīqah*) of a child with the recitation of the *Basmala*. The words of the *Basmala* are recited softly and then the cleric spits into the ears of the newborn. Usually the child's name is given at the same time. According to the Jakhanke, this seals his Muslim identity and guards him against dangers from the spirit world.[5] This can be supplemented from documentary sources. Mungo Park, during a stay at Kamalia in southeastern Bundu, attended the naming ceremony of a child who was seven or eight days old. The local inhabitants call the occasion *ding koon lee*, a Mandinka term also employed by the Jakhanke which means literally, 'the child's head-shaving'. A festival meal is provided called *dega*, made of pounded corn and sour milk, and rich parents may kill a goat or sheep for the occasion. A Muslim cleric presides whether or not the child's parents are Muslims. He says a long prayer over the *dega* meal first, with everybody placing their right hands on the brim of the calabash. The cleric then takes the child in his arms and says a second prayer asking for the blessing of God upon the child and upon those present. At the end of the prayer he whispers a few sentences into the child's ear, and spits three times into its face. Then he declares the name of the child aloud before returning it to its mother. After that the child's father distributes the *dega* meal in small balls to everyone there. An announcement is made asking for the names of everyone in the town who is ill and such persons receive a generous portion of the *dega* meal now believed 'to possess great medical virtues'.[6]

The next stage in the life of the child as far as the cleric is concerned is at the initiation into Qur'ān school. At that point the cleric receives the child by writing a part of the *Basmala* into the palm of its hand. The child then licks it. Normally, enrolment takes place on a Wednesday.[7] After the ceremony the child is given two balls of pounded meal, one in each hand. It takes the balls home after the cleric has said prayers over them and gives one to its father and the other to its mother.[8] Extensive reference to prayer in Qur'ān schools has been made in Chapter 7.

It may be useful at this stage to consider the category of festival prayers, namely, the *ᶜīd al-aḍḥā*, or Bairam festival. It is rather elaborately and ornately observed. Timed to coincide with the *ḥājj* to Mecca, it involves the slaughter of sacrificial animals. One traveller gives a description of this or a similar occasion in central Guinea. In this instance, all the men were armed with guns, lances, bows and arrows, which were laid aside during the actual prayers. The chief of the area attended the festival prayer on horseback with a 200 to 300 strong escort. The *imām* came later, preceded by one Mamadi Sanici (Ar. Muḥammad Sanūsī), who may possibly have been his *nā'ib* (assistant) but is described as 'chief magistrate'. The *imām* was ornately dressed in a fine scarlet mantle trimmed with gold lace at the fringes, which had been given him by one Major Peddie at Kakandi (Guinea). Both the *imām* and his *nā'ib* were accompanied by escorts carrying white silk banners which were marked by a red figure, probably a crescent or a star, although the source says it was in the shape of a heart. Music was provided by two large drums. The account continues: 'The almamy repeated the prayer with an air of sincere devotion. It was a solemn spectacle to behold so numerous an assembly all kneeling in adoration of their God ' (Caillie 1830: I 266-8). At the end of the prayers the congregation waited to hear the *khuṭbah*, sermon. 'Old men formed a canopy with some white pagnes' beneath which the *imām* sat and 'read a long prayer in Arabic...After this prayer Mamadi Sanici, the chief, harangued the people - asked them to transfer their trade to Wassoulou, Baleya, and the Futa Jallon, saying the road to Bouré was very dangerous and all dealings in that part must be suspended. Then the crowd dispersed' (*ibid*: 268). Women attended on that occasion, but although they joined in the prayers they were seated at some distance from the men. It may be observed that the disquisition on current trade conditions came after the prayer rite proper and did not therefore form any part of the formal devotions. Another festival prayer is the *ᶜīd al-fiṭr* performed at the end of Ramaḍān.

There are random references in documentary sources to prayer activity by clerics, ranging from the obligatory *ṣalāt* to occasions of *duᶜā* (pl. *adᶜiyah*) involving outsiders. This material will be presented before consideration of the important *ṣalāt al-istikhārah*. Jobson refers to Muslim clerics worshipping God, probably a reference to *ṣalāt*. He also says that there is no day of abstinence among the clerics although Friday is regarded as a day of public prayer ([1623] 1968: 84-5). Another story also seems to involve a *ṣalāt* prayer. A cleric arrives at a river bank in the morning, accompanied by his slaves. One of the slaves is carrying a big gourd which he fills with water from the river and takes to the cleric who is waiting at some distance from the river. The cleric uses the water to wash with. Then a second gourd is filled and taken to the cleric who proceeds to wash his hands. A third gourd is brought and the cleric washes his face and then he kneels to pray. He prays first towards the east (*qiblah*) and then towards the west after which he concludes the prayer (*taslīm*) (*ibid*: 87-8).

In *ṣalāt*, obligatory prayer strictly speaking, performed by and required only of Muslims, there is little the cleric can do to include outsiders, and as far as the Jakhanke, always living among strangers, are concerned this imposes a real restriction. But ways have been found to compensate for this apparent limitation, largely through the practice of spontaneous prayer in which both Christians and pagans can be included. By the practice of providing prayer protection for trade caravans, for example, the cleric in general was attempting to infiltrate a buoyant circle of small-scale entrepreneurs with a considerable range of operation. Jobson describes a hazard-fraught river scene where a cleric was accompanying a cattle caravan during a crossing, and, standing in the canoe in which they were travelling, the cleric offered prayers for the protection of the cattle against attack from crocodiles. The cleric, as an extra precaution, was attended by a man with a drawn bow ([1623] 1968: 21). Park observed that the schoolteacher and two of his slave merchants sat between members of a trade coffle (caravan) and the townspeople at a public meeting place. They engaged in a long spontaneous prayer, led by the cleric, after which they walked around the coffle three times (presumably for protection), making marks with the end of their spears. They ended the ritual by muttering something 'by way of a charm'.[9] Examples of prayers for trade caravans can be multiplied, but they do not add much to the general impression we have already formed of clerical involvement with long-distance trade.[10]

The inclusion of outsiders, such as pagans and Christians, in spontaneous or supererogatory prayer is well attested. Park describes one public occasion, this time the appearance of the new moon, when 'Pagan natives, as well as Mahomedans, say a short prayer... This prayer is pronounced in a whisper - the party holding up his hands before his face; its purport (as I have been assured by many different people) is to return thanks to God for His kindness through the existence of the past moon, and to solicit a continuation of His favour during that of the new one. At the conclusion, they spit upon their hands, and rub them over their faces' (Park [1799] 1969: 208; see Soleillet 1887: 460).

We have fuller details of the celebration of New Year's Day among the Jakhanke. This falls in the month of Muḥarram in the Muslim calendar. The New Year celebrations are accompanied by prayer devotions, concluding with a recitation of *ṣūrah al-ikhlāṣ* (cxii) one thousand times. New Year's Day is called by the Jakhanke *Musu-koto salo*, literally, 'old women's prayer'. It is followed by the month of *ṣafar al-khayr* which is celebrated by another elaborate prayer ritual, called *kekoto salo*, literally, 'old men's prayer'. Prayer devotions pervade this occasion, and ideas and notion borrowed from the African cosmology are sustained by supporting them on Qur'ānic foundations. It is believed that during that time of the year 23,000 dangers descend on the world in the form of material deprivation, disease, or spirit-possession. A formidable prayer structure is erected to provide protection for man. A *nāfilah ṣalāt* is performed consisting of four *rukūᶜ*. Each *rakaᶜa* is accompanied by a recitation of the *Fātiḥah*, the opening chapter of the Qur'ān, followed by *ṣūrah al-kawthar* (cviii) ten times, *ṣūrah al-ikhlās* (cxii) fifty times, *ṣūrah al-nās* (cxiv) and *ṣūrah al-falaq* (cxiii) once each. All these *ṣūrāt*, except the *Fātiḥah*, form part of the earliest Meccan *ṣūrāt*. After this a prayer is recited and a part of it written on wooden slates and then washed off; the liquid is subsequently dispensed as an extra precaution against the malevolent forces represented by the 23,000 dangers.[11] The potency of the spirit world is a recognition shared with pagan populations, and in the clerical endeavour to provide preventive or curative prayers the distinction between Islamic and pagan medical procedure becomes tenuous and fluid. At a later stage of this discussion the pagan parallel is treated more fully (p. 207ff.).

The use of one particular form of prayer among the Jakhanke may now be looked at more closely. This is *ṣalāt al-istikhārah*, which has already been mentioned, which also concerns their peculiar involvement in the West African *jihād* tradition.

Al-istikhārah

Before discussing its importance in Jakhanke relations with *mujāhidūn* in the nineteenth century and its use in other spheres of Jakhanke activity, we first examine the form and content of *al-istikhārah*. According to one authority the term means 'entrusting God with the choice between two or more possible options, either through piety and submission to His will [such people are called *akhyār*], or else through inability to decide for oneself, on account of not knowing which choice is the most advantageous one [these are called *mustakhīrūn*]' (Fahd 1974: 259).[12] *Al-istikhārah* can be a very complex discipline. In undertaking it, 'the cleric advises his client to recite certain Qur'ānic phrases after each *rakᶜa* of the next ritual prayer, then shielding his mouth with his hand to whisper his request. After that he must lie down where he will not be disturbed, on the right side, placing his right hand under his ear. He receives the answer in the form of a dream which the cleric interprets. He prays two *rakᶜas*, incorporating a *ṣūrah* appropriate to the request, recites a *dhikr* [litany] of one of the names of God until he is almost asleep when he makes his request, and continues with the *dhikr* until he falls asleep' (Trimingham 1959: 123). There is no limit of time or space determining when the dream will in fact occur.

According to Daumas and de Chancel (1856), *al-istikhārah* can be the means of obtaining knowledge about the true state of affairs. For example, the author says that when he undertook *al-istikhārah*, he received information about the state of his family. The method is described in some detail. After defining it as the procedure by means of which man gains a means of communication with God through dreams, he goes on to say that in order to obtain this a man of faith performs the ablution (*wuḍū*) as for *ṣalāt*, in the first half of Thursday night. Then in the second half he performs two *rukūᶜ* during which he recites the following prayer:

> Dieu de l'univers, j'implore de ta bonté que cette nuit tu me montres en rève ce qu'il est bon que je sache. Par le grandeur du Prophète - que la prière et le salut soient sur lui - s'il y a du bien ou du mal, fais-le-moi voir. O mon

> Dieu, lorsque tu dis d'une chose 'koun' (sois), elle est; ton ordre est entre la *kaf* et le *noun*...Je te supplie, par ton nom sublime et révéré, par le livre des destinées que tu as écrit, par tes prophètes, par tes apôtres, par le saint marabout *un tel*, de me manifester ta volonté. Je te le demande de les sept cieux et tous les anges qu'ils renferment, par les sept terres et tous le animaux et les oiseaux qu'elles nourrissent, par la mer, par les fleuves et tout ce qu'ils contiennent de précieux et de merveilleux; car tu as le pouvoir sur toutes choses. (Daumas et de Chancel 1856: 23-4)

Thus prepared the individual lies down on his right side, next to the tomb of the saint in whose name he has made the invocation, and God will show him in a dream what he has asked for, good or bad. He will act according to what he has seen.

It is clear from this description that *al-istikhārah*, unlike *khalwah*, can be performed by any Muslim, indeed by any 'man of faith' ('un homme de foi'). For an uninitiate, on the other hand, it is dangerous to tamper with *khalwah*. There is a tradition which says that some men engaged in *khalwah* were visited by *jinn*. The latter brought them news of al-Ḥājj ᶜUmar whom they wanted to meet but had not been able to up to that point. However, on other occasions men in *khalwah* received strange visitations, and 'some came out of *khalwah* silent, some came out saying do thus and so, and some came out insane.'[13]

According to a Jakhanke cleric, *al-istikhārah* is opened with a recital of the *Basmala*, followed by the *Fātiḥah* up to verse 5, then a portion of a *ṣūrah* is recited after which the intention (*niyāh*) is declared. Then follows *ṣūrah al-ikhlāṣ* (112), *ṣūrah al-falaq* (113) and *sūrah al-nās* (114). The rest of the *Fātiḥah* is recited to the end. The individual then cups his hands and spits into them. This procedure sets the individual up for the next two stages: declaring the request and adopting the proper position for sleep. When the individual gets an answer involving a dream he generally resorts to the cleric for interpretation.[14]

Al-istikhārah and the Senegambian Jihād Wars

> The King has asked and given us a choice of taking up arms and joining battle, and, on the other hand, building a fortress. We have said, if we are asked to build a fortress we shall build it, and if we are asked to take up arms and join battle, we shall build a fortress. We are entirely at his beck and call. (Traditional Jakhanke saying, Senegambia; see Chapter 4).

It is convenient to consider in the discussion of *al-istikhārah* the nature and extent of Jakhanke involvement in the West African *jihād* tradition since this potentially shows a measure of divergence from their pacific tradition. Although the Jakhanke have not themselves taken up arms against their political rulers, they have been instrumental in providing prayer support for military figures, either by remaining at home and engaging in specialised prayers for their clients or by directly aiding the cause of their spiritual protégés by specifically assigning clerics to war leaders. At the outset of a campaign prayers may be offered, or before a battle guidance and protection can be sought through prayer. In some cases the Jakhanke may even be involved in prayer-duels with their opponents, and this is to be distinguished from undertaking prayer assignments on behalf of their clients in order to subdue opposing forces.

Prayer was thus the most prominent form of Jakhanke participation in the nineteenth century *jihād* wars of Senegambia. This was a service the Jakhanke cleric gave in common with other Muslims in different parts of the Western Sudan and Fisher (1971) provides information on the military association of *al-istikhārah* in the wider African Muslim content. Trimingham writes that the Fulbe leaders 'who initiated jihads during the last century went into retreat before the announcement of their mission and before undertaking an expedition, consequently their followers regarded their orders as the oracle of God.' [15] Elsewhere he is more specific: 'jihad leaders of the last century all employed the dream method (*ṣalāt al-istikhārah*). Before making a decision they went into retreat to receive guidance...' (1968: 84).

Fode Kabba Doumbuya (d. 1911), the Senegambia *mujāhid*, opened his military operations with a request to the Jakhanke clerics to perform *al-istikhārah* for him. There is an abundance of material in oral sources. Fode Kabba was himself of Jakhanke stock. His mother's father was Jaghun Fode, also known as Jagha Salimu, of Didécoto, Bundu, the brother of Karamokho Ba. Fode Kabba's mother was Hawa Gassama.[16] He and his father, Bakary Doumbuya, left Bundu-Gumbael and came to Niani-Tantukunda where Fode Kabba was placed under the personal tutorship of Simoto Kemo (see Map 5). His father left there and travelled to Niani-Dobo and to Kerewan-Dumbokono, Fuladu East. Bakary Doumbuya carried on some commercial activity alongside his normal teaching functions, and when he came to Fuladu East he took control of a transit port called Pirifu on the river Gambia, now no longer extant. By assuming control of Pirifu, Bakary Doumbuya came into direct conflict with the commercial oligarchy of neighbouring Chakunda. The people of Chakunda forced their way into Pirifu to collect customs dues and Bakary Doumbuya and his party turned them away. Incensed at the way they were treated, the people of Chakunda resolved to bring force to bear. An attack was launched against Pirifu which was successfully resisted. At this point Bakary Doumbuya asked the Jakhanke clerics of Bundu to perform *al-istikhārah* for him and advise him of what the future held in store. The results predicted that conflict on a major scale was inevitable and Bakary Doumbuya was advised to take certain precautions, including making an offering of a slaughtered bull. Soon after that a second attack was launched against Pirifu which met with the same fate as the first one. At this point Fode Kabba joined forces with his father and together they sacked Chakunda and a number of other towns in the Upper Gambia region. At Songkunda, however, they met with stiff resistance and were repulsed. Fode Kabba then turned to Alfa Molo, the Fula warrior, for support, and a precarious alliance was formed which soon failed.[17]

Although the Jakhanke performed prayers for Fode Kabba and his following, they refused to take part in military operations because of what was described to me as a fundamental scruple that Fode Kabba's military operations had none of the characteristics of a *jihād* and that even if such operations could qualify as one the Jakhanke would not be able to provide material support beyond a token blessing. They were prepared to see the early stages of the conflict as preventive action (Jakhanke: *monebai*) but were reluctant as a group to endorse the later stages.[17] But this attempt to make a neat and sharp distinction between preventive war and offensive operations may represent a mythical ideal rather than practical reality. The Jakhanke have had plenty of time to work out such a theory.

According to another oral account, before opening his operations Fode Kabba appealed to the Jakhanke for support, including the performance of *al-istikhārah*. To justify this appeal to his fellow Muslim Jakhanke, Fode Kabba compared his career to that of the Prophet at Medina. His daily regime was self-consciously Muslim: strict adherence to the five daily prayers, an observance of Muslim dietary rules (such as a prohibition on consuming carrion or flesh not properly bled according to rules of *dhabaḥ*, pork, and reptiles), and a ban on alcoholic drinks. A Jakhanke cleric, Fode Bakary, from the Darame *qabīlah*, was adopted by Fode Kabba as his war chaplain. At a critical stage in the proceedings when Fode Kabba, shunned by most of the Jakhanke, which much depleted his moral and spiritual reserves, faced the combined fire of the English and the French and defeat was inevitable, a number of people were evacuated from Medina (Fogny) to Morikunda (Casamance). These included Buraima Doumbuya, Fode Kabba's eldest son, Sidiya Darame and Ba Jimmo Darame, both sons of Fode Bakary Darame. Sidiya Darame was later fetched from Morikunda by a relative of his, Ta Mbemba, and came to settle in Danfakunda, Upper Gambia, where he became the leader of the Jakhanke clerical establishment.[18]

It is not, however, true that the Jakhanke allied themselves with war leaders only on the condition that they espouse the cause of Islam. An example is the career of Musa Molo (see Quinn 1971: 437-40; also Marty 1915/6: 448-52). Musa Molo was essentially a secular military leader, and his movement, directed initially against local aristocracies like the Mandinka of Firdou who had been defeated by Alfa Molo, his father, before the latter's death in 1881, was aimed at restoring Fulbe hegemony in Senegambia. He had no explicit religious programme except a longstanding feud with Fode Kabba. Musa Molo was in touch with the Jakhanke and had as cleric-in-attendance Fode Shaykhu Silla, originally of Bundu-Banī Isrā'ila (see pp. 162-3). He performed prayers for Musa Molo and followed his campaigns. But Fode Shaykhu broke with Musa Molo when he learned of the latter's plans to attack Jarra-Bureng. The leading Jakhanke cleric at Bureng was Muḥammad Sanūsī, a refugee from Bundu which he had abandoned following disagreements with the *mujāhid*, Momodou-Lamin (see p. 85). He came to Bureng before he moved finally to Kounti. Fode Shaykhu, concerned for Muḥammad Sanūsī's safety, leaked the news of Musa Molo's impending attack, and after this incident he appears to have severed all connections with Musa Molo.[19]

Prayer also figures prominently in the split between Momodou-Lamin and the Jakhanke of Bundu (see pp. 80-88). It is reported that after fruitless attempts to secure the collaboration of the Bundu Jakhanke, Momodou-Lamin turned to one Fode Ansumana Darame for help, presumably because both came from the Darame *qabīlah*. It is said that when Fode Ansumana received the message he turned his prayer rug right side down, and proceeded to lead the prayers from that position. His meaning is said to be that he and his people valued no submission other than the one to God, even if that was to be at some cost, and that whichever way they turned, or were made to turn, it would have to be in the direction of prayer to God. They would give their loyalty to Momodou-Lamin, that is, they would never betray him and would pray for him, but would never surrender that loyalty in his cause. Momodou-Lamin, riled by this rebuff, threatened to crush Fode Ansumana and his party by superior military force. Fode Ansumana answered by vowing to disinherit Momodou-Lamin through special prayer techniques. With that impasse reached Fode Ansumana and his party evacuated Bundu-Bakadaji, which Momodou-Lamin sacked, and came to Gamou, or Gamon, where they were welcomed by the chief, Filifeng.[20] From Gamon, Fode Ansumana and his people crossed a river at Kulontu where he is reported to have caused the river to part by special prayer, *ᶜilm al-asrār*.[21] Shortly after he was established at Jimara-Bakadaji, Musa Molo, in alliance with some European forces, rounded up Momodou-Lamin and cornered him at Niani-Kayaye where he was captured and beheaded.[22] Musa Molo seized the wife of Momodou-Lamin and brought her alive to Fode Ansumana at Bakadaji, who subsequently married her, thus fulfilling the prophecy he had made to Momodou-Lamin in Bundu about disinheriting him. About twelve years had elapsed from the time of the split between Fode Ansumana and the death of Momodou-Lamin (1887).[23]

Jakhanke links with Samori Toure (d. 1898), though most important for the trade benefits, also featured prayer support which in its turn ensured rewards for the Jakhanke. Samori himself is said to have been initiated into the Tijāniyāh Ṣūfī *ṭarīqah* by one al-Ḥājj Mukhtār Jabi at the latter's *zāwiyah* in Mecca and to have provided contacts for him in Bunduku.[24] This is a rather surprising story, for if, as seems likely, al-Ḥājj Mukhtār Jabi was a Jakhanke it would have been highly unusual for him to be a Tijānī *muqaddam*. The claim for Samori's Tijānī affiliation must similarly remain an open question. Nevertheless, Samori was in active contact with Jakhanke clerics who prayed for the success of military operations by Samori's forces. Samori rewarded such prayer efforts liberally, often in the form of captives.[25] A Bundu Jakhanke cleric, Bakari Jabi, once went to pay Samori a visit. Samori, appreciative of the honour, gave him fifteen slaves as a gift, but this got Bakari Jabi into trouble after he returned to Bundu. Boubakar Saᶜada, then reigning in Bundu, an ally of the French who had rewarded him with the Légion d'Honneur (Rançon 1894a: 107), seized the slaves and placed Bakari Jabi under strict surveillance because of suspected links with Samori with whom the French were at war.[26] The reference to Samori's contacts with clerics in Bundu is confirmed by another account which says that Sillacounda and Samecouta, both centres in eastern Bundu in the area called Niokholo, had a glut of captives taken in Samori's wars (P. Smith 1965a: 255-6). One local informant recalls the time when his father went on horseback to supervise slaves working on the farms (*ibid*).

Touba itself appears to have participated widely in prayer activity for military purposes. Dr Gouldsbury, who visited the town in June, 1881, described it as the largest town in the region with about 800 houses. He noted especially its immense religious/clerical stature and called it 'the Canterbury of the country. When the Foulahs are about to make war they send to Toobah to invoke the prayers of its priests for success in their enterprise.'[27]

Prayer and the Foundation of Clerical Centres

The Jakhanke have used prayer, including *al-istikhārah*, as part of the process of community renewal (*tajdīd*), particularly in the area of undertaking new ventures and founding new centres. As we have seen Banī Isrā'ila is said to have been founded following *al-istikhārah* which was accompanied by the miraculous presence of the Prophet in the company of Jacob and others (see p. 49). In this instance *al-istikhārah* was confirmed by a request-granting dream, *ru'yā al-ṣāliḥah*. The Silla Jakhanke henceforth looked to Banī Isrā'ila as their spiritual home. Similarly, Karamokho Ba is said to have founded Touba following a dream (*ru'yā al-ṣāliḥah*) by his senior wife, Nana-Ba, and some prayer devotions (*TKB*: fo. 5). Karamokho Ba's miracles also involved prayer and dreams. For example, after he had performed specialised devotions which *TSK* (fo. 7) describes as *ᶜilm al-asrār*, he had a dream in which God answered his prayers and he was then able to perform the miracle of removing an impediment to shipping in a river in what is now Sierra Leone, which service earned him the reward of a princess as wife (see p. 101 above).

The role of prayer in Jakhanke clerical activity dates from very early times and bears the imprint of al-Ḥājj Sālim Suware himself. In the story of the Kabba *qabīlah* we have seen how the two sons of Hamjatou Kabba, Yaᶜlā and ᶜAmārah, relinquished their title to the gold inheritance which their father left for them and instead allowed al-

Ḥājj Sālim to keep it for his own use. Al-Ḥājj Sālim in turn endowed the Kabba *qabīlah* through them with a power of prayer so that the Kabba became pre-eminent for their efficacious prayers (*mustajību al-daᶜwāt*) (see p. 42 ; and *TSK*: fos 4-5). On religious ceremonial occasions, the Jakhanke have a tradition that the Kabba-Jakhite *qabīlah* shall lead in the performance of the supererogatory prayer of *duᶜā*. The founding of a separate Kabba-Jakhite clerical order is traced back to the time when they first assumed this role.

Sainthood (Wilāyah) and the Cult of Saints among the Jakhanke

The question of saints in Islam, particularly in Ṣūfī Islam (cf Goldziher [1889/90] 1967/71: II 259 ff), is of cardinal importance, and we should expect the Jakhanke clerics, already familiar with sources on the Ṣūfī way, to pay some attention to it in their clerical life and practice. The traditional attitude of outside students of West African Islam has, however, been to relegate it to an insignificant position. Yet there is incontrovertible evidence that a considerable tradition of saint veneration has been maintained among the Jakhanke, and the problem is to define this tradition in such a way that it is not made to resemble a full-blown cult.

Marty, for example, emphasises that the cult of saints does not exist among Muslims in Black Africa, including the Jakhanke, in the way that the cult is prominent among the Moors and in the Sahil region. He says, 'Il est encore inexact de dire que les tombeaux des saints de Touba [Binani] attirent les pèlerins. Ces pieuses visites aux sépultures des grands marabouts, si en honneur en Afrique du Nord, sont absolument inconnues en pays noir, chez les Diakanké comme chez les autres peuples islamisés' (Marty 1915/6: 359). Trimingham also writes that while the cult of saints 'is the focal point of the religion of the whites of Sahara and Sahil regions and amongst Negro people (Wolof in particular) in the Senegal and borderland regions influenced by Moors [it] is not an integral part of the religious life of most West African Negroes' (1959: 88).

This is surprising, particularly when it is realised that among the Jakhanke the saint cult persists in embryonic form in 'the continuity of veneration after death' which Trimingham regards as the crucial test of the existence of the cult (*ibid*: 89). While the cult certainly is not a prominent feature of West African Islam, nevertheless an active prayer devotion exists around the tombs of saints. This is not confined to the Jakhanke. ᶜUthmān dan Fūdī's sacred remains, as well as those of his relatives, are preserved in Sokoto at the memorial tomb, *Hubbaru*, which has become an imposing mausoleum in the religious landscape of Sokoto and the surrounding areas. Pilgrims flock there from numerous parts of West Africa and devotees surround the richly adorned tomb uttering supplicatory and intercessory prayers.

Among the Jakhanke there is a similar practice. For example, the burial ground of Karamokho Ba became such a centre of pilgrimage. People undertook long journeys to have their various petitions made at the side of his grave as well as those of his relatives. Such veneration of the dead, although it never grew into a cult with special ritual features and an independent religious code, has its source in a similar environment of ancestral worship. Soriba describes the pilgrimage scene at Karamokho Ba's tomb and says the *ziyārah* there is another of the miracles vouchsafed to him, of even higher merit, *ziyārah ḍarīḥahu fahadhihi hiya ghāyah al-karāmah min Allāh taᶜālā*... (the pilgrimage to his tomb and this was the utmost limit of a miracle from God the Almighty...').[28]

The tradition of prayers at the graveside of Muslim saints may not be connected with a saint cult in the technical sense of that term, but it is part of the phenomenon of saint veneration and wonder-working widely diffused in West African Islam. A well-known case is that of the *qāḍī* ᶜUthmān Darame of Tendirma. His tomb became a popular religious centre where prayers were offered for the cure of various ailments. The author of *Ta'rīkh al-Fattāsh* says that an active devotional life continued at the tomb which was located behind the main mosque of Tendirma: all wishes made there were fulfilled and diseases cured (Kaᶜti 1913: 169-71, Ar. 90-1). It would appear that ᶜUthmān Darame acquired a strong religious following in his lifetime, represented in one instance by a miracle which occurred when uncooked rice left for him by his mother in the dish was later discovered changed into a cooked meal enhanced with various spices and condiments, and that after his death people still continued to believe that some spiritual efficacy attached to his tomb.

The tombs of founders of Jakhanke clerical centres are consistently venerated. The site of the grave of al-Ḥājj Sālim Suware became a treasure of religious feeling and devotion at Diakha-Bambukhu.[29] Mama

Sambou's grave, or the one alleged to have been his, was a centre of attraction for successive clerical generations at Sutukho. It is claimed that the *sulṭān* Muḥammad Rimfa (of Kano) asked to be buried at the site of the grave where ᶜAbd al-Raḥmān Jakhite was buried so as to benefit from the latter's *barakah*.[30] Karamokho Bekkai's tomb in Nibrās continued as a centre of pilgrimage for private religious groups. Muḥammad Sanūsī Silla, the founder of Kounti, was buried on the left side of the *miḥrab* on the outer verandah of the main mosque, and prayers are offered at his graveside.[31] Such holy grave-sites were invariably visited and prayers offered before any important project or venture was undertaken, or for health, blessing, protection and guidance. Acceptance into Jakhanke clerical communities, an easy matter in general, was facilitated by the presentation of guests and visitors at the tomb of the original founder, for the belief is held that even after death the spirit of the pious patriarch continues to keep guard over the centre to preserve it. This is also related to the concept of sainthood (*wilāyah*), for the Jakhanke patriarchs are held to be saints whose intercession on behalf of their members is sought and prayed for.

The Jakhanke view is contained in a section of Soriba (n.d.: 199) which goes into considerable detail on the qualifications for sainthood, and since this discussion follows closely on an earlier one on the miracles of Karamokho Ba it is relevant to an understanding of the prayer power attributed to holy men. One of the important qualifications is the capacity for inner spiritual reform evidenced by his headship of a Ṣūfī order (*iṣṭilāḥ al-ṭā'ifah al-ṣūfiyāh*). A saint must consequently be prominent in divinely attested works, to be distinguished sharply from acts of revolt or rebellion (*maᶜṣiyah*). His second qualification is to shun all works of violence and causing harm and to rely solely on God, the true reality, keeping in mind and being on his guard about things which concern His praise. His capacity for distinguishing between various classes of wrong and disobedience must be unimpaired and his resolve to conform to divine norms unwavering (*ibid*). The saint is required to do this in consonance with the Qur'ānic verse which says: 'God is the protector of those who believe' (ii: 258). His third quality is to make common cause with the upright (*al-ṣāliḥīna*), following the verse in the Qur'ān: 'Thou art our Protector. And help us against the people of the unbelievers' (ii: 286). Both Qur'ānic verses contain the root *walī* (pl. *awliyā*) saint. Some stress is put on the fact that God is on the side of the faithful, and the saint is a leader among such people. Furthermore, a saint is expected to be in close communion with God if he is to benefit from the numerous spiritual gifts bestowed on the *awliyā* (Soriba n.d.: 199).

Trimingham writes that the veneration of saints, so prominent among the Jakhanke, 'is a different thing from the power of *barakah* and on the border line with magic' (1959: 89). But this distinction does not exactly fit the case. The example of Shaykh Fanta Madi Kabba (1878-1955), a Jakhanke cleric popularly ascribed the honorific 'Sharīf of Kankan' and of wide religious renown throughout the Western Sudan, is a well-attested instance of a man who rose to the status of a saint to whom numerous miracles and wonders were attributed (*ibid*). The Jakhanke themselves encourage visits to the tombs of saints, usually founders of flourishing clerical centres. The evidence is that all the outward forms of a cult of saints are maintained even though the full doctrine of cult worship or a culture of ritual veneration is certainly missing. What is therefore surprising is not the presence of vestiges of a cult, but that, given the bridge of such close resemblances, the Jakhanke do not seem to have gone over completely to the cult. All the necessary criteria for the emergence of saint cults exist in Jakhanke Islam except for a predilection for saint worship among adjacent populations. This is crucial, for there is little doubt that the Jakhanke, so conscious of good public relations and alert to the advantages of rendering religious or clerical services, would have exploited to the full a commodity which they have in abundant supply. 'But with Negroes in general, although public opinion canonizes devotion, learning, or manifestation of power in the living, no account is taken of these same men when dead. This is perhaps related to the fact that pagan Sudanese pay little attention to the graves of ancestors once the full ceremonies have been accomplished. This is connected with their idea of the personality of man which is severed from the disintegrating corpse, whereas Islamic belief links the soul with the corpse, one day to be resurrected, which it visits and to which honour can therefore be paid' (Trimingham 1959: 90-91).

The Power of Prayer to Curse

A category of prayer for which the evidence is very weak indeed among the Jakhanke is prayer used as a curse, that is to say the exploitation of prayer to harm, thus inducing fear and respect for the cleric.

There are many examples of this category in other parts of Muslim Africa, but the Jakhanke are not known to have used prayer in this way. The instances when prayer has been used as a weapon are those in which the Jakhanke have been in conflict with their neighbours: the example of Fode Ansumana Darame and Momodou-Lamin is one case (see pp. 195-6). and another is the example of Karamokho Ba and Bakari Tamba who had imprisoned Karamokho Ba's son (see p. 109). In neither instance, however, did the use of prayer appear effectively to prevent acts of hostility, and in the second example it is not even certain that prayer came into it, although the religious stature of Karamokho Ba carried weight in itself. In the Momodou-Lamin episode what happened was a fulfilment of a prayer prophecy. Outside the Jakhanke tradition, however, prayer has sometimes acted to protect apparently exposed or vulnerable Muslim individuals and groups.[32]

In one example, however, prayer ceremonies appear to have played a major role in preserving a Jakhanke clerical community from outside interference, a form of protection against the harmful effects of political intervention from the state. In the time of the Mali empire, the corporate clerical integrity of the Jakhanke in the holy town of Gunjūr was not only safeguarded but became the basis on which they received political deference. What prayer might have afforded to them by way of protection they obtained through a reputation for saintliness and religious power. On the night of the 26th Ramaḍān, the king would visit Gunjūr and make a food offering which he gave to children. The food would be consumed and afterwards the children would pray and call down blessings on the king. This prayer ritual was the only occasion on which the king would enter the clerical town; for the rest of the time he would act only through the *qāḍī* of Gunjūr, (Ka^{c}ti 1913: 315; see also p. 28).

Dreams and Dream-Interpretation

Prayer and dreams overlap to a considerable extent in Jakhanke clerical activity and, as we have seen, in *ṣalāt al-istikhārah* the two are inseparable. In that context prayer is the medium through which dreams, particularly 'Prospective Dreams' (ones in which the dreamer receives messages of the prospects of a venture) are incubated (see Faraday 1972: 167-73).

Jakhanke notions about dreams derive mainly from the definitive Islamic work on the subject, *Ta^{c}ṭīr al-Anām fī Ta^{c}bīr al-Manām* by ^{c}Abd al-Ghanī al-Nābulsī (1641-1731). This is a two volume manual of nearly 700 pages. There is a smaller, more popular work, *Ta^c^bīr al-Ru'yā* attributed to Muḥammad bin Sīrīn (d. 728). Bin Sīrīn is also quoted as the author of another popular work on dreams which appears to be widely use in Black Africa (Trimingham 1959: 122). A tradition attributed to the Prophet is quoted to provide normative support for dream activity. According to al-Nābulsī, 'the Prophets used to think of dreams as divine inspiration (*al-waḥī*) and to see them as concerning sacred laws (*al-yuhimmu fī sharā'i^c^i al-aḥkām*): "thus Prophecy has passed, and only the envoys of glad tidings (*mubashshirāt*) remain - sound dreams which a man sees or which are shown to him in sleep."'[33] Al-Nābulsī makes a distinction between different types of dream which provides the accepted orthodox framework for dream classification. There are three broad types: dreams of good news from God which are sound dreams recorded in the Ḥadīth; dreams of ill-omen from Satan; and finally, dreams that originate from auto-suggestion or from the self (*ru'yā mimma yuḥaddathu bihi al-mar' nafsihi*).[34] Al-Nābulsī gives a detailed account of the origin of dreams (and visions) in Islamic thought and although the tradition goes back to Joseph, the archetypal dreamer (*ṣūrah* xii), the sanction for it is derived directly from the experience of the Prophet himself - a far more convincing argument than pronouncements attributed to the Prophet. In a tradition (Ḥadīth) originating from the Prophet's wife, ^c^Ā'isha (local variant Aisatou), it is reported that the Prophet told Abū Bakr of a dream he once had. He said that he saw Abū Bakr and himself raised on a ladder and then Abū Bakr climbed two steps on the ladder and turned to him and said: 'Oh, Apostle of God, God has rushed to your side with His mercy. I shall outlive you by two and a half years' (Nābulsī n.d.: I 3). According to the account this dream experience preceded the granting of the spirit of Prophetic revelation (*al-waḥī*) and it is the close connection between *al-waḥī* and *ru'yā al-ṣāliḥah* which has enabled Muslim authorities to list *ru'yā al-ṣāliḥah* as a forty-sixth part of Prophecy (Sīrīn n.d.: 3). Al-Nābulsī (*loc. cit.*) goes even further and claims dreams are an integral part of sound faith: 'He who does not believe in dreams does not believe in God and the Last Day.' To quote al-Nābulsī again: 'The knowledge (or science) of dreams is the first science since the beginning of creation and has never ceased to be bestowed on all Prophets...who were instructed regarding the science until their Prophethood was demonstrated by means of it' (n.d.: I 3). In the case of the Prophets this science of dreams includes both the faculty of dreaming and the gift of dream-interpretation (*ta'wīl al-ru'yā*), that is, the power to penetrate immediately to the meaning of dreams, to be distinguished from other kinds of dream analysis (*ta^c bīr al-ru'yā*) by means of acquired skills.

Dreams played a significant role within the Jakhanke clerical order, similar in fact to the role they played in the general Islamic Ṣūfī tradition. This is a vast subject in itself, and its serious investigation is only just beginning (see Grünebaum and Caillois 1966 *passim*). Trimingham says that dreams form an important part of the formation of a new Ṣūfī *ṭā'ifah*, order, and observes that among the Khalwatiyāh the members 'cultivated the practice of dream-interpretation (*ta^c bīr al-ru'yā*), so much so that some of the leaders have said that it is the pivot (*madār*) upon which their Path rests' (1971: 158, quoting al-Sanūsī). He also quotes ibn ^cAtā Allāh's definition (*Miftāh al-Falāh*, II 95) of what seems to be a visionary experience. In this connection a vision of al-Khaḍir (cf Qur'ān xviii: 64-81), 'the spirit of Islamic gnosis', is important in respect of sainthood and the founding of a new *ṭā'ifah*. People who dream this way can equally have a vision, the former experienced while sleeping and the latter while awake.[35] The ethical theologian, Abū Ḥamid al-Ghazālī was under the instruction of his guide and master (*murshid*) Yūsūf al-Nassāj in Ṭūs when, in his own words, he 'was vouchsafed revelations (*wāridāt*) and saw God in a dream'.[36] No hard and fast line seems to be drawn between dreams and visions and both are central to the religious code of Ṣūfī brotherhoods as well as commonplace in the religious experience of the Jakhanke.[37]

In the dream which ^cĀ'isha reported from the Prophet, in which the missionary character of Islam is described, Abū Bakr is said to have remarked to the Prophet that the black and white figures which appeared in the dream indicated that the Prophet's following would embrace the Arab race and non-Arab peoples as well. Two remarks may be made about this statement: a) that the intimation of the death of the Prophet in the dream is now further strengthened by a reference to the success and completion of his mission, and b) that the phrase about God's mercy is now expanded by including in that a universal submission to the Prophet's message. Both that dream and the notion of a missionary enterprise find parallels in Jakhanke tradition. Al-Ḥājj Sālim Suware is said to have left Mecca on his last pilgrimage and embarked for Black Africa on a proselytising mission following a dream (*ru'yā*).

Sometimes dreams may play a significant role in situations of tension and conflict. The tensions which contributed to the break-up of the early Jakhanke community at Diakha-Bambukhu were, for a time at least, held in check by the intervention of al-Ḥājj Sālim in a dream where he appeared to the *qabīlah* leaders responsible for the city. In some situations dreams can play a part in helping to resolve difficulties or clear up a state of indecision. Into this class fall the dreams of many clerics which helped them to decide which place to adopt as a centre. The Silla Jakhanke date the foundation of their separate order to the dream which Fode al-Hasan and his maternal uncle, Muḥammad Darame, had at Banī Isrā'ila. Fode Maḥmūd Jīlānī, the eminent Bundu Jakhanke leader who opposed Momodou-Lamin's *jihād*, was instructed in a dream to found a centre and call it Jīlānī, hence his *nasab*. The village of Jīlānī become an important centre for the Jakhite-Kabba *qabīlah* of Senegambia. Fode Maḥmūd later abandoned Jīlānī, following disagreements with Momodou-Lamin who sacked it, and came to Pakeba (*TKQ*: fo. 6: see p. 84). In one instance a cleric was warned by a dream to vacate a town because of impending danger: Muḥammad Sanūsī Silla was living in Bureng when his father appealed to him in a dream to abandon the town because of an imminent attack. The story says this was a persistent dream which occurred three times.[38] A little later, news of Musa Molo's impending attack was leaked to Bureng (see p. 195). Muḥammad Sanūsī's father, Marang Burema, had been a clerical ally of al-Ḥājj ᶜUmar Ṭāll, and died soon after he left Bundu at a place called Sollu.[39]

Similarly, the Karambaya *qabīlah* of Touba faced a difficult time in this century. One source of anxiety was the dwindling number of students who came there, the cause of which they attributed to changed political circumstances. The death and the events surrounding the last unhappy years of Karamokho Sankoung (see Chapter 6) also seemed to be portents of an inauspicious future. Eventually, around 1955, the Karambaya *qabīlah* evacuated Touba under Sankoung's eldest two sons and heirs, al-Ḥājj Banfa and al-Ḥājj Soriba, and came to Macca-Kolibantang, Senegal. According to local accounts Sankoung himself had prophesied as a result of a dream that his heirs would transfer to Niani Santo, i.e. Upper Niani, where Macca-Kolibantang is situated.[40] Macca-Kolibantang has become a prosperous clerical centre under al-Ḥājj Soriba's pastoral guidance.

The emergence of the Jabi-Gassama lineage into prominence in the person of Karamokho Sankoung's great-grandfather, Karamokho Ba, is itself tied up in part with 'lucid dreams' or, more suitably, 'dreams of knowledge'.[41] Karamokho Ba appears to have used dreams widely in his scholastic career. The birth of his sixth son and heir, Muḥammad Taslīmī, was dreamt about by somebody else and accordingly reported to him (see p. 101). The creation of the successful clerical centre at Touba was similarly dreamt about, in this case by his senior wife, Nana-Ba. In a dramatic setting, news of the death of Shaykh Mukhtār al-Kuntī was miraculously brought to him in a vision while he was leading public prayers (see pp. 108-9). The famous miracle which he performed for King Ishaq Kamara when he removed an impediment to shipping in the local river was recommended to him in a 'Precognitive Dream' (see *TSK*: fo. 7).

Current interest in dreams and dream-interpretation runs very high, although Jakhanke clerics are chary about discussing the dreams of their clients. A few typical examples may be cited. There is a strong tradition among the Jakhanke of the ascent to heaven of the spirits of famous clerics which after death carry out intercessory functions on behalf of their communities. Reports of such ascensions proliferate. It is in this context that the following dream story is set. The leader of the Kounti Jakhanke clerical order, Muḥammad Khalīfa Silla, testifies before a public meeting that three years before the founder of that clerical centre, Muḥammad Sanūsī, ascended into heaven he (Khalīfa Silla) had a dream about it,which he promptly reported to his companions.[42] In a further example, this one involving dream-interpretation, a member of the clerical community had a dream which he reported to the leader. In his dream he saw a woman with legs outstretched plaiting the hair of her husband. The leader of the clerical community interpreted the dream to mean that the woman would conceive and bear a baby girl. When the husband of the woman heard of the dream story he came to see the leader and left some religious offerings.[43] This story is an ideal type for expansion and interpolation, and local versions vary. Some say that the woman was barren until the dream, others that the couple were past child-bearing age. In another dream story, the uncle of Muḥammad Khalīfa Silla dreamt that he saw his own sister laughing and dancing in the nude. Muḥammad Khalīfa interpreted this to mean that a divorce was imminent, which did indeed come to pass.[44] A member of the clerical community, in another example, had a dream which the cleric interpreted to mean an impending epidemic. The cleric then proceeded to prescribe preventive measures for the community. Some 100 Qur'ān verses were written down and washed off as holy water. Animal manure was picked up and mixed with the holy water and the mixture was used for drinking and washing.[45]

Religious Healing

The dream story about the imminent epidemic which was averted by dispensing a prescription for internal and external use is one example of how dreams, prayer and healing are interconnected in general clerical practice. As in certain aspects of prayer and dream activity, in healing the Jakhanke have served a wide religious constituency. Although they have operated in the same area as the traditional herbalists, Jakhanke clerics have not penetrated this area of traditional healing in any depth. They have for the most part limited their activities to utilising the sacred language of the Qur'ān, a province within which they are immune from competition from local non-Muslim priestly clans.

A general, ill-defined area of healing activity is the provision of amulets. Trimingham has indicated the role Islamic amulets played in preparing pagan cultures for the greater infiltration of Islamic elements by weakening the earlier pagan traits. For example, among the pagan Bambara, the phrase *bisimịlay* (Ar. *bismillāh*, in the name of Allāh) is used by the Bambara in sacramental invocations and magical incantations because it is believed to be a phrase of power. The word *ṣadaqah*, freewill offerings, is used for offerings to the gods. Similarly amulets are accepted from Muslim clerics, who also transmit other aspects of the material culture of Islam, without there being any observable shift of allegiance away from the pagan religious culture (Trimingham 1959: 34-5). Since the adoption of amulet-use is several stages removed from an articulate Islamic faith, it bears more of the characteristics of pagan culture than Muslim. What distinguishes Islamic amulets from pagan ones, apart from the sacred Arabic language, is mainly the procedural elements employed to decide whether the means, not the ends, are lawful (*ḥalāl*) or unlawful (*ḥarām*). But this exercise does not change the aims or goals for which amulets might be intended, and what the Muslim cleric offers in its making is a regularised procedure rather than a completely different substitute. The cleric is not denying but rather borrowing and inflating a pagan concept and tradition of spirit-power and control (*ibid*: 112-13). *Taṣrīf*, which equips him in this matter, is the means by which the cleric works out an accommodation to a pagan practice. The path of transition which pagans may eventually adopt is thus facilitated by the cleric.

The Jakhanke use the term *ḥijāb*, plural *ḥujub*, for an amulet.[46] It is also used to mean any phrase from an Islamic ceremony or prayer devotion which is believed to be infused with *barakah* and which is efficacious when retained on one's person, either in the form of a memorised formula or as an amulet. Such *barakah*-charged formulae can also be written down on Qur'ān slates and washed off, the mixture serving as medicine. As a rule, such amulets serve an all-purpose function.

Jobson, visiting the Senegambia region, describes in some detail the function and nature of amulets which he calls 'Gregories'. He says:

> The Gregories bee things of great esteeme amongst them, for the most part they are made of leather of severall fashions, wounderous neatly, they are hollow, and within them is placed, and sowed up close, certaine writings, or spels which they receive from their Mary-buckes [clerics], whereof they conceive such a religious respect, that they do confidently beleeve no hurt can betide them, whilst these Gregories are about them...([1623] 1968:64)

Jobson goes further to tell of the medicinal value of these amulets: they are used for all sorts of maladies and for any swellings or sores on the body; for protecting horses and other animals; men also adorn their weapons with them (*ibid*: 64). Amulets are also used on drinking occasions, and Jobson describes the custom of the King of Casa (his religion is not stated) of pouring a small quantity of liquor on one of the amulets (*ibid*: 77).

Mungo Park provides numerous details on the many uses to which amulets (he calls them, after the Mandinka word, 'saphie') can be put.[47] This is his description:

> These saphies are prayers, or rather sentences from the Koran, which the Mohamedan priests write on scraps of paper, and sell to the simple natives, who consider them

> to possess very extraordinary virtues. Some of the Negroes wear them to guard themselves against the bite of snakes or alligators, and on this occasion the saphie is commonly enclosed in a snake's or alligator's skin, and tied round the ankle. Others have recourse to them in times of war, to protect their persons against hostile weapons; but the common use to which these amulets are applied is to prevent or cure bodily diseases, to preserve from hunger and thirst, and generally to conciliate the favour of superior powers under all circumstances and occurrences of life. ([1799] 1969: 28)

In practice clerics write the requests of their clients inside these amulets in vague and general language. In one amulet, for example, Marty found the following instructions:

> Talisman capital contre tout mal terrestre, provenant de la lance, du sabre, du couteau, de la pierre, du bois, du sultan et des sultans musulmans ou infidèles, mâles ou femelles, tous sans exception. Que personne ne craigne Mamadou Daī. Aucun mal de ce bas monde ne l'atteindre jamais. Par la permission de Dieu Très-Haut, et par la vertu de la cavale Bouraq et du Coran sublime. (1921: 484)

The amulet formula is usually surrounded on the four corners by the archangels: Gabriel, Michael, Ezrael and Ezrafael. Many have the names of the Prophet and God written at the centre, surrounded by Qur'ānic verses. The proximity of amulet-therapy to pagan notions is pointed out by Marty:

> Il est curieux de constater que l'amulette islamique est considérée comme un des grands préservatifs contre les maléfices des agents du fétichisme, ce qui implique donc la croyance à la puissance de ces agents et à la réalité de leur action, tant religieuse que magique. (1921: 484-5)

Psychological disorders and mental ill-health, including various types of phobia and manic-depression, form a significant part of the cases with which Jakhanke clerics deal. Here the cleric is able to relate the Qur'ānic ideas on *jinn*, incorporeal beings inhabiting the terrestrial world, to local notions about spirit power (Trimingham 1959: 103). In one centre in Senegambia there is a vigorous tradition of psychological healing. The story is told of a Jakhanke cleric, Karamokho Sanūsī Suware, who lived and died at Pakao-Sumbundu, and was endowed with powers of exorcism: he would first appeal to the *jinn* to go out of their hosts, and then, if that gentle approach failed, he would resort to harsh words of rebuke and exorcism. On one occasion, Karamokho Sanūsī's father, Momodou-Lamin Suware, who lived at Touba where he was a contemporary of Karamokho Taslīmī, confronted a maniac whom he cured simply by staring into his eyes. A schizophrenic was once cured, presumably by the source of this information, by reciting certain verses from the Qur'ān.[48] There are more precise details available on this question of curing schizophrenia. The first four verses of *ṣūrah al-jinn* (lxxii) are copied from the Qur'ān and written down on a slate and washed off. The liquid is then collected in a container and the patient rubbed with it. Similarly, the mixture can be used for washing the patient. In one example both amulet and prayer are used: this is where a person in the grip of fear or in danger of exposure to the evil eye can recite the last two verses of *ṣūrah al-qalam* (lxviii: 50-52) for self-protection. It is said that the practice goes back to the Prophet for at one Friday *ṣalāt* he recited these verses himself. Later, after the Friday *khuṭbah*, his disciples asked him the significance of the verses. He explained that someone who possessed an evil eye could encompass the death of another person. The recitation of these verses could prevent this.[49] These verses are used for the health and stability of the psychologically insecure and in cases of excessive neurosis.

There are other healing activities concerned with general disorders and preventive work, as well as safety from danger and an assurance of spiritual well-being. Physical ill-health receives some attention but not nearly as much as the other aspects. There is little activity in cases of bodily harm such as fractures, septic wounds, trachoma or other forms of blindness. A person suffering from 'stomach ache', not precisely defined, can be cured through the application of verses 73 to 85 of *ṣūrah al-mu'min* (xl).[49] If such a person died after reciting these verses, his sins would be forgiven, a heuristic clerical device to help protect their own reputation. Another set of verses which is believed to have a wide protective spectrum is verses 129 to the end of *ṣūrah al-tawbah* (ix), popularly known by the opening phrase, '*laqad jā'kum*'. Upon reciting these verses a person is shielded from danger and death that particular day. The story is told of a man who was chased by brigands, who during the hot pursuit managed to recite these verses to good effect: the brigands went temporarily blind and lost their way, enabling the man to escape.[49] A man of prayer but of low popular esteem used to recite these verses and as a result he had a dream one night. In the dream he saw an animal sitting on the lap of the Prophet who expressed his fondness of the animal by gently stroking it. The dream, according to the way a cleric interpreted it, indicated a man's closeness to the Prophet even though in the eyes of ordinary people he was no more than an animal. Explained thus, the man in question acquired an enhanced status and gained recognition.[49]

Two final issues should be considered: the first is the use of power over disease and death as a weapon against other people and the second is the contrast between religious healing and faith healing, with the subsidiary issue of similarities with African Christian examples. As in the case of prayer, the evidence for the use of the power over disease and death either as a deterrent against hostile acts from anti-clerical individuals or groups or as a weapon of punishment is slender. There are no traditions which to my knowledge link the Jakhanke clerics to this practice, and, as we have already seen, even when a conflict breaks out between the Jakhanke and their neighbours the deterrent prayer does not seem to have been effective. There are numerous instances among non-Jakhanke of the use of prayer to retaliate against an injury or wrong or as a threat to force reluctant clients into compliance. I was myself present on one occasion when the diviner, a pagan Fula, told how he was preparing measures to harm a former client of his because the latter had failed to pay the agreed sum for a service he rendered. His comment about clients who did faithfully discharge their obligations was that such clients made the widescale use of the fatal curse difficult to justify! I do not know whether the defaulting client, a highly placed civil servant, complied in the end. When I reported details of this story to a Jakhanke cleric who lived in the same town, without divulging any names because of the rule of secrecy, it was remarked that such activities of harming people or holding them to ransom were not in the way of God.

Nevertheless, the practice of harming through prayer and the fatal curse is widespread in Muslim Africa. It is reported that the first Muslims in Kano in the fourteenth century subdued their opponents by praying successfully against them and they were all struck blind (an instance cited by Fisher 1973: 28). Walad Abū Ṣādiq, the saint from the Nilotic Sudan, in what appears to be Muslim in-fighting, cursed a judge with skin disease because the judge had criticised his marital irregularities (*ibid*).

As to the distinction between religious healing and faith healing, it is one current in Jakhanke clerical practice itself, although the distinction is not an exclusive one: a person taking part in religious healing can pass into the category of faith healing, and vice versa. Faith healing in this tradition requires an initial attitude of faith in the client that the cleric possesses the power to heal so that he is prepared to repose all confidence in him. Religious healing does not require this attitude, so that a schizophrenic or an epileptic in deep coma can be submitted to the methods of religious healing. Whereas faith healing requires the active presence and participation of the client, religious healing does not. A parent can represent his or her child in religious healing but not in faith healing. The prior psychological disposition of trust and reliance on the cleric is essential to faith healing: sometimes that trust and reliance are elicited or prompted by the personal charisma or *barakah* of the cleric and sometimes they depend on an implicit conviction of the utility of Islam.

Faith healing, as opposed to religious healing, is known to have played a prominent role in West African Christianity, for example the Aladura Christian movement. Their founder, Joseph Shadare was guided in a dream during an influenza epidemic in 1918 to form prayer groups (Turner 1967: I 9). The West African patriot and Anglican Bishop, James Johnson, approved the early work of the prophet Garrick Braide in Eastern Nigeria, 'who for seven years healed the sick without taking a penny in return' (Ayandele 1970: 356-7). In the Independent African Church tradition there is a strict insistence that both herbal traditional and modern medicine should be altogether excluded from among religious devotees.[50] Along with this has gone the insistence that, for a person to receive faith healing, conversion was necessary. (For faith healing in general see Fisher 1973: 25-35.)

There is for the Jakhanke a further, perhaps secondary, distinction between religious healing and faith healing. Faith healing can be effected at religious shrines, such as the tombs of saints,[51] and, much more pertinent, it is often practised by clerics as it obviates requiring their clients to be able to manipulate religious symbols. Often a prayer, deeply intoned and whispered into the ear or over the head or outstretched hands of the client is enough. Once the conditions of faith healing are fulfilled, the cleric can, and many in fact do, apply the techniques of religious healing to augment the processes of faith healing. A client can approach a cleric on the basis of faith in him, and the cleric may deliver a powerful prayer on his client's behalf. He may then proceed to prescribe certain procedures for the client in the same way as he will for religious healing. The example of the Senegalese Mouride Brotherhood makes this abundantly clear: a *murīd*, accepting the all-embracing efficacy of his *shaykh*'s *barakah*, is entitled to protection by his *shaykh* from spiritual dangers and to healing in times of illness. At the outset the *murīd* places himself in the hands of the *shaykh* 'like a corpse in the hands of the embalmer', as the vivid phrase has it. As a result the *murīd* receives some of the benefits of his *shaykh*'s *barakah* through direct or indirect physical contact (Cruise O'Brien 1971: 97). Following this, the *shaykh* can, in the event of an illness, perform the functions of the traditional healer and magician. 'Even the Khalifa-General [Head of the Brotherhood] will prepare an amulet under certain conditions, and although payment is not demanded, a gift in return is normal. Others will attempt to cure *ṭālibés* of various illnesses, both physical and mental, through the use of invocations, certain herbs, and holy water' (*ibid*: 105). A final comment: in faith healing the living and the dead can be called upon to cure; in religious healing both client and cleric are in the land of the living.

NOTES

1 Qur'ān xxx: 17; xx: 130; xvii: 80; xi: 116; iv: 104; ii: 40. One Muslim authority comments on the later increase of this number: 'The fact, however, that the prayers were fundamentally three is evidenced by the fact that the Prophet is reported to have combined these four prayers into two, even without there being any reason. It was in the post-Prophetic period that the number of prayers was inexorably fixed without any alternative to five, and the fact of the fundamental three prayers was submerged under the rising tide of the Ḥadīth which was put into circulation to support the idea that the prayers were five' (Rahman 1968: 33).

2 The Qur'ānic basis for *du*ʿ*ā* is in ii: 182: 'And when My servants question thee concerning Me - I am near to answer the call of the caller [*dā*ʿ*wah al-da*ʿ*i*] when he calls to Me; so let them respond to Me.'

3 'The advantage of appointing forty days is that, on the completion of this period, the manifestation begins to appear' (Suhrawardī, trans. 1891: 43). Also al-Ḥājj Soriba Jabi, Macca-Kolibantang, 9/12/72.

4 All these types of prayers are known among the Jakhanke and were discussed at various meeting with al-Ḥājj Shaykh Sidiya Jabi and al-Ḥājj Soriba Jabi, among others.

5 Al-Ḥājj Madi Hawa, Jarra-Barrokunda, 17/11/72.

6 Park [1799] 1969: 206-7. Park says he attended such naming ceremonies four times at different places and did not observe any variation of the formalities.

7 Al-Ḥājj Mukhtār Jabi, Sutukung, 16/11/72.

8 Muḥammad Kebba Silla, Sutukung, 16/11/72.

9 Park [1799] 1969: 249. The reference to spears could suggest that clerics were usually armed but in fact such weapons as they had were carried either for ceremonial purposes or for self-protection, as clerics were normally exempt from bearing arms, see Jobson ([1623] 1968: 99).

10 See, for example, Moore 1738: 102; Mollien 1820; 147, 153; Park [1799] 1969: 32, 250. See also p. 55 ff above.

11 Al-Ḥājj Madi Hawa, Barrokunda, 17/11/72.

12 The prayer is of considerable antiquity. Ibn Khaldūn says he has employed it with excellent results (in *al-Muqaddimah*); ibn Baṭṭūṭa found it a reliable medium (trans. 1929: 10). Tradition indeed credits the Prophet with performing *al-istikhārah* by doing two *rukuʿ*, one a prayer emphasising God's omniscience and omnipotence and the other referring to the subject of consultation (Fahd 1974: 259).

13 Fisher 1970: 64. In discussing dreams of men of *khalwah* the Ṣūfī Qādirī manual makes confused uninterpretable dreams a distinct possibility and danger (Suhrawardī quoted in *ibid*: 51f).

14 Muḥammad Khalīfa Silla, Kounti, 30/11-1/12/72. Marty gives a less specific description of *al-istikhārah* (1920: II 299). This matter of prayer-exercises in the context of dream inducement has wider significance and interest than the specific Jakhanke clerical example. A popular manual directed at introducing a wider audience to the subject gives the following description:

> Prayer is the shield which safeguards the etheric body, and the sleeper now rests with the knowledge that he is available to receive instruction if such can be conveyed to him at the time. Upon entering the sleep state, a sudden dramatic switch is thrown in the mind. The feeling nature is replaced by the mental nature which becomes a reservoir of potential reception. Mind alone does not have motivation or will but is influenced by a greater force than it possesses; this force is similar to the life within a flower which sprouts the seed and pushes its new growth upward through the soil. (Street 1971: 18-19)

For a thorough investigation of the phenomenon of dreams and dream-interpretation see Faraday 1972. The author appears to be in danger in this work of an over-concentration on the psychological significance of dreams and puts less emphasis on the social and practical side.

15 Trimingham 1959: 122. Alfa Ibrahima, also known as Karamokho Alfa, creator of the Futa Jallon theoratic state, is said to have told his wife that he saw in a dream the Prophet, who charged him with a mission

to evangelise. This was apparently the fruit of a retreat which lasted 7 years, 7 months and 7 days. He launched his *jihād* in 1725 as a result of this dream. He died in 1775 (Marty 1921: 3-4). A comparable story of divine commissioning is recounted by ᶜUthmān dan Fūdī (Hiskett 1973); he was enturbaned and invested with the 'sword of truth' (Ar. *sayf al-ḥaqq*) to prepare him for his mission.

16 Charlotte Quinn is confused about Fode Kabba's family background. She says his family 'were Jakhanke Mandingo, a people from Futa Tuba who spoke a dialect of Mandingo different from that of their neighbours in the Gambia states' (1972: 172).

17 Karamokho Sankoung Jabi, Nibrās, 4/12/72. See p. 245-6; and Chapter 4 for a parallel in the case of Momodou-Lamin.

18 Al-Ḥājj Khousi Darame, *imām*, Danfakunda, 12/12/72. During Sidiya Darame's tenure it was decided to upgrade the *masjid* to a *jāmiᶜ*, but Sidiya died before he saw the completion of the scheme.

19 Muḥammad Khalīfa Silla, grandson of Muḥammad Sanūsī, Kounti, 30/11-1/12/72.

20 Al-Ḥājj Janko Darame, Jimara-Bakadaji, 11/12/72.

21 This is a familiar theme in Jakhanke clerical activity. Karamokho Ba was reported to have performed a miracle involving the removal of a large rock in the river. To prevent ᶜAbd al-Raḥmān's departure from Mali all the normal crossing facilities at the river (Niger?) were withdrawn. When ᶜAbd al-Raḥmān arrived at the crossing and found the boats tied at the opposite side of the river, he performed a special prayer and caused the tide to recede and he and his party crossed. (Ḥājj 1968: 9-10; see pp.29-30).

22 For differing accounts of the death of Momodou-Lamin, see pp. 89 and 93 n. 47.

23 Al-Ḥājj Janko Darame, Jimara-Bakadaji, 11/12/72.

24 Holden 1970. This Bunduku is in the Ivory Coast just across the border from modern Ghana.

25 Al-Ḥājj Shaykh Sidiya Jabi, Brikama, 28/10/72.

26 Al-Ḥājj Fode Jabi, grandson of Bakari Jabi, Sandu-Jakhaba, 9/2/73.

27 Gouldsbury 1881. I am grateful to Boubacar Barry for bringing this reference to my attention.

28 Soriba n.d.: 196. In the wider setting of saint veneration in Islam, the visit to the tombs of saints is also important, for it is widely held that 'the saints cure sickness and their prayers are always granted, every saint is a *mujāb al-duᶜā*' (Goldziher [1889/90] 1967/71: II 269).

29 In Niokholo and Dentilia the descendants of al-Ḥājj Sālim considered themselves the inheritors of al-Ḥājj Sālim's *barakah* and

guardians of his saintly relics. At Sillacounda in Niokholo, for example, the Suware clan retained custodial rights over the town, and in an emergency or change of political regime, they dug up the 'amulets' which they believed contained the secrets of al-Ḥājj Sālim and used them to stabilise the town (P. Smith 1965b: 279).

30 Ḥājj 1968: 20. The phrase is *la^{c}allī ajidu barakatuhu*. See p. 31 above.

31 Field-notes on site; Muḥammad Khalīfa Silla, grandson of Muḥammad Sanūsī, Kounti, 1/12/72.

32 A story is recounted of Da, the early nineteenth century Bambara king of Segu, who, in spite of repeated warnings by a *sharīf*, or descendant of the Prophet, began to oppress the Muslims in his area, and was suddenly smitten with illness. When he appealed to a cleric for healing he did not obtain it and instead was told that a frightful fate would soon overtake him: his power would be checked that year, his favoured son would not succeed him and he himself would never be cured. Sometimes clerics, through prayer, inflicted terrible diseases upon those who had abused religious men, diseases which the inflicting cleric removed only after complete repentance and recompense. For those examples see Fisher 1973: 28.

33 Nābulsī n.d.: I 2. The tradition cited as the Prophet's words in the latter half of the quotation has been preserved by al-Bukhārī (d. A.D. 870), *Saḥīḥ*, 91: 5. My translation throughout this passage.

34 *ibid*: I 3. Al-Nābulsī then gives a detailed list of how to recognise dreams which are false and those which are true.

35 This is Trimingham's distinction (1971: 159), but this appears too rigid, although it would be right to say that visions occur during waking hours (and sometimes also in sleep) while dreams take place only in sleep. However, this is a slippery problem. See Fisher, H.J.: 'The Ivory Horn: Oneirology, Chiefly Muslim, in Black Africa', paper submitted to Seminar on Conversion to Islam, Centre for International and Area Studies, University of London, 7/5/73.

36 Reported by Muḥammad al-Murtaḍā, *Itḥāf al-Sāda*, I 9, quoted in Trimingham 1971: 33n. A conflicting tradition is reported by Grünebaum and Caillois 1966: 16.

37 In a different tradition, it is said that Peter the Hermit, who canvassed the idea of the Crusades in Mediaeval Europe, based support for the idea on the dream in which he heard the call to prepare for armed assault (Mackay 1892: II 6).

38 Al-Ḥājj Khousi Silla, Brikama, 11/11/72.

39 *ibid*. Sollu was a town on the boundary between Bundu and Bambukhu, and it was a base of operations for al-Ḥājj ^{c}Umar. For this, see Oloruntimehin 1972: 77.

40 Al-Ḥājj Soriba Jabi, Macca-Kolibantang, 9/12/72.

41 These 'dreams of knowledge' are ones in which the subject is aware,

or made aware, of what is taking place even though he may be asleep. In *khalwah*, for example, to take a specific prayer type, a cleric may receive guidance through the appropriate manifestation (*kashf mujarrad*) as the reward and proof of his deed, i.e. the prayer-retreat. Suhrawardī writes: 'In the midst of *dhikr*, it sometimes happens...from things felt (this world) that they become concealed (in unconsciousness); and that to them become revealed, as to the sleeper of hidden matters. It, the Sufis call *wāqiᶜah* (dream)' (1891: 48, see also pp. 43, 49). Such a category of dreams is classified as dreams from God which only eminent clerics receive. They are perspicacious dreams in which the disguise screen is stripped away and replaced by the direct guidance principle. (Cf Trimingham 1959: 123n.)

42 Kounti, 30/11-1/12/72. It may be pointed out here that the fact of the reporting of the dream to outsiders a considerable time before the event does not necessarily prove the veracity of the dream, and that in this case at any rate the dream method may have been employed to prepare the clerical community for accepting the story once it was reported to them.

43 Muḥammad Khalīfa Silla, Kounti, 30/11-1/12/72.

44 *ibid*. The preponderance of dreams needing interpretation is not unrepresentative, although there are dreams which the dreamer himself can interpret.

45 *ibid*.

46 The concept of *ḥijāb* is widely used in Muslim tradition, but one of its distinctive features is its occurrence in mystical as well as clerical activity. In this connection, one authority defines the concept of *ḥijāb* as 'mystical separation, a supernatural isolation, a supraterrestrial protection, in fact an amulet (*ṭilasm*) which renders its wearer invulnerable and ensures success for his enterprises. A *shaykh* or *faqīr* writes cabbalistic signs and Qur'ānic verses on a sheet of paper which, for a small sum, he gives to petitioners. These writings are considered to be most efficacious and to have the power to attract a husband's love, to cure a sick person, and to render a barren woman fertile and even to protect from bullets. They are worn around the neck and must never be taken off' (Chelhod 1971). But it is not strictly true that amulets, once put round the neck must never be taken off. Some amulets, like the ones which render a person bullet- or knife-proof, must be taken off when the person goes to bed, and some must be removed during *ṣalāt*. Many amulets are worn across the shoulder like a sash, some are carried in pockets, others tied around the waist and still others tied above the knee or carried inside hats. When amulets are not carried on the person they can be placed in one of several places: inside suitcases, across entrances, buried in the ground or tucked away under the eaves. Mungo Park mentions amulets as being tied around the ankle and carried as portable sheaths. In the latter case the amulets were made out of horns ([1799] 1969: 28). Jobson gives many details on the way amulets were to be found tied to various parts of the body ([1623] 1968: 64).

47 The origin of the Mandinka word *safe* in unclear. The nearest Arabic word is *sifā'a*, meaning medicament, and with a slight vowel shift the Mandinka word can be derived. But this is all speculative.

48 Al-Ḥājj Madi Hawa, grandson of Karamokho Sanūsī Suware, Jarra-Barrokunda, 17/11/72.

49 All these details derive from information provided by al-Ḥājj Madi Hawa in a written statement quoting the actual verses as well as the treatment method.

50 West African Islamic clerics generally, and the Jakhanke in particular, do not appear to make this kind of rigid distinction between religious healing and herbal or modern medicine. However, the *shuyūkh* of the Mouride Brotherhood, for example, have resisted modern dispensaries because they challenge their control of healing procedures (Cruise O'Brien 1971: 232).

51 In the 16th century, for example, the tomb of the *qāḍī* ᶜUthmān Darame was popular for this reason: any petitions brought there were always answered, and the sick healed (Kaᶜti 1913: 171).

CHAPTER NINE

SLAVERY, ISLAM AND THE JAKHANKE

The social and educational organisation of a Jakhanke clerical establishment required a good supply of manpower, and indeed the very continuity of the Jakhanke clerical tradition in the past depended on the availability of extra labour which would free Jakhanke children, another potential source of labour in the family, for a full-time educational career. The acquisition of slaves and their widespread and large-scale employment by Jakhanke clerics were essential to the clerical enterprise. Ritual restrictions as well as the social taboos of inferior status and separate quarters distinguished the slaves from their free Jakhanke masters. After a time slaves not only served an economic function but also a ceremonial one as their masters began to measure the prestige and importance of a clerical order by the size of slave quarters existing in it. Even when it became uneconomical to acquire slaves, either because of slave over-population in one particular centre or later through the legal penalties imposed by colonial administrations,[1] slavery still continued among the Jakhanke, who had come to attach a special ritual and social significance to owning slaves. Indeed for many purposes the institution of slavery continues to exist today and slave families remain distinctly separate from the free-born.

The Historical and Religious Origins of Slavery

The origin of slavery is obscure and the date of its appearance in Africa uncertain. It would seem, however, that at a very early date slaves formed an important item of tribute payment imposed by political rulers on their vassals or subordinates. Nubia, for example, had to provide as *baqṭ*, an annual tribute, to Egypt numerous slaves, many of whom were obtained from her southern neighbours (Hasan 1967: 43, 46). The black slaves supplied in this way were used as domestic servants, labourers and troops. The practice was very important as a source of cheap labour during the first two centuries of Islam, giving rise to traditions traced back to the Prophet to the effect that 'He who has no friend should take a friend from the Nubians', and 'Your best captives are the Nubians' (Hasan 1967: 43; cf Irving 1850: 239).

The penetration of Islam into Black Africa seems to have encouraged the widescale practice of slavery. Although slaves were also taken from other sources, such as punishment for economic insolvency, theft and similar offences,[2] by far the greatest numbers came from commerce and war.[3] The introduction of Islam by the sword further helped to spread the institution of slavery. 'With the spread of Islam in negro Africa and intensification of Moroccan pressure in this direction, beginning in the last centuries of the Middle Ages, the question of the legality of subsequent sales had to be put to some great jurists; they answered circumspectly, giving the dealers the benefit of the doubt as to the origins of individuals offered for sale' (R. Brunschvig 1960: 32). Trade and war in this context were not mutually exclusive means of acquiring or making slaves. The high demand for slaves, which was everywhere a feature of markets at one time or another, encouraged the forcible capture of weaker neighbours in the event of a dispute.

We shall return later to the wider question of the status of slaves in Islam. We may briefly point out here, however, that although Islamic Law considerably ameliorates, some would even say potentially abrogates, the servile condition, nevertheless custom, history and economic gain have combined to produce an enduring tradition of slavery among the dark-skinned populations of Africa, often on the pretext that the slaves were non-believers but sometimes even in flagrant disregard of that pretext.[4] In Islamic Law the effects of slavery are mitigated by three fundamental principles: restrictions on its origin, that is, it can be imposed only in circumstances of obstinate unbelief and refusal to submit to the *jizyah*, payment of tax; the legal rights of slaves; and, finally, facilities for and recommendation of manumission (Schacht 1964: 127). While we are justified in pointing to the fact and practice of slavery among the Jakhanke and other Muslims, it should be borne in mind that, when followed in spirit, the Law acted as a solvent on the proliferating slave-camps into which plundered peoples were concentrated. But caution is necessary in thus invoking the enlightened power of the

Law, for the slave-dealer who suffers its reprimand for taking with the left hand may offer generous ransom with the right and thus leave his critic without resource.[5]

Such dexterity among slave-dealers is commonplace in African history, for by placing Black Africa under a mythological curse the slavers were able to quarry from its ravaged ruins without the fundamental deterrent of conscience. The whole project became waterlogged with easy gain, and the bursts of humane sentiment we may get here or of genuine kindness there were insufficient altogether to drain the swelling. The task of putting in fetters the children whose Hamitic ancestors bore the original curse proved as little difficult to justify as it was rewarding. One story makes this point particularly clearly, and since it also dispose of the possible suspicion of religious bias it bears quotation in full. Captain Theophilus Conneau records a conversation with Ama-De-Bella ("Ahmadou Billo"), brother of the king of Futa Jallon:

> I desired him to tell me if these wars of devastation commanded by the Holy Book, were not more frequently instigated by interest in the great profits his Mahometan countrymen reaped from the results. I gently insinuated my belief that he himself would not undertake to storm one of the well-fortified Caffree towns if not prompted by a successful booty of slaves. After a minute's consideration he replied with some humour that Mahometans were no better than Christians; the one stole, the other held the bag; and if the white man...would not tempt the black man with them, the commands of the Great Allah would be followed with milder means. Somewhat convinced on the subject, I retired from the field of controversy with a flea in my ear. ([1854] 1976: 69-70)

The Qur'ān positively enjoins the taking of slaves in *jihād* (see Baillie [1869/75] 1957: 363ff):

> When you meet the unbelievers, smite their necks, then, when you have made wide slaughter among them, tie fast the bonds [of slavery]...[6]

This Qur'ānic injunction on making slaves from religious wars is, however, propounded alongside various rulings on the manumission of slaves, a question which receives an elaborate and complex treatment in Muslim law books. Some of that material, in the Qur'ān and in the Law, may be presented with a view to indicating the extent to which due recognition is accorded in Islam to slavery as a social institution.

In one place the Qur'ān makes the freeing or ransoming of slaves one of the fulfilling obligations of true piety (Ar. *al-birra*), alongside belief in God:

> True piety is this: to believe in God, and the Last Day, the angels, the Book, and the Prophets, to give of one's substance, however cherished, to kinsmen, and orphans, the needy, the traveller, beggars, and to ransom the slave... (ii: 172)

In similar vein, the Qur'ān enjoins believers to make available free-will offerings for the ransoming of slaves (ix: 60). Manslaughter committed by a Muslim against a fellow Muslim can be compensated for by setting free a slave (iv: 94). Expiation for perjury can be obtained among other means by freeing a slave (v: 91). These and numerous other regulations are laid down precisely in Muslim Law (see Qayrawānī 1945: 220-30, 262, 272).

Such data provide incontrovertible proof that a real distinction exists in Islam between bond and free and that such distinction as exists places the class of slaves in an inferior, disadvantaged category. According to these tenets the Jakhanke did not err in recognising and exploiting this class of bondsmen, and, when pressure was brought to bear by colonial administrations, they only tempered the harshness of a slave condition by reducing the work-load and offering various forms of dispensation in observance of the injunction of the Prophet when he urged 'kindness to slaves'.[7] The rest of the discussion will be concerned primarily with the way the Jakhanke acquired slaves and the role such slaves played in Jakhanke society. Attention will also be drawn to those institutions in which traces of slavery have survived.

Methods of Acquiring Slaves

The Jakhanke acquired slaves through straight purchase, pious gifts, inheritance, and as rewards for clerical service. In their contacts with Samori in the nineteenth century they obtained a substantial quantity of slaves, mostly by direct purchase: Samori would supply slaves and in return received salt, strips of locally woven cloth, gold and cash.[8] As we have already noted, the Jakhanke provided prayer support for Samori, and for this service they were rewarded with slaves (see p.196-7). Samori's contacts with the Jakhanke in Bundu seem to have been extensive. For example, two prominent clerical centres in Niokholo Samécouta and Sillacounda, flourished from the captives that came from Samori's wars (P. Smith 1965a: 255-6).

Prayer support for a warrior in exchange for slaves was not necessarily confined to those instances in which the Jakhanke had no moral objection to the worthiness of his cause. It is not certain whether they in fact identified their clerical interests with Samori's revolution but they also provided prayer support for Musa Molo, from whom they obtained slaves (see p. 195), although it was generally known that Musa Molo was fighting not a *jihād* but a political war directed at anti-Fulbe circles, sometimes including local Muslim resistance. Indeed, two of Musa Molo's implacable enemies were Fode Kabba and Momodou-Lamin, both previously aligned with the Jakhanke, and Molo's stiffest resistance came from sources of Muslim strength, while his own men were for the most part the staunchly anti-Muslim Fulbe (Quinn 1971: 437, 438). On one occasion Musa Molo came to ask for prayer support for a military expedition he was about to undertake. After a successful expedition he returned to this particular clerical centre, Jimara-Bakadaji, and gave a number of slaves as reward.[9] After his wars with Dikor Kumba at Patta, Musa Molo brought six slaves (three male, three female) to Fode Ansumana.[9] When a Jakhanke cleric was approached by a prospective warrior requesting his clerical services, he was normally paid, after victory, ten male and ten female slaves.[10] Such transactions make it clear that slaves were a staple economic commodity and an indispensable part of a prosperous community. The Jakhanke regarded them in this way and obtained by prayer and other types of clerical activity what other people might obtain through warfare.

One of the largest centres of slave concentration among the Jakhanke was at Touba, where at one point the number of slaves reached 11-12,000.[11] Karamokho Ba himself represents the archetypal image of the successful cleric to whom slaves were given as pious gifts.[12] Imām ᶜAbd al-Qādir Bademba, of the Soriya faction, for example, heaped honours on him and made him a personal gift of seven slaves and a thoroughbred horse (*TKB*: fo. 4). The creation of a separate clerical order in the Khairabaya Jabi *qabīlah* was a direct result of the large number of slaves Karamokho Ba's brother, Muḥammad Khaira, brought back from his travels and handed over to Karamokho Ba as pious gifts made by the latter's sympathisers and friends.[13] Karamokho Ba is reported to have been so pleased by the unexpected size of these pious gifts that he bestowed a special blessing on Muḥammad Khaira as resuit of which the latter and his descendants evolved into a powerful separate *qabīlah*.[13] A good supply of slaves continued to flow into Touba under Karamokho Ba's successors for, apart from the voluntary (but numerous) pious gifts important political rulers made to the Touba clerics, it was standard practice for ex-students to make yearly donations. The cleric who undertook a *tournée pastorale* was also likely to acquire a good number of slaves as pious gifts. Karamokho Qutubo, for example, on the one occasion when he travelled from Touba to Mauritania, gathered in the friendly places he passed through, in addition to a huge following of students, a number of slaves.[14]

For Karamokho Sankoung more precise details are available. He personally owned some 1,200 slaves, most of them pious gifts from contemporary political figures. Samori is said to have given him many slaves; Alfa Yahya, the nineteenth century Fula leader from Labé, on one occasion gave him about forty; Modi Sellou, a local Fula leader, once gave him seventeen slaves and another Fula patron, Tcherno Dama, gave him eight.[15] A successful fellow-cleric in Kankan, Daye Kabba, once gave Sankoung eight slaves as a personal gift and another local patron was Alfa Ālimu from Labé who is said to have given him many slaves.

A good number of slaves at any one time in Touba were born in slavery and over a generation or two a significant increase in their numbers resulted from this natural process. Jakhanke clerics inherited the slaves of their fathers, and the possibility of a thinning out of the slave population was removed through the device of a rigid caste system out of which neither slaves nor their descendants could break. The Jakhanke rules applying to the inheritance of the father's property, which included slaves, were very rigid.

Slaves in Jakhanke Traditions of Dispersion

In Serakhulle traditions slaves are mentioned from the beginning of their dispersion. The stories have a legendary flavour but there is no reason to suppose that the slave element was an invention by later Serakhulle communities heavily committed to the slave trade. One version says that when Dinga, the ancestor of the Serakhulle, was on his travels he was accompanied by a slave, Biranin Tunkara, who acted as his bodyguard. From Diakha-Masina (referred to in the source as Dyara-Ba) Dinga went to a country called Darega where he found a well named *kire gede*. In charge of it was a slave woman called Terigabe Senewali. She was under orders from her master not to let any one drink from the well. But Dinga and his travelling party would not be restrained and a contest of magical powers ensued in which Senewali spat in Dinga's face which made him blind. A leading travelling companion, Suduro, came to Dinga's rescue and cured him (Ch. Monteil 1953: 371).

Mama Sambou's sister, Tenenkuta Jabi, was accompanied by a slave girl when she fled from Sutukho. She crossed at Fattatenda to the district of Jimara where she and her slave girl went into hiding in a cave until a hunter came upon them there.[15] Slaves also figure prominently in that most characteristic form of Muslim mobility: the *ḥājj*. Momodou-Lamin was accompanied home from the pilgrimage by ten slaves who carried his gifts of 300 copies of the Qur'ān. The slaves were sumptuously dressed, marching pompously (Marty 1915/6: 280; Fisher 1970: 59n).

Slaves were of considerable importance in the initial founding of Jakhanke clerical centres. There is scant information on the founding of Sutukho, but Jobson says that when he visited it he found slave quarters into which slaves were strictly segregated by their clerical masters (Jobson [1623] 1968: 101). Many of these were descended from slave families whose origins probably date back to the founding of the town. Didécoto, already described, included caste families as well as slaves at its inception (see p. 47). Karamokho Ba went to old Touba with a good supply of slaves, and these, and many more who were acquired later, transferred to Touba itself to be utilised in the practical business of helping to build the new clerical centre. In a non-clerical context slaves were prominent at Nāta, founded by Ba Gassama after a split with the Touba leadership. Nāta does not appear to have become a clerical centre and in fact Ba Gassama's reputation was as a slaver and not as a cleric (Suret-Canale 1970: 68). Nevertheless, his decision to leave Touba and settle at Nāta was facilitated by the large number of slaves he possessed. The main force he deployed to found the village consisted of slaves, in the manner and following the examples of other Jakhanke centres. When he returned to Touba he was accompanied by 300 slaves (see pp. 128-32).[15]

The prosperous Darame Jakhanke centre in the Gambia, Jimara-Bakadaji, was founded with slave assistance. The leader of the slave quarter when Fode Ansumana established it in 1885 was Bamba Sise, himself a slave. Other sections were Sidibekunda, headed by Tuman Sidibe, Jakhitekunda, Jallokunda (Fulbe), Dembelekunda, Sankarakunda (Bambara), Konatekunda, Sisekunda II, Tarawarekunda (Bambara), Sanekunda, Susokunda and Jallokunda II (Fulbe).[16] Sectional heads of the slave quarters reported directly to the general head who co-ordinated efforts and organised the slaves into task force units.[17] Fode Ansumana continued to add to the number of slaves he owned through pious gifts and purchase.

When Karang Sambu Lamin migrated to Sutukung, he had a number of slaves in his following (see p. 168). Dembele was the senior slave; his children were Sara, Yahya and Mama; the others were Kali, Jaydatou, Nyimma, Fode Modou, Wonto and her son Muḥammad-Lamin (the latter named after Karang Sambu Lamin) and a daughter.[18] Sutukung was already a strong community when Karang Sambu Lamin came there so that his slaves were not instrumental in founding the centre but his own clerical practice was strengthened through the utilisation of his slaves. Indeed, after he was persuaded to come to Sutukung through what the sources describe as the unanimous and collective pressure of the Sutukung Muslim community, he was given extra slaves to help him to settle down.[19]

The Use of Slaves in Agriculture

The use to which slaves were and still are put in Jakhanke clerical centres follows a standard pattern. A substantial proportion is employed in farm labour. One Jakhanke elder made an explicit point of this when he said that the Jakhanke have traditionally acquired slaves in order to put them to farm work and that way relieve pressure on the children of clerics who were then put into full-time education.[20] Jakhanke involvement in agriculture has been extensive, and the attention given to this aspect of their work is in direct proportion to the size of their educational establishments. Slaves provided the food base of such educational establishments until slavery was banned by colonial administrative decree, when a new form of bondage was grafted on to existing institutions to make up the manpower shortage.

There are numerous references in documentary sources to the use of slaves on farms (see p. 57 ff above). According to one estimate, in the eighteenth century, about three quarters of the population of the Senegambia region were slaves and most of these were employed in agricultural labour (Park [1799] 1969: 16). In Niani one account estimates identical figures for slave and free and adds that most of the slaves were employed in farm labour (Durand 1806: 44). Another source says that slaves spent two-thirds of the working day on the farms of their masters, and the other third on their own farm (Reade 1864: 582).

The use of Qur'ān school pupils on the farms of their Jakhanke teachers was similar to the use of slaves and has already been described (see pp. 151-4). It was normal practice in Jakhanke schools that when a student enrolled he was regarded as the domestic slave of the teacher. For all practical purposes he followed the same work schedule as other slaves, with the slight difference that he received a modicum of education while in residence. Some idea of the transaction between the parents of students and the schoolteachers is given by Mungo Park. In order to gain the release of the student the parents had to bring a slave or the price of one. If he could not be redeemed by his parents, the student was required to work on the farms of the teacher until the latter decided to release him (Park [1799] 1969: 243). Park estimated that the price of a prime male slave ranged from £18 to £20 (*ibid*: 18) but periodic fluctuations in the market naturally affected the figure.

The theory that Qur'ān school students were in a state of redeemable servitude gained some notoriety after the institution of slavery had been abolished. The Jakhanke clerics did not directly resist the colonial law which forbade them to keep and maintain slaves but, while they complied with the regulations, they at the same time fostered and exploited notions of servitude among the people, some of them ex-slaves, to whom they offered Qur'ān schooling. Under the innocent cover of their educational institutions they maintained the same degree of control as before over their ex-slaves while simultaneously increasing the range of their clientele to surrounding areas. While professing their compliance with the will of their political overlords, they put to double effectiveness the legitimate offer of education. Their tradition of co-operating with political rulers was maintained, but it was given a twist.

Marty (1921) has made similar observations, and although he is not a disinterested witness, representing as he does the colonial administration which was attempting to abolish slavery, nevertheless his account contains elements which are pertinent to the issue. He writes that in all the local villages the old ties which bound slaves to their masters in the days before emancipation tended to repeat themselves, but this time in the guise of the familiar religious set-up. Marty confirms that many Jakhanke slave masters kept in contact with their ex-slaves and began operating Qur'ān schools in those areas where liberated slaves went to settle. Whereas previously Jakhanke clerics made only token efforts to provide instruction for their slaves, they now pursued this line of activity with energy and determination, and such services as they rendered were initially provided free. But beneath the seemingly generous nature of such activity they fostered a set of obligations and binding considerations from which the Jakhanke clerics derived material gain and religious power. Marty continues:

> Et l'on peut constater que l'ex-captif se transforme en client religieux et rapprend le chemin de la case de son maître pour lui porter des présents. Ce n'est plus au patron qu'il obéit, c'est au Karamoko qu'il rend hommage.[21]

The extension of educational services to pupils from the class of ex-slaves enabled the Jakhanke clerics to cope with the serious and sudden drain on their economy which emancipation foisted upon them. A number of women slaves were attached to their Jakhanke patrons as concubines and others were formally pronounced free just to become the legal wives of their masters (Marty 1921: 119). The practice of redeeming a *ṭālib* at the termination of his studies with a slave or the price of one was no longer enforced in precisely the same terms, but the concept of ransom (Ar. *fidan*) has survived in another form in that parents are expected to give some sort of remuneration to the cleric according to their means. The unspecified character of the transaction usually means that students, and/or their parents, live in a state of continuous obligation to clerics. It is not uncommon, for example, for students to render an annual homage to the cleric involving agricultural produce, livestock, cloth and cash. In addition many send their own sons to their old teachers, and in this sense the bonds are passed from parent to child.

A regular feature in clerical centres is that successors to the leadership tend to be chosen from the younger sons of the clerical leaders. In the context of plural marriages and the wide age differentials between clerics and their wives, this results in enormous variations between the age span of one clerical dynasty and another. One example is given of a man who, had he lived, would have been aged 120 in 1966, and his son, the incumbent clerical leader, who was 65, while the designated leader, a son of the incumbent was aged eight (Wilks 1968: 171). Alongside this feature of uneven dynastic chronologies is the extent to which clerical centres will enrol all the male children of the clerical lineage in full-time education, leaving slaves and other students to carry out essential work on the farms. Thus the economic strength of a clerical establishment, deriving in the past mostly from slave manpower, ensures a correspondingly secure clerical future. In the absence of slave labour, many clerics now look for those students who, for various reasons, are willing to place themselves in bondage to the cleric in return for free education. Such students, usually coming from some considerable distance away, may take a longer time than normal to complete their course. In the meantime they supply the cleric with the necessary manpower resources for supporting a system of full-time education for the children of the centre.[22]

In spite of the evident extensive survival of traces of slavery in Jakhanke educational work, the comparison can be taken too far. There is no parallel, for instance, to the numerous legal and ritual restrictions imposed on slaves. As will presently be made clear, slaves constituted a class of deprived members of the clerical community, and the chains of caste inferiority were automatically riveted on their children. Slaves were totally denied civil status, and their exclusion from responsible office was reinforced by the entire weight of Islamic Law, Muslim social practice and traditional stigma. However oppressed his Qur'ān school counterpart may be, a wide chasm still divides him from the restrictions and ritual inhibitions with which the slave is burdened.

The Legal Position of Slaves

Islamic Law and Muslim customary practice, respectively Sharī^{c}ah and *^{c}ādah*, coincide at numerous points to define the position of the slave in the Muslim community. There are some generalised rulings. Slaves as such do not inherit, and their property remains the property of the owner. Under certain circumstances, as when a slave has signed a contract (*kitābah*) with his master stipulating the payment of a fixed sum in exchange for freedom, a slave (he is called *mukātab*) regains some of his personal rights.[23] In place of a *kitābah* a legal formula will suffice. Another category of slave is the *mudabbar*: the master has promised that after his death the slave can regain his freedom. This is qualified by the fact that if the slave is owned by more than one master (such a slave is termed *mushtarak*), then compensation is to be paid to the co-owner (Qayrawānī 1945: 220 ff.; H. Fisher and A. Fisher 1971: 55). There is a difference between the two types of slave: a *mukātab* slave, but not a *mudabbar*, is recommended to attend Friday Congregation Prayer. Also, a *mukātab*, unlike a *mudabbar*, can make a vow and keep it provided it does not interfere with the payment for his freedom (Ishāq 1956: 87, 139; H. Fisher and A. Fisher 1971: 47-8, 55-6). The evidence of a slave is not admissible in court, but his confession, in certain matters, may be (Qayrawānī 1945: 258, 262; H. Fisher and A. Fisher 1971: 7).

Among the Jakhanke similar restrictions are in force in some cases even today. *ᶜIddah*, the required waiting period before a divorce becomes absolute, is two months for slaves while for others it is three months.[24] While the *zakāt*, the obligatory alms, are mandatory on all free-born Muslims they are not required of the slave in the same way. A slave's property or the *zakāt* due on it is made over to his master.[25] A master gives alms for his slave at the annual *zakāt al-fitr*. A slave cannot assume the office of an *imām*, and this is a general rule in Islamic Law and practice, although some *madhāhib*, schools of thought, have different rulings on this, allowing a slave to lead public prayers provided this function carries no juridical or similar responsibilities (R. Brunschvig 1960). Among the Jakhanke even the descendants of a slave emancipated before his death cannot fill any important religious office. Slaves are also excluded from leadership of a *majlis*, the school or educational organisation. The *ḥājj* is not enjoined upon them (although as will be shortly discussed there is provision in Islamic Law for slaves to make the *ḥājj*), nor can they make the animal sacrifice at the pilgrimage feast, the *ᶜīd al-aḍḥā*. The matter of oath-taking is of no consequence since among the Jakhanke there is a tradition of refusal of oaths. But a slave cannot qualify as a competent witness before a consistorial assembly. He cannot substitute for the free man. His word against that of a free-born person is null and void. The tradition which makes the Friday Congregation Prayer mandatory for all Muslims except slaves (V. Monteil 1964: 110) is observed, and since the class of *mukātab* slaves exists only as a legal fiction this ruling affects all slaves.

The structure of such disabilities is further reinforced by local custom and practice. In one community, where slaves have for more than three generations achieved a statutory emancipation, the appearance of a subservient slave ethos is carefully maintained even today. In this setting slaves provide labour on the farms of their masters; they pound their couscous and thresh their rice; they undertake the building of their houses; they go on errands. The children of these slave families go to study under their parents' masters. At the circumcision ceremony circumcised slaves look after the children of their masters, constantly attending to their needs; bringing them food and presents, and providing all the necessary equipment for the passing out ceremony. The duration of the circumcision confinement varies, but the usual length is about two months.[26] At weddings slaves carry on their heads the bridal trousseau for which they may receive gifts. Slaves may accompany their masters on long journeys and carry the luggage required for the trip. They may not eat from the same dish as their masters, or in some cases as any free-born person. After the slaughter of an animal in the community slaves (and leather-workers) do the flaying. The head of the animal and the skin are taken by them.[27]

From a slightly different tradition, an equivalent set of conventions is observed towards slaves. After his master, or his master's wife, has been away on a journey, a slave goes to meet him (or her) and, in the case of able-bodied slaves, he bears his master on his back and brings him home. In cases where a slave is unable to do this, he will nevertheless make a token offer and then carry his master's baggage. Upon reaching home the slave washes the feet of his master as a symbol of his subservience and brings him a calabash of fresh milk to drink. Slaves cannot marry without first obtaining the authorisation of their master. They do, however, possess their own compounds and are Muslims.[28]

In discussions elsewhere with Jakhanke clerics some of these points were repeated. A marriage contract cannot be undertaken without prior authorisation (*idhn*) from the master.[29] A slave thus authorised is called a *ma'dhūn*, and he may also engage in trade for his master. A slave can apply for the *mukātab* status, but even here he is at the complete mercy of his master who determines the amount to be paid and the method of payment. It can be a prohibitive price that he is asked to pay, which completely negates any advantages that the right was supposed to have given him in the first place.[30]

Marriage rules are different for slaves. The children of slave parents inherit the slave status of their parents. If a slave man marries a free-born girl the children belong to the owner of their father. If a slave woman marries a free man, their children are free.[31] Jakhanke clerics can emancipate their female slaves and marry them subsequently, a practice for which support is found in the Qur'ān, *ṣūrah al-nisā'i* (iv: *passim*). However, according to strict Islamic Law slave wives must be someone else's slaves, and one's own slaves can be taken only as concubines (Qayrawānī 1945: 178). Slave women thus married are liable to half the chastisement of free women if they contravene the marriage rules.[32] But although technically a slave woman stands on an equal footing with the free co-wives, she occupies an inferior status in the domestic management of the home. Muslim Law allows a man up to four wives,[33] but that number can in effect be increased by taking slave women as concubines. The four legitimate wives of a household take turns in managing the domestic affairs, including the supervision of any female slaves (see also Park [1799] 1969: 205), but a slave woman married in such a household would be given menial tasks and no corresponding responsibility in running the home.[34] For example, she would pound the couscous normally used for breakfast, and husk the rice. It was not common, in the days before emancipation, for slave women to own property in the form of rice-fields, instead they worked on the fields of their mistresses. In some cases slave women did own fields, but the produce from then belonged to the household in which they lived and was not eligible for the *zakāt*.[35] The children of such slave women were, however, free of any legal restrictions.

The Ceremonial Functions of Slaves

The ceremonial role of slaves in clerical centres, which their descendants continue to fulfil, has been touched on. In the circumcision ceremony they take leading parts. They provide the ceremonial robes of the initiates, robes fashioned in the traditional style of a fully fledged hunter. At weddings they carry the bridal trousseau, and they sometimes play the role of matchmaker by running errands. After the slaughter of a sacrificial animal, as at the Bairam Festival, it is customary for slaves to be apportioned the head and skin of the animal. A slave goes out to meet a returning master, and provides the ceremonial washing of feet, followed by a calabash of fresh milk. When the cleric goes on a journey his slave will usually lead the way, sometimes carrying a staff in his hand. The legal ruling that in certain infringements of the religious code a slave can be freed as legal restitution was not always kept, but instead clerics made pious food offerings for slaves to consume. This is done in the spirit of the Qur'ānic verse which enjoins the provision of free-will offerings (*al-ṣadaqāt*) for the relief of the needy, including slaves (ix:60). The religious education, if any, slaves received was minimal, so that they did not join prayers or hold religious office among the Jakhanke. Similarly, slaves are not prominent in pilgrimage rites among the Jakhanke, but in Islamic Law slaves can attend the pilgrimage in the company of their masters and be adorned with the pilgrimage vestments (*al-iḥrām*). Having accomplished the *ḥājj* that way they qualify automatically for enfranchisement (Ishāq 1956: I 142).

Information on the ceremonial and similar functions of slaves is provided by outside observers. One incident already described concerns a cleric who came to a river bank accompanied by his slaves. One of the slaves carried a large gourd which he filled with water from the river and brought to the cleric who was waiting a short distance away. The cleric used the water to wash himself with. A second gourd-ful was brought and the cleric washed his hands. With the third and final ration of water he washed his face and then commenced performing the *ṣalāt* (Jobson [1623] 1968: 87-8; see p.189). On the prestige or decorative value of slaves, one writer, a century later than Jobson, gives some details. According to him domestic female slaves not yet fallen into a state of concubinage, had an easier life than the average slave. They were lavishly dressed, and sometimes better furnished with clothes and jewellery than their masters' wives. They were known, for example, to have coral, amber and silver pieces on their person which were reckoned to be worth £20 or £30 sterling (Moore 1738: 29ff.). Mungo Park describes the Bairam Festival (*ᶜīd al-aḍḥa*), called locally *banna salee*, in the Jarra area. The slaves were magnificently attired on that day and provided with lavish meals. They seem to have taken full part in the festivities of the day, and Park reported no constraint on them ([1799] 1969: 127). It is doubtful, however, whether slaves also attended the *ᶜīd al-aḍḥa* community prayers, and the expectation would be that they stayed away from that part of the proceedings. René Caillie, who describes the *ᶜīd al-aḍḥa* prayer and says that the chief attended the prayer with an escort of up to 300, does not refer to slaves forming part of the retinue (1830: I 266-8; see p. 188 above).

Emancipation and Jakhanke Attitudes

Slave families, as we have seen, have continued to be attached to their Jakhanke clerical patrons long after emancipation. Local colonial administrations enforced the emancipation decrees of the 1890s through a series of measures. In the Gambia Protectorate the travelling commissioner, Cecil Sitwell, conducted a survey on the south bank of the river and reported on the state of the slave trade in the area. He noted, among other things, that there was a buoyant traffic in slaves, particularly those captives taken from Fode Kabba's *jihād* (Sitwell 1893. See pp.193-5). In an earlier period, the Administrator of the territory, Cooper, estimated that the profits from the trade in slaves amounted to some 500%, and in the same period he observed that 'there is hardly one single exception where produce is not bought by traders in this river through the medium of slaves.'[36] A Slave Abolition Ordinance was enacted in 1906 and put into effect. Among its provisions were that if a slave set foot on English soil at Bathurst (now Banjul), Albreda or MacCarthy Island he was granted automatic enfranchisement, and slaves anywhere became automatically free after the death of their master.[37] The Gambia colony did not have sufficient police or military force to put many of these provisions into effect, and consequently numerous slave families continued to live in bondage to their masters. In addition, since so much of the effectiveness of the Ordinance depended on individual slaves taking the initiative and travelling to Crown possessions to achieve free status, very few did, and most were content to seek relief within conditions of slavery. It was under such circumstances that Jakhanke clerical patrons retained their slaves. For many of these slaves the ties with the old patterns of living were too strong to snap by what amounted to a personal repudiation of their servile status.[38]

The slaves of Karang Sambu Lamin, for example, did not begin dispersing before the 1940s, well after the death of Karang Sambu himself. At Bakadaji slave compounds still exist and slaves continue to honour some of the old obligations to their masters' families. Slave groups and other castes still exist at Bani-Kantora and Bani-Sami, although in the latter it is the Joune, Dhahaba and similar caste families who predominate. Some descendants of slaves live in Wuli-Bani, a Jakhanke clerical centre in the same area as Sandu-Jakhaba. There is also widespread use of the Jola ethnic group, the target of numerous Muslim military operations in the Casamance region, as domestic slaves. In fact one Jakhanke cleric says that the Kujabi and Sambu Jola, two of the most numerous of the Jola families, were originally descended from the slaves of Mama Sambou Gassama.[39]

The disruption of Touba's clerical activity by the mass emancipation of slaves has to be analysed in the light of the close connection between a strong agricultural basis, supported by slave labour, and a successful clerical enterprise based on family tradition. Jakhanke distrust of French motives was exacerbated by the rigid French stand on the question of slaves. Two accounts, already given, say that in one day the French, who had a *poste* in Touba, freed some 4,800 slaves (see p. 136-7). One account says the figure was far greater, involving some 8,000 slaves.[40] Whatever Touba's slave population (and one reliable estimate puts it at 11,000) even the lower of these two figures is a drastic cut for a single day. It is impossible for the outsider to assess the psychological impact of such measures, so that we must rely on al-Ḥājj Banfa Jabi and al-Ḥājj Soriba Jabi to tell the story of how the Jakhanke felt among themselves. The consequences of such a policy for the continued existence of the Touba clerical establishment were immediate and far-reaching (see Chapter 6).

Jakhanke accounts suggest that the French did not make what to them was a crucial distinction between slaves destined for a clerical centre and slaves owned and utilised by mercantile interests. Here Banfa and Soriba's attitude to Ba Gassama, who operated as an independent commercial agent in the buying and selling of slaves, was one of mistrust and disapproval. Ba's political intentions were also suspect. As their subsequent readjustment to statutory emancipation showed, the Jakhanke believed that the institution of slavery was itself akin to traditional notions of client status (*mawlā*) and patronage (*riʿāyah*), notions which survived slavery in the form outlawed by the French. Beneath the Jakhanke attitude towards the French role in emancipation, which they saw as a clumsy if costly misunderstanding, was a feeling of bewilderment and numbness. Jakhanke explanations of their experience at Touba during those crucial years reveal this. All the available accounts look to a wider issue for the source of the dénouement at Touba, which they find in French antipathy to Islam.[41] Only that kind of set policy on the part of the French could explain why they came down heavily on the Touba Jakhanke, an analysis which more accurately reflects the confusion of the Touba clerics than the realities of French policy.

Strongly implanted in the Jakhanke mind is the idea that the French were opposed to the Islamic clerical solidarity which they represented and this was why they, the French, outlawed slavery which they knew to be the mainstay of the Touba clerical practice. In seeking to explain the motives of the French, the Jakhanke have admitted and expounded the paramount role slavery played in their clerical work. Once the element of slave labour was removed, it was merely a matter of time before the clerical establishment contracted to a small nucleus whose long-term survival would in fact depend on finding student-substitutes for direct slave labour. The eventual arrest and exile of Sankoung, and the repercussions which that led to in Touba, hastened Touba's decline. Although it was to make a brief and fitful rally after the return of Sankoung from exile, it had lost the basis on which to effect a permanent and stable recovery. The result was further dispersions both in the direction of ex-slave settlements, where previous bonds of servitude were reasserted in less onerous ways, and in other places where student labour was easy to obtain and retain.

As to the meaning and significance of the acquisition and ownership of slaves for their tradition of political neutralism and military pacifism, the Jakhanke defend themselves by a dexterous combination of principle and expedience: the one requiring them to insist on their traditional independence, and the other allowing them a tolerable margin of activity in slavery. But this is fraught with hazards which only agile or well-placed clerics can sidestep. It requires a cleric of exceptional powers of discernment to be able to avoid the losing side in a dispute or escape the consequences of defeat. Either could bring the loss of slave revenue and possibly the threat of political or military action. However, Touba proved that with a secure clerical reputation, the Jakhanke were able to take and keep slaves with no more compromise of their tradition than a supple conscience would dictate.

NOTES

1 As we have seen,the abolition of slavery in the interior was undertaken by the French in their West African colonies from 1905. In the Gambia the Slave Abolition Ordinance was promulgated in 1906. However, the process was always a slow one. It was not until 1922 that the French finally suppressed public slave dealing in Morocco and c. 1930 that their control of the Saharan interior was sufficient to effectively end the trade. In Northern Nigeria although abolition began in 1907 a new order was still required in 1936 to make the abolition mandatory. (See R. Brunschvig 1960: 39.)

2 See Park [1799] 1969: 222ff; Moore 1738: 29 for examples in Black Africa. Punishment for theft and insolvency as a source of slaves is of great antiquity, see, e.g. Leviticus 25: 39; Deuteronomy 15: 12; Exodus 22: 2-4.

3 'Slaves by peaceful means tended, from an early date, to compete with the forcible method' (R. Brunschvig 1960: 32).

4 Aḥmad Bābā (1556-1627), a Sudanic scholar, wrote a short treatise on slavery, the *Miᶜrāj*, in which he argues forcefully that the reason and grounds for slavery are non-belief, not the colour of a person's skin, referring in this to the widescale practice of using colour as a justification for enslavement. (See Bābā 1977.) Over three hundred years later Aḥmad Bābā was quoted with approval by the 19th century Moroccan, al-Nāṣirī, who said that in view of the serious doubt surrounding the true state of Blacks enslaved it is better to presume their freedom until incontrovertible proof can be advanced to the contrary, and in that process the testimony of slave-dealers and traders should be dismissed *a priori*: they are tainted witnesses. He writes: '...we would say that even if there were no more than a strong doubt in this matter...there would be...a case for preventive action, which is a principle of the Holy Law...sufficient to oblige one to cease having anything to do with an evil which is derogatory to honour and religion.' (Text given in Hunwick 1976.)

5 The *askiya* Dawud of Songhay (reigned 1549-83) gallantly rewarded the clerics of Timbuktu with numerous slave cargoes. When in one instance his generosity was repudiated he sought to redeem himself by granting further batches of slaves (Kaᶜti 1913: 196, 198; Ar. 106).

6 Qur'ān xlvii: 4. Elsewhere an oblique reference can be found, ix: 14. After the famous Battle of Badr, the Prophet ordered that some of the Meccan captives could secure their redemption on condition that each captive taught ten Medinan Muslims how to write, this at a time when the early Muslim recruits were mostly illiterate (Muir 1858/61: I ix).

7 Qayrawānī 1945: 323. This sentiment was expressed by a local Mandinka Muslim to Dr Blyden in Liberia: 'O man of understanding, be not arrogant over your slave or make yourself superior to him. Seek with kindness what God has decreed to you of profit from him...' (Blyden 1888: 364-5). It is evident here that slavery is believed to be God's decree. Discretional manumission does not alter or weaken the force of the law concerning it.

8 Al-Ḥājj Shaykh Sidiya Jabi, Brikama, 28/10/72. Samori is said to have been enslaved himself in adolescence. Some traditions say that he bound himself to slavery to redeem his mother. (See Hargreaves 1963: 244; also Person 1968/70: I *passim*.)

9 Al-Ḥājj Janko Darame, Jimara-Bakadaji, 11/12/72. See pp. 85-6. For Jakhanke opposition to Samori in Touba, see Person 1974.

10 Al-Ḥājj Shaykh Sidiya Jabi, Brikama, 28/10/72.

11 11,000 is the estimate given by Al-Ḥājj Soriba Jabi, Macca-Kolibantang, 9/12/72; 12,000 by Ba Fode Jakhabi, Georgetown, 2/12/72. The number is unexpectedly large but there is no reason to suspect deliberate invention.

12 *TKB* lists numerous concubines of Karamokho Ba and his successors.

13 Al-Ḥājj Shaykh Sidiya Jabi, Brikama, 28/10/72.

14 Al-Ḥājj Mbalu Fode Jabi, Marssassoum, 18/1/73. Mbalu Fode is the grandson of Qutubo through his father Karamokho Madi, also known as al-Maghīlī.

15 Al-Ḥājj Soriba Jabi, Macca-Kolibantang, 9/12/72.

16 Al-Ḥājj Janko Darame, Jimara-Bakadaji, 11/12/72. Many of these names were adopted by the slaves in recognition of their master's name. Sisekunda, for example, was owned by the Sise clerics. But names like Jallokunda indicate the Fula ethnic group from which the slaves originally came.

17 Al-Ḥājj Janko Darame, Jimara-Bakadaji, 11/12/72.

18 Al-Ḥājj Mukhtār Jabi, Sutukung, 16/11/72.

19 Muḥammad Kebba Silla, Sutukung, 16/11/72 (on tape). This source says that Karang Sambu Lamin was invited to a solemn community meeting as he prepared to leave Sutukung after a brief second visit. The meeting reminded him of an earlier promise he had made about adopting Sutukung as his home and held him to honour it. At that time Karang Sambu was teaching at Niamina-Jāfai. See pp. 167-9 for an account of Karang Sambu.

20 Shaykh Farūqi Jakhabi, Sutukung, 16/11/72.

21 Marty 1921: 135. For the establishment of Qur'ān schools among ex-slaves, see *ibid*: 146 and p. 171 ff. above.

22 Cf Wilks 1968: 171. Al-Ḥājj Madi Hawa, in his mid-sixties, had numerous students from a fair distance, and not only the children of his three brothers but his own teenage brother have been fully occupied with education, a privilege some clerics in weak centres cannot enjoy.

23 Qayrawānī 1945: 222-4. Upon default of payment such a slave forfeits his rights to emancipation and the part of the sum already paid.

24 Kalāmullāh Sise, Jimara-Bakadaji, 11/12/72. Cf R. Brunschvig 1960.

25 Kalāmullāh Sise, *loc. cit.* ; Ishāq 1956: 114, 120. In Shāfi[c] law the *zakāt* is similarly not required of a slave (Chodjā[c] 1935: 17).

26 Park says that at the ceremonies he attended it took two months and more for full recuperation [1799] 1969: 203-4.

27 This information comes from a public meeting in which the subject of the interview was Kalāmullāh Sise, Jimara-Bakadaji. Perhaps as the result of a long process of conditioning, the slave families of Bakadaji are claimed to be the most ardent defenders of their own low caste status.

28 Notes taken from a conversation with Mrs Fatumata Sise, Serrekunda, Feb. 1973. The example here refers to Bani-Kantora.

29 Al-Ḥājj Soriba Jabi, Macca-Kolibantang, 9/12/72; also Qayrawānī 1945: 180.

30 Al-Ḥājj Soriba Jabi, *loc. cit.* According to this source, a slave master can compute on a daily basis and estimate the number of years a slave is likely to be in active service, and the sum arrived at that way is put to the charge of the slave.

31 Al-Ḥājj Soriba Jabi, *loc. cit.*

32 This is based on the explicit ruling of the Qur'ān, iv. 30.

33 iv. 3; also Qayrawānī 1945: 178. Concubinage (*istisrāt*) is part of the same process as marriage of slave women (xxiv: 32). The special provision in the law which recognises the taking of an unlimited number of concubines removes the pressure for taking slave women as co-wives. The Qur'ān, however, encourages the latter course, iv: 28.

34 Commenting on the society of Murzuq, which is known to be atypical, Nachtigal said that concubines were sometimes preferred to wives since the threat of resale acts as a check on fidelity. Nachtigal goes on: '...if one considers also that a slave girl, apart from the stronger motive for fidelity...is also by nature more industrious, more obedient and less demanding, one cannot wonder that in these regions many prefer lawful concubinage, and in many houses where there are legitimate wives, the master's preference goes to his slave girl.' ([1879/89: I 102-3] 1974: I 95)

35 The *alkali* and others, Jimara-Bakadaji, 11/12/72.

36 CO/87/109, 6th January, 1876, cited in Quinn 1972; 139-40.

37 The Slave Abolition Ordinance, Ref. 2/96, 1906, Records Office, Banjul.

38 In parts of Guinea, for example, the descendants of slaves still maintain their separate caste distinctions and their Fulbe patrons restrict them socially. See Derman 1973: 27-42 ff.

39 Al-Ḥājj Soriba Jabi, Macca-Kolibantang, 9/12/72. This may be a reference to the captives Mama Sambou presumably acquired during his

military operations in Fogny, an area of Jola concentration. A story has it that the Jola gave him the name Sambou as a substitute for Shu^{c}aibou because of a linguistic modification which still occurs in the Jola language.

40 Ba Fode Jakhabi, Georgetown, 2/12/72.

41 Ba Fode Jakhabi, *loc. cit.*, says that while the French were making life difficult for the Touba Jakhanke they had also taken similar actions against Muslim insurgents in Senegambia: Ma Ba, Lat Dior, Saer Mati Ba, Al-Bouri Ndiaye, all of them allies in a common cause against the French, Fode Kabba and others. For this theme in Senegambian history, see Klein 1972. In general see also pp. 77 ff and 132 ff above.

CHAPTER TEN

CONCLUSIONS

Some general conclusions may now be attempted. Since their emergence sometime between the twelfth and thirteenth century under al-Ḥājj Sālim Suware, the Jakhanke have adopted a consistent policy of clerical pacifism and political neutrality. They have acted as advisers, counsellors and chaplains to rulers and princes and even warriors without compromising their neutral stand. This tradition, beginning with al-Ḥājj Sālim himself, endured well into modern times. It is a test of the significance of this tradition that the Jakhanke were able to participate fully in the acquisition and use of slaves without a corresponding involvement in war and politics or commerce. Their wide-ranging dealings with warriors and political leaders left their neutral reputation largely intact. The slavery issue is also an important factor in determining Jakhanke involvement in trade. The wide use to which slaves were put has already been indicated but, although slaves were an important economic commodity in most parts of Africa at the time, the Jakhanke appear not to have taken part in the slave trade as professional slave merchants. A close examination of the sources from which they acquired slaves reveals the same pattern of clerical interest: slaves came as pious gifts, votive offerings, rewards for religious service, and payment for educational work. When slaves were purchased it was to strengthen the clerical establishment and enhance its teaching function. Up to the time of the abolition of slavery and the emancipation of slaves in the African interior early this century, the Jakhanke continued to cling to their slaves as inalienable property. The record shows no rush to sell or emancipate slaves even when under pressure from the French. Tradition and profession had come to make slaves an inseparable part of the clerical life.

The precise manner of the evolution of Jakhanke clericalism is not difficult to outline. Al-Ḥājj Sālim brought with him a clear set of rulings on religion and war and founded the clerical vocation on the basis of repudiation of war and of political office. Sometime probably in the thirteenth century the Jakhanke splintered off from their Serakhulle background and developed into a religious elite. Recognised by affluent trading communities as religious and educational masters, they received generous patronage which further bolstered the clerical vocation. It was obvious, particularly in the heyday of Diakha-Bambukhu, that the clerical vocation was in itself a rewarding enterprise and that political leaders could be brought to acknowledge its autonomy. Thus it came about that from the earliest days the Jakhanke lived in what outside observers called clerical/maraboutic republics, 'de "noyautage", sous forme de collectivités disséminées un peu partout, et aussi de la constitution de gros centres quasi-exclusivement musulmans' (Ch. Monteil 1926: 598). The importance of these clerical cells in the dissemination of Islam cannot be over-emphasised.

The missionary theme in Jakhanke Islam is underpinned by the educational function of clerical centres. Education served many purposes. It spread knowledge of Islam; it created an instructed body of believers; it produced a distinct class of teachers and educated men; it produced a cadre of students devoted to their teachers and to Islam through study; it led to mobility as students, teachers and whole communities followed the educational trail in search of improvement. The student is instructed, the cleric rewarded and the community renewed through participation in the educational process.

The reforming capacity of education, what in other sources is referred to as literacy, is an acknowledged fact (Fisher 1969: 247). Equipped with sufficient knowledge of the literary sources of religion, the cleric and his community were able to embark on a programme of purification and renewal. There was no need to resort to military solutions in the maintenance of Islamic standards. In situations of conflict, and the consequent disruption of life that followed, the Jakhanke abandoned their centres and withdrew to a quieter life where they used the educational instrument to perpetuate their vocation. Dispersion thus helped them both to escape military confrontation and to preserve their pacific tradition. The implications of this for accepted ideas on the correlation between militancy and the Islamic reform tradition are striking. The role of pacific clerics in carrying through projects of Islamic reform is significant. A high level of literacy did not in their case lead to adopting arms to reform Islam: education, more than war, was the means of sustaining the missionary impulse and reform. In the light of this there is a need to revise previous controversial categorisations of the African Muslim *ᶜulamā* of the times of the *jihād* wars as *ᶜulamā al-su'i*, venal malams, who were opposed to the *jihād* programme of reform and supported the status quo because they benefited by it. Jakhanke clerics do not fall into such a category for they repudiated *jihād* leaders because principle and practice demanded it, not because they were venal, in collusion with wicked rulers. Their clientele, the so-called compromising Muslims, similarly need to be reassessed in terms of their positive contribution to gradual, peaceful reform. Thus Islamic reform according to this new understanding becomes a process rather than a precise programme of revolutionary change.[1]

Travel and mobility acted in like fashion to maintain and rejuvenate the clerical vocation. Examples of students embarking on *shaykh*-seeking; of clerics, both young and old, travelling to acquire knowledge and experience; of pilgrims benefiting from the journey to and from Mecca, and of schools bivouacked along the travel path have already been discussed and are too numerous to need detailed listing here. Two examples may suffice to show the much wider occurrence of the travel theme. In Adamawa (present day Cameroun) the German traveller, Heinrich Barth, in 1851, met an Arab who had come there from Jedda. This Arab, 'with the title of *sharīf*', came to Adamawa by way of Waday and Logon and was engaged in constructing a warm bath for the leading cleric of the place, as he had done for the *sulṭan* of Waday (Barth [1857] 1965: II 155). Barth observes that 'this very man was a remarkable example of those saintly adventurers so frequently met with in Negroland...' (*ibid*: II 156). The other example is the history of the first published account (1854) of the Kanuri language, spoken by Muslims in the Lake Chad area in northeastern Nigeria, which was prepared in Freetown by Sigismund Koelle, working with freed slaves, and subsequently checked and corrected in Cairo by another scholar working with students at Al-Azhar (Fisher 1969: 248). The impact of Qādirī teachings through such mobility is a sufficiently large topic in itself to merit a more detailed inquiry, but enough is known of the contacts between Jakhanke clerics and the Kunta Qādirī *shuyūkh* for us to appreciate the connection. Dervish activity, for example, focused on travel and associated it closely with the figure of Jesus, 'because, during the whole course of his life, he was in *safar* [travelling]; and for the safety of his faith, never stayed in [one] place' (Suhrawardī 1891: 26).

The religious basis of Jakhanke clericalism has been expounded in the thematic chapters. In some of their practices the Jakhanke were in clear contravention of the strict interpretation of the Law. Mālikī Islam, to which they belonged, though tolerant to a certain degree of assimilating local customary practice (*ᶜurf* or *ᶜādah*), is nevertheless normally insistent on prescriptive rulings on matters of orthodox behaviour. In the matter of *ṣalāt* regulations, for example, the Jakhanke clerics have exceeded the limits of the law by incorporating features of traditional ritual. The New Year rituals, to take one instance, show unmistakable identity with traditional practice. The whole area of divinatory practice, to take a different example, is overlaid with traditional religious nuances, however impressive the Islamic parallels. In a matter such as marrying concubines the clerics were again in ostensible breach of the law. They did not moreover adhere strictly to the law on prohibited degrees of marriage, some clerics marrying their brothers' daughters (*banāt al-akhi*) on which there is a specific legal interdiction (Qur'ān iv: 26; Levy 1957: 104). What is surprising, however, is that literate clerics have taken part in practices for which weak Muslims were previously censured. But, largely immune from the radical effects of the *jihād* propaganda, the Jakhanke clerics were able to combine their man-for-all-seasons attitude with a reform outlook, an option that less educated clerics failed to pursue.

The involvement of Jakhanke clerics in indigenous religious practice and usage underlines an assumption maintained throughout this book, namely, the indigenous character of clerical Islam in West Africa. The incidence of foreign missionary influence among the Jakhanke is slight, and surprisingly few Jakhanke even went on the *ḥājj*. Clerical sources pay more regard to local saintly personages, dead and living, than to Middle Eastern ones. Without being insulated against the universal claims of the faith which they embraced so wholeheartedly, the Jakhanke succeeded in maintaining an independent tradition in African Islam, a blend of local resources and outside inspiration. In their educational and religious work the clerics have expressed this local understanding in terms of natural events, such as birth, and environmental influences, such as education. They have consequently been prominent in both areas, praying for fertility and baptising infants, on the one hand, and, on the other, providing instruction for children and leadership to the people.

The specific contribution of Islamic Ṣūfī ideas to Jakhanke clericalism needs emphasising once again. A tentative area for investigation has been indicated in chapter 7 where the educational setting is used to identify possible parallels. Part of the difficulty is related to the elusiveness of Ṣūfīsm itself, a multi-faceted movement spawning theistic as well as non-theistic ideas. The organisational stimulus and parallel, however, are less difficult to reconstruct. The dominant role of the *murshid* or *shaykh* vis-à-vis the *murīd* or *ṭālib*, the place of *awrād* (sing. *wird*, litanies) in clerical devotion, stages of initiation into the clerical vocation, including the colourful and symbolic turbaning ceremony, ideas of *barakah* and saintly power, the use of mystical *salāsil* (sing. *silsilah*) to link renowned personalities with existing movements of renewal, the charismatic foundation of clerical centres and the mystical notions of education all confirm the Ṣūfī interest. The practice of establishing a *modus vivendi* with political rulers is strongly reminiscent of a tradition in Ṣūfīsm which sought to influence political affairs.[2] However, clerical pacifism among the Jakhanke is derived directly from the teachings of al-Ḥājj Sālim rather than being taken from a Ṣūfī source.

Religious pacifism, founded upon al-Ḥājj Sālim's clerical legacy, became the cornerstone of Jakhanke identity. That this principle should have led Jakhanke clerics to co-operate with the colonial overlords is inevitable: the same logic dictated their relations with pre-colonial rulers. In fact it is in their relations with local political figures that the Jakhanke best demonstrate the independence of their clerical tradition.

Two final points may be made in conclusion. One relates to the possible effect of Jakhanke pacific teachings on war and politics, in particular the nineteenth century *jihād*, and the other to the continuing tradition of Jakhanke clericalism in Senegambia.

The story of Jakhanke opposition to Momodou-Lamin has already been told in chapter 4. A similar quarrel developed with Fode Kabba (d. 1911) in the Casamance (see pp. 193-5). It is instructive to examine how Fode Kabba, like Momodou-Lamin, suffered as a result of Jakhanke pacifist teachings which over the years succeeded in alienating large numbers of Muslims from the *jihād* cause. Fode Kabba tried to raise a standard of revolt in the Casamance, using religion as a rallying cry.

The clerics and their communities, however, boycotted him. Faced with the split in Muslim ranks Fode Kabba harnessed his war chariot to political movements in the area. His chief ally in the Casamance was a Mandinka insurgent, Sounkary, with whom he mobilised against the French at Carabane and Sédhiou in 1876-77 (see, for example, Leary 1971: 237-41). Sédhiou had already been the scene of a Muslim struggle in the early parts of the nineteenth century, when the marabout of Pakao, Doura, led engagements against the pagan Jola and Balanta of Sédhiou, forcing them to retreat to Fogny and destroying the region of Boudhié. Doura had occupied Sédhiou with his principal *ṭullāb* from 1840-49 (Marty 1915/6: 496). He died in 1864; to be succeeded by his son, Sounkary, who immediately tried to supplant French power in the Casamance by a coalition of local dissidents. After a period of prayer and fasting Sounkary, with Fode Kabba's blessing, was joined by Fode Lende of Yacine and together they led a *jihād* against the French in 1881 (Leary 1971: 238). But Sounkary received divided support from the Muslims and indeed both Fode Madia of Ndiama, the clerical seat of Fode Kadiali of Jakhanke inspired fame, and Famara Manneh of Kaabu spurned him.

The despair of Islamic militants in areas strongly influenced by the Jakhanke tradition suggests a major pacifist category in African Islam. I have dwelt on this point in parts of chapter 1. Since Islamic militancy has come to be regarded by some schools as a necessary prerequisite of reform, it is important to stress here the peaceful sources of religious renewal. That some mixing of traditional African religious materials and Islam takes place in this gradual process seems inevitable, but that is not for lack of an adequate understanding of the literary sources of the faith. Muḥammad Fāḍil Fadera, for example, a Senegambian scholar brought up in the spirit of the Jakhanke clerical tradition, writes (n.d.) that there is nothing in the authoritative legal sources of Islam to back Aḥmadiyāh strictures against amulets and similar practices in African Islam. At the heart of the dispute is the trustworthiness of Aḥmadī credentials, not the propriety of indigenisation. It shows how an educated cleric, fluent in the broad Islamic tradition, can uphold local innovative forms of Islam against explicit outside criticism.

Finally we come to the continuing relevance of al-Ḥājj Sālim's legacy. The story is told of how President Sekou Toure of Guinea, accompanied by President Léopold Sedar Senghor of Senegal, visited the

Jakhanke clerics settled at Macca-Kolibantang. During the visit Sekou Toure requested that al-Ḥājj Banfa Jabi return to Touba in Guinea which he had left. Banfa, according to himself, declined the invitation, thus keeping in step with a venerable tradition of avoiding direct political sponsorship of the clerical vocation. Al-Ḥājj Mbalu Fode Jabi of Marssassoum, the son of Karamokho Madi, similarly turned down many invitations to travel to Dakar on the occasion of the visit of the late King Faisal of Saudi Arabia, although he finally agreed under continuous pressure to meet the royal visitor. Karang Sambu Lamin of Sutukho, to go slightly further back in recent history, refused to be subsidised from the district coffers of the colonial administration for fear of undue political influence (see p.169). To take a completely different example, Wilks (1968) refers extensively to the *Ta'rīkh al-Madaniyya*. I have been able to consult this document closely, and its author, al-Ḥājj Marhaba, was in fact originally a member of the Jabi-Gassama *qabīlah* at Touba, of the same *nasab* as al-Ḥājj Banfa and al-Ḥājj Mbalu Fode. Al-Ḥājj Marhaba left Accra recently to go to Bobo-Dioulasso in Upper Volta as *muftī*. The *Ta'rīkh al-Madaniyya*, like numerous other similar documents, is steeped in the legacy of al-Ḥājj Sālim, and its existence in modern Ghana is an indication of the range of influence of that legacy.

These references conclude our study aptly by bringing together the themes of unity in the Jakhanke tradition, a unity of practice as well as of endurance, and of geographical range. Al-Ḥājj Sālim could not have wished for a more faithful and enduring tribute to his style and vision.

NOTES

1 Wilks describes this process in terms of *tajdīd*, renewal. He argues that the tendency towards assimilation is counteracted by a constant concern for the reinvigoration of the content of Muslim culture: '...the necessary preconditions of *tajdīd* are, first, the presence throughout society of a basic level of literacy and, second, the existence within society of a basic educated elite - the *ᶜulamā* - able to maintain links with the wider Muslim community and, through the study and interpretation of basic expositions of the Islamic sciences, to preserve conformity between local practice and the general precepts of Islam' (1968: 165).

2 Farid al-Din Attar, the 13th century Persian Ṣūfī, tells an anecdote about the Ṣūfī saint who, by being present at the court of the prince,

was able to plead the cause of pious Muslims some of whom were critical of associating with earthly rulers (*Tadhkirat-al-Awliyā*, tr. in Arberry 1966: 263). Mukhtār al-Kuntī for similar pious reasons withdrew from politics but continued to exercise a deep influence on public affairs through his *jāh*, spiritual rank, and diplomacy (see Baṭrān 1971: 290-322).

GLOSSARY OF ARABIC AND LOCAL TERMS

For ease of reference singular and plural forms are listed separately where they begin with different letters. Words are Arabic unless otherwise indicated.

adab, literature, literary style
^{c}ādah, custom, local practice
ādhān, the call to prayer
ad^{c}iyah, sing. *du^{c}ā*, supplicatory, voluntary prayers
aḥādīth, sing. *ḥadīth*, traditions going back to the Prophet, based on *isnād*
aḥzāb, sing. *ḥizb*, divisions (sixteenths) of the Qu'rān
^{c}ālim, pl. *^{c}ulamā*, one trained in the religious sciences, orthodox scholar, malam
alkali, political office,head of a village (Ar. *al-qāḍī*)
amīr, ruler, prince
^{c}amm, paternal uncle
ansāb, sing. *nasab*, lineage
^{c}aqīqah, naming ceremony on the eight day after birth
aṣl, pl. *uṣūl*, root, source of Islamic law (Sharī^{c}ah)
^{c}aṣr, *ṣalāt al-*, afternoon ritual obligatory prayer
assa, found, create
awliyā, sing. *walī*, saints
awrād, sing. *wird*, prayers, 'collects', phrase-patterned devotions

banna salee (Mand.), Bairam festival
barakah, holiness, spiritual power of virtue
bashīr, pl. *-ūn*, missionary
basmala, the opening phrase used in every *ṣūrah* of the Qur'ān with one exception
bay^{c}ah, pledge or vow of allegiance, contract
bayt al-māl, charitable endowment
bid^{c}ah, pl. *bida^{c}*, blameworthy innovation, heresy
bismillāh, in the name of Allāh

dar al-ḥarb, sphere of war
dar al-Islām, sphere of peace
dawlah, regime, political order
dhabaḥ, ritual slaughter of animal
dhikr, litany, spiritual exercise of recollection
ding koon lee (Mand.) naming ceremony on eighth day after birth
du^{c}ā, pl. *ad^{c}iyah*, supplicatory voluntary prayer, supererogatory prayer exercises

fanna, pl. *funūn*, branch of formal Islamic education
faqīh, pl. *fuqahā*, one trained in *fiqh*, jurisconsult
far^{c}, pl. *furū^{c}*, branch, tributary
farīḍah (*farḍ*), pl. *farā'iḍ*, obligatory ritual prayer and religious duties
fātiḥah, al-, opening chapter of the Qur'ān
fatwah, legal opinion
fayḍ, pl. *fuyūḍ*, outpouring, emanation, divine grace
fidā'atu (*fidā'ah*), the possession of special religious powers and advantages, instrumental or applied religion, the practical utility of religion. (The Jakhanke use the word almost synonymously with Ar. *fā'idatu, fā'idah*.)
fidan, ransom
fiqh, Islamic jurisprudence, religious law
fitnah, violent strife
fode (Mand.), one invested with the turban authorising him to practise as a cleric

gandu (Hausa), slave fields
garanke (Mand.), leatherworkers

ḥadīth, pl. *aḥādīth*, tradition going back to the Prophet, based on *isnād*
ḥājj (*al-ḥājj*), annual ritual pilgrimage to Mecca in month of *Dhū al-ḥijjah* (title of a pilgrim to Mecca)
ḥalāl, lawful, permitted
ḥarām, (lit.) sacred; forbidden, unlawful
ḥarth, farming
ḥijāb, pl. *ḥujub*, veiling, mystical separation, secret prayer, amulet
hijrah, withdrawal, departure
hiyāl, legal casuistry
ḥizb, pl. *aḥzāb*, division (one sixteenth) of the Qur'ān

ʿibādah, pl. *-āt*, canonical rites in which worshipper's relationship is expressed
ʿīd al-aḍḥā, feast of sacrifice at the *ḥājj*, Bairam festival
ʿīd al-fiṭr, feast of ending the fast of Ramaḍān
ʿiddah, prescribed waiting period of three months before divorce is absolute
idhn, authorisation (of a slave)
ijābah al-duʿā, al-, gift of efficacious prayer
ijāzah, pl. *-āt*, authorisation, license, approval
ijmāʿ, consensus of Muslim community, source of Islamic law
ʿilm, pl. *ʿulūm*, higher knowledge, advanced religious studies
ʿilm al-asrār, esoteric knowledge, secret power, charismatic endowment
ʿilm al-awfāq, science of magic squares or amulet-making
imām (*imām ratti*), leader in public worship (chief *imām*)
irādah, aspiration of *murīd* to undertake journey of soul to God
ʿishā', ṣalāt al-, obligatory evening prayer
isnād, the ascription of prophetical tradition, chain of transmitters, educational licence
istighfār, asking forgiveness of God
istikhārah, al-, asking God for guidance and choice
iʿtikāf, spiritual withdrawal, retreat
iʿtizāl, seclusion, retreat

jāh, spiritual rank
jāmiʿ, main mosque
jeli (Mand.), griot
jihād, struggle, religious war, striving along the Ṣūfī path
jinn (pl.), a category of incorporeal spiritual beings
jins, race, species
jongkunda (Mand.), slave caste

kāfir, pl. *kuffār*, infidel, unbeliever, pagan
kalām, *ʿilm al-*, scholastic theology
karāmah, pl. *-at*, grace, miracle
karamokho (Mand.), teacher, holy person (derived from Ar. *qara'a*, to read)
kashf mujarrad, unveiling, stripping away of veil, perspicacious revelation
khāl, maternal uncle
khalīfah, pl. *khulafā'u*, vicar, deputy, successor
khalwah, retreat, seclusion in prayer from three to forty days
khirqah, patched garment of dervish, Ṣūfī symbol of religious status or office
khuṭbah, homily delivered at Friday and festival prayers
kitābah, contract

laibe (Mand.), woodcutters caste
laqab, honorific, sobriquet, nickname
lawḥ, tablet, wooden slate used in Qur'ān schools
lēro (Mand.), writing paper
lūghah, linguistics, language study

madār, pivot
madhhab, pl. *madhāhib*, Sunni juridical school, one of four schools of thought
ma'dhūn, slave given authorisation (*idhn*) by his master to undertake business normally reserved for the freeborn

madīḥ, pl. *madā'iḥ*, eulogy on the Prophet
mafhūm, evident interpretation, making intelligible, understood
majlis, pl. *majālis*, gathering, assembly, educational establishment (among Jakhanke)
majnūn, pl. *majānīn*, one possessed by *jinn*, madman
Mālikī, school of *imām* Mālik ibn Anas
mandūb (pl.), recommended or meritorious acts
maqām, *maqāmah*, stage or degree on Ṣūfī path, status
ma^crifah, insight
masjid, minor mosque
mawlid, birthday of Prophet or important saint
miḥrab, niche in the wall of a mosque indicating *qiblah*
mu'adhdhin, one who calls to prayer
mu^callim, teacher, traditional scholar (Hausa: *malam*)
mudabbar, slave promised emancipation after death of master
muftī, canon lawyer authorised to pronounce *fatwah*, legal opinion
muhājir, pl. *muhājirūn*, migrant, émigré, Muḥammad's companions on the *Hijrah*
mujāb al-du^cā, one whose prayers are always granted
mujaddid al-dīn, renewer of the faith, strengthener of religion
mujāhid, pl. *-ūn*, leader in *jihād* or Holy War
mujtahid, diligent, industrious, authority on independent application of Sharī^cah rules
mukātab, slave who has a contract (*kitābah*) by which he can buy his freedom
mulk, political rule, office, kingdom
muqaddam, sectional leader in a Ṣūfī order; recognised hierarchy in Ṣūfism
murābiṭ, dweller in a *ribāt*, professional religious person (Fr. *marabout*)
murīd, novice, aspirant, disciple, student
murshid, Ṣūfī guide or director, teacher
mushtarak, slave owned by more than one master
mustajībū al-da^cwāt (pl.), efficacious prayers
mutafannin, versatile scholar, one who knows many branches (*funūn*) of learning
mutawallī, *amīr al-*, subordinate district chief
Mu^ctazilah, mediaeval Islamic rationalist school, Mutazilites

nafs, lower self, carnal spirit
naḥw, grammar, philology
nā'ib, deputy, assistant
najdah, courage, vigour, military valour
nasab, pl. *ansāb*, lineage, patronymic
naw^c, kind, branch
naw mini (Mand.), ceremony of canonical investiture of a *tafsīr* scholar
nawo, (Mand.), turban
nisbah, affinity, genealogical tradition
niyāh, intention
noro (Mand.), scent of holiness
numu (Mand.), smith
nūr, light, divine effulgence
nyamakala (Mand.), members of a caste occupational group (tanners, musicians, woodcarvers, etc.)

qabīlah, pl. *qabā'il*, family or clan grouping, common ancestry or paternity
qāḍī, Muslim judge or magistrate
Qādirī, Qādiriyāh, one of the Muslim brotherhoods prevalent in West Africa
qasm awwal, al-, first order, group, class
qiblah, direction of prayer, facing Mecca (see *miḥrab*)
qirā'ah, diligence in learning
qiyās, analogical deduction, a process of legal reasoning employed in *fiqh*
quṭb, pole, axis

rakᶜah (*rakaᶜa*), pl. *rukūᶜ* (*rakaᶜāt*), cycle of word and act of prostration in *ṣalāt*
Ramaḍān, Muslim month of fasting
ribāṭ, religious hospice, retreat house, Ṣūfī centre
rijāl al-ṣāliḥīna, sing. *rajul*, the upright men, i.e. the leaders of the clans (*qabā'il*) as a group
riwāyah, tradition, chain of transmission
riyāḍah (or *-at*), retreat in prayer
runde, *rounde* (Fula), slave village
ru'yā (*taᶜbīr al-*) (*ta'wīl al-*), dream (dream-interpretation) (gift of dream-interpretation)
ru'yā al-ṣāliḥah, request-granting dream

ṣadaqah, pl. *-āt*, free-will offering
safar, travel, journey, religious itinerancy (Fr. *tournée pastorale*)
salāt, obligatory ritual prayer
ṣalāt ᶜalā al-nabī, calling down blessings on the Prophet
ṣalāt al-istikhārah, prayer of asking God for guidance and choice
ṣalāt nāfilah, meritorious ritual prayer additional to prescribed prayers
sālihīna, upright, righteous
samako (Mand.), platform from which teacher supervises students
seno (Mand.), farming
shaqīqah, pl. *-āt*, uterine brother
sharīᶜah, (lit.) path to be followed; exoteric revelation, Muslim Law
sharīf, one who claims descent from the Prophet
shawkah, military prowess
shaykh, pl. *shuyūkh*, religious title given to respected or venerated Muslim leader, guide, director
Shīᶜī, Muslim adhering to the party recognising ᶜAlī as the Prophet's heir (as opposed to Sunnī)
silsilah, pl. *salāsil*, chain, lineage chain of spiritual descent
siyām, *ṣawm*, fasting
Ṣūfī, Muslim mystic
Sunnī, orthodox Muslim as distinct from Shīᶜī Muslim
ṣūrah, pl. *ṣūrāt*, a chapter of the Qur'ān

tāᶜa, *imām al-*, commander of obedience
taᶜbīr al-ru'yā, skill or craft of dream-interpretation
tafrīq, dispersion
tafsīr, exegesis of the Qur'ān
taḥiyāh, act of greeting in ritual *ṣalāt* (end of second *rakaᶜa*), greeting of Prophet during *mawlid*
taḥlīl, dispensation, accepted past rulings of the Patriarchs
ṭā'ifah, association, organisation, Ṣūfī order
tajdīd, renewal
takbīr, act of formal opening of *ṣalāt* with words *'Allāh Akbar'*
ṭālib, pl. *ṭullāb*, advanced Qur'ān school student
taᶜlīm, teaching, instruction
talqīn, giving secret instruction, act of initiation
taqlīd, established Muslim practice
ta'rīkh, pl. *tawārīkh*, history, historical or genealogical account
ṭarīqah, pl. *ṭarīqāt* (*ṭuruq*), Ṣūfī path mystical method or system for traversing the path
tartīl, recital of the Qur'ān
taslīm, surrender, act of formal terminating of *ṣalāt*
taṣrīf, discipline of grammar, conjugation; (among Jakhanke) occult powers of clerics
tawakkul, trusting in God
tawallā, to make a gift
tawḥīd, theology, the Unity of God
ta'wīl al-ru'yā, gift of dream-interpretation, immediate insight into dreams
tcherno (Fula), cleric
Tijānī, Tijāniyāh, one of the Muslim brotherhoods prevalent in West Africa
ṭilasm, amulet
tilmīdh, pl. *talāmīdh*, elementary Qur'ān school pupil
tungi (Mand.), educational centre housed in a building

ᶜulamā, sing. *ᶜālim*, those trained in the religious sciences, orthodox scholars
ᶜulūm, sing. *ᶜilm*, higher knowledge, advanced religious studies
ummah, community
ummī, enlightened illiterate
ᶜurf, customary practice
uṣūl al-fiqh, sing. *aṣl*, fundamental principles of Islamic jurisprudence

walā (Mand.), Qur'ān school wooden slate
wali, pl. *awliyā*, protector, saint, political office as in *amīr al-mutawallī*, subordinate district chief
wāridāt (pl.), revelations (in the sense of mystical enlightenments)
wilāyah (*walāyah*), sainthood, sanctity, spiritual office or jurisdiction
wird, pl. *awrād*, prayer, 'collect', phrase-patterned devotion
wuḍū, ritual ablution before *ṣalāt*

zāhid, pl. *zuhhād*, ascetic devotee
zāwiyah, pl. *zawāyā*, religious retreat or centre
zayt (*zayyāt*), olive oil (dealer in olive oil)
zakāt, obligatory alms
ziyārah, pilgrimage to local holy places, visit to saints' tombs
ẓulm, error, political oppression

ARCHIVAL AND LOCAL SOURCES

ARCHIVES AND ABBREVIATIONS USED IN THE TEXT

AFD Archives Fédérales de Dakar, Senegal. This was most useful for Chapter 6,especially collections in Session de 1911, listed under Camille Guy in the Bibliography below.

ANSOM Archives Nationales Section Outre-Mer, Paris, France, housing the Archives Ministère de la France d'Outre-Mer (AMFOM). This was particularly used for Chapters 4 and 5, especially Mission Galliéni - Campagne 1886-7; Mission de Capitaine Martin en Bambouk; Correspondences de la Ministère des Colonies MC/I série Sénégal et Dépendances 1850-86 folios 37-73; MC/IV série Sénégal: Expansion territoriale et politique indigène 1820-95, folios 24, 50, 60, 104-5, 127.

IFAN Institut Fondamental de l'Afrique Noire, Dakar, Senegal.

PROB Public Records Office, Banjul, the Gambia. This contains, for example, a report listed under C. Sitwell in the Bibliography below and the Slave Abolition Ordinance, 1906, Ref. 2/96.

PROL Pblic Record Office, London, UK. This was used for an account listed under M.D. Gouldsbury in the Bibliography below.

TAWĀRĪKH OBTAINED IN SENEGAMBIA

TBI *Ta'rīkh* on the Silla of Banī Isrā'ila, obtained from al-Ḥājj Khousi Silla, Brikama. It is a short manuscript and is widely available in the Silla community. It was also the manuscript used and commented upon by de Mézières (1949).

TKB *Ta'rīkh* on Karamokho Ba of Touba. Its author was Karamokho al-Maghīlī (Madi) (b. 1855) who started compiling it under the direction of Karamokho Qutubo. It was finally verified by Karamokho Sankoung, the last clerical head of Touba before the manuscript was finished. The present *Ta'rīkh* was submitted to Sankoung's eldest sons, al-Ḥājj Banfa Jabi and al-Ḥājj Soriba Jabi, and to Karamokho Madi's son, al-Ḥājj Mbalu Fode Jabi. It exists in several different versions.

TKQ *Ta'rīkh* on the Kabba-Jakhite *qabīlah*, obtained in Kuntaur-Fulakunda from the estate of the late al-Ḥājj Kemoring Jakhite.

TSB *Ta'rīkh* on Sālim (Gassama) of Touba (Karamokho Ba) by al-Ḥājj Mbalu Fode Jabi of Marssassoum. Part of an extended treatment of the family of Karamokho Ba through Karamokho Qutubo.

TSK *Ta'rīkh* on al-Ḥājj Sālim Suware and Karamokho Ba, compiled by al-Ḥājj Banfa Jabi and disseminated by his students. The present *Ta'rīkh* was shown to Banfa for his approval of using it as a source.

PRINCIPAL INFORMANTS IN INTERVIEWS

Most of the place names may be found on Map 5, p. 161.

DARAME, al-Ḥājj Janko, grandson of Fode Ansumana, Jimara-Bakadaji.
DARAME, al-Ḥājj Khousi, *imām*, Danfakunda.
DERRI, al-Ḥājj Nfanding, Kounti.
GASSAMA, al-Ḥājj Denano, Sandu-Chowdukunda.
HAWA, al-Ḥājj Madi (or Momodou), Jarra-Barrokunda.
JĀBAI, Njari, *Alkali*, Wuli-Sutukho.
JABI, al-Ḥājj Almamy, Wuli-Sutukho.
JABI, al-Ḥājj Banfa, son of Karamokho Sankoung, Macca-Kolibantang.
JABI, al-Ḥājj Fode, Sandu-Jakhaba.
JABI, al-Ḥājj Mbalu Fode, son of Karamokho Madi, Marssassoum.
JABI, al-Ḥājj Mukhtār, brother of al-Ḥājj Shaykh Sidiya Jabi, Jarra-Sutukung.
JABI, al-Ḥājj Shaykh Sidiya, son of Karang Sambou Lamin, Jarra-Sutukung, resident at Kombo-Brikama and then at Brufut.
JABI, al-Ḥājj Soriba, son of Karamokho Sankoung, Macca-Kolibantang.
JABI, al-Ḥājj Soriba ibn Banfa, Macca-Kolibantang.
JABI, Alieu Sajjalī, Nibrās.
JABI, Karamokho Sankoung (Muḥammad Taslīmī), grandson of Karamokho Qutubo, Nibrās.
JAKHABI, Ba Fode, *imam*, Georgetown.
JAKHABI, Shaykh Farūqi, Jarra-Sutukung.
JAKHITE, al-Ḥājj Ba, Wuli-Sutukho.
JAKHITE-KABBA, al-Ḥājj Ansumana, grandson of Fode Maḥmūd Jīlānī, Jarumekoto.
JAKHITE-KABBA, Muḥammad Lamin, Kuntaur-Fulakunda.
JAKHITE-KABBA, Yusufa, ex-Kuntaur-Fulakunda.
JIKINNE, Ibrahima, ex-Jarra-Sutukung, resident at Farafenyi.
JIKINNE, Maḥmūd Jīlānī, Jarra-Sutukung.
JIKINNE, Muḥammad Gallo, Jarra-Sutukung.
SILLA, al-Ḥājj Bubakar, Jarra-Barrokunda.
SILLA, al-Ḥājj Khousi, Komba-Brikama.
SILLA, Khalīfa, Jarra-Sutukung.
SILLA, Kunnadiya, Kuntaur-Jakhaba.
SILLA, Muḥammad Kebba, Jarra-Sutukung.
SILLA, Muḥammad Khalīfa, grandson of Muḥammad Sanūsī Silla, Kunti.
SILLA, Mukhtār, brother of al-Ḥājj Khousi Silla, Kombo-Brikama.
SISE, al-Ḥājj Ibrahima (Tankular Sise), Kiang-Jiroffe.
SISE, Kalāmullāh, Jimara-Bakadaji.

BIBLIOGRAPHY

Journal abbreviations used:

BCEHS de l'AOF *Bulletin du Comité d'Etudes Historiques et Scientifiques de l'Afrique Occidentale Française*
BSOAS *Bulletin of the School of Oriental and African Studies* (London)
Bull. IFAN *Bulletin de l'Institut Français* [later *Fondamental*] *de l'Afrique Noire* (Dakar)
JHSN *Journal of the Historical Society of Nigeria*

ABUN-NASR, J.M. 1965 *The Tijaniyah: A Sufi Order in the Modern World.* London.
ADANSON, Michael 1759 *A Voyage to Senegal, the Isle of Gorée and the River Gambia.* London.
AJOSE, O.A. 1957 'Preventive Medicine and Superstition in North Nigeria', *Africa* XXVII (3).
AKINJOGBIN, I.A. 1967 *Dahomey and its Neighbours 1708-1818.* London.
ANAWATI, M.M. & L. GARDET 1961 *La mystique musulmane.* Paris.
ANCELLE, J. 1887 *Les explorations au Sénégal.* Paris.
ANDERSON, Benjamin 1971 *Journeys to Musadu.* London.
ANDERSON, J.N.D. 1954 *Islamic Law in Africa.* London.
ANDRAE, Tor 1960 *Muhammad: The Man and his Faith.* New York.
ARBERRY, A.J. 1943 *An Introduction to the History of Sufism.* London.
—— 1950 *Sufism.* London.
—— 1964 *The Koran Interpreted.* London.
—— 1966 *Muslim Saints and Mystics.* London.
ARCIN, André 1907 *La Guinée française: races, religion, coutume, production, commerce.* Paris.
—— 1911 *Histoire de la Guinée française.* Paris.
ARKELL, A.J. 1955 *A History of the Sudan to 1821.* London.
ARKLEY, Alfred S. 1965 *Slavery in Sierra Leone.* M.A. dissertation, Columbia University, New York.
ARMSTRONG, R. 1964 *The Study of West African Languages.* Ibadan.
ARNAUD, Robert *et al.* 1923 'Vestiges de la vénération du feu au Soudan', *Rev. d'Ethnog. et des Trad. Pop.* 4 (14).
ARNETT, E.J. 1922 *The Rise of the Sokoto Fulani.* Lagos.
ARNOLD, T.W. 1965 *The Preaching of Islam.* London.
AUBERGER, M. 1913 'Etude sur Dia', *Document IFAN* XVIII, 3/1, Archives de Ké-Macina, Dakar.
AUBERT, A. 1923 'Légendes historiques et traditions orales', *BCEHS de l'AOF* IV.
AYANDELE, E.A. 1970 *Holy Johnson.* London.
BA, Hampaté & J. DAGET 1962 *L'empire peul du Macina.* Paris.
BĀBĀ, Aḥmad 1977 *Mi^{c}rāj.* Edited by Bernard Barbour and Michelle Jacobs. Princeton University Conference Paper, June. (Author 1556-1627.)
BAILLIE, Neil B.E. [1869/75] 1957 *A Digest of Moohummudan Law.* London. Reprinted in Lahore.

BAKRĪ, al- 1965 *Kitāb al-masālik wa al-mamālik/Description de l'Afrique Septentrionale*. Ed. and tr. by M.G. de Slane. Paris. (Original, 11th C.)

BARBOT, Jean 1732 'A Description of the Coasts of North and South Guinea', in *A Collection of Voyages and Travels*, ed. Awnsham Churchill. Vol. V. London.

BARTH, H. [1857] 1965 *Travels and Discoveries in North and Central Africa 1849-55*. Reprint, 3 vols. London.

BATHILY, A. 1970 'Mamadou-Lamine Daramé et la résistance anti-impérialiste dans le Haut-Sénégal (1885-7)', *Notes Africaines* (IFAN) 125 (Jan.).

BAṬRĀN, Abdal Azīz ᶜAbdallāh 1971 *Sidi Mukhtār al-Kuntī and the Recrudescence of Islam in the Western Sahara and the Middle Niger c. 1750-1811*. Ph.D. thesis, University of Birmingham.

—— 1973 'A Contribution to the Biography of Muḥammad ibn ᶜAbd al-Karīm (ᶜUmar Aᶜmar) al-Maghīlī al-Tilimsānī', *J. of Af. Hist.* XIV(3).

BAṬṬŪṬA, ibn 1929 *Riḥlah*. Tr. H.A.R. Gibb. London. In Arabic, 1964, Beirut. (Original, 14th C.)

BEHRMAN, Lucy 1966 'The Islamisation of the Wolof by the End of the 19th Century', in *Boston Papers in African Studies*, vol. II, ed. J. Butler.

BELL, R. 1926 *The Origins of Islam in its Christian Environment*. London.

BELLO, Muḥammad 1957 *Infāq al-Maisūr*. Edited by C.E.J. Whitting, London. (Author d. 1837.)

BENTON, P.A. 1971 *Kanuri Readings*. London.

BINGER, L.G. 1891 *Esclavage, islamisme, christianisme*. Paris.

—— 1892 *Du Golfe au Niger de Guinée*. 2 vols. Paris.

BLAKE, J.W. 1942 *Europeans in West Africa 1450-1560*. Hakluyt Society, ser. 2, no. 86.

BLASDELL, R.A. 1940 'The Use of the Drum for Mosque Services', *Muslim World* 30: 41-5.

BLYDEN, E.W. 1888 *Christianity, Islam and the Negro Race*. London.

BOAHEN, A.A. 1964 *Britain, the Sahara and the Western Sudan, 1788-1861*. London.

BOCARDÉ, B. 1849 'Notes sur la Guinée portugaise ou Sénégambie méridionale', *Bull. de la Soc. de Géog.* (Paris), sér. 3, XII.

BOER, T. de 1967 *The History of Philosophy in Islam*. New York.

BOILAT, P.-D. 1853 *Esquisses Sénégalaises*. Paris.

BOULÈGUE, Jean 1966 'Contribution à la chronologie du royaume du Saloum', *Bull. IFAN* XXVIII, sér. B, no. 31.

—— 1969 *La Sénégambie du milieu du XVᵉ siècle au début du XVIIᵉ siècle*. Thesis, Univ. of Paris.

BOULNOIS, J. & B. HAMA 1954 *Empire de Gao*. Paris.

BOUTILLIER, J.L., P. CANTRELLE, *et al.* 1962 *La Moyenne Vallée du Sénégal*. Paris.

BOVILL, E.W. 1958 *The Golden Trade of the Moors*. London.

BOWDICH, T.E. 1825 *Excursions in Madeira and Porto Santo*. London.

BRELVI, M. 1964 *Islam in Africa*. Lahore.

BRENNER, Louis 1973 *The Shehus of Kukawa*. London.

BRIGAUD, F. 1962 *Histoire traditionelle du Sénégal*. St. Louis, Senegal.

BRIGGS, L.C. 1960 *Tribes of the Sahara*. Cambridge, Mass.

BROOKS, E.H. 1964 *The City of God and the City of Man in Africa*. Lexington, Kentucky.

BRUN, P.J. 1910 'La totémisme chez quelques peuples du Soudan

Occidental', *Anthropos* 5.

BRUNSCHVIG, R. 1960 '[c]Abd', *Encyclopaedia of Islam.* New Edition. Vol. I. Leiden.

BRUNSCHWIG, H. 1963 *L'avènement de l'Afrique noire.* Paris.

CAILLIE, Réné 1830 *Travels through Central Africa to Timbouctou and the Great Desert to Morocco Performed in the Years 1824-28.* 2 vols. London.

CANOT, T. 1928 *Adventures of an African Slaver: Being a True Account of the Life of Captain Theodore Canot...as Told in the Year 1854...* London.

CARDAIRE, Marcel 1954 'L'Islam et la terroir africain: Bamako', *Bull. IFAN.*

CARRIERE, F. & P. HOLLE 1855 *De la Sénégambie française.* Paris.

CHAILLEY, M. 1962 'Aspects de l'Islam au Mali: notes et études sur l'Islam en Afrique noire', *Recherches et Documents du CHEAM.* (Paris) I: 9-51.

CHATELIER, A. le 1899 *L'Islam dans l'Afrique occidentale.* Paris.

CHELHOD, J. 1971 'Hidjāb', *Encyclopaedia of Islam.* New Edition. Vol. III. Leiden.

CHENGUITI, ech-, Ahmad Lamine 1953 *El-Wasīt.* Tr. Mourad Teffahi. Saint Louis, Senegal. Etudes Mauritaniennes 5. (See also Shinqītī).

CHODJĀ[c], Abū 1935 *Abrégé de la loi musulmane selon le rite de l'Imām al-Shāfi[c]ī.* Tr. and ed. G.-H. Bousquet. Extrait de la *Revue Algérienne, Tunisienne et Marocaine de Législation et de Jurisprudence.* Paris.

CISSOKO, S.M. 1972 'L'empire de Kabou XVIe-XIXe'. Paper presented at the Manding Conference, SOAS, London.

CLAPPERTON, H. 1829 *Journal of a Second Expedition into the Interior of Africa.* London.

CLERCQ, A.J.H. de 1861/1919 *Recueil des traités de la France 1713-1906.* 23 vols. Paris.

COELHO, Lemos de 1953 *Duas descrições seiscentistas da Guiné.* Lisbon.

COHEN, Abner 1971 'Cultural Strategies in the Organisation of Trading Diasporas', in *The Development of Indigenous Trade and Markets in West Africa,* ed. C. Meillassoux. London. 266-81.

CONNEAU, Capt. Theophilus [1854] 1976 *A Slaver's Log Book or 20 Years' Residence in Africa.* Complete, original manuscript, New Jersey. (Previously ed. Brantz Mayer, 1854, and numerous other editions.)

COOKSEY, J.J. & A. McLEISH 1931 *Religion and Civilisation in West Africa.* London.

CORNEVIN, R. & M. 1964 *Histoire de l'Afrique des origines à nos jours.* Paris.

COULSON, N.J. 1964 *A History of Islamic Law.* Edinburgh.

——— 1969 *Conflicts and Tensions in Islamic Jurisprudence.* London.

CRAGG, Kenneth 1955 'Each Other's Face: Pilgrimage Prayers (min manāsik al-ḥājj)', *Muslim World* (July).

——— 1956 *The Call of the Minaret.* New York.

——— 1957 'Ramaḍān Prayers from *Mukhtaṣar Ad'iyat*', *Muslim World* (July).

——— 1965 *Counsels in Contemporary Islam.* Edinburgh.

——— 1970 *Alive to God: Christian and Muslim Prayers.* London.

CROWDER, M. 1966 *The Story of Nigeria.* London.

——— (ed.) 1971 *West African Resistance.* London.

CRUISE O'BRIEN, D. 1967 'Towards an Islamic Policy in French West Africa', *J. of Af. Hist.* VIII(2).

——— 1970 'The Saint and the Squire: Personalities and Social Forces in the Development of a Religious Brotherhood', in *African Perspectives*, ed. C. Allen and R.W. Johnson. London.

CRUISE O'BRIEN, D. 1971 *The Mourides of Senegal*. London.

CULTRU, Prosper 1910 *Histoire de Sénégal du XVe siècle à 1870*. Paris.

CURTIN, Philip D. 1971a 'Jihad in West Africa: Early Phases...', *J. of Af. Hist.* XII(1).

—— 1971b 'Pre-colonial Trading Networks and Traders: The Diakhanké', in *The Development of Trade and Markets in Pre-colonial West Africa*, ed. C. Meillassoux. London.

—— 1972 'The Western Juula in the Eighteenth Century'. Paper presented at the Manding Conference, SOAS, London.

—— 1973 'The Lure of Bambuk Gold', in *J. of Af. Hist.* XIV.

—— 1975 *Economic Change in Precolonial Africa: Senegambia in the Era of the Slave Trade*. Madison, Wisconsin.

CURTIN, Philip D. & A. Neil SKINNER 1971 'Saki Olal N'diaye: the story of Malik Sy', *Cahiers d'Etudes Africaines* 43.

CUTTER, C.H. 1968 'The Politics of Music in Mali', *African Arts* (Spring).

DARCY, J. 1904 *France et Angleterre: cent années de rivalités coloniales: l'Afrique*. Paris.

DAUMAS, E. [1851] 1971 *The Ways of the Desert*. Transl. London.

DAUMAS, Le Général E. & A. de CHANCEL 1856 *Le grand désert: itinéraire d'une caravane du Sahara au pays des nègres (royaume de Haoussa)*. Paris.

DEHAINI, A.R. 1965 *Arabic Teaching in Private Primary Schools in Western Nigeria*. Report, Ibadan.

DELAFOSSE, M. 1912 *Haut-Sénégal-Niger*. 2 vols. Paris.

—— 1913 *Traditions historiques et légendaires du Soudan occidentale*. Paris.

DEMANET, l'Abbé 1767 *Nouvelle histoire de l'Afrique française*. 2 vols. Paris.

DERMAN, W. 1973 *Serfs, Peasants and Socialists: A Former Serf Village in the Republic of Guinea*. Berkeley, California.

DESCHAMPS, H. 1962 *Le Sénégal et la Gambie*. Paris.

DIETERLEN, Germaine 1951 *Essai sur la religion Bambara*. Paris.

DIOP, Cheik Anta 1960 *L'Afrique noire pré-coloniale*. Paris.

DODGE, B. 1961 *Al-Azhar: A Millenium of Muslim Learning*. Washington, D.C.

DOUCOURÉ, Boubou 1940 'Notice sur l'origine des habitants de Goumbou, subdivision de Nara, cercle de Nema', *Bull. IFAN* 2 (3/4).

DOUGHTY, C.M. 1923 *Travels in Arabia Deserta*. London.

DRETKE, J. 1965 *The Muslim Community of Accra*. M.A. dissertation, Univ. of Legon.

DUMONT, Fernand 1974 *L'Anti-Sultan ou al-Hajj Omar Tal du Fouta: combattant de la foi (1794-1864)*. Dakar and Abidjan.

—— 1975 *La pensée religieuse d'Amadou Bamba: fondateur du Mouridisme sénégalais*. Dakar and Abidjan.

DURAND, J.L.P. 1802 *Voyage au Sénégal (1785-86)*. Paris. Tr. into English, 1806, London.

EARTHY, E.D. 1955 'The Impact of Mohammedanism on Paganism in the Liberian Hinterland', *Numen* II.

EAST, R.M. 1934 *Stories of Old Adamawa*. Lagos and London.

EVANS-PRITCHARD, E.E. 1949 *The Sanusi of Cyrenaica*. London.

FADERA, Al-Ḫājj Muḥammad Fādilu n.d. [?c. 1969] *Kitāb Taḥdhīr Ummah al-Muḥammadiyāh min Ittibā^c al-firqah Aḥmadiyāh* (A Warning to the Muslim Community on the Dangers of Following the Ahmadiyah Sect). Dakar.

FAGE, J.D. 1969 *A History of West Africa: An Introductory Study*. London.

FAGE, J.D. & R. OLIVER 1970 *A Short History of Africa*. London.
FAHD, Toufic 1966 *La divination arabe: études religieuses, sociologiques et folkloriques sur le milieu natif de l'Islam*. Leiden.
—— 1974 'Istikhārah', *Shorter Encyclopaedia of Islam*. London and Leiden.
FAIDHERBE, L.L.C. 1856 'Populations noires des bassins du Sénégal et du Haut-Niger', *Bull. de la Soc. de Géog.* ser. 4, XI.
—— 1889 *Le Sénégal: la France dans l'Afrique occidentale*. Paris.
FARADAY, Ann 1972 *Dream Power: The Use of Dreams in Everyday Life*. London.
FARUKI, K.A. 1954 *Ijma and the Gate of Ijtihād*. Karachi.
—— 1962 *Islamic Jurisprudence*. Karachi.
FARUQI, I.R.A. 1965 'History of Religions: Its Nature and Significance for Christian Education and the Muslim-Christian Dialogue', *Numen* 12.
FERNANDES, Valentin [1506/10] 1951 *Description de la côte occidentale d'Afrique*. Tr. T. Monod, A. Teixeira da Mota & R. Mauny. Bissau.
FISHER, H.J. 1961 'Early Muslim-Western Education in West Africa', *Muslim World*.
—— 1969 'Islamic Education and Religious Reform in West Africa', in *Education in Africa*, ed. Richard Jolly, Nairobi.
—— 1970 'The Early Life and Pilgrimage of al-Ḥājj Muḥammad al-Amīn the Soninké (d. 1887)', *J. of Af. Hist.* XI(1).
—— 1971 'Prayer and Military Activity in the History of Muslim Africa South of the Sahara', *J. of Af. Hist.* XII(3).
—— 1973 'Hassebu: Islamic Healing in Black Africa', in *Northern Africa: Islam and Modernisation*, ed. M. Brett. London.
—— 1975 'The Modernisation of Islamic Education in Sierra Leone, Gambia and Liberia', in *Conflict and Harmony in Education in Tropical Africa*, ed. G.N. Brown & M. Hiskett. London.
FISHER, H.J. & A.G.B. FISHER 1971 *Slavery and Muslim Society in Africa*. London.
FISHER, H.J. & V. ROWLAND 1973 'Firearms in the Central Sudan', in *J. of Af. Hist.* XII.
FLUEGEL, Gustave 1842 *Concordantiae Corani Arabicae*. Leipzig.
—— 1883 *Corani Textus Arabicus*. Leipzig. (Repr. 1965.)
FODÉ, al-Ḥājj Mbalu 1972 *Majmūʿa Khuṭbah Dīniyāh*. Dakar.
FORBES, J.G. 1904 'Native Methods of Treatment in West Africa', *Journal of the Africa Society* III.
FOX, William 1851 *A Brief History of the Wesleyan Missions on the Western Coast of Africa*. London.
FREY, H. 1886 'Rapport Frey', Archives Nationales, Section Outre-Mer (ANSOM), Sénégal, IV 85a.
—— 1888 *Campagnes dans le Haut-Sénégal et dans le Haut-Niger 1885-6*. Paris.
FROELICH, J.C. 1962 *Les Musulmans d'Afrique noire*. Paris.
FYFE, C. 1962 *A History of Sierra Leone*. London.
FYZEE, A.A.A. 1964 *Outlines of Muhammadan Law*. London.
GABRIELI, F. 1968 *Muhammad and the Conquests of Islam*. London.
GALLIÉNI, J.S. 1891 *Deux campagnes au Soudan français, 1886-88*. Paris.
GAMBLE, D.P. 1949 *Contributions to a Socio-economic Survey of the Gambia*. London.
GAUDEFROY-DEMOMBYNES, M. 1954 *Muslim Institutions*. London.
GHAZĀLĪ, Abū Ḥāmid al- [1109/10] 1964 *Naṣīḥat al-Muluk/Counsel for Kings*. Tr. F.R.C. Bagley. London.
GIBB, H.A.R. 1947 *Modern Trends in Islam*. Chicago.

GIBB, H.A.R. 1953 *Mohammedanism*. 2nd ed. London (1st ed. 1949; 2nd ed. reprinted in 1969.)
—— 1962 *Studies in the Civilisation of Islam*. Edited by S.J. Shaw and W.R. Polk. London.
—— 1970/1 'The Heritage of Islam in the Modern World', *J. of Mid. East Stud.* 1 (1) ; 1 (3) ; 2.
GLUCKMAN, M. 1955 *Custom and Conflict in Africa*. Glencoe, Ill.
GOITEIN, S.D. 1959 'The Origin and Nature of the Muslim Friday Worship', *Muslim World* 49 (July).
GOLBERRY, Sylvain 1802 *Fragments d'un Voyage en Afrique 1785-87*. 2 vols. Paris.
GOLDZIHER, Ignaz 1917 *Muhammad and Islam*. New York.
—— [1889/90] 1967/71 *Muslim Studies*. Tr. & ed. C.R. Barber & S.M. Stern. 2 vols. London.
GOODY, Jack 1970 'Reform, Renewal and Resistance: A Mahdi in Northern Ghana', in *African Perspectives*, ed. C. Allen & R.W. Johnson. London.
GOUILLY, Alphonse 1952 *L'Islam dans l'Afrique occidentale française*. Paris.
GOULDSBURY, M.D. 1881 *Expedition to Upper Gambia, August 1881*. Public Records Office, London, Enclosure 1 in no. 17 (June 22, 1881).
'Government and Islam in Africa' 1921 *Muslim World* XI.
GRAY J.M. 1966 *A History of the Gambia*. New York and London.
GRAY, Richard 1964 *A History of the Southern Sudan*. London.
—— 1973 Review article of D.W. Cohen: *The Historical Traditions of Busoga*. *BSOAS* XXXVI (1).
GRAY, William & Staff Surgeon DOCHARD 1825 *Travels in Western Africa 1818-21*. London.
GRÜNEBAUM, G.E. von 1953 *Mediaeval Islam*. Chicago.
—— 1970 *Classical Islam*. London.
GRÜNEBAUM, G.E. von & R. CAILLOIS 1966 *The Dream and Human Societies*. Los Angeles.
GUY, Camille 1911a 'Proposition d'internement d'indigènes de la Guinée pour faits d'insurrection contre l'autorité de la France'. Report by the Governor of the Colonies and Lt-Governor of Guinea. Archives Fédérales de Dakar (AFD), 84, Session de 1911.
—— 1911b 'Internement d'Alfa Yaya, de son fils Mody Aguibou et de son conseiller Oumarou Koumba'. Report in Archives Fédérales de Dakar (AFD), Session 1911, 20th June.
ḤĀJJ, M.A. al- 1968 'A 17th Century Chronicle on the Origins and Missionary Activities of the Wangarawa', *Kano Studies* 1(4).
HALSTEAD, J.P. 1964 'The Changing Character of Moroccan Reformism: 1921-34', *J. of Af. Hist.* 435-47.
HAMET, Ismael 1920 'Littérature arabe saharienne', *Revue du Monde Musulman* 4e Année, Oct. 194-213.
HAMLYN, W.T. 1931 *A Short History of the Gambia*. Bathurst.
HARGREAVES, J.D. 1963 *Prelude to the Partition of West Africa*. London.
—— 1966 'The Tokolor Empire of Ségou and its Relations with the French', in *Boston University Papers on Africa*, vol. II, ed. J. Butler. Boston.
HASAN, Yusuf Faḍl 1963 'Penetration of Islam in Eastern Sudan', *Sudan Notes and Records* 44.
—— 1967 *The Arabs and the Sudan*. Edinburgh.
HECQUARD, H. 1851 *Voyage sur la côte et dans l'intérieur de l'Afrique occidentale*. Paris.
HILL, Christopher 1966 *Society and Puritanism in Pre-revolutionary England*. London.

HILL, Polly 1972 *Rural Hausa*. London.
HISHĀM, ibn 1858/60 *Sīrat Rasūl Allāh*. Ed. F. Wüstenfeld. Göttingen.
HISKETT, M. 1957 'Material Relating to the State of Learning among the Fulani', *BSOAS* XIX(3).
—— 1960 'Problems of Religious Education in Muslim Communities in Africa', *Overseas Education* (London).
—— 1962 'An Islamic Tradition of Reform in the Western Sudan from the 16th-18th Centuries', *BSOAS* XXV(3).
—— 1971 'The Song of the Shehu's Miracles: A Hausa Hagiography from Sokoto', *Af. Lang. Stud.* XII.
—— 1973 *The Sword of Truth: The Life and Times of Shehu Usuman dan Fodio*. New York.
HISKETT, M. & A.D. BIRAR 1962 'The Arabic Literature of Nigeria to 1804', *BSOAS* XXV(1).
HITTI, P.K. 1967 *History of the Arabs*. London.
HODGE, Carleton T. (ed.) 1971 *Papers on the Manding*. Bloomington, Indiana.
HODGES, Cornelius [1689/90] 1924 'The Journal of Cornelius Hodges in Senegambia', *Eng. Hist. Rev.* 39.
HODGKIN, R.A. 1957 *Education and Change*. London.
HODGKIN, T. 1962 'Islam and National Movements in West Africa', *J. of Af. Hist.* 3(2).
—— 1963 'Islam, History and Politics', *J. of Mod. Af. Stud.* 1(1).
—— 1971 *Nigerian Perspectives*. London.
HOGBEN, S.J. & A.H.M. KIRK-GREENE 1966 *The Emirates of Northern Nigeria*. London.
HOLDEN, Jeff 1970 'The Samorian Impact on Buna', in *African Perspectives*, ed. C. Allen & R.W. Johnson. London.
HOLDEREN, P. 1939 'Note sur la coutume Mandingue du Ouli', in *Coutumes juridiques de l'Afrique occidentale française*. Vol. I: *Sénégal*. Paris.
HOLT, P.M. 1958a *The Mahdist State in the Sudan*. London.
—— 1958b 'The Sudanese Mahdia and the Outside World 1881-89', *BSOAS* XXI(2).
—— 1966 *Egypt and the Fertile Crescent, 1516-1922*. London.
HOPEWELL, James F. 1958 *Muslim Penetration into French Guinea, Sierra Leone and Liberia before 1850*. Ph.D. thesis, Columbia Univ.
HOVELACQUE, Abel 1889 *Les nègres de l'Afrique sub-équatoriale*. Paris.
HUMBLOT, P. 1918 'Du nom propre et des appellations chez les Malinké des vallées du Niandan et du Milo', *BCEHS de l'AOF*. 1: 519-42.
HUNTLEY, H.V. 1850 *Seven Years' Service on the Slave Coast of Western Africa*. 2 vols. London.
HUNWICK, J.O. 1965 *Report on a Seminar on the Teaching of Arabic in Nigeria*. Ibadan and Kano.
—— 1966 'Religion and State in the Songhay Empire 1464-1591', in *Islam in Tropical Africa*, ed. I.M. Lewis. 296-317.
—— 1972 'The Word made Book: Review Article of J. Goody (ed.), *Literacy in Traditional Societies*', *Trans. of the Hist. Soc. of Ghana* XIII(2).
—— 1976 'Black Africans in the Islamic World...' Department of History Seminar Paper, University of Ghana, 24 Nov.
HUXLEY, Elspeth 1954 *Four Guineas: A Journey through West Africa*. London.
INNES, Gordon 1972 'The Kingdom of Kaabu in Gambian Mandinka Oral Tradition'. Paper presented at the Manding Conference, SOAS, London.
IRVING, Washington 1850 *Lives of the Successors of Mahomet*. Leipzig.

ISHĀQ, Khalīl ibn 1956 *Abrégé de la loi musulmane selon le rite de l'Imām Mâlek*. Vol. I: *Le Rituel*. Tr. G.-H. Bousquet. Alger.
JAMBURIAH, Omar 1919 'The Story of the Jihad of the Foulahs', *Sierra Leone Studies* III.
JEAN-LÉON L'AFRICAIN (Leo Africanus) 1956 *Description de l'Afrique*. 2 Vols. Tr. A. Epaulard. Paris (Original, 16th C.)
JEFFERY, A. 1938 *The Foreign Vocabulary of the Qur'ān*. Baroda.
——— 1958 *Islam: Muhammad and his Religion*. New York.
——— 1962 *Reader on Islam*. The Hague.
JOBSON, Richard [1623] 1968 *The Golden Trade or a Discovery of the River Gambia, 1620-21*. London.
JOHNS, A.H. 1961 'The role of Sufism in the spread of Islam to Malaya and Indonesia', *J. of the Pakistan Hist. Soc.* 9.
JOHNSON, G.W. 1973 *The Emergence of Black Politics in Senegal: The Struggle for Power in the Four Communes, 1900-1920*. London.
JOHNSTON, H.A.S. 1967 *The Fulani Empire of Sokoto*. London.
JOSHI, R.B. 1962 'Was Sankara Influenced by Islam?', *Oriental Thought*. 6(IV).
JUNGE, W. 1952 *African Jungle Doctor*. London.
KABA, Lansiné 1972 'The Mandinka-Mori of Baté, Guinea: a Preliminary Survey for Research in Ethno-history'. Paper presented at the Manding Conference, SOAS, London.
KANE, Cheikh Hamidou 1962 *L'aventure ambiguë*. Paris.
KANYA-FORSTNER, A.S. & C.W. NEWBURY 1969 'French Policy and the Origins of the Scramble for Africa', *J. of Af. Hist.* X.
KA^C^TI, Maḥmūd al- 1913 *Tarīkh al-Fattāsh*. Tr. O. Houdas & M. Delafosse. Paris. (Reprinted 1965; original, 16th-17th C.)
KENSDALE, W.E.N. 1955 'Field Notes on Arabic Literature in Western Sudan', *J. of the Roy. Af. Soc.*
KEREKES, T. (ed.) 1961 *The Arab Middle East and Muslim Africa*. London.
KESBY, J.O. 1963 'Islam in Senegal', *Islamic Quarterly* 7.
KHADDURI, Majid 1955 *War and Peace in the Law of Islam*. Baltimore.
KHALDŪN, ibn 1968 *Histoire des Berbères*. Tr. and ed. M.G. de Slane. 5 vols. Paris, (Original, 14th C.)
KLEIN, M. 1966 'The Moslem Revolution in 19th Century Senegambia', in *Boston Papers in African Studies*, ed. J. Butler. Boston.
——— 1968 *Islam and Imperialism in Senegal: Sine-Saloum 1847-1914*. Edinburgh.
——— 1972 'Social and Economic Factors in the Muslim Revolution in Senegambia', *J. of Af. Hist.* XIII(3).
KOELLE, S.W. 1854 *A Grammar of the Bornu or Kanuri Language*. London.
KOUROUBARI, A. 1959 'Histoire de l'Imam Samori', *Bull. IFAN*. sér. B.
KUNTĪ, Shaykh Mukhtār al- n.d. *Kawkab Waqqād*. Printed and distributed privately by al-Ḥājj Banfa Jabi.
LABAT, J.-B. 1728 *Nouvelle relation de l'Afrique occidentale*. 5 vols. Paris.
LABOURET, H. 1934 'Les Manding et leur langue', *BCEHS de l'AOF* XVII.
LAMMENS, H. 1928 *Les Chrétiens à la Mecque à la veille de l'hégire: l'Arabe occidentale avant l'hégire*. Beirut.
LANDAU, R. 1958 'The Karaoune at Fez', *Muslim World* XLVIII.
LANE, Edward W. 1966 *Manners and Customs of the Modern Egyptians*. London.
LANGE, D. & S. BERTHOUD 1972 'L'intérieur de l'Afrique occidentale d'après Giovanni Lorenzo Anania (XVIe siècle)', *Cahiers d'Histoire Mondiale* (Unesco) XIV/2.
LAST, D.M. 1967a *The Sokoto Caliphate*. London.

LAST, D.M. 1967b 'A Note on the Attitude to the Supernatural in the Sokoto Jihād', *JHSN* IV(Dec.).
—— 1970 'Political Dissent in Hausaland', *Africa* XL (3).
LAST, D.M. & M.A. al-ḤĀJJ 1965 'Attempts at Defining a Muslim in 19th Century Hausaland and Bornou', *JHSN* III(2).
LAUGHTON, John 1938 *Gambia: Country, People and Church in the Diocese of Gambia and Rio Pongas.* London.
LEARY, F.A. 1971 'The Role of the Mandinka in the Islamisation of the Casamance', in *Papers on the Manding*, ed. C.T. Hodge. Bloomington.
LEMAIRE, J.J. [1682] 1887 *Voyage to the Canaries, Cape Verd and the Coast of Africa.* Tr. E. Goldschmid. Edinburgh.
LESLIE, J.A.K. 1963 *A Survey of Dar es-Salaam.* London.
LEVTZION, N. 1968 *Muslims and Chiefs in West Africa.* London.
—— 1971 'A 17th Century Chronicle by ibn al-Mukhtār: A Critical Study of the *Ta'rīkh al-Fattāsh*', *BSOAS* XXXIV.
—— 1972 'The Differential Impact of Islam among the Soninké and the Manding'. Paper presented at the Manding Conference, SOAS, London.
—— 1973 *Ancient Ghana and Mali.* London.
LEVY, R. 1957 *The Social Structure of Islam.* London.
LEWICKI, T. 1969 *Arabic External Sources for the History of Africa to the South of Sahara.* London.
—— 1970 'Les origines de l'Islam dans les tribus berbères du Sahara occidentale: Musa ibn Nusayr et ᶜUbayd Allāh ibn al-Ḥabḥāb', *Studia Islamica* XXXII.
—— 1971 'Un état soudanais médiéval inconnu: le royaume de Zafun(u)', *Cahiers d'Etudes Africaines* XI.
LEWIS, Bernard 1950 *The Arabs in History.* London.
—— 1971 *Race and Color in Islam.* New York.
LYNCH, H.R. 1967 *Edward Wilmot Blyden: Pan-African Patriot.* London.
MACDONALD, Duncan B. 1965 *The Religious Attitude and Life in Islam.* Beirut.
MACKAY, C. 1892 *Extraordinary Popular Delusions and the Madness of Crowds.* 2 vols. London.
MAGE, M.E. 1868 *Voyage dans le Soudan occidentale (Sénégambie-Niger): 1863-66.* Paris.
MARTIN, B.G. 1963 'A Mahdist Document from Fouta Jallon', *Bull. IFAN* sér. B, XXV(1/2).
—— 1971 'Al-Ḥājj ᶜUmar Tall, Samori Turé and their Fore-runners', in *Papers on the Manding*, ed. C.T. Hodge. Bloomington, Ind.
MARTY, P. 1915/16 'L'Islam en Mauritanie et au Sénégal', *Revue du Monde Musulman* XXXI.
—— 1920 *Etudes sur l'Islam et les tribus du Soudan.* Vol. II. Paris.
—— 1921 *L'Islam en Guinée.* Paris.
—— 1922 *Etudes sur l'Islam en Côte d'Ivoire.* Paris.
MASRI, F.H. el- 1963 'The Life of Shehu Usuman dan Fodio before the Jihad', *JHSN.*
MASSIGNON, Louis 1954 *Essai sur les origines du lexique de la mystique musulmane.* Paris. 2nd ed.
MAUNY, R. 1961 *Tableau géographique de l'ouest africain.* Dakar.
MEILLASSOUX, Claude (ed.) 1971 *The Development of Indigenous Trade and Markets in West Africa.* London.
MÉNIAUD, Jacques 1931 *Les pionniers du Soudan.* 2 vols. Paris.
MÉZIÈRES, A. Bonnel de 1949 'Les Diakhanké de Banisiraïla et du Bondou...', *Notes Africaines* (IFAN) 41 (Jan.).
MITCHINSON, A.W. 1881 *The Expiring Continent.* London.

MOISTER, William 1866 *Memorials of Missionary Labours in Western Africa, the West Indies and the Cape of Good Hope.* London.
MOLLIEN, Gaspard 1820 *Travels in Africa to the Sources of the Senegal and Gambia in 1818.* London. 2nd ed., 1825.
MONTEIL, Ch. 1915 *Les Khassonké.* Paris.
—— 1926 'Etat actuel de nos connaissances sur l'Afrique occidentale française: le coton chez les noirs', *BCEHS de l'AOF* 9(4).
—— 1928 'Le site de Goundiourou', *BCEHS de l'AOF* 11(4).
—— 1929 *Les empires du Mali: étude d'histoire et de sociologie soudanaises.* Reprinted, 1968, from *BCEHS de l'AOF* 12(3/4).
—— 1953 'La légende de Ouagadou et l'origine des Soninké', *Mémoires de l'IFAN* 23 (Mélanges Ethnologiques).
MONTEIL, V. 1961 'Contribution à l'étude de l'Islam en Afrique noire', in *Colloque sur les religions.* Abidjan.
—— 1964 *L'Islam noir.* Paris.
MOORE, Francis 1738 *Travels into the Inland Parts of Africa.* London.
MORGAN, John 1864 *Reminiscences of the founding of a Christian Mission on the Gambia.* London.
MOUBARAK, Y. 1958 *Abraham dans la Koran.* Paris.
MUḤAMMAD, ᶜAbdullāh bin [1813] 1963 *Tazyīn Waraqāt.* Ed. and tr. M. Hiskett. Ibadan.
MUIR, Sir William 1858/61 *The Life of Mahomet.* 4 vols. London.
—— [1898] 1963 *The Caliphate: Its Rise, Decline and Fall.* Reprinted, Beirut.
MUNAJJID, Salāh al-Dīn 1963 *Mamlakah Māliyah ᶜind al-jughrafiyīn al-Muslimīn.* Beirut.
NĀBULSĪ, ᶜAbd al-Ghanī al- n.d. *Taᶜṭīr al-Anām fī Taᶜbīr al-Manām.* 2 vols. Cairo. (Author lived 1641-1731.)
NACHTIGAL, G. [1879/89] 1971→ *Sahara and Sudan.* Tr. A.G.B. Fisher & H. Fisher. Several vols. forthcoming.
NADEL, S.F. 1954 *Nupe Religion.* London.
NAQAR, O. al- 1972 *The Pilgrimage Tradition in West Africa.* Khartoum.
NDIAYE, Francine 1968 'La colonie du Sénégal au temps de Brière de l'Isle 1876-1881', *Bull. IFAN,* sér. B, XXX(2).
NIANE, Djibril Tamsir 1971 *Sundiata: An Epic of Old Mali.* London.
NIANE, D.T. & J. SURET-CANALE 1965 *L'histoire de l'Afrique occidentale.* Paris.
NJEUMA, M.Z. 1969 *The Rise and Fall of Fulani Rule in Adamawa: 1809-1901.* Ph.D. thesis, Univ. of London.
NOIROT, E. 1889 *A travers le Fouta-Diallon et le Bambouc.* Paris.
NYAMBARZA, Daniel 1969 'Le marabout El-Hadj Mamadou-Lamine d'après les archives françaises', *Cahiers d'Etudes Africaines* IX(1).
OGILBY, J. 1670 *Africa, being an Accurate Description...,* London.
OLIVER, R.A. 1961 *The Dawn of African History.* London.
OLORUNTIMEHIN, B.O. 1968 'Muhammad Lamine in Franco-Tukulor Relations 1885-87', *JHSN* 4(3).
—— 1971 'Senegambia - Mahmadou Lamine', in *West African Resistance,* ed. M. Crowder. London. 80-110.
—— 1972 *The Segu Tukulor Empire.* London.
OWEN, Nicholas 1930 *Journal of a Slavedealer, 1746-57.* Ed. E. Martin. London.
PADEN, John N. 1973 *Religion and Political Culture in Kano.* California.
PADWICK, C.E. 1957 'The Language of Muslim Devotion: IV: Petition and Greeting', *Muslim World* (Oct.).
—— 1961 *Muslim Devotions.* London.
PALMER, H.R. 1908 'The Kano Chronicle', *J. Roy. Anthr. Inst.* XXXVIII.

PALMER, H.R. 1914 'An Early Fulani Conception of Islam', *Journal of the Africa Society*.

—— 1928 *Sudanese Memoirs*. Reprinted 1967, London.

PANIKKAR, K.M. 1964 *The Serpent and the Crescent: A History of the Negro Empires of Western Africa*. London.

PARK, Mungo [1799] 1969 *Travels in Africa 1795-97*. London. Reprinted in Everyman ed.

PARRINDER, E.G. 1951a 'Ibadan Annual Festival', *Africa* XXI(1).

—— 1951b *West African Psychology*. London.

—— 1953 *Religion in an African City*. London.

—— 1954 *African Traditional Religion*. London.

—— 1969 *Religion in Africa*. London.

PEEL, J.D.Y. 1968 *Aladura: A Religious Movement among the Yoruba*. London.

PELLAT, Ch. 1971 *'Al-Ḥarīrī'*, in *Encyclopaedia of Islam*. New Edition, vol. III. Leiden.

PERSON, Yves 1962 'La jeunesse de Samory', *Revue Française d'Histoire d'Outre-Mer* XLIX.

—— 1968/70 *Samori: une révolution dyula*. 3 vols. Dakar.

—— 1974 'The Atlantic Coast and the Southern Savannahs', in *History of West Africa*, ed. A.D. Ajayi & M. Crowder. Vol. 2. London.

PETERSON, E.L. 1959 'ᶜAli and Muᶜāwiyah: The Rise of the Umayād Caliphate, 656-661', *Acta Orientalia* XXIII

PIRAJNO, Denti di- 1955 *A Cure for Serpents: A Doctor in Africa*. London.

PLANHOL, Xavier de 1968 *Les fondements géographiques de l'histoire de l'Islam*. Paris.

POLLET, Eric & Grace WINTER 1971 *La société soninké (Dyahunu, Mali)*. Brussels.

PROUDFOOT, L. 1954 'Muslims among Akus in Freetown', *Africa* XXIV(3).

—— 1959 'Mosque Building and Tribal Separation in Freetown', *Africa* XXIX(4).

—— 1961 'Towards Muslim Solidarity in Freetown', *Africa* XXXI.

QAYRAWĀNĪ, ibn Abī Zayd al- 1945 *La Risālah: ou épître sur les éléments du dogme et de la loi de l'Islam selon le rite mâlikite*. Tr. and ed. L. Bercher. Alger, (Original, 10th C.)

QUELLIEN, N. 1910 *La politique musulmane dans l'Afrique occidentale*. Paris.

QUINN, Charlotte A. 1968a 'Niumi: A Nineteenth Century Mandingo Kingdom', *Africa* XXXVIII.

—— 1968b 'Maba Diakhabou - Scholar-Warrior of the Senegambia', *Ta'rīkh* 2(3).

—— 1971 'A Nineteenth Century Fulbé State', *J. of Af. Hist.* XII.

—— 1972 *Mandingo Kingdoms of the Senegambia*. London.

RAFFENEL, Anne 1856 *Nouveau voyage dans le pays des nègres*. 2 vols. Paris.

RAHMAN, F. 1968 *Islam*. New York.

RANÇON, A. 1894a *Le Bondou*. Bordeaux.

—— 1894b *Dans la Haute-Gambie*. Paris.

READE, W.W. 1864 *Savage Africa*. London.

REEVE, H.F. 1912 *The Gambia, its History: Ancient, Mediaeval and Modern*. London.

REICHARDT, C.A.L. 1876 *Grammar of the Fulde Language*. London.

ROBERT, Maurice 1929 'Quelques règles de droit coutumier malinké en Haute-Guinée', *BCEHS de l'AOF*. 12.

ROBERTS, S.H. 1929 *The History of French Colonial Policy 1870-1925*. London.

RODNEY, Walter 1968 'Jihad and Social Revolution in Futa Djalon in the 18th Century', *JHSN* IV(2).
—— 1970 *A History of the Upper Guinea Coast 1545–1800*. London.
RODRIGUES, J.H. 1965 *Brazil and Africa*. Berkeley.
RONCIÈRE, Ch. de la 1919 'Une histoire du Bornou au XVIIe siècle', *Revue de l'Histoire des Colonies Françaises* VII(2).
ROSENTHAL, E.I.J. 1958 *Political Thought in Medieval Islam*. London.
ROUCH, J. 1953 *Contribution à l'histoire des Songhay*. Dakar.
ROWLANDS, E.C. 1959 *A Grammar of Gambian Mandinka*. London.
RUSSELL, A.D. & A. al-M. SUHRAWARDY 1906 *First Steps in Muslim Jurisprudence*. London.
RUXTON, F.H. 1916 *Maliki Law*. London.
RYAN, Patrick J. 1975 *Imale: Yoruba Participation in the Muslim Tradition*. Ph.D. thesis, Harvard University.
SABATIÉ, A. 1925 *Le Sénégal*. St. Louis, Senegal.
SA^cDI, al- [1913/4] 1964 *Ta'rīkh al-Sūdān*. Tr. Octave Houdas. Paris.(17th C
SADLER, G.W. 1950 *A Century in Nigeria*. Nashville, Tenn.
SAINT-PÈRE, J.H. 1925 *Les Sarakollé de Guidimakha*. Paris.
SALENC, Jules 1918 'La vie d'al-Hadj Omar, traduction d'un manuscrit arabe de la Zaouia Tidjania de Fez', *BCEHS de l'AOF*.
SANNEH, L.O. 1972 'The Origin and Dispersion of the Jakhanke'. Paper presented at the Manding Conference, SOAS, London.
—— 1974a *The History of the Jakhanke People of Senegambia: A Study of a Clerical Tradition in West African Islam*. Ph.D. thesis, University of London, on which the present book is based.
—— 1974b 'Senegambia at a Slow Pace', *Africa Magazine* (Feb.).
—— 1975 'Field-work among the Jakhanke of Senegambia', *Présence Africaine* 93.
—— 1976a 'The Origins of Clericalism in West African Islam', *J. of Af. Hist.* XVII(1).
—— 1976b 'Slavery, Islam and the Jakhanke People of West Africa', *Africa* XLVI(1).
—— 1977 'Islamic Slavery in the African Perspective'. Princeton University conference paper, June.
SAUNDERS, J.J. 1965 *A History of Medieval Islam*. London.
SCHACHT, J. 1950 *The Origins of Muhammadan Jurisprudence*. London.
—— 1959 'Islamic Law in Contemporary States', *American Journal of Comparative Law*.
—— 1964 *An Introduction to Islamic Law*. London.
—— 1965 'Notes on Islam in East Africa', *Studia Islamica* 23.
SCHWAB, G. 1947 *Tribes of the Liberian Hinterland*. Cambridge, Mass.
SHAH, Idris 1971 *The Sufis*. London.
SHINQĪṬĪ, al- 1911 *Al-Wasīt fī tarājim udabā Shinqīṭ*. Cairo. Tr. into French, 1953, see Chenguiti above.
SĪRĪN, Muḥammad bin n.d. *Ta^cbīr al-Ru'yā*. Cairo. (Author d. 728.)
SITWELL, Cecil 1893 *South Bank Report*. Public Record Office, Banjul, Ref. 76/19.
SKINNER, David E. 1971 *Islam in Sierra Leone in the Nineteenth Century*. Ph.D. thesis, University of California.
1972 'The role of the Mandingos and Susus in the Islamisation of Sierra Leone'. Paper presented at the Manding Conference, SOAS, London.
SMITH, H.F.C. 1961 'A Neglected Theme of West African History: The Islamic Revolutions of the 19th Century', *JHSN* 2(2).
SMITH, Marshall G. 1953 'Secondary Marriage in Northern Nigeria', *Africa* XXIII(4).

—— 1966 'The Jihad of Shehu dan Fodio: Some Problems', in *Islam in Tropical Africa*, ed. I.M. Lewis. London.

SMITH, Mary 1954 *Baba of Karo*. London.

SMITH, Pierre 1965a 'Les Diakhanké: histoire d'une dispersion', extrait de *Cahiers du CRA*, in *Bull. et Mém. de la Soc. Anthr. de Paris*, sér. XI,8: 231-62.

—— 1965b 'Notes sur l'organisation sociale des Diakhanké. Aspects particuliers à la région de Kédougou', *Cahier du CRA*, in *Bull. et Mém. de la Soc. Anthr. de Paris*, ser. XI, 8: 263-302.

SOH, Siré-Abbas 1913 *Chroniques du Foûta Sénégalais*. Ed. M. Delafosse & H. Gaden. Paris.

SOLEILLET, Paul 1887 *Voyage à Ségou*. Ed. G. Gravier. Paris.

SORIBA, al-Ḥājj (Al-Ḥājj Ibrahima Jabi) n.d. *Kitāb al-Bushrā: Sharḥ al-Mirqāt al-Kubrā*. Tunis.

SOUTHERN, Bella 1952 *The Gambia: The Story of the Groundnut Colony*. London.

STENNING, D.J. 1959 *Savannah Nomads*. London.

STIBB, Captain 1738 'Voyage up the Gambia in the Year 1723', in *Travels into the Inland Parts of Africa*, ed. Francis Moore.

STREET, Noel 1971 *Dreamer Awake: A Guide to Dream Study*. Miami, Florida.

SUHRAWARDĪ, al 1891 *Al-ᶜAwārif al-Maᶜārif/Bounties of Divine Knowledge*. Tr. Wilberforce Clarke. Calcutta. In Arabic, 1939, Cairo. (Author lived 1145-1234.)

SULE, A.O. 1969 *Islam in Aide Clan, Etsako Division of Mid-Western State of Nigeria*. Long Essay, Dept. of Arabic and Islamic Studies, Ibadan Univ.

SURET-CANALE, J. 1961 *L'Afrique noire: occidentale et centrale*. Paris.

—— 1964 'A propos du Ouali de Goumba', *Recherches Africaines*.

—— 1970 'Touba in Guinea: Holy Place of Islam', in *African Perspectives*, ed. C. Allen & R.W. Johnson. London.

TANŪKHĪ, Sayd Saḥnūn al- 1906/7 *Al-Mudawwana al-Kubrā*. Cairo. (Author d. 854.)

TARDIFF, Jean 1965 'Aspects de l'histoire et de la situation socio-economique actuelle (Kédougou)', extrait de *Cahiers du CRA*, in *Bull. et Mém. de la Soc. Anthr. de Paris*, sér. XI, 8.

TAUXIER, L. 1921 *Le noir de Bondoukou*. Paris.

—— 1937 *Moeurs et histoire des peulhs*. Paris.

TERRIER, Auguste et Charles MOUREY 1910 *L'expansion française et la formation territoriale. (L'oeuvre de la Troisième République en Afrique Occidentale.)* Paris.

TORREY, Ch. 1933 *The Jewish Foundations of Islam*. New York.

TOURNEAU, R. 1969 *The Almohad Movement in North Africa in the 12th and 13th Centuries*. London.

TOYNBEE, A. 1957 *Christianity among the Religions of the World*. New York.

TREMEARNE, A.J.N. 1913 *Hausa Superstitions and Customs*. London.

—— 1914 *The Ban of the Bori*. London.

TRIAUD, J.-L. 1973 *Islam et sociétés soudanaises au moyen-âge*. Paris and Ouagadougou.

TRIMINGHAM, John Spencer 1955 *The Christian Church and Islam in West Africa*. London.

—— 1959 *Islam in West Africa*. London.

—— 1962 *A History of Islam in West Africa*. London.

—— 1968 *The Influence of Islam upon Africa*. London and Beirut.

—— 1971 *The Sufi Orders in Islam*. London.

TRIMINGHAM, J.S. & C. FYFE 1960 'The Early Expansion of Islam in Sierra Leone', *Sierra Leone Bulletin of Religion* 2(2).
TURNER, H.W. 1967 *History of an African Independent Church*. 2 vols. London.
TYAM, Mahammadou Aliou 1935 *La vie d'al-Hadj Omar, qacida (ode) en poular*. Tr. Henri Gaden. Paris.
cUMARI, ibn Faḍl Allāh al- 1927 *Masālik al-abṣār fī mamālik al-Amṣār/ L'Afrique moins l'Egypt*. Tr. M. Gaudefroy-Demombynes. Paris. (Original, 14th C.)
URVOY, Y. 1949 *Histoire de l'empire du Bornou*. Paris. Reprinted, 1968, Amsterdam.
VILLARD, A. 1943 *Histoire du Sénégal*. Dakar.
VUILLET, Jean 1952 'Recherches au sujet de religions professées en Sénégambie, anciennement ou à l'époque actuelle', *Comptes Rendus Mensuels des Séances de l'Acad. des Sci. Coloniales* XII(viii): 413-26.
WAD, Daif Allāh 1930 *Ṭabaqāt Awliyā' al-Sūdān*. Cairo.

WALCKENAER, Baron Charles Athanase 1826-31 *Histoire générale des voyages*. 11 vols. Paris.
WALDMAN, M.R. 1965 'The Fulani jihād: A Reassessment', *J. of Af. Hist.* VI(3).
WALZ, Terence 1972 'Notes on the Organisation of the African Trade in Cairo, 1800-1850', extrait des *Annales Islamologiques* (Cairo) XI.
WASHINGTON, Captain 1838 'Some Accounts of Mohammedu-Sisei, a Mandingo of Nyani-Maru on the Gambia', *J. of Roy. Geog. Soc.* VIII.
WATT, W. Montgomery 1962 *Muhammad at Medina*. London.
—— 1967 'The Conception of *Imān* in Islamic Theology', *Der Islam*.
WELLHAUSEN, J. 1964 *The Arab Kingdom and its Fall*. Beirut.
WELMERS, W.E. 1960 *The Mande Languages*. Georgetown Univ. Monograph Series 2, Washington, D.C.
WENSINCK, A.J. 1965 *The Muslim Creed: Its Genesis and Historical Development*. London.
WESSELS, A. 1972 *A Modern Arabic Biography of Muḥammad: A Critical Study of Muḥammad Ḥusayn Haykal's Ḥayāt Muḥammad*. Leiden.
West African Sketches 1824 Compiled from the Reports of Sir G.R. Collier, Sir Charles MacCarthy, etc. London.
WESTERMANN, D. 1912 'Islam in the Sudan', *International Review of Mission*.
WHITCOMB, Thomas 1972 'A Western Saharan Clerical Tribe: The Tajakant'. African History Seminar paper, SOAS, London, 31 May.
WILKS, I. 1963 'The Growth of Islamic Learning in Ghana', *JHSN* II.
—— 1968 'The Transmission of Islamic Learning in the Western Sudan', in *Literacy in Traditional Societies*, ed. J. Goody. London.
WILLIS, J.R. 1966 Review of *Tijaniyāh* by J.M. Abun Nasr, *Research Bull. of Centre of Arabic Documentation* 2(1).
—— 1967 '*Jihād fī sabīl li llāh*: Its Doctrinal Basis in Islam and some Aspects of its Evolution in 19th Century West Africa', *J. of Af. Hist.* VIII.
—— 1970 *The Jihād of al-Hajj cUmar al-Fūtī: Its Doctrinal Basis...* Ph.D. thesis, Univ. of London.
WOLF, Eric 1951 'The Social Organisation of Mecca and the Origins of Islam', *Southwestern Journal of Anthropology* 7.
—— 1969 'On Peasant Rebellions', *International Social Science Journal* XXI(2).
WOOD, W. Raymond 1967 'An Archeological Appraisal of Early European Settlements in the Senegambia', *J. of Af. Hist.* VIII(1).

YA^{c}QŪBĪ, al- 1892 *Kitāb al-Buldān*. Leiden. (Original, 9th C.)
YĀQŪT 1866/73 *Mu^{c}jam al-Buldān*. Ed. F. Wüstenfeld. Leipzig. (Original, 13th C.)
YOUNG, H.B. 1946 'Islam in West Africa', *Muslim World*. 36.
ZIADEH, Nichola 1958 *Sanūsīyah: A Study of a Revivalist Movement in Islam*. Leiden.

INDEX

For Product Safety Concerns and Information please contact our EU
representative GPSR@taylorandfrancis.com
Taylor & Francis Verlag GmbH, Kaufingerstraße 24, 80331 München, Germany

www.ingramcontent.com/pod-product-compliance
Lightning Source LLC
Chambersburg PA
CBHW070608270326
41926CB00013B/2465
* 9 7 8 1 1 3 8 5 9 7 9 2 1 *